The Political Economy of
the Latin American Motor
Vehicle Industry

The Political Economy of the Latin American Motor Vehicle Industry

edited by Rich Kronish and Kenneth S. Mericle

The MIT Press
Cambridge, Massachusetts
London, England

Sponsored by the Joint Committee on Latin American Studies of the Social Science Research Council and the American Council of Learned Societies.

This book was set in Palatino
by The MIT Press Computergraphics Department
and printed and bound by Halliday Lithograph
in the United States of America.

Library of Congress Cataloging in Publication Data

Main entry under title:

The Political economy of the Latin American motor vehicle industry.

  Bibliography: p.
  Includes index.
  1. Automobile industry and trade—Latin America.
  2. Automobile industry workers—Latin America.
  3. Corporations, Foreign—Latin America. 4. Industrial relations—Latin America.
  I. Kronish, Rich.
  II. Mericle, Kenneth S.
  HD9710.L32P64   1984   338.4′76292′098   83–17535
  ISBN 0–262–11089–X

To Becca, David, Judy, Katie, Mindy, and Morgan

Contents

8 **Bargaining Relations in the Colombian Motor Vehicle Industry** 231
   Michael Fleet

9 **The Development of the Latin American Motor Vehicle Industry, 1900–1980: A Class Analysis** 261
   Rich Kronish and Kenneth S. Mericle

Introduction

The automobile has had a unique significance in modern industrial society. From its emergence as an important item of mass consumption in the United States during the 1920s, the automobile has had a profound impact on advanced capitalist societies. It has both shaped the structure and productive processes of capitalist economies and defined the lifestyles of the consumer society.

The social and economic impact of the development of the industry in the Third World has been no less dramatic. This book examines the emergence and growth of the motor vehicle industry in Latin America, the area of the Third World where the industry is most advanced. It explores what occurs when the premier product of industrial society is produced and consumed in a context of dependency and underdevelopment. Although the essays in this book do not employ the same level of analysis or theoretical perspective, each essay does address some aspect of this question.

We focus most of our attention on Argentina, Brazil, and Mexico. These three countries were the first in Latin America and among the first in the Third World to progress beyond simple vehicle assembly and to install production operations. Today their industries are among the largest and most important in the Third World. Colombia, the fourth country discussed in this book, provides an example of a late-arriving industry in a smaller and less developed economy with market and industrial conditions typical of many Third World countries now considering motor vehicle production.

Throughout Latin America large transnational corporations (TNCs) of American as well as German, French, and Italian origin dominate the industry. These firms are among the largest industrial corporations in the world and account for a large share of total foreign direct investment in the Third World. They are very powerful political and economic entities wherever they are found, but their power is especially pronounced in the dependent economies of the Third World.

The relationship between the TNCs and host-country governments constitutes an important analytical theme of this book. There is some disagreement among the authors about the nature of this relationship. Some emphasize the conflictual aspects of this relationship. By contrast, others conceive the TNC–host government relationship primarily in terms of cooperation and support. There is, however, no disagreement about the centrality of this relationship. Government policies have established the parameters that define the basic characteristics and performance of the Latin American vehicle industries. Indeed the formulation and implementation of government policies affecting motor vehicle production and consumption have determined in large measure the fate of these industries.

A second important theme in this book is the role and impact of labor. The significance of this theme derives in part from the relative inefficiency and high cost of vehicle production and the resulting pressure on labor costs in the Latin American industries. In addition its significance derives from market considerations, for in the Third World only a small segment of the population is wealthy enough to consume and operate an automobile. Motor vehicle production thus has tended to encourage and sustain, and indeed be dependent on, a highly inequitable distribution of wealth and income. Under these circumstances the political strength and militance of the auto workers, the auto workers' role within the urban working class as a whole (whether privileged aristocracy or vanguard element), and the nature and success of government labor and income policies all have had profound consequences for the development of the industry.

Exploration of these two themes encompasses a broad range of issues that arose in the Latin American context but are common to all underdeveloped countries embarking on the path of motor vehicle production. These issues entail the following questions. How important will the industry be in the overall industrialization strategy? What role will TNCs play in the development of the industry? What inducements will be offered and what constraints imposed on the TNCs? What are the social and political consequences of developing the industry? What social and political conditions encourage or discourage growth of the industry? How does the industry stimulate or restrain overall economic growth? How do the TNCs' global strategies mesh with domestic development objectives? Although it cannot be predicted if the Third World countries now initiating or contemplating the installation of motor vehicle industries will duplicate the experience of the Latin America industries, nevertheless the answers provided by the Latin American experience to these questions have enormous relevance for the global development of the industry and indeed for capitalist development throughout the Third World.

The Political Economy Essays

These three essays examine the formation and evolution of the Latin American industries. All three stress the significance of the structural problems encountered by the industries. These problems include the fragmentation of the terminal sector (too many firms producing too many models for a small market), insufficient parts and materials infrastructure (especially in the light of high domestic content requirements), high production costs, insufficient effective markets, and excess capacity. Although these problems are fairly well documented in other works, the chapters in this book transcend the existing literature by explicating and analyzing the political and economic processes that first produced industries with these characteristics and then generated policies designed to ameliorate or solve the structural problems.

The main contribution of Mericle's chapter on the Brazilian industry lies in its discussion of the conditions that stimulated rapid growth in an industry that suffered from the structural problems associated with low-volume, high-cost production. Mericle documents a consistent and comprehensive pattern of government support for the TNCs that now totally dominate the Brazilian industry. He argues that the industry was the principal beneficiary of the regressive and authoritarian social policies of post-1964 military governments in Brazil. By encouraging income concentration and effective social control, particularly of the working class, these policies helped create near-optimal conditions for the production and consumption of automobiles and made the motor vehicle industry the leading sector in a general economic boom. Mericle also illustrates how the internal and external contradictions of this growth model have generated economic and political problems that have adversely affected the fortunes of the industry during the past decade.

Jenkins's chapter on Argentina describes an industry that, in contrast to the Brazilian industry, has never escaped its stagnationist tendencies.

Jenkins argues that initial government policies strengthened these tendencies while also contributing to the denationalization of its terminal sector. Jenkins then traces government efforts to restructure the industry along the lines of the Brazilian Model, attributing the failure of these efforts to the relative strength of the working class and to Argentina's dependent position within the world economy.

In the final chapter in this section, Kronish examines the changing relationship between the Latin American industry and the world industry as a whole. He shows that the vehicle-producing industries that emerged in Latin America in the late 1950s and the 1960s were relatively isolated. In recent years, however, the TNCs have begun integrating their Latin American subsidiaries with the rest of their worldwide operations, prompting increases in both Latin American exports and, to a lesser extent, imports. Kronish roots these developments in the dynamics of the vehicle industries of the developed countries. More specifically he argues that the interplay of two factors—the intensification of TNC competition for markets with the continuing conflict between labor and capital in the industry in the developed countries—has encouraged the transnational producers to develop export production outside the traditional vehicle-producing areas. Kronish then identifies the factors that have influenced the TNCs' choice of particular Third World countries as export sites.

The Labor Essays

Most studies of economic development, dependency, and specific industries in the Third World consider workers only as a passive object of the industrialization process. The approach is similar to that of neoclassical economics: labor is another abstract factor of production. By contrast the chapters in this section conceive of industrialization as a dialectical process in which labor is both subject and object. Indeed they argue that the attitudes and actions of the auto workers have had a major impact on the development of the Latin American motor vehicle industry, affecting both supply and demand conditions. They show that at certain key times the auto workers have spearheaded opposition to government income concentration policies and thereby constituted a significant barrier to the expansion of demand for automobiles. At the same time, the militance, consciousness, and organizational capacity of the auto workers on the shop floor have affected the TNCs' ability to limit labor costs and control the production process, matters crucial to firm profitability and performance.

Kronish and Mericle's comparative essay formulates this analysis of labor's influence on the development of the essay, and the full argument is elaborated there in the concluding chapter of this book. The essays in this section examine various pieces of the overall theme as it is played out in different national contexts.

Humphrey examines the wages and working conditions of Brazilian auto workers. Contrary to widely held opinion in Brazil, Humphrey argues that conditions in the plants do not support a view of auto workers as a privileged labor aristocracy within the working class. Humphrey finds that Brazilian auto workers work at an intense pace at predominantly unskilled and semiskilled jobs while confronting high turnover rates and arbitrary dismissals and with little opportunity for occupational mobility. For almost fifteen years following the 1964 coup, the auto companies suppressed grievances based on these conditions through a mixture of coercion and intimidation, with the aid of the Brazilian government. Since 1978, however, the auto workers have openly challenged this pattern of domination, opposing both the auto companies and the Brazilian government. Indeed Humphrey argues that the auto workers' actions now constitute a vanguard role in the struggle for economic and political change.

Evans, Hoeffel, and James trace the emergence of the Argentine auto workers in the decade leading up to the military coup of 1976 as a militant social force. They show that the Argentine auto workers consistently challenged government economic policies, often in highly dramatic and effective fashion, while simultaneously fashioning a shop floor organization that effectively blocked the auto companies' efforts to increase labor productivity through speedup measures and the like. The authors examine the historical context shaping this "rebellious reality," thereby clarifying the relationship between the auto workers' role in the *Cordobazo* and other antigovernment mass mobilizations and their struggle on the shop floor for improved working conditions.

Roxborough examines the policies and internal structures of the unions of Mexico's motor vehicle industry. He shows that throughout the 1960s these unions were largely dominated by conservative leaders affiliated with the Confederacion de Trabajadores Mexicanos (CTM), who relied on a mixture of special favors and coercion to provide a stable and relatively passive labor force to the industry. Subsequently, however, several unions broke away from the CTM and formed independent unions. Roxborough shows that these unions, as well as two others that remained loosely within the CTM orbit, tend to be more militant and democratic than the remaining CTM-affiliated unions. Roxborough analyzes the origins of this development and its likely impact on the future development of the industry.

The Bargaining Essays

The essays in this group explore the bargaining process between the TNCs and the Latin American governments at critical junctures. Unlike much of the other literature on bargaining, the essays in this book make a serious attempt to specify both the common and the conflicting interests of the TNCs and the governments. The chapters evaluate specific attempts to alter the behavior of the TNCs in a direction consistent with the goal of national economic growth. They also evaluate specific attempts by the TNCs to influence policy formulation and implementation in a direction consistent with the goals of profit maximization and growth.

Bennett and Sharpe examine the negotiations that took place between the Mexican government and the TNCs at the time of the creation of the Mexican automobile industry (1960–1964). They show that although there were significant differences between the two parties concerning the actual issues on the bargaining table (for example, domestic content requirements and the number of participating firms), conflict occurred within a context of cooperation and mutual interest. Bennett and Sharpe then analyze the bargaining process itself. They argue that the TNCs effectively mobilized their home-country governments to exert pressure on the Mexican government. By contrast the Mexican government failed to exploit its major source of potential power (the pattern of oligopolistic competition among the TNCs), permitting the TNCs to prevail at the bargaining table.

Fleet's chapter on the Colombian industry provides a second illustration of the TNC–host government bargaining process. The chapter makes an additional contribution to the book by addressing the case of the development of the industry in a smaller, late-arriving country. Fleet shows that despite limited bargaining power, the Colombian government took advantage of TNC competition and negotiated fairly favorable contracts. Fleet also demonstrates, however, the failure of the Colombian government to enforce these contracts. This failure has permitted the TNCs to minimize investment in Colombia, using it instead as a profitable outlet for parts and components produced elsewhere in their international structures.

Concluding Essay

Kronish and Mericle's comparative essay on Brazil, Argentina, and Mexico serves to draw together and provide an overview to this book. On the one hand, it explicitly formulates and elaborates the book's principal themes concerning the significance of labor and the relationship between the TNCs and the Latin American governments. On the other hand, it provides a comparative and historical examination of the three principal industries. On this basis Kronish and Mericle identify similarities and differences in the development of the three industries. They find that all three have been prone to stagnation and thus required extensive government support. National patterns of support and intervention have varied considerably, however, reflecting to a significant degree different content requirements. In Brazil and Argentina very high content requirements (90 percent or more) exacerbated structural problems and made the success of government efforts to expand effective demand through income concentration crucial to industry expansion. Kronish and Mericle show by contrast that the far greater reliance of the Mexican industry on imported parts and subassemblies exacerbated balance-of-payments difficulties and prompted the government to emphasize export promotion. Government efforts in all three countries to expand effective demand and/or promote vehicle exports in turn have implied significant challenges to the working class in general and to the auto workers in particular. Kronish and Mericle demonstrate that the success of these efforts has depended on the relative strength of the auto workers, with very different consequences in Brazil, Argentina, and Mexico.

Conclusion

This book is distinctive, for it provides a comparative analysis of the political economy of development of a single industry in a number of different national settings. Most industry-based comparative studies of Third World industrialization are more narrowly focused on the economic structure of the industry. We are particularly fortunate to have a kind of natural experiment with four distinct outcomes in the cases of Brazil (full integration with very rapid growth), Argentina (full integration with stagnation), Mexico (intermediate integration and steady growth), and Colombia (low integration and restrained growth). The book will contribute to a fuller understanding of the international development of the leading consumer durable in the world. It addresses many theoretical issues relevant to the development of the industry throughout the Third World and thus should be of broad interest to students of development.

The Political Economy of
the Latin American Motor
Vehicle Industry

1

The Political Economy of the Brazilian Motor Vehicle Industry

Kenneth S. Mericle

The Brazilian motor vehicle industry is the eighth largest in the world. In 1980 it produced over 1 million vehicles, making it by far the most important consumer durables industry in the Third World.[1] Under the direction of the Brazilian government, the industry has progressed from an embryo of scattered assembly operations to a fully integrated manufacturing industry in a period of twenty years. From its origin as a low-volume, high-cost producer serving a highly protected domestic market, the industry has become an increasingly cost-effective supplier of parts and vehicle exports to the world market. Virtually all of the capital in the terminal sector of the industry and much of that in the parts sector is foreign owned or controlled. Large transnational corporations (TNCs) offer the same range of products and use many of the same production techniques as they do in their home country operations. By any measure the industry is the epitome of successful import substitution industrialization.

The industry also typifies the recent dynamism of Brazilian capitalism. As a key lead sector of the growth model, the industry played a critical role in stimulating the so-called Brazilian miracle. During the peak years of 1968 through 1974, industry output grew at a compound annual rate of 22.0 percent, over twice as fast as the 11.2 percent for the economy as a whole.[2] Because of its size and interdependence with the rest of the economy, both as a consumer of parts, components, and raw materials (especially steel, rubber, plastics, and nonferrous metals) and as a stimulator of downstream development in auxiliary services and infrastructure, the industry has had a profound impact on the whole course of Brazilian development.

But the industry also provides a dramatic illustration of the irrationalities of Brazilian capitalism. In Brazil the lavish consumption patterns of advanced capitalism coexist with some of the worst poverty in the

Western Hemisphere. Automobiles roll off the assembly line at the same time as many Brazilians suffer from malnutrition, substandard housing, inadequate medical care, and a host of other social problems. When the automobile boom began in 1968, per capita gross domestic product was about $318.[3] At that level of development, automobiles had little to do with the needs of the average citizen. The existence of the industry depended and continues to depend on a style of consumerism that prevails in advanced capitalist countries; to replicate these consumption patterns in Brazil introduces tremendous strains on the society, economy, and environment. For upper-income groups the automobile is the symbol par excellence of the industrial boom and their participation in it. For the average Brazilian the automobile boom means traffic congestion, noise and air pollution, accidents, and alterations in land-use patterns, all of which have seriously eroded the quality of life in Brazilian cities. More important, the centrality of the motor vehicle industry in Brazilian development implies that much of the nation's human and natural resources are unavailable for alternative uses that would better serve the Brazilian people.

It is impossible to understand the pattern of economic growth in Brazil in the late 1960s and early 1970s and its social and political prerequisites and consequences without understanding the role played by the motor vehicle industry. As the most successful example of motor vehicle manufacturing in the the Third World, it also represents an important case in the international expansion of the industry.

This chapter analyzes the growth of the industry from its inception to the present. My explanation of the evolution of the industry stresses the importance of the intervention of the Brazilian state, which has been comprehensive and fundamental in shaping the industry. Thus at one level, this chapter is a study of the relationship between a powerful, authoritarian Third World state and a group of the largest and most powerful TNCs in the world.

In the case of the Brazilian motor vehicle industry, the state-TNC relationship has been primarily a supportive one in which the TNCs have been the beneficiaries of a broad range of policies engineered by the state. Conflict has not been absent from this relationship, but it has been limited in scope and secondary in importance. When the state has taken measures not in the narrow short-run interests of the industry, it has usually attempted to ease the burden with compensatory programs while simultaneously pursuing programs that would create and recreate conditions supportive of long-run growth.

The second theme in my analysis of the industry focuses on the relationship between the state and the working class. My argument is that the restrictive labor policies of the Brazilian government were conducive to the development of the industry, which required a highly skewed pattern of income distribution to generate demand for its main product, the automobile. The industry is also highly vulnerable to job actions and strikes and hence a major beneficiary of the repression of these activities by the state.

My analysis thus emphasizes class conflict and the role of the state in structuring class relations as important influences on the development of the industry. It also emphasizes that state intervention was crucial to the development of the industry and that the defining characteristics of the state's relationship to the TNCs were support, cooperation, and protection rather than conflict and antagonism.

The evolution of the industry can be divided chronologically into four phases: installation, 1919–1961; stagnation, 1962–1967; accelerated expansion, 1968–1974; and retrenchment, since 1975.

Installation, 1919–1961

The installation phase comprises a period of laissez-faire development that lasted until the early 1950s and a period of planned development in which the state supervised the installation of full-scale manufacturing operations in Brazil. The most important aspect of government policy was a decision in 1956 that established the conditions for participation in the industry in its move from assembly to manufacturing. All terminal sector firms were required to obtain virtually 100 percent of parts and components within Brazil. Despite this stringent requirement, eleven firms went ahead with investments in the terminal sector.

The 1956 decision raises a number of interesting issues, particularly since Brazil was the first of the three large producing countries in Latin America to attempt the move from assembly to manufacturing. Why did the Brazilian policy makers decide to move so decisively toward manufacturing? Why did they insist on such a restrictive domestic content requirement? Why did they invite seventeen firms to invest in the terminal sector and accept the projects of eleven of them?

Prior to World War II activity in the Brazilian motor vehicle industry was almost entirely confined to final assembly operations. By the mid-1920s Ford, General Motors, and International Harvester had established low-volume assembly lines that depended entirely on imported parts and components. The industry stagnated during the depression when the stock of motor vehicles in Brazil shrank from 250,000 in 1930 to 160,000 in 1940.[4] Entering World War II, Brazil's vehicle stock was depleted, and those that existed were old and badly in need of repair. Demand for vehicles was strong at a time when Brazil was cut off from normal sources of supply. A domestic parts sector soon began to flourish in this protected wartime market. In 1950 one hundred firms were engaged in parts fabrication and assembly operations as compared to the three assemblers and only five parts firms in 1941.[5]

The emerging parts industry was soon threatened with extinction as normal trade channels reopened after World War II. During the war Brazil had accumulated substantial foreign exchange reserves, much of which was used to import motor vehicles in the immediate postwar period. Between 1946 and 1952 imports of motor vehicles, mostly from the United States, averaged $114.3 million per year.[6] A similarly large inflow of inexpensive imported parts threatened local producers with bankruptcy. In addition to this threat, motor vehicle and parts imports were contributing to a steady deterioration in the Brazilian balance-of-payments position.[7] The balance-of-payments difficulties reached crisis proportions with the collapse of the world price of coffee at the end of the Korean war boom.

In an effort to stem the inflow of imports and protect the nascent parts industry, the Brazilian government undertook its first systematic efforts to promote the development of a domestic industry. Aviso 288 of the Bank of Brazil prohibited the importation of 104 parts then being produced in the country, thus guaranteeing a market for the Brazilian producers. In general terms the measure limited the concession of import licenses to those parts not produced in Brazil. Final assembly received a large boost in July 1953 with the issuance of aviso 311, which prohibited the importation of nonessential assembled motor vehicles, a measure whose effectiveness is illustrated by the fact that the total value of vehicle imports dropped from $198 million in 1952 to $21 million in 1953.[8] The parts sector received further stimulus in January 1954 when new regulations on the importation of completely knocked down (CKD) vehicles were issued. The new regulations required that CKDs could not be imported as self-contained units but rather would be required to use any individual parts available from manufacturers in Brazil. After 1956 the law of similars, a measure stating that any product locally manufactured could be imported only at prohibitive cost in import duties, provided further protection for the industry. The combined impact of these measures was dramatic. By 1956 520 factories were producing parts compared to 100 in 1950; 8 firms were assembling vehicles compared to 3 in the prewar period.[9] Thus the process of import substitution was well underway before the Brazilian government issued the decree establishing the basic plan for the manufacturing phase.

In June 1956 the Brazilian government created the Automotive Industry Executive Group (GEIA) to supervise the planning and development of an industry capable of producing a full range of motor vehicles in sufficient quantity to meet domestic demand, from parts and components made in Brazil.

In a series of administrative decrees, GEIA established the guidelines for nationalizing the content of vehicles in each major branch of the industry. Firms that chose to participate were given three and one-half years to meet 90 to 95 percent by weight domestic content requirements. The requirements were later increased to 100 percent with a 1 percent tolerance limit on automobiles and 2 percent on commercial vehicles. Given the state of the industry in 1956, these plans were ambitious. During that year Brazilian-made parts accounted for an average of 43.0 percent of the weight of the vehicles assembled in Brazil.[10] Nevertheless it is important to bear in mind that a substantial parts sector existed in Brazil at the time GEIA made its nationalization decision and that the nationalization policy represented only the final step in a policy of protection and import substitution that began in the early 1950s.

In effect GEIA invited terminal sector firms to gamble on the future viability of the Brazilian market. The 100 percent content requirement meant that the cost of vehicles would be high, at least in the short run. From the point of view of participating firms, the key issue was whether the market could absorb sufficient quantities of high-priced vehicles to ensure profitable production runs.

GEIA's conditions of participation provided incentives that greatly reduced the riskiness of this venture. The most important incentive was access to the growing and protected Brazilian market. For all practical purposes failure to establish production facilities in Brazil was to forfeit participation in a market for motor vehicles and parts, which had very attractive long-run growth prospects.

A second set of incentives reduced the effective out-of-pocket cost of the investments. This was accomplished through fiscal incentives and foreign exchange advantages that GEIA made available to participating firms. The fiscal incentives included total exemption of imported machinery and equipment from duties and sales tax, total exemption of complementary parts (not produced in Brazil) from duties, and special access to short- and long-term credit.

The foreign exchange advantages had two key provisions: government guarantees of the availability of foreign exchange for the importation of parts (working capital could be raised in Brazil and readily converted to hard currencies for crucial parts imports in the installation phase), and government subsidies of foreign equipment imports by guaranteeing the availability of hard currency at favorable exchange rates.[11]

Although these incentives were far less important than market considerations in a firm's decision to invest, they considerably reduced the costs involved in the original round of investments.[12] One study estimates that eighty-nine cents in exchange and fiscal subsidies were granted for each dollar invested in the industry between 1956 and 1961.[13] Once a firm had decided to invest, it could not compete without access to the incentives. Thus, based on its power to grant the incentives, GEIA was able to channel investments and bargain over the nature of the projects. In the original round of bargaining, which ended December 31, 1957, GEIA approved the investment projects of seventeen firms in various segments of the terminal sector of the industry. Eleven firms actually carried out their plans and initiated production.

Two factors appear to have been particularly important in shaping government policy toward the motor vehicle industry in the post-World War II period. First, the isolation of the depression and World War II permitted a group of Brazilian industrialists to get established in the parts sector. This group had an important direct stake in the postwar development of the industry. It is likely that they saw themselves as the principal beneficiaries of high domestic content requirements. Second, the post-Korean war balance-of-payments crisis illustrated Brazil's vulnerability in the international economy and the role of motor vehicle imports in contributing to that crisis. The protective measures of the 1950s came in response to both of these factors. By 1956, when the decree was issued, the direction of the industry was clearly established.

The TNCs that responded to the decree may have preferred lower domestic content requirements, but there is no evidence to suggest that they were hostile to the principle of establishing manufacturing facilities. In fact the TNCs had been involved from the early 1950s in discussions about the form of the decree, including the content of the incentive program.[14] Given the potential payoff, the relatively low initial investment cost, and the certainty of losing the entire market if they did not invest, it is not surprising that the eleven firms were willing to participate.

On the issue of why GEIA permitted eleven firms to enter, several points can be advanced. First, several auto firms already had assembly operations in Brazil, a fact that must have strengthened their ability to bargain with the agency. Furthermore to expel any of these firms would have been interpreted as a hostile act against foreign capital as a whole, which would have made the whole venture less attractive to potential participants. Second, Brazil was the first Third World country to experiment with motor vehicle manufacturing. There was no previous experience on which either the agency or the firms could rely. Possibly neither agency nor firms were fully aware of the consequences that fragmentation would have for production costs. Third, conventional economic analysis suggested to the policy makers that competition was desirable. If the seven major product lines of the industry are considered separately, we find the following: two firms producing buses; three firms each producing jeeps, station wagons, light trucks, and heavy trucks; four firms producing medium trucks; and six firms producing automobiles. Assuming the desirability of competition within product lines, the possibility of some attrition (which in fact did occur) and the lack of compelling a priori reasons why firms should produce in more than two or three product lines, the industrial organization that emerged seems more comprehensible.

Stagnation, 1962–1967

By the end of 1961 the Brazilian motor vehicle industry, though highly fragmented, was capable of producing a full range of vehicles from parts and components produced almost entirely in Brazil. But production grew very slowly, and profits were difficult to realize. In part the stagnation that occurred during this period was due to the inherent structural problems of the industry; in part, it was the consequence of the economic and political turmoil sweeping the country. The key development of the period was the military coup in April 1964. Although stagnation continued for the first few years following the coup, the military government initiated a series of policies that restored economic and political stability and led to a partial resolution of the structural problems. During the immediate postcoup period foreign capital consolidated its control of the terminal sector. Also during this period the state enacted the labor policies on which the subsequent accelerated development of the industry was based.

Structural problems

The structural problems of the industry had three main dimensions: excessive fragmentation, which resulted from the division of a small market among too many producers; chronic underuse of installed capacity, which resulted from a failure of the market to grow as anticipated; and the high cost of Brazilian-made parts, which terminal sector firms were compelled to use because of domestic content requirements. The major consequence of these three problems was that production costs were very high in spite of the availability of low-wage labor.

The impact of fragmentation can be clearly illustrated by data on production runs. In 1962 six firms were producing cars; the largest, Volkswagen, turned out fewer than 54,000 vehicles. Willys Overland was the largest of five light vehicle producers, producing about 28,000 units. Ford, with about 15,000 vehicles, led six firms in the bus and truck segment. It has been estimated that the optimal production run for a single basic vehicle type is 240,000 units per year; assembly operations become viable at about 120,000 units per year.[15] By 1967 the production run of Volkswagen's basic 1200/1300 sedan had reached 91,821 units, but it was the only model produced in Brazil that even approached an economically efficient level for assembly operations. Thus during the stagnation period, eleven firms scrambled to capture a share of a market incapable of supporting a single technically efficient producer in each of its three major segments.

The high-cost problem resulting from excessive fragmentation was exacerbated by the low rates of capacity utilization. Throughout the 1960s the industry was heavily overcapitalized, which meant that the price structure reflected a disproportionately high level of fixed cost. It has been estimated that 40 to 50 percent of installed capacity was unutilized during the stagnation period.[16] Firms that entered during the installation phase had planned their investments for a market that failed to materialize. The result was that plant and equipment that lacked sufficient scale to be technically efficient if run at full capacity was rendered even less efficient by underutilization.

The high cost of parts was the result of government protection and market fragmentation. Fragmentation meant a proliferation of models requiring thousands of different parts. Production runs could never be large enough to justify efficient mass production techniques; instead inefficient job shop production characterized the sector. The main impact of protection was to reduce competitive pressures on costs by eliminating competition from foreign-produced parts. Terminal firms had no choice but to obtain parts in Brazil. They could either purchase parts from high-cost Brazilian suppliers or produce the parts themselves. The main competitive check on the Brazilian suppliers was thus the terminal firm's ability to internalize production; however, this approach was constrained by higher labor costs and smaller production runs since they were producing only for their own use. In some cases competitive pressures among Brazilian suppliers may have provided an impetus to reduce production costs; however, it is likely that neither supplier-supplier nor supplier-terminal firm competition could generate anywhere near the pressure that would have resulted from an opening of the market to competition from foreign imports.

The structure of the Brazilian industry made it a high-cost operation. A leading expert on motor vehicle production in the Third World attributes high production costs to three factors: limited domestic markets, the proliferation of vehicle models and plants, and high domestic content requirements.[17] The Brazilian experience suggests a fourth factor: inefficient use of production facilities due to underutilization of existing capacity. Data for 1965 illustrate the magnitude of these problems in Brazil. During that year the eleven terminal sector firms produced eighty-eight models in a combined production run of 185,173 units, which represented about 50 percent capacity utilization. The average domestic content by weight of these vehicles was 98 percent.[18] A vehicle that cost approximately $1,660 to manufacture in Detroit cost $3,000 in Brazil.[19]

High tax rates also contributed to high sales prices. A federal value-added tax and a state sales tax added 24 and 17 percent, respectively, to the factory cost of an automobile. On the average taxes accounted for about one-third of the sales price of motor vehicles.

The combined impact of high production costs and high taxes resulted in a very high priced vehicle. In the first quarter of 1968 the Brazilian retail list price for the standard Volkswagen sedan, probably the most efficiently produced vehicle in Brazil at the time, was $2,660; a Ford Galaxie sold for $7,000.[20] These two vehicles were selling in the United States during the same period for $1,699 and $2,971, respectively.[21]

The industry was in a paradoxical situation: it appeared to need higher production runs in order to cut costs and lower prices, but higher production runs could be justified only on the basis of higher sales, which appeared to depend on lower prices. Facing this situation, most firms seemed content to ignore the possibility of significantly reducing costs and concentrated instead on increasing their share of the stagnant, low-volume, high-cost, and highly protected market.

The structural problems of the industry persisted throughout the mid-1960s, and by 1967 total production had expanded only 17.9 percent over the 1962 level. Of the major product groups, only automobile production increased during this period. There were really no effective short-run actions that the terminal firms could have taken to resolve their structural problems.

Economic and political crisis

The economic and political crisis that shook Brazil in the early 1960s and the measures taken by the military regime to resolve it were factors critical to the future development of the industry. Economic indicators for 1963 summarize some of the more important economic dimensions of the crisis. During that year, per capita gross domestic product declined by 1.3 percent in real terms, the rate of inflation reached 78 percent, and the net flow of foreign investment was negative.[22] Foreign investors were losing confidence in the country. The U.S. government and the International Monetary Fund were demanding responsible fiscal and monetary actions. Workers were striking and seriously disrupting production. In the face of these problems, the government of João Goulart seemed incapable of constructing a consistent, coherent economic policy.

The political dimensions of the crisis were equally dramatic. The wage struggles of the working class were accompanied by political demands and a major mobilization behind a radical reform program.[23] Rural workers demanded land reform and backed their demands with land seizures and armed confrontations. A radicalization process occurred even among the lower ranks of the military. The country was in a state of political upheaval in which the current distributions of income and wealth were under attack, the role of foreign capital was being assailed, and and the basic development model was subject to serious questioning. As this mass movement grew and became more militant and more strident, various segments of the dominant class increasingly interpreted it as a threat to property interests. Populist President Goulart, who vacillated between attempting to control the movement and encouraging further mobilization and militancy, seems finally in early 1964 to have opted for the mobilization strategy and militant pursuit of the reform program.

It was with the clear support of the dominant class and much of the middle class that the military staged its coup and launched a systematic attack on the working class. Leaders of the mobilization were subject to arrest, torture, and assassination. Labor unions were seized and their leaders replaced by state-appointed bureaucrats. All of the popular movements that participated in the mobilization were quickly crushed.

The coup represents a key turning point in the development of the industry. Prior to the coup political and economic disruption contributed to its stagnation. The future course of foreign participation in the industry was uncertain. Had the radical reform movement been successful, foreign firms could have expected, at worst, nationalization and, at best, state-directed development with a heavy emphasis on commercial and transit vehicles. They also could have expected increasingly independent and militant trade unions.

Instead the military intervened and initiated its attack on the working class. Between 1964 and 1966 the military government imposed a tight austerity program aimed mainly at controlling inflation by depressing the wages of urban workers. During this period the average real value of the minimum wage declined by 28.5 percent relative to precoup levels.[24] In 1965 and 1966 the government tightly controlled most wages and salaries. The wage policy contributed to income concentration by constraining the wages of workers in rapidly growing sectors of the economy where productivity gains have been tremendous, causing a concentration of income within the wage and salaried sector.[25] A variety of other measures were necessary complements to the wage policy. The right to strike was eliminated, legal job security provisions were seriously undermined, and the comprehensive control provisions in the labor law were revitalized and used to prevent further mobilization by the trade unions. The military established a system of controls that they used successfully until the late 1970s to prevent any further mobilization and to eliminate virtually all open manifestations of conflict in the industrial relations system.[26]

Political developments were equally ominous. In effect the government eliminated all potential sources of opposition except the church. Various military regimes outlawed all existing political parties, removed elected officials from office, forcefully dissolved the Brazilian Congress, instituted press censorship, and until the late 1970s repressed virtually all open dissent.

Direct participants in the mass movements of the early 1960s were not the only groups to suffer. The tight money policies of the austerity program pushed many businesses to bankruptcy. In some cases foreign firms were able to acquire Brazilian firms at bargain prices. The middle class also felt the squeeze. Small businesses suffered because of the decline in popular purchasing power, and middle-class wage earners were subject to the constraints of the wage policy. By 1967 the military, by tenaciously following its austerity program, had alienated much of its precoup support. Inflation had been brought under control but at great political expense. The regime needed desperately to develop a broader base, and in order to do so, it was crucial that real growth be restored in the economy. Production of automobiles would be at the center of the growth strategy.

Motor vehicle industry in the crisis

Stagnation was not primarily the result of problems on the supply side of the industry. The terminal sector firms had significant excess capacity throughout the stagnation period. Firms encountered some problems in developing reliable sources of key parts and ensuring supplies of basic materials like steel, rubber, and nonferrous metals; however, these problems were more likely to cause disruption and inconvenience rather than to constitute a constraint on production. If anything, these production-related problems grew worse during the accelerated expansion of the industry after 1968.

The credit shortage affected both the supply and demand side of the motor vehicle market. During the mid-1960s Brazilian financial institutions were unable to finance the working capital necessary to maintain inventories and to purchase parts, let alone to provide the consumer credit necessary to finance automobile sales. The tight money situation was most acute during the 1964–1966 austerity period, although in 1965 the government began to permit the federal savings and loans banks (Caixas Econômicas Federais) to finance automobile sales. By 1967 the credit situation began to loosen significantly.[27]

The potential strength of the automobile market was demonstrated by the resourcefulness and determination that the middle class exhibited during the tight money period. A significant portion of automobile sales, possibly 30 to 40 percent of the total, resulted from group-buying arrangements known as *consórtia* in which group members pooled contributions and purchased cars from the pooled funds. Raffles were held to determine which group member received the automobile in any given month.[28]

The firms best equipped to compete during the stagnation period were the larger producers and those with solid foreign connections. Size was important in gaining an edge on production costs, and foreign connections greatly facilitated access to low-cost credit. Table 1.1 shows the profit rates of the eleven original producers for the period from 1966 to 1980. It also includes late entrants Fiat and Volvo.

In the 1966–1968 period the only firms to show consistent profits were three of the high-volume producers: Volkswagen, General Motors, and Mercedes-Benz. The performance of Ford and Willys Overland, the other two major producers, was inconsistent. None of the low-volume producers—FNM, International Harvester, Scania-Vabis, Simca, Toyota, and Vemag—made significant profits during this time.

A number of changes occurred in the structure of the industry in the latter half of the 1960s. In November 1966 Chrysler International acquired 92 percent of Simca, the parent corporation of Simca do Brasil. Chrysler then acquired the facilities of International Harvester, which had ceased producing because of sustained losses. In October 1967 Ford acquired Willys Overland by purchasing controlling shares from Kaiser and Renault. Volkswagen acquired control of Vemag in 1966. And Alfa Romeo gained control over the Brazilian government's firm, Fábrica Nacional de Motores. A final change came in 1969 when Saab merged with Scania in Sweden, and the name of the Brazilian affiliate was modified to reflect the parent's new structure.

The net results of the consolidations were the disappearance of four of the original participants, the reentry of Chrysler, and virtually total denationalization of the terminal sector as the three firms with the most significant Brazilian participation—FNM, Willys Overland, and Vemag—all passed to foreign control.

Summary

Events occurred during the stagnation period that partially transformed the industry and, more important, totally transformed the industry's political and economic environment. First, the threat posed by the reform movement was eliminated. The movement was thoroughly and completely crushed by the military. Total transformation of the development strategy and the industry was no longer at issue.

Table 1.1
Profit rates of firms in the terminal sector of the Brazilian motor vehicle industry,
1966–1980

Firm	Return of net book value (%)[a]						
	1966	1967	1968	1969	1970	1971	1972
Fabrica Nacional[b] de Motores	3.8	(9.4)	(12.0)	(58.1)	(3.9)	(14.5)	NA
Fiat							
Ford	(2.8)	(6.1)	9.6	0.3	(17.2)	(14.0)	14.0
General Motors	5.1	3.3	8.4	12.1	22.5	31.5	26.0
International Harvester	(19.2)	(29.4)	(32.2)	(2.8)			
Mercedes-Benz	10.2	8.5	11.7	13.6	1.9	5.8	14.5
Scania Vabis[c]	(0.6)	(1.5)	3.8	2.4	11.4	13.0	42.5
Simca[d]	1.6	(77.4)	(9.7)	16.4	NA	(54.6)	(78.1)
Toyota	(13.2)	NA	(7.6)	(9.2)	(5.5)	8.8	(11.4)
Vemag	(48.9)	(5.3)	6.8	10.3	20.7	20.6	21.1
Volkswagen	5.1	6.5	11.5	7.6	18.9	21.1	20.8
Volvo							
Willys Overland	11.3	0.0	(0.8)				

Source: "Quem é Quem na Economia Brasileira," *Visão*, September 7, 1967, and later issues.
Notes: a. Percentage of net income before tax on net book value (capital plus free reserves plus deferred receipts less deferred expenditures). Figures in parentheses indicate losses.
b. After 1977, the data refer to Fiat Diesel.
c. After 1969, the data refer to Saab-Scania.
d. After 1966, the data refer to Chrysler.

1973	1974	1975	1976	1977	1978	1979	1980
NA	NA	NA	0.0	(28.0)	(65.1)	(393.1)	
		NA	(35.4)	(87.1)	(190.3)	(41.3)	(115.5)
21.5	12.3	13.3	(11.6)	(17.3)	35.2	27.1	46.3
9.5	(8.1)	0.5	(1.4)	(86.8)	(9.7)	(38.2)	44.2
14.4	25.4	18.3	33.0	33.6	28.5	23.4	31.0
46.9	38.3	24.1	4.9	14.7	4.0	31.5	68.9
1.5	(365.9)	NA	(97.2)	(44.0)	(20.9)	(178.8)	
(5.5)	(5.1)	5.6	20.2	28.1	22.5	25.4	21.4
17.7	12.7	9.6	12.8	15.6	19.3	18.4	(8.0)
					0.1	(1.5)	(19.9)

Second, the state itself was partially transformed. Prior to the coup the executive branch shared governing power with the Congress and the courts. The political system was open and competitive, and political parties operated freely. A populist had captured the presidency, and although he was weak and indecisive, he nevertheless drifted far enough with the events to alienate most of the upper class. By contrast the military centralized power in the executive branch, repressed political opposition, and used its power to restore stability in the economy and establish conditions for a capitalist growth spurt. This meant that the industry could expect to deal with a powerful, unified, and authoritarian state that could largely ignore popular pressures because of the political vacuum it had created.

Third, the new military government established a set of labor policies with two principal consequences for the industry. The labor policy weakened the position of the industry's own labor force and hence reduced the possibility of disruption and the ability of workers to benefit during the expansion of the industry. It also weakened the position of the working class in general, making it impossible for the labor movement to challenge effectively the distributional consequences of the labor policies and development model. Of particular importance to the industry was the fact that most of the benefits of the model accrued to the upper-income groups, which consumed automobiles.

Fourth, the economic pressures of the period led to a restructuring of the terminal sector and a nearly total elimination of Brazilian capital from that sector. The future role of the national bourgeoisie was limited to the parts sector, and their influence has declined over time even there.

By 1967 the military government was able to ease the most restrictive fiscal and monetary aspects of the austerity program, and the full impact of the changes were about to be felt in the economy and the industry. A period of unprecedented growth was about to commence.

Accelerated Expansion, 1968–1974

A growth strategy centering on consumer durables and especially automobile production was both economically and politically expedient for the military regime. The sector was characterized by excess productive capacity and hence was capable of responding rapidly with increased production. The government created effective demand by making consumer credit available and by pursuing income-concentration policies. By transferring effective purchasing power to the upper and upper-middle classes, the military simultaneously created a market for consumer durables and deepened its base of political support. By the early 1970s the growth strategy was fully in place, upper income groups were prospering, political support for the military regime was expanding, and the motor vehicle industry was experiencing explosive growth.

Demand and growth

The importance to the industry of income concentration is suggested by the 1960 and 1970 data on income distribution. During that period the top 10 percent of income earners increased their share of total income from 39.7 to 47.8 percent.[29] All other population deciles received lower shares of total income in 1970 than they had in 1960. The impact of this concentration process on average incomes within population deciles is also highly revealing. The average real income of the top decile rose by 66.9 percent during the decade, while that of the second highest decile rose 34.8 percent, the third 20.9 percent, and the fourth, fifth, and sixth, 7.7, 6.3, and 9.5 percent, respectively. In absolute terms these comparisons are even more striking. The average income of the top decile increased by 545 cruzeiros per month between 1960 and 1970. For the remaining 90 percent of the population, the total increase in average incomes for the nine population deciles totaled only 234 cruzeiros. In other words the vast majority of the benefits of economic growth during the decade accrued to the top 10 percent of income earners.

Income concentration was very beneficial to the motor vehicle industry. In 1970 the average income of the top decile of the population was approximately $300 per month.[30] It is highly unlikely that at this income level the automobile-consuming segment of the population penetrated much below this top decile. By massively increasing the purchasing power of this group of high-income consumers, the income-concentration process greatly stimulated the effective demand for automobiles and played a major role in the rapid expansion of the industry in the late 1960s and early 1970s.

More recent data illustrate that income concentration continued to occur at least until the mid-1970s. By 1976 the top decile had increased its share to 51.4 percent of the country's total income.[31] The average monthly income of the top decile in 1976 had increased to approximately $670, while the second decile from the top averaged $203 per month.[32]

The upper class has managed to gain an even larger share of a much larger pie. They continued to constitute the heart of the market for new automobiles, although, as the data suggest, the market had begun to broaden with rapid economic growth.

A second factor that stimulated effective demand for motor vehicles was the mobilization of consumer credit. In 1970 consumer credit amounted to 9.7 billion cruzeiros. This figure grew to 14.1 billion in 1971, 22.3 billion in 1972, 37.1 billion in 1973, and reached 40.9 billion cruzeiros by June 1974. An estimated 50 to 60 percent of this total was used to finance automobile purchases.[33]

As expansion of the industry progressed, it developed a self-perpetuating mechanism. Higher-capacity utilization and new, more efficient investments lowered production costs, and part of the savings was passed on to dealers and consumers. By 1974 real wholesale prices of automobiles were approximately 75 percent of their 1969 level, and they continued to fall in the latter half of the decade.[34] Scattered evidence on consumer prices suggests declines of similar magnitude.[35] Thus falling prices became a third factor in the expansion of the demand for vehicles.

One final factor was critical to the expansion of the industry: the rapid rate of growth in the economy as a whole. Between 1968 and 1974 real gross domestic product grew at a compound annual rate of 11.2 percent. The motor vehicle industry was growing almost twice as fast at a rate of 22.0 percent. In effect the motor vehicle industry was one of the most important leading sectors in an economy-wide growth boom. By linkage effects, both forward and backward to other industries, the motor vehicle industry further contributed to the demand for its own product.

The impact of these factors on the growth of the industry was dramatic. Total production of vehicles more than tripled between 1968 and 1974 (see table 1.2). All five of the major firms experienced substantial growth.[36]

The differential growth rates of the three major market segments during this period are shown in table 1.3. All segments of the market experienced rapid growth, but the automobile sector was by far the most dynamic portion of the industry.

Initially firms in the terminal sector could meet the buoyant demand in the post-1968 period with existing facilities by bringing into production the excess capacity that had characterized the industry throughout the stagnation period. As existing facilities began to be strained in the early 1970s, terminal sector firms undertook a massive

Table 1.2
Motor vehicle production by major firms in Brazil, 1968–1980

Year	All firms	VW	Ford	General Motors	Mercedes-Benz	Chrysler	Others[a]
Production in 1968 (units)	279,715	154,972	69,379	24,987	16,736	8,564	5,077
Production indexes							
1968	100	100	100	100	100	100	100
1969	126	115	128	211	103	138	95
1970	149	150	110	281	106	162	99
1971	184	190	138	333	119	207	97
1972	218	217	171	418	157	211	101
1973	261	236	213	563	195	430	113
1974	324	296	254	730	224	449	236[b]
1975	332	324	246	696	261	286	292
1976	352	342	248	725	292	325	514[c]
1977	329	305	188	616	316	257	1,735
1978	380	335	226	779	351	198	NA
1979	368	315	225	752	328	185	NA
1980	416	332	238	927	359	166	NA
Market share in 1977 (%)	100.0	51.4	14.2	16.7	5.8	2.4	9.6

Source: ANFAVEA, Notícias de ANFAVEA, various issues.
Notes: a. For 1968–1971, "others" denotes the following firms: Fábrica Nacional de Motores (FNM), Saab-Scania, Toyota, Industria Automotores do Nordeste, and Puma. Industria Automotores do Nordeste ceased production in early 1972.
b. FNM began producing automobiles in 1974, which accounted for about one-half of the 1973–1974 increase in the "others" category.
c. Fiat initiated production in 1976.

Table 1.3
Motor vehicle production by major market segment, 1968–1980

Year	Automobiles and station wagons	Light vehicles[a]	Trucks and buses
Production in 1968 (units)	202,841	29,080	47,471
Production indexes			
1968	100	100	100
1969	138	93	95
1970	169	103	89
1971	216	120	91
1972	251	154	117
1973	296	200	149
1974	368	241	185
1975	381	237	187
1976	408	214	202
1977	380	112	243
1978	454	143	212
1979	NA	NA	NA
1980	482	244	245

Source: ANFAVEA, *Notícias de ANFAVEA,* various issues.
a. Includes jeeps and pickup trucks.

round of new investment in which their net book value more than doubled between year-end 1968 and year-end 1973. Data from the Council of Industrial Development (CDI), the agency that replaced GEIA and other similar groups, document the expansion of the industry. Between 1971 and 1973 the CDI approved projects in the parts and terminal sectors of the industry valued at $1,477 million (approximately two-thirds was destined for the terminal sector of the industry).[37] A number of major terminal sector projects were approved during this period: a joint venture by Fiat, the state of Minas Gerais, and the Italian government's investment corporation capable of producing 190,000 automobiles annually and an additional 155,000 motors for export; expansion of the Volkswagen complex at São Bernardo do Campo to increase daily production from 1,600 to 2,500 vehicles; construction of a new four-cylinder motor plant with 255,000 annual capacity and expansion of facilities for the introduction of Ford's Maverick; construction of a diesel motor plant by General Motors; and introduction of a new car and expansion of existing production capacity by FNM (Alfa-Romeo). The installed capacity of the terminal sector expanded enormously as these projects were completed, reaching an estimated 1.5 million units by 1975.[38]

Politics of the boom

The relationship between the military regime and the TNCs was clearly symbiotic during this period. The regime administered the repressive policies that stimulated the growth of the industry, and the TNCs helped generate political support for the regime. Repression of the working class was fundamental and essential to this system. In the absence of repression, income concentration would have been challenged. Workers and their trade unions would have demanded redistribution policies and supported their demands with militant activity. The industry could not have expanded as it did had it not been for the role the state played in crushing the labor movement and controlling the working class.

The domination of the industry by the TNCs was greatly enhanced during this period. TNCs controlled all of the massive new investments in the terminal sector, as well as much of the capital that flowed into the parts sector.[39] Brazilian private capital declined greatly in relative importance and ceased to play an important role in shaping the industry.

Developments in the industry reflected the broader changes occurring in the Brazilan economy where foreign capital dominated the dynamic consumer durable sector, and the state increased its relative importance both as a regulator of the development process and as a direct participant, particularly in infrastructural investments. National capital, which tended to be concentrated in consumer nondurables, grew far more slowly and declined in relative importance compared to foreign and state capital; however, the sheer dynamism of the Brazilian economy provided all segments of capital with opportunities to diversify and grow. The boom also provided substantial benefits for the traditional petit bourgeoisie and the salaried middle class, especially those elements whose skills were in short supply in the dynamic upper segments of the labor market. From the commencement of the boom in the late 1960s until deterioration of the economic situation in the mid-1970s, there was remarkable unity among the segments of the economic elite in their support of the growth strategy and the authoritarian regime that directed it.

Retrenchment, 1975–1980

The quadrupling of oil prices in late 1973 and subsequent balance-of-payments problems have had profound implications for the whole pattern of economic growth in Brazil and especially for the motor vehicle industry. The impact on the industry is reflected in production figures. Between 1968 and 1974 production leaped ahead at a compound annual rate of 22.0 percent. Between 1974 and 1980 the annual rate of increase was only 4.3 percent. The slowdown is even more dramatic when one considers that Fiat inaugurated a large-scale production facility precisely when the fortunes of the industry began to sour.

The dramatic decline in the growth of the industry is largely the result of government measures designed to limit the expansion of the domestic market for automobiles. At the same time the state has attempted to aid the industry by subsidizing and promoting export activities to offset the decline of the domestic market. Both sets of measures have their roots in the balance-of-payment crisis that arose in the mid-1970s. The oil crisis in 1973 and the serious deterioration in the Brazilian balance of trade that followed served as the impetus for a change in direction of state policy in regard to the industry. State intervention during the mid-1970s focused on reducing the contribution of the industry's negative trade balances and the buildup of foreign debt. The industry has entered a period of retrenchment in which the domestic automobile market will play a far less important role in industry growth and profitability.

Balance of payments and foreign debt

Historically Brazil has been successful in maintaining surpluses in its balance of trade. Between 1946 and 1970 exports exceeded imports in all but three years (1952, 1960, and 1962);[40] however, the situation changed drastically in the 1970s as deficits became the norm. Table 1.4 presents the Brazilian balance of payments from 1970 through 1980. The deterioration of the trade balance in the mid-1970s is readily apparent. This deterioration was not caused by declining or stagnating exports, which in fact grew throughout the period. Rather, the problem arose on the import side. Between 1970 and 1974 imports increased fivefold. In 1974 the trade deficit reached a record $4.7 billion. Between 1974 and 1978 the total volume of imports stabilized largely because the government established a restrictive import control program in

Table 1.4
Brazilian balance of payments and foreign debt, 1970–1980

Account	1970	1971	1972	1973	1974	1975	1976	1977	1978	1979[a]	1980
1. Trade balance	232	−341	−244	7	−4,690	−3,499	−2,151	97	−1,024	−2,840	−2,828
Exports	2,739	2,904	3,991	6,199	7,951	8,670	10,126	12,120	12,659	15,244	20,132
Imports	−2,507	−3,245	−4,235	−6,192	−12,641	−12,169	−12,277	−12,023	−13,683	−18,084	−22,960
2. Services[b]	−815	−980	−1,250	−1,708	−2,433	−3,213	−3,860	−4,020	−4,975	−7,199	−9,500
3. Transfers	21	14	5	27	1	0	6	6	72	18	150
Current transactions (1 + 2 + 3)	−562	−1,307	−1,489	−1,688	−7,122	−6,712	−6,011	−3,917	−5,927	−10,020	−12,178
4. Net capital flow[c]	1,015	1,846	3,492	3,512	6,254	6,161	8,298	4,863	9,439	6,936	9,362
5. Errors and omissions	−92	−9	436	355	−68	−399	150	−316	368	−130	−683
Balance of payments (1 + 2 + 3 + 4 + 5)	545	530	2,439	2,179	−936	−950	2,437	630	3,880	−3,215	−3,499
6. Gross foreign debt	5,295	6,622	9,521	12,571	17,166	21,171	25,985	32,037	43,511	49,904	54,400
7. International reserves	1,187	1,746	4,183	6,416	5,269	4,041	6,544	7,256	11,895	9,689	6,911
Net foreign debt (6 + 7)	4,108	4,876	5,338	6,156	17,131	19,442	17,131	24,781	31,616	40,215	47,489

Source: *Conjuntura Econômica*, various issues.

a. Preliminary estimates.

b. Includes balance for travel, transportation, insurance, capital income (interest, profits, and dividends), government transactions, management fees and technical assistance, patents and royalties, and various miscellaneous services.

c. Includes inflows of investments, loans and financing, less amortization payments, plus the net flow of short-term loans.

1975.[41] Nevertheless in spite of the controls and in spite of accelerated export promotion activities, the trade deficits remained a serious problem in every year except 1977, totaling $16.9 billion for the 1974–1980 period.

Remarkably these trade deficits have not developed into a serious balance-of-payment crisis, particularly in the light of the magnitude of the additional outflows in the service account. Outflows for services have increased from $815 million in 1970 to $9.5 billion in 1980. The most important items in the service account are the various forms of repatriated income on foreign loans and direct investments (for example, interest, profits, and royalties). The trade account and the service account are the two main components of current transactions that were in deficit every year of the 1970s. Two factors have been particularly important in offsetting this massive outflow in current transactions: inflows of foreign direct investment and a massive increase in Brazil's externally held debt. The net annual flows of these two items appear on line 4 of table 1.4 as net capital flow. The buildup of debt is documented in the last row of the table. Net foreign debt increased by approximately $41.3 billion from the beginning of 1973 until the end of 1980. Foreign direct investment expanded by approximately $9.3 billion during the same period.[42]

The conclusion one is forced to draw from these data is that the Brazilian government is mortgaging the country's future in order to meet its current international obligations. Trade deficits and service payments are being financed through increased foreign penetration of the Brazilian economy, a penetration that implies even more massive outflows of capital in the future. The country is caught in a vicious cycle: to solve its immediate problems, it must incur potentially more serious future problems. Foreign investors must be attracted, and foreign loans must be obtained. The situation is highly precarious, and yet the investments and loans keep flowing in. It is a tribute to the underlying strength of the Brazilian economy and to the sophistication of Brazilian technocrats that the confidence of foreign investors has remained reasonably high.

As long as foreign capital can be attracted, the cycle of increased debt and foreign ownership can continue, but the danger of a loss of confidence is always present. As foreign debt grows, so does wariness. If banks refused to make new loans, corporations refused to make new investments, and they all tried to repatriate as much income as possible, the present equilibrium between current account deficits and capital account inflows would collapse. Overnight service payments would explode, capital inflows would be reduced to a trickle, and balance-of-payments disaster of major proportions would be at hand. Clearly all of the important actors have an interest in avoiding this situation. Nevertheless it is rational for a bank or corporation to protect itself as the risks increase. But a solution that is rational for each and every individual translates into a disaster for the system if collectively pursued by the individual actors. Under the circumstances, it is incumbent on the state to impose higher-order system rationality.

One aspect of the higher-order rationality involves sophisticated management of the debt with the object of lengthening payback periods in order to smooth and stretch out the outflows of interest and am-ortization payments. Given the size of the current debt, Brazilian tech-nocrats have a considerable amount of bargaining power in debt renegotiation. One need only imagine Brazil as the lead domino in an international moratorium movement to have discovered the worst nightmare of international banking executives.[43] But this nightmare is shared by the Brazilian technocrats. Moratorium is very risky. Brazil's growth model is based on the total economic integration of the country within the international capitalist economy. A threat to that economy is a threat to the technocrats and the Brazilian upper class as a whole. Moderation and reasonable behavior are clearly in order. Concessions have been and will continue to be made to the technocrats, and in return they manage the long-run solution to the problem, a solution that ultimately must center on the trade account. The outflows in the service account can be delayed through debt management and, in ex-treme cases, through measures like freezes on the repatriation of profit, but eventually the claims of the foreign sector must be met. To do otherwise would imply a transformation of the whole development model and a secession from the international capitalist economy. Thus it is not at all surprising that the technocrats have established com-prehensive programs to restrict imports and expand exports.

Role of the motor vehicle industry

During the early 1970s the motor vehicle industry was responsible for large outflows in the trade account. By far the most important factor in the 1974 import explosion was the rise in the cost of petroleum. In 1973 imports of petroleum and petroleum derivatives cost Brazil $680 million,[44] the 1974 cost was approximately $2.7 billion.[45] It has been estimated that 60 percent of Brazil's petroleum imports were consumed by motor vehicles in 1974, much of it by private passenger cars.[46] Between 1968 and 1974 automobiles accounted for 82.6 percent of the total number of vehicles produced by the industry. At the new price levels of petroleum, the cost of organizing an urban transportation system around private ownership of the automobile was enormous for a country at Brazil's level of development. From a macroeconomic perspective Brazil's auto fleet became a serious liability.

The industry also depended heavily on foreign sources of technology. During the accelerated expansion from 1968 to 1974, the industry grew twice as fast as the economy as a whole. This expansion required huge outlays for imported machinery and equipment, particularly during the investment boom of the 1970s. Of the investment projects approved by the CDI in 1973, a key year in the investment boom, the industry accounted for 29 percent of the total imports of machinery and equipment of the entire manufacturing sector.[47]

The motor vehicle industry was also an important consumer of imported raw materials. In the case of steel, one source estimated that the motor vehicle industry used about 660,000 tons in 1974, or approximately one-quarter of total steel imports.[48] The industry probably consumed a disproportionate share of nonferrous metals, rubber, and plastic imports also.

Thus, in the early 1970s, the motor vehicle industry was responsible for a substantial share of petroleum, machinery and equipment, and raw materials imports. Together these three items accounted for 67.5 percent of the total imports in 1974.[49]

The industry also generated balance-of-payments outflows in the service account. The terminal sector of the industry is almost completely foreign owned, as are many of the major parts firms. In 1973 these two sectors accounted for 14.6 percent of all registered foreign capital in Brazil.[50] If the foreign firms in the industry had repatriated profits equal to 12 percent of registered capital in that year, $71.3 million would have left the country.[51] In fact scattered evidence indicates that profit remittances were probably lower than 12 percent.[52] But accounting profit is only one of several means by which money is repatriated, and it may not be the most important in the case of the motor vehicle industry. For example, in the period from January 1965 to July 1975, the Volkswagen subsidiary remitted profits of $70.6 million to its German parent, while remittances in payments for technology totaled $208.5 million.[53] In late 1975 General Motors do Brasil had an officially registered capital of $38 million and an additional $200 million in the form of loan capital.[54] As a cost item, interest payments on the loan capital represent a convenient and unchallenged flow of resources back to the parent. In the General Motors case, this flow dwarfed profit remittances. Taken together remittances of the industry in the service account (profits, royalties, and interest) probably had a large negative impact on the balance of payments.

A more exact indicator of the overall, direct impact of the industry on the balance of payments can be gained from a study by the Brazilian government of the 115 largest foreign-owned firms in Brazil.[55] The balance-of-payments accounts for 1974 of the automobile firms parallel those of the nation as a whole in some interesting ways. First, trade account had a $208 million deficit. Second, service payments represented another important outflow of $71 million. Taken together the service and trade accounts produced a large deficit in current transactions of $279 million. Third, the current transactions deficit was offset in part by a large inflow of capital in the form of new foreign obligations ($193 million).[56] In short the industry is a prime example of the mechanism by which foreign control of the Brazilian economy is extended and deepened. It is important to bear in mind that these data do not include the value of imported oil consumed by Brazil's vehicles.

Given the magnitude of its adverse impact on current transactions, the industry, not surprisingly, began to fall from favor as the centerpiece of the growth model. In fact 1974 represents an important turning point. From that point forward the motor vehicle industry has been affected by government policies designed to prevent a balance-of-payments crisis. The specific interests of the industry in maintaining an accelerated rate of expansion in the domestic market have been sacrificed by the government in favor of the general interests of the upper class in maintaining stability in the international economy.

Domestic stagnation

The government responded to the oil crisis by increasing the purchase price of gasoline. Between January 1973 and April 1977 the price of a gallon of regular gasoline rose by 242 percent in real terms, reaching $1.70.[57] The government also tightened consumer credit terms on automobile loans; it decreased the maximum installment period from thirty-six to twenty-four months and required a 30 percent down payment.[58] The combined effect of these two measures was to raise substantially the income levels necessary to purchase and operate an automobile, thus decreasing effective demand.

In the area of import controls, the government launched an immediate attack on the former privileged status of the industry. In late 1974 the CDI removed automobile assembly from the list of industries that qualified for exemptions.[59] This meant that any imported equipment for expansion of existing facilities or new investments was subject to the general import policies, which were undergoing a tightening process in 1974 and 1975. From a situation in which imports were readily available at international prices, the TNCs moved to a situation in which they faced high duties, some outright import bans, and from late 1975 on, a system under which they were required to place on deposit with the central bank the equivalent of the f.o.b. value of the imported goods 360 days prior to delivery. The deposits were refunded, but they drew no interest and were not subject to monetary correction, which meant that their real value declined dramatically, thus substantially raising the actual cost of the imported goods.[60] The only possibility of escaping this situation was through participation in the export promotion program, one dimension of which was the restoration of the major import concessions. The message to the automobile producers was clear: any major future expansion was contingent on a commitment to export.

The rapid deceleration of growth in the domestic market led to a profit squeeze in the 1974–1976 period for the automobile producers (see table 1.1). Chrysler's losses were staggering, with recovery complicated by the firm's emphasis on larger cars. Ford showed a loss in 1976 and by early 1977 claimed to be losing $250 on each vehicle sold in Brazil.[61] General Motors suffered its first loss in over a decade in 1974; in 1975 it barely broke even; and from 1976 to 1979 it registered consistent losses. Fiat, in attempting to carve out a share of the shrinking automobile market, was allegedly selling vehicles at a price 7 percent below production costs, a strategy that produced staggering losses in the 1976–1980 period.[62] Perhaps because of high volume and rapidly expanding export business, Volkswagen was able to remain profitable until 1980 when it too finally suffered losses.

Faced with a relatively stagnant demand for automobiles after 1974, the producing firms sought to maintain profit margins by raising prices and increasing per unit profits. In this attempt, they initially encountered stiff opposition from the price control agency, which not only did not allow the higher markups but refused to permit full pass through of cost increases. The net effect of this confrontation was to reduce the firms' incentive to expand automobile sales. Once again the message was clear: automakers must shift their product mix in favor of commercial vehicles, improve the fuel efficiency of automobiles, and begin to produce for export.

In July 1977 the terminal sector of the industry was granted an exemption from the price control system.[63] One interpretation of this event is that the government perceived that its message had been heeded and the industry deserved respite. But this view ignores the actions the TNCs had been taking in their own defense. Their bargaining chips were their workers. In early 1977 the large automobile producers engaged in a round of layoffs and threatened further permanent reductions of their labor forces.[64] Probably because of the general climate of heightened political tension in the country, the government let it be known that it preferred reductions in overtime and short-term layoffs to the permanent dismissals. In April the government granted the exemption from the price controls in return for collaboration in avoiding dismissals. The automobile firms began an immediate round of price increases.

Export promotion

The pressures on motor vehicle firms to participate in the export incentive schemes became acute in the mid-1970s. In addition to coercive measures—stagnation of the domestic automobile market, disqualification of the industry from import incentives, the price-cost squeeze, and constant pressure from the government—the vehicle firms had strong positive reasons for entering the program. Most important were the lucrative financial inducements and the competitive advantage over nonparticipating rivals provided by the export program. By 1976 all of the important terminal sector firms had succumbed to the combination of pressures and incentives and had signed export contracts under the Special Fiscal Benefits for Exports (BEFIEX) program. General Motors, Ford, and Volkswagen are each committed to programs in excess of $1 billion in exports over a ten-year period. The volumes for the other firms are as follows: Chrysler, $314.5 million; Saab-Scania, $415.4 million; Mercedes-Benz, $500 million; Fiat, $550 million; and FNM, $400 million.[65] Volvo, the latest entrant in the industry, began to participate in BEFIEX as soon as production began in 1977.

The impact on the volume of exports has been very impressive, growing from $76.2 million in 1973 to $1,512.3 million in 1980.[66] From the BEFIEX exports should be subtracted parts and components imports, which, according to the program, can constitute up to one-third of the total value added in Brazil. But even if this deduction is made, the large net positive impact of the program remains impressive.

Participating firms were granted a number of lucrative financial advantages.[67] From a profit perspective, the most important benefits were derived from a federal and a state tax credit.[68] In reality the two tax credits constituted an outright export subsidy. The taxes were waived on export sales. In addition the firm received a credit payable against taxes due on goods produced for the domestic market. The credit was equal to the value of the taxes waived on export sales.

An example will clarify how the system worked.[69] Suppose a firm exported $100 million worth of vehicles and sold $400 million worth in Brazil. Taxes equal to $30 million would be waived on the export sales, and the firm would receive an additional $30 million credit against the $120 million in taxes due on domestic sales. This example illustrates a number of interesting points. First, Brazilian state and federal governments stood to lose $60 million in tax revenues for every $100 million sold in the export market rather than the domestic market. Second, the exporting firm gained a $30 million advantage on each $100 million it exported in comparison to its nonexporting competitors in Brazil.[70] Third, the exporting firm gained a $30 million advantage on each $100 million it exported in comparison to its competitors in the export market. The example clearly reveals the competitive pressures that forced all of the motor vehicle firms into the program and reveals the incentives for parent firms to reduce production in home country facilities in order to create space for the products of their Brazilian subsidiaries.[71] Finally, it also reveals the extraordinary lengths to which the Brazilian government went in order to promote motor vehicle exports. Who wins and who loses? The answer is painfully obvious. The winners are the participating TNCs, while the losers are the workers in the export markets who are dislocated from their jobs and the Brazilian people who must make up $60 million in lost taxes or forgo $60 million in public services.

In spite of the advantages of this program to the firms, its long-run viability is not a forgone conclusion. There is a problem with resistance from workers in the export markets whose jobs are threatened with extinction. Brazilian export subsidies on a variety of products were attacked in the United States as early as 1976.[72] With respect to protectionism, the automobile firms derive a distinct advantage from their broadly based international structure and their practice of worldwide sourcing. This permits Ford, for example, to ship Brazilian four-cylinder motors to Canada for installation in vehicles that ultimately will be sold in the United States. If the motors entered directly, they would be subject to the same pressures applied to other subsidized Brazilian exports.

A second problem results from intrafirm rivalry. Two events at Volkswagen provide examples. In the first, the parent company effectively cut off access of its Brazilian subsidiary to an attractive market in Algeria and claimed the market as its own.[73] In the second, the Mexican subsidiary began to export models not produced in Europe to West Germany and other European countries, a market previously promised to the Brazilian subsidiary.[74] The problem can be stated in general terms as one of too many export commitments and too few markets for the exported goods. If Spain, Brazil, Mexico, and Argentina all have similar export promotion strategies, if markets in the non-oil-producing Third World are stagnating for the same reasons that the Brazilian market is stagnating, if workers in the rich countries are increasingly effective in protecting their jobs, then where will the exported products be absorbed? In particular how will the TNC, which has signed contracts with two, three, four, or more countries, meet its obligations, and what recourse will the country or countries have if it does not? The answers to these questions are not clear, but it seems likely that if problems arise for one firm, they will probably arise for all. Under such circumstances effective discipline will be difficult for governments to administer. In the meantime firms participate and collect lucrative subsidies.

One interesting issue has not been addressed thus far; it relates to the ability of the industry to compete in world markets in the absence of the export subsidies. Two aspects of the Brazilian industry are particularly relevant with respect to this issue. The first concerns the structure and scale of the industry. In spite of excessive fragmentation in the Brazilian industry, considerable specialization occurs within major product groups. The vast growth of the domestic market from 1968 to 1974 has produced a situation in which certain firms within certain product groups have begun to achieve reasonably high levels of production in terms of the minimum requirements for technical efficiency. For example, automobile production reached 512,946 units at Volkswagen, 164,729 at General Motors, 124,656 at Ford, and 97,302 at Fiat in 1978. The totals for light vehicles were less impressive: 18,570 at General Motors, 13,967 at Ford, and 5,605 at Volkswagen. In the truck and bus segment Mercedes produced an impressive 58,766 units, while Ford built 18,104 and General Motors 11,437. When combined with relatively low-cost Brazilian labor, this implies a cost structure that is probably quite competitive. These five firms accounted for 96.6 percent of the vehicles produced by the industry in 1978. Volkswagen has clearly arrived at an efficient scale of operation. Mercedes-Benz is probably close in the truck and bus category where scale requirements are not nearly as high as in automobile production. Ford and General motors have passed the minimum scale for automobile assembly operations. It seems possible that the cost structure of the industry has reached or is approaching an internationally competitive position, which implies that the export subsidies could be eliminated if less costly incentives or coercive measures could be discovered.

The second aspect of the industry that relates to this issue is the export-oriented nature of the latest round of investments. Many of these projects were designed specifically for an export market. They employ the latest technologies and are planned for optimal output levels regardless of domestic market demand. Ford's new motor plant is one example; when built, it was capable of producing 255,000 four-cylinder motors for which the demand in Brazil in the late 1970s was about 120,000 units. Fiat's new complex has a motor facility that produces 150,000 units beyond Brazilian needs. In the case of investments of this sort, the firms face the choice of exporting or letting the facilities remain idle. The existence of the export-incentive program was clearly the salient factor in the firms' decisions to make these investments, but once the facilities are in place, the existence of the incentive is irrelevant. The firms have no real choice but to export.

The State, the TNCs, and the Working Class: Autos in the 1980s

In the 1980s the Brazilian motor vehicle industry will be capable of producing at least 1.5 million vehicles per year. Its products are being exported in large volumes, a process that will probably continue even if export subsidies are eliminated. In quantitative terms, the industry is probably the most successful case of import substitution industrialization in the Third World.

I have traced the evolution of the industry through its various stages of development by focusing primarily on the relationship between the

Brazilian state and the TNCs that dominate the industry. In each stage the actions of the state have had a major impact not only on the economic performance of the industry but also on its structure and operating policies. Overall the relationship between the state and the firms has been harmonious and mutually supportive. Even when the continued rapid growth of the industry began to threaten the entire growth model and the state took action to slow the growth of the domestic market, it sought to ease the burden by providing TNCs with lucrative incentives to expand export sales.

All indications are that the state will continue its supportive policies in the 1980s. It is committed to a massive program of developing alcohol as a vehicle fuel. In this regard the state and the TNCs have entered a formal accord with the following provisions: the firms have promised to produce 900,000 vehicles that operate on 100 percent alcohol between 1980 and 1982; they have promised to convert 270,000 existing vehicles to 100 percent alcohol operation during the same period; and the state has promised to guarantee the supply of alcohol fuel for these vehicles in the main service stations of Rio de Janeiro, São Paulo, and other states where the vehicles will be authorized for sale.[75] If this program is successful, macroeconomic constraints on the growth of the domestic market will ease.

The future of the industry will also depend on the outcome of political and social changes that began in the late 1970s. The Brazilian working class is again threatening to become an important political force in shaping the industry. In fact the working class has always had an important influence on the industry. In the early 1960s the radicalization of the workers contributed to the stagnation of the industry and threatened the future of foreign participation in the industry. In the late 1960s and early 1970s the total domination of the labor movement was crucial to the success of the income concentration policies that helped create the dynamic market for automobiles. The domination of workers within the industry allowed the TNCs to reap virtually all of the gains of rapidly increasing productivity. Between 1966 and 1974 output per worker in the terminal sector of the industry jumped from 4.37 to 8.41 units per year.[76] Workers in the industry had serious grievances during this period: dangerous and unhealthy working conditions, a very intense pace of work, severe and arbitrary authority on the job, and a total lack of job security. Nevertheless the domination of the labor movement was so complete that these grievances were effectively suppressed. The state administered the repressive labor policies that made this situation possible.

In the late 1970s the whole authoritarian labor structure came under attack. Workers in the motor vehicle industry played a vanguard role in job actions in 1977 and major strike movements in 1978, 1979, and 1980, movements that revitalized the unions. Labor is demanding larger wage increases, recognition of union stewards, restoration of legal job security, and the right to strike. The labor movement is also a key element in the movement to democratize the country. The state has responded to these developments with a mixture of cautious concessions and repression. The TNCs have tightened their internal security measures.

Although the outcome of these struggles is difficult to predict, the renewed militancy of auto workers portends increasingly difficult day-to-day labor relations and more resistance to speedups at a time when an uncertain profit picture makes labor docility and increased productivity particularly important to the TNCs. The renewed vitality of the labor movement could mean an end to the income concentration process that has been so beneficial to the industry. This also is occurring at a time when the high cost of purchasing and operating a vehicle has restrained the growth of the domestic market. The days of easy growth and easy profit are over; the days of increased competition and conflict have begun.

Notes

1. The source of all production data used in this chapter is the manufacturers' association for the terminal sector of the industry, the Associação Nacional dos Fabricantes de Veículos Automotores (ANFAVEA). Detailed production data are published in the monthly newsletter, Notícias de ANFAVEA.

2. Source of motor vehicle data is ANFAVEA. The figure for economy represents the compound annual growth rate of real gross domestic production. Conjuntura Econômica 31, no. 7 (July 1977). Both growth rates are calculated for a seven-year period over the base-year totals for 1967.

3. World Bank, World Bank Atlas: Population, Per Capita Product and Growth Rates (Washington, D.C., 1977), p. 6.

4. José Almeida, A Implantação da Indústria Automobilística no Brasil (Rio de Janeiro: Fundação Getúlio Vargas, 1972), p. 8.

5. Ibid., pp. 8, 11.

6. This figure does not include 1950, for which data were not available. Fundação IBGE, Comércio Exterior do Brasil (Rio de Janeiro: various issues).

7. In 1952 motor vehicles (including assembled passenger cars, trucks, buses and other road motor vehicles and unassembled chassis but excluding parts and components shipped separately from chassis) accounted for 12 percent of total Brazilian imports. Source for total Brazilian imports is *Conjuntura Econômica* 29, no. 1 (January 1975): 74.

8. Fundação IBGE, *Comércio Exterior do Brasil*.

9. Almeida, *A Implantação da Indústria Automobilística no Brasil*, p. 23.

10. Ministério da Indústria e Comércio, cited by ibid., p. 45.

11. Almeida, *A Implantação da Indústria Automobilística no Brasil*, p. 33.

12. On the relative importance of incentives and market considerations, see Lincoln Gordon and E. Grommers, *United States Manufacturing Investment in Brazil: The Impact of Brazilian Government Policies, 1946–1960* (Cambridge: Harvard University Press, 1962), esp. chap. 4.

13. Almeida, *A Implantação da Indústria Automobilística no Brasil*, p. 41.

14. Gordon and Grommers, *United States Manufacturing Investment*, pp. 47–48.

15. Jack Baranson, *Automotive Industries in Developing Countries* (Washington, D.C.: International Bank for Reconstruction and Development, 1969), pp. 29, 73.

16. José Almeida, "A Evolução da Capacidade de Produção da Indústria Automobilística Brasileira no Período 1957–1969," *Pesquisa e Planejamento* 2, no. 2 (June 1972): 60.

17. Jack Baranson, "Will There Be an Auto Industry in the LDC's Future?" *Columbia Journal of World Business* (May–June 1968): 52.

18. A complete listing of all models produced from 1957 to 1971 can be found in ANFAVEA, *Indústria Automobilística Brasileira* (São Paulo, 1972). Data on percentage of Brazilian content attained is published annually in IBGE, *Anuário Estatístico do Brasil* (Rio de Janeiro, various years).

19. Baranson, "Will There Be an Auto Industry?" p. 52.

20. Economist Intelligence Unit, "The Brazilian Passenger Car Industry," *Motor Business*, no. 55 (July 1968): 40.

21. *Automotive News 1968 Almanac* (Detroit: Slocum Publishing Co., 1968), pp. 66, 78.

22. *Conjuntura Econômica* 28, no. 5, p. 145; 29, no. 12, p. 88.

23. See Timothy F. Harding, "The Political History of Organized Labor in Brazil" (Ph.D. diss., University of Wisconsin, 1974).

24. For an analysis of the Brazilian government's labor and wage policy, see Kenneth S. Mericle, "Conflict Regulation in the Brazilian Industrial Relations System" (Ph.D. diss., University of Wisconsin, 1974). Minimum wage data appear on p. 10.

25. Ibid., pp. 252–299.

26. See Mericle, "Conflict Regulation," and Kenneth Mericle, "Corporatist Control of the Working Class: Authoritarian Brazil since 1964," in James Malloy, ed., *Authoritarianism and Corporatism in Latin America* (Pittsburgh: University of Pittsburgh Press, 1977).

27. Sam Morely, "Inflation and Stagnation in Brazil," *Economic Development and Cultural Change* 19, no. 2 (January 1971).

28. Economist Intelligence Unit, "Brazilian Passenger Car Industry," pp. 40–41.

29. There is now a vast literature on the Brazilian income distribution. The data presented here are from Carlos Langoni, *Distribuição de Rendas e Desevolvimento Econômico de Brasil* (Rio de Janeiro: Expressão e Cultura, 1973). Langoni had best access to government data, and thus his figures are probably most reliable. Most authors do not dispute that income concentration occurred during the 1960s; however, there is great disagreement over the causes of concentration. In addition to Langoni, some of the major contributions to this debate include: G. S. Fields, "Who Benefits from Economic Development? A Reexamination of Brazilian Growth in the 1960's," *American Economic Review* 67 (1977): 570–582; A. Fishlow, "Brazilian Size Distribution of Income," *American Economic Review* 62 (1972): 391–402; R. Hoffmann, "Considerações Sôbre a Evolução Recente da Distribuição da Renda no Brasil," *Revista de Administração de Emprêsas* 13 (1973): 7–17; R. Hoffmann and J. C. Duarte, "A Distribuição da Renda no Brasil," *Revista de Administração de Emprêsas* 12 (1972): 46–66; and J. Wells, "Distribution of Earnings, Growth and the Structure of Demand in Brazil during the 1960's," *World Development* 2 (1974), published in Portuguese in R. Tolipan and A. Tinelli, *A Controvérsia sôbre Distribuição de Renda e Desenvolvimento* (1975). An excellent review of this literature is contained in Edmar Bacha and Lance Taylor, "Brazilian Income Distribution in the 1960's: 'Facts,' Model Results and the Controversy," Discussion Paper 34 (Cambridge, Mass.: Harvard Institute for International Development, 1977).

30. This calculation is based on average monthly income of 1,360 cruzeiros converted to dollars at the average exchange rate prevailing in 1970 ($1 = 4.564 cruzeiros).

31. The 1976 data have rekindled the income distribution debate. *Estudos Econômico* 11, no. 1 (January–March 1981) is devoted entirely to the subject. The data reported here are from Marcos G. da Fonseca, "Radiografia da Distribuição Pessoal de Renda no Brasil: Uma Desagregação dos Indices de Gini," *Estudos Economicos* 11, no. 1 (January–March 1981): 13.

32. These figures are reported in 1970 dollars. The data are reported by Fonseca in 1970 cruzeiros. The average monthly income was 3,056 cruzeiros (1970), converted to dollars at the average exchange rate prevailing in 1970 ($1 = 4.564).

33. Carlos Alberto Wanderley, "Novas Prioridades de Indústria Mudam Ação das Financeiras," *Jornal do Brasil*, September 8, 1974.

34. These figures are based on an index constructed by dividing the wholesale price index for motor vehicles by the consumer price index for Rio de Janeiro with January–June 1969 = 100 as the base for both indexes. The price data are published in *Conjuntura Econômica* 35, no. 3 (March 1981) and earlier issues.

35. "Indústria Automobilística: Sem Orelhas Vermelhas," *Visão*, September 23, 1974, p. 68.

36. The phenomenal growth of General Motors was the result of the commencement of passenger car production in 1968. Until that year GM had produced exclusively for the slower-growing light vehicle and truck and bus sectors of the market. Mercedes, which produces trucks and buses exclusively, did not experience rapid growth until that sector of the market started to expand in 1972. The data on market shares in table 1.2 are slightly misleading because most of the major producers tend to concentrate on certain segments of the market. Market shares based on number of vehicles produced understates the importance of Mercedes, Chrysler, and others, all of which produce higher-priced vehicles; Volkswagen's market share tends to be overstated because of an exclusive focus on the lower end of the market. Market shares by sales were as follows in 1973: Volkswagen, 33.3 percent; General Motors, 24.3; Ford, 19.9; Mercedes, 11.2; Chrysler, 6.7; and others (FNM, Saab-Scania, and Toyota), 4.5. These figures are calculated from data in "Quem é Quem na Economia Brasileira," *Visão*, August 31, 1974. Final sales data do not provide an accurate measure of the relative importance of the firms in the economy due to different levels of vertical integration.

37. Ministério da Indústria e do Comércio, Conselho de Desenvolvimento Industrial, *Relatório 1973* (Rio de Janeiro, 1974).

38. José Almeida, "Perspectivas da Indústria de Veículos no Brasil," *Revista de Administração Pública* 8, no. 1 (January–March 1974): 318.

39. By 1973 TNCs controlled or owned outright twelve of the top twenty-five parts firms and participated as minority joint-venture partners in three more. Among the next twenty-five, seven were wholly owned or controlled by TNCs, and one was a minority joint venture. The twenty-three firms accounted for 63.2 percent of the sales of the top fifty group. Data are from "Quem é Quem na Economia Brasileira," pp. 197, 201.

40. *Conjuntura Econômica* 29, no. 1 (January 1975): 74.

41. For details on the import-control program, see *Business Week*, January 12, 1976, and *Business Latin America*, February 18, 1976.

42. Data on foreign investment flows are from the balance-of-payments capital account published in *Conjuntura Econômica*. For historical data see vol. 29, no. 12 (December 1975). The most recent data are usually published in the February issue. These data include only the net flow of new foreign investment into Brazil. They do not include reinvestments. The Banco Central do Brasil reports an increase in the stock of registered foreign capital (investments and reinvestments) of $14.1 billion between December 1972 and December 1980. *Boletim Mensal do Banco Central do Brasil* 17, no. 10 (October 1981) and earlier issues.

43. In June 1976 U.S. banks held $10.4 billion of the $25 billion total external Brazilian debt. See *Conjuntura Econômica* 31, no. 5 (May 1977).

44. Banco Central do Brasil, *Boletim do Banco Central do Brasil: Relatório Anual 1973* 10, no. 3 (March 1974): 77.

45. *Conjuntura Econômica* 29, no. 12 (December 1975): 77.

46. "Freire Recomenda Modelos Mais Econômicos e maior Segurança," *Jornal do Brasil*, September 6, 1974.

47. In 1973 the CDI approved investment projects that included $1,228 million worth of machinery and equipment imports. Of this total 29 percent was destined for the motor vehicle sector. Given the lead times necessary for carrying out investment projects, one would expect that most of the machinery and equipment in the 1973 projects was imported in 1974 and after. The CDI-approved projects do not include machinery and equipment for small-scale projects and for normal replacement purposes. Thus a significant share of imports are not included in the CDI total. Of the actual CDI projects, some were probably cancelled. On the other hand, firms traditionally have understated the share of machinery and equipment that is to be imported (as opposed to purchased by Brazil) in their proposals to the CDI. The source of the data on CDI projects is Ministério da Indústria e do Comércio, Conselho de Desenvolvimento Industrial, *Relatório 1973* (Rio de Janeiro, 1974).

48. Marcos Pereira Vianna, "Evolução Automotiva Conduz as Vanguardas Mundiais," *O Estado de São Paulo*, September 8, 1974, p. 58.

49. *Boletim Mensal do Banco Central do Brasil* 17, no. 10 (October 1981). Of $12.6 billion of total imports, machinery and equipment totaled $3.1 billion. Petroleum (fuels and lubricants) equaled $2.8 billion, and raw materials (including cast iron and steel, nonferrous metals, plastics, and rubber) were $2.6 billion.

50. *Banco Central do Brasil* 10, no. 3 (1974): 233.

51. Registered foreign capital in these two sectors totaled $594.3 million on June 30, 1973. Ibid., p. 233. The actual value of assets of these firms was much higher because of debt financing.

52. A recent study by the Brazilian government lists actual profit remittances for 1974 at $27 million. The study is reported in *Business Latin America,* June 16, 1976. In August 1974 the president of one of the major U.S. firms in the terminal sector claimed in an interview with me that all profits of the company had been reinvested in the late 1960s and early 1970s.

53. *Latin America Economic Report,* January 9, 1976.

54. Ibid.

55. Reported in *Business Latin America,* June 16, 1976.

56. Ibid.

57. Gasoline prices are published in *Conjuntura Econômica* 31, no. 2 (February 1977): 70.

58. *Business Latin America*, July 28, 1976, p. 234.

59. Ibid., September 18, 1974, p. 300.

60. *Business Week*, January 12, 1976, p. 38.

61. *Latin America Economic Report* (March 25, 1977), p. 47.

62. Ibid., October 7, 1977.

63. Ibid.

64. Ibid., March 11, April 8, October 7, 1977.

65. BEFIEX Program, cited by Ronald E. Muller and David H. Moore, "Case One: Brazilian Bargaining Power Success in Befiex Export Promotion Program with the Transnational Automotive Industry" (paper prepared for the United Nations Center on Transnational Corporations, New York 1978).

66. *Boletin Mensal do Banco Central do Brasil* 17, no. 10 (October 1981) and earlier issues. These data include all Brazilian exports for the transportation material industry. Export of motor vehicles and motor vehicle parts constitute the vast majority of exports from this sector.

67. See, for example, Kenneth S. Mericle, "The Brazilian Motor Vehicle Industry: Its Role in Brazilian Development and Its Impact on United States Employment" (unpublished paper, 1975).

68. The federal tax is a value-added tax payable on all products produced in Brazil. The state tax is a sales tax.

69. In this example, we are assuming that the firm exports goods to which it has contributed an added value of $100 million. As presented, the example in the text overstates the value of the tax credits since, on export products worth $100 million, the terminal sector firm could not possibly be responsible for the full value. Perhaps a more realistic situation would be one in which exports equal $200 million, value added by the exporting firm equals $100, and the rest of the example does not change. The situation described in the text was adopted to simplify exposition; the principles illustrated in the example do not change if the more realistic situation is used.

70. The waiving of exports from the two taxes does not affect the firm's position relative to its competitors in the home market. The tax waiver affects only the firm's ability to compete in the export market. However, the credit, since it can be used to offset local taxes, does provide the exporting firm with a clear advantage over its nonexporting competitors.

72. Ford has been accused of reducing production of four-cylinder motors at its Ohio plant in order to allow its Brazilian motor plant to supply a Canadian assembly operation that services the entire North American Market. See *Latin America Economic Report*, July 23, 1976, p. 115.

72. Contervailing duties were imposed on shoes, leather handbags, and soybean oil in 1976. See *Business Latin America*, May 26, 1976, p. 161. In 1977 coun-

tervailing duties were imposed on Brazilian scissors and cotton yarn. See ibid., September 21, 1977, p. 298.

73. *Latin America Economic Report,* March 3, 1978, p. 69.

74. Ibid.

75. *Wall Street Journal,* September 10, 1979, and "Brazil: Gearing up to Produce the All Alcohol Car," *Business Week,* October 1, 1979, pp. 60–61.

76. The source of these data is ANFAVEA.

2

The Rise and Fall of the Argentine Motor Vehicle Industry

Rhys Jenkins

In 1959 the Argentine government embarked on a major project to develop a national vehicle industry through the attraction of foreign investment by the world's leading car manufacturers. Today that project is in a state of crisis. The world's second largest transnational corporation (TNC), General Motors, after two decades of production in Argentina, has decided to give up manufacturing vehicles there. Argentina has fallen further behind Brazil in terms of vehicle output, has been overtaken by Mexico, and is on the verge of falling behind Venezuela. What went wrong? Was this a case of bad planning by the government of an underdeveloped country? Or was it a case of underdevelopment promoted by TNCs?

Origins of the Argentine Motor Vehicle Industry

A first attempt at local motor vehicle assembly was made by an Argentinian, Horatio Anasgasti, using imported Bleriot parts from France in the early part of the century, but this venture failed. In 1916 Ford set up one of its earliest overseas assembly plants in Buenos Aires. General Motors set up a subsidiary in 1925, and Chrysler began assembly a few years later. By the late 1920s sales of vehicles in Argentina were running at over 50,000 a year and reached a peak of 76,561 in 1929.[1] More than half of total sales were accounted for by the three U.S. firms, the only companies whose scale of operation justified local assembly. Their cost advantage over firms that imported assembled vehicles was increased in 1931 by changes in the Argentine tariff giving a 30 percent discount on CKD (completely knocked down) and 15 percent on SKD (semiknocked down) imports of cars and trucks.[2] In the 1930s the three U.S. firms had an even greater share of the total market.

The interruption of supplies of imported parts and the increasing age of the Argentine vehicle stock led to a rapid growth of repair shops and workshops producing parts up to the end of World War II. Employment increased threefold and value added two and a half times between 1935 and 1946.[3] After the war some of these firms enjoyed a continued expansion, with their products being incorporated by local assemblers.

In the early 1950s the Peron government attempted to promote the development of a vehicle manufacturing industry. In 1951 decree 25.056/51 declared the motor vehicle industry of national interest and granted exchange and import privileges for a period of five years. Two years later, in 1953, the Peronist regime, faced with a falling level of accumulation and a deteriorating balance-of-payments position, changed its attitude toward foreign capital, passing law 14.222. Although the main objective of the law was to attract foreign capital, it attempted to impose a measure of control by limiting profit remittances to 8 percent of the original investment.

The degree to which the industry developed following these measures was limited. The state-owned IAME (Industrias Aeronáuticas y Mecánicas del Estado) began producing vehicles in 1951 on a small scale. In the following year Mercedes-Benz began producing chassis for trucks and buses and a car for use mainly as a taxi. The main entrant to the industry before 1959 was Industrias Kaiser Argentina (IKA) in 1955, which alone accounted for $8 million of the $12 million of foreign investment authorized under law 14.222. Kaiser, however, was not a major force in the international motor vehicle industry, and the investment in Argentina was seen as a means of disposing of part of the company's plant in the United States where the firm had failed in competition with the Big Three U.S. manufacturers. Total output of vehicles in Argentina over the entire 1950s was less than 100,000, of which less than 40,000 were cars (see table 2.1).

Significantly in the period up to 1959, no Argentine government had succeeded in getting a major company to set up a manufacturing plant in the country. Despite sales of around 20,000 in the late 1920s and a subsequent reduction in their Argentine market because of problems in importing parts, neither Ford nor GM decided to move from assembly to local manufacture. Ford, whose assembly plant had to close in 1948 because of import restrictions, did not take advantage of the Peron decrees.[4] GM, whose Overseas Policy Group considered manufacturing

Table 2.1
Production of cars and commercial vehicles, 1951–1978

	Cars	Commercial vehicles	Total
1951	18	90	108
1952	62	907	969
1953	63	3,011	3,074
1954	173	3,186	3,359
1955	235	6,156	6,391
1956	326	5,617	5,943
1957	5,461	10,174	15,635
1958	14,310	13,524	27,834
1959	18,290	14,662	32,952
1960	40,154	49,194	89,348
1961	78,274	57,914	136,188
1962	90,648	39,232	129,880
1963	75,338	29,561	104,899
1964	114,617	51,866	166,483
1965	133,734	60,802	194,536
1966	133,812	45,641	179,453
1967	130,297	45,021	175,318
1968	127,965	43,011	170,976
1969	153,047	65,543	218,590
1970	167,000	52,599	219,599
1971	193,105	60,132	253,237
1972	200,885	67,706	268,591
1973	219,439	74,303	293,742
1974	212,088	74,224	286,312
1975	185,162	54,874	240,036
1976	142,072	51,445	193,517
1977	168,126	67,230	235,356
1978	134,118	45,757	179,875

Source: Asociación de Fábricas de Automotores (ADEFA).

in Argentina after World War II, decided that assembly would be economically more sound.[5]

Undoubtedly this lack of investment prior to 1959 reflected in part
the general attitude of foreign capital toward the Peronist government
in the postwar period. Between 1951 and 1955 the annual average of
new direct foreign investment in Argentina (including reinvestment)
was only $3.1 million and accounted for only 1 percent of new foreign
investment in all of Latin America. Following the overthrow of Peron,
foreign investment increased sharply, to over $60 million a year in
1956 and 1957.[6] In the case of the motor vehicle industry, it also reflected
the situation in the world industry in this period, which was dominated
by the three U.S. firms, especially Ford and GM, which as late as 1954
accounted for almost two-thirds of world car production. The subsequent
recovery and growth of the European producers reduced their share
to less than a half by 1958.[7] In the early 1950s, however, the Big Three
did not feel threatened by the possibility of investment in Argentina
by European competitors. TNC suspicion of Peron and the absence of
competitive pressure from European firms were more important than
the size of the potential market (which was considerable given the age
of the existing stock of cars after the war) or the lack of supporting
industrial development in postponing the major development of the
industry in Argentina until the 1960s.

Establishment of Large-Scale Manufacturing

The establishment of the motor vehicle industry as a large-scale manufacturing operation and the consolidation of control of the terminal
sector by TNCs coincides with the period of civilian rule in Argentina
between the election of Arturo Frondizi and the military coup in 1966.
The September restoration, which overthrew Peron, reestablished the
position of the agricultural oligarchy and saw the dismantling of the
apparatus of populist nationalism established during the previous decade. The Instituto Argentina de Promoción de Intercambio (IAPI) was
abolished, credits to small and medium-sized firms cut, the peso de-
valued, and exchange controls removed. The result was a substantial
shift in income toward agricultural profits as agricultural prices
improved.

Despite the economic liberalization policies of the military, it was
not until the election of Frondizi in 1958 (following a secret pact with
Peron) that foreign capital began to flow into Argentina on a massive

scale.[8] Nevertheless many of the favorable conditions required by foreign capital had already been laid prior to his election with the change in the government's attitude toward labor, the incorporation of Argentina in the IMF and the World Bank, and the application of a stabilization policy. Despite a history of anti-imperialist rhetoric, Frondizi pursued an explicitly *desarrollista* policy, characterized by an increased integration with foreign monopolies and the negotiation of credits through the International Monetary Fund (IMF). The main beneficiaries of these policies, in addition to foreign capital, were the oligarchy and large national capital. The result was that small and medium firms and a large part of the middle and working classes became increasingly disillusioned.[9]

The attraction of foreign capital was regarded as an alternative to imposing restrictions on domestic consumption, which would permit industrialization without requiring political repression.[10] Law 14.780 of 1958 provided favorable conditions for foreign capital wishing to invest in Argentina. Unlimited profit remissions and repatriation of the original investment were both allowed. Investment was permitted in the form of capital goods, raw materials, and intangibles as well as foreign exchange, and foreign capital was guaranteed equal juridical treatment with national capital. Authorizations of foreign investments leaped from $42 million between 1956 and 1958 to over $200 million in 1959. The share of foreign firms in industrial production, which fluctuated between 18 and 19 percent from 1955 to 1959, moved sharply upward to reach 24.7 percent by 1962.[11]

The specific legislation designed to promote the development of the motor vehicle industry was decree 3693 of 1959. Indeed the industry was one of the key sectors of the *desarrollista* program together with chemicals, petrochemicals, and metallurgy. Between 1959 and 1962 over $500 million of foreign investment was authorized, of which almost $100 million was in the motor vehicle industry.[12] Although not all the investments authorized were undertaken, the period did show a substantially higher inflow of foreign capital than previous or subsequent years.[13]

Decree 3693 set the framework for the organization of the motor vehicle industry over a five-year period, giving certain advantages to firms that submitted production plans for the local manufacture of cars and trucks with an increasing incorporation of local parts. The main benefits were duty-free imports of machinery and equipment required for investment and preferential duties on imports of parts and com-

Table 2.2
Permitted imports in the Argentine automotive industry (percent c.i.f. value)

Class	Type	1960	1961	1962	1963	1964
A	Commercial vehicles	45	40	35	30	20
B	Cars 190–750 cc	45	40	35	25	10
C	Cars 750–1,500 cc	40	35	30	20	10
D	Cars 1,500–2,500 cc	35	30	25	15	10
E	Cars more than 2,500 cc	30	25	20	15	10
F	Others	20	15	10	5	5

Source: Industrias Kaiser Argentina, *La Industria Automotriz Argentina* (Buenos Aires, 1963), pp. 34–35.

ponents up to a maximum percentage of the c.i.f. (cost, insurance, freight) value of the vehicle. (See table 2.2.) The preferential duty was 20 percent in category A (commercial vehicles), with a further 5 percent that could be imported at the 100 percent duty and the remainder up to 60 percent at 300 percent. For the other categories the preferential rate was 40 percent, and again the remainder up to 60 percent could be imported at 300 percent (reduced to 200 percent in June 1960). A further 10 percent of the annual amount imported was allowed to cover losses and replacement of parts with an import duty of 100 percent. In 1960 imports of assembled vehicles were prohibited, although a nominal rate of protection was fixed at between 400 and 500 percent for cars and 35 to 40 percent for trucks.

The terms of the decree proved highly attractive to foreign capital, hardly surprising in view of the fact that up to 66 percent of all the c.i.f. value of cars (including the allowance for losses of parts) could be imported and that in the first year of operation for a car between 750 cc and 1500 cc the duty would only be 62 percent of the c.i.f. price (40 percent at 40 percent, 20 percent at 200 percent, and 6 percent at 100 percent). In a situation of acute supply shortage and prohibitive import duties on assembled cars, local prices were between two and two and a half times the c.i.f. price of an assembled vehicle. This meant that with a minimal amount of local manufacturing, substantial profits could be realized.[14]

The immediate response to the decree was twenty-three proposals to manufacture vehicles in Argentina. Some never began production and others produced only a few hundred units, but fifteen firms produced in excess of 5,000 vehicles during the five-year period 1959–1960 to 1964.[15] Although there is obviously truth in the charge that some firms never intended manufacturing locally and were merely taking advantage of the program to assemble largely imported cars, it is also clear that a significant number of firms were interested in establishing a presence in the industry. Ten of the dozen largest vehicle producers in the world in the late 1950s entered the Argentine industry, all but one of them (BMC) through direct investment.

The large number of entering firms has led some commentators to suggest that the government's concessions were excessively generous.[16] Although this may apply to the firms that began manufacturing simply to make short-term profits, it would be misleading to suggest that incentives could have been fine tuned to lower levels, which would have led to the entry of a far smaller number of firms, consonant with the size of the local market. Such a view ignores the highly interdependent nature of corporate behavior in the motor industry, which provides an almost classic example of oligopolistic reaction.[17] Under these circumstances, a decision to invest in the industry by leading TNCs will lead others to invest in order to avoid future exclusion from an important market. If incentives are not sufficiently attractive, no investment is generated. If they are sufficiently attractive, then a number of firms will enter, irrespective of market size.

The question remains, however, given the intense competition to enter, why did the government fail to use its potential bargaining strength to obtain the entry of a small number of firms on more favorable terms through direct control of the number of plants and firms permitted? A senior government official provided the official rationale:

The means to obtain these objectives [i.e., the development of the motor vehicle industry] was through a regimen of open competition, where there would be room for all the interested parties which complied with certain common requirements. From the struggle for a hungry, but restricted market, the most competent and efficient firms should emerge, without any prior exclusions and without any discretionary powers on the part of government officials which would permit erroneous interpretations. We received clear instructions from the President to this effect. Only the fulfillment, or otherwise, of the basic requirements of the agreed plans should establish differences.[18]

As subsequent experience was to show, such reasoning was fundamentally flawed. First, there is no guarantee that the most efficient firms technically will necessarily survive where some firms have the backing of the vast financial strength of multinational parents. Second, price competition will not necessarily be the result of a greater number of firms in a market that remains oligopolistic. Finally, despite the free entry of all firms, the industry was subject to numerous discretionary controls, including government approval of output for each firm's production plan.

An alternative explanation that seems more plausible is that the Frondizi government, which was anxious to attract foreign capital and create a favorable impression in international financial circles, was reluctant to appear to be controlling the entry of such capital. Law 14.780 on foreign investment represented a sharp break with the Peronist legislation in permitting unlimited remittance of profits and repatriation of capital, and it may have been considered unwise to discourage the inflow of capital in any way. Indeed it is possible that political pressure was brought to bear on the government by the companies to ensure the acceptance of their proposal.

In 1961 the government revised decree 3693/59, introducing decree 6567/61. The new decree made some modifications in the permitted import content for vehicles, spelled out the method for calculating import content, which the original decree had not done, required a minimum investment of 200 million pesos by the end of 1961, and permitted a higher import content for firms introducing a new model. The new decree followed pressure from the U.S. companies to modify the initial legislation, and it was only after it was passed that Ford, GM, and Chrysler began producing cars in Argentina (originally they had produced only manufactured trucks).[19] Paradoxically the one type of vehicle where a large number of firms had not entered under the 1959 decree was category E, cars of more than 2,500 cc. Here IKA had the possibility of achieving significant economies of scale. The result of entry by the U.S. firms was that the market came to be divided between four firms, and the opportunity for specialization was lost. This supports the view that pressure from the major companies may have contributed to the excessive fragmentation of the industry.

In its anxiety to attract foreign investment, the Argentine government not only failed to impose any restrictions on foreign firms entering the terminal industry but also largely ignored the interests of national capital as exemplified by the parts industry. The parts industry grew rapidly before and during World War II and continued to expand from the late 1940s when difficulties in importing again increased demand. The industry's output in 1954 was estimated at 4,000 million pesos (at 1963 prices).[20] Local capital dominated the sector, and as late as 1964 foreign firms accounted for less than one-fifth of the output of parts and components.[21] In contrast to the other major Latin American countries, Brazil and Mexico, the Argentine legislation was confined to the terminal industry and placed no limitations on the vertical integration of these firms. Thus while the parts producers welcomed the decision to develop a local motor vehicle industry, they regretted the failure of the government to give equal treatment to the parts suppliers and to prevent vertical integration by the terminals.[22] Despite pressure throughout the 1960s, parts firms were unable to obtain more favorable treatment from successive governments. Consequently the foreign car manufacturers, in addition to producing their own stampings and engines (in all cases), also made their own forgings (Fiat, IKA), castings (IKA, Ford), axles (Fiat, Ford, GM, Peugeot, Citroen), transmissions (Fiat, IKA, Peugeot, Chrysler), and suspensions (Fiat, IKA, Ford, GM, Peugeot).

Growth and Denationalization, 1959–1965

The Frondizi government's policy of economic expansion based on large inflows of foreign capital was successful in bringing about significant growth in 1960 and 1961, particularly in those sectors where foreign investment was concentrated—petroleum, consumer durables, and petrochemicals. The inflow of capital meant that expansion did not lead immediately to a balance-of-payments crisis; however, the growth of import-intensive industries meant an increase in imports of over $250 million in 1960 and $210 million in 1961.[23] Imports of parts for the motor industry alone went up by $65 million in 1960 and almost $40 million in 1961, accounting for more than one-fifth of the total increase in imports.[24]

A reversal in the inflow of foreign capital precipitated the recession of 1962 and 1963. Vehicle output fell, and a number of smaller firms went out of business. After 1963 production recovered rapidly, reaching almost 200,000 cars and commercial vehicles in 1965. By 1965 the number of firms in the terminal industry had been reduced to thirteen compared to twenty-one in 1960. This process of concentration accentuated by the recession was also facilitated by the increase in local content requirements and changing market conditions. The permitted import content at preferential rates of import duty was reduced to 20 percent for commercial vehicles and 10 percent for cars. The large backlog of demand for cars was eliminated, and the extremely favorable market conditions in the early years of the industry came to an end.

This process of concentration was accompanied by a displacement of national capital from the terminal industry as the TNCs extended their control. In 1960 majority foreign-owned firms accounted for only one-third of Argentine vehicle output, but by 1965 they had increased their share of production to around 60 percent. A number of foreign firms began production in Argentina with only a minority shareholding in a locally owned company (see table 2.3). Of these firms, Chrysler, Citroen, and Peugeot later increased their holdings to obtain majority and eventually virtual total ownership. The U.S. Big Three, which began by producing trucks, entered the car market in 1962 when this segment was clearly viable. In a situation of substantial excess capacity (around 40 percent by the mid-1960s), foreign firms squeezed out financially weaker national competitors by offering favorable terms on consumer credit and updating their model ranges.

Locally owned firms, lacking financial resources, were in a poor position to resist these pressures. Two strategies were open to them: find a foreign company that would provide the necessary financial backing or attempt to obtain government support. Siam di Tella Automotores, the largest wholly Argentine company in the industry, tried both strategies. After the decision of the U.S. companies to produce cars and faced with a falling market share, Siam approached BMC, whose models they produced, offering the British firm up to 50 percent of the company, but this was turned down.[25] Siam then proposed a merger of the five remaining locally owned companies (excluding IKA), which would be competitive with state support. The government was asked to provide over $14 million in financial support but did not.[26] Eventually Siam was taken over by IKA, a merger that compounded IKA's problems.

The period 1959 through 1964 saw the bulk of the foreign investment authorizations in the motor vehicle industry. One estimate put the total authorized by mid-1964 at $144.1 million,[27] whereas in the period 1965 through 1970, authorizations fell to only $15.5 million.[28] The amount actually invested by the motor vehicle manufacturers up to mid-1964 was considerably lower, only $33.1 million. In fact during this period, when new foreign investment in the industry was heaviest, the outflow of profit remittances was even greater, reaching $52.3 million.[29] Thus within a very short period the impact of the industry on the capital account of the balance of payments became negative.

Most of the new investment in the industry by foreign companies was in plant and equipment. Of $225 million of foreign investment

Table 2.3
Firms in the Argentine motor industry

Firm	Licensor	Cars	Trucks	Foreign ownership (1961)
Ford	Ford	x	x	100%
GM	GM	x	x	100%
Chrysler-Fevre	Chrysler	x	x	Majority
Fiat	Fiat	x		Majority
IKA	Kaiser/Renault	x	x	Minority
Mercedes-Benz	Mercedes		x	Majority
Siam di Tella	BMC	x	x	0
Autoar	NSU	x	x	0
Cisitalia	Abarth/Cisitalia (?)	x		Minority
Citroen	Citroen	x	x	Minority
Dinborg	Borgward	x	x	0
DINFIA	Borgward (engine)	x	x	0
Fáb. de Autos Utilitarios	Fuldamobil	x		0
Goliath Hansa	Goliath Hansa	x		Minority
IAFA	Peugeot	x		Minority
IASF	DKW	x	x	Minority
ITA	Porsche (parts)	x		0
Isard	Hans Glass	x		0
Los Cedros	Studebaker/Heinkel	x	x	0
Metalmecánica	BMW/Simca	x		0
Onfre Maimon	Villers	x		0
Panambi	Messerschmitt	x		0

authorized in the transport equipment sector (mainly motor vehicles) between 1954 and 1972, 93 percent took the form of goods.[30] GM, for example, was authorized to invest $14 million by decree 11625/59 in order to manufacture trucks and diesel engines in Argentina. This was to come entirely in the form of imports of machinery and equipment and special tools, and a further $6 million of local expenditure was to be financed by reinvested local profits. The ability to undertake the investment without any dollar outflow from the United States was an important consideration for GM.[31] Part of the equipment imported in this way was secondhand. The most notorious case was Kaiser, which imported machinery and equipment that was over twenty years old. Ford also imported secondhand machinery from Canada. A study carried out in 1967 indicated that almost a quarter of the equipment in use at the time was more than ten years old.[32] The use of secondhand machinery gave considerable scope for manipulation of prices (transfer pricing) in order to give the firm's assets a greater book value or, in the case of a joint venture, in order to obtain a greater share of the company.[33]

The Consolidation of Foreign Domination, 1966–1970

The Onganía regime, which came to power in the 1966 coup, represented the consolidation of the position of monopoly capital in Argentina. Particularly from March 1967 the government applied an economic program that represented the hegemonic domination of foreign monopoly capital.[34] In contrast to previous stabilization policies, the benefits of devaluation and anti-inflationary measures did not accrue to agricultural exporters. The industrial sector was the main beneficiary of these policies, and within it monopoly capital was particularly favored, as indicated by the increased share of the largest one hundred companies in industrial production in this period.[35]

The installation of Juan Carlos Onganía in power saw the final shake-out of locally owned firms in the terminal sector of the motor industry. By 1968 foreign control was virtually complete. Siam di Tella had gone out of business, IKA was taken over by Renault, and Industria Automotriz Santa Fe was on the brink of bankruptcy. Only the state-owned DINFIA (formerly IAME) remained. This period also saw an extension of foreign control over the parts industry with a number of locally owned firms being taken over by foreign companies (see table 2.4). By the early 1970s over sixty foreign firms controlled more than 40 percent

Table 2.4
Locally owned parts producers taken over by foreign capital

Transferred firm	Purchasing firm	Country
Thompson Ranco	Thompson Products	United States
Indeco S.A.	Federal Mogul	United States
Suavegom	Dow Chemical	United States
Transax	Ford Motor Co.	United States
Acinfer S.A.	Ford Motor Co.	United States
Argelite	Holley	United States
Beciu S.A.	Eaton	United States
Armetal S.A.	Bud	United States
Resortes Argentina S.A.	Associated Spring	United States
Resortes Sachs S.A.	Isringhausen GBM	West Germany
Agrometal Ingersol	Borg Warner	United States
Byron Jackson S.A.	Borg Warner	United States
Bendix S.A.	Bendix	United States
Proyectores Arg.	Cibie	France

Source: J. E. Corradi, "Argentina," in R. H. Chiloate and J. C. Edelstein, *The Struggle with Dependency and Beyond* (New York: John Wiley and Sons, 1974), table 1.

of the sales of the parts industry (excluding tires), double their share less than a decade earlier.[36]

After an initial period of stagnation (1966–1968) vehicle production increased substantially, reaching a peak of 293,742 units in 1973. Nevertheless, despite renewed growth, there was considerable cause for concern. One of the problems that aroused most concern was the continuing high cost of locally produced vehicles. In 1967 it was estimated that cars produced in Argentina sold on average at 122 percent above their prices in the country of origin; the corresponding figure for trucks was 85 percent.[37] In 1968 another estimate found that the average price to the dealer of Argentine cars was 102 percent higher than the f.o.b. price, and the price to the public was 135 percent higher.[38] Thus despite reductions in the relative price of cars compared to other domestic prices since the early 1960s, Argentine-produced cars continued to sell at more than twice their international price.

Despite the concentration of production in the industry, labor productivity did not increase significantly during the 1960s. Throughout the decade it took on average around 250 man-hours to produce a vehicle, although it had been lower in 1960 and 1961 when a significant

Table 2.5
Man-hours per vehicle produced, 1960–1976

Year	Man-hours
1960	233.9
1961	227.6
1962	277.2
1963	293.6
1964	253.9
1965	242.1
1966	268.8
1967	244.6
1968	244.5
1969	237.9
1970	249.0
1971	218.3
1972	214.7
1973	218.1
1974	241.8
1975	276.5
1976	309.3

Source: ADEFA.

proportion of parts and components were imported (see table 2.5). An international study indicated that labor productivity in the motor industry of Argentina was a quarter of U.S. levels and less than half of European levels in 1965.[39]

The major factors accounting for the high price of locally produced cars have been the large number of firms, the wide variety of models produced, and the frequency with which models are changed. Although the number of firms in the industry was reduced from twenty-one in 1960 to thirteen in 1964, the number of models produced increased from 50 to 57.[40] Despite a further reduction in firms to ten by 1972, the number of models in production had increased to 120.[41] The scale problem has been compounded by the fact that the foreign companies in the industry have followed a policy of frequent model changes. In the large car segment of the market, GM, Chrysler, and Ford changed their models between 1965 and 1967, and IKA supplemented its range by introducing the Torino. In 1969 and 1970 Chrysler, GM, and IKA changed their models, and Ford introduced the Fairlane. In medium-sized cars, Fiat replaced the 1100 by the 1500 in 1963, the 1500 by the 1600 in 1969, and the 1600 by the 125 and 127 in 1971 and 1972. SAFRAR introduced the Peugeot 404 in 1962, the 504 in 1968, and the 404 Diesel in 1971. In the 1970s U.S. producers expanded into the medium-sized car market, with Chrysler introducing the Dodge 1500 in 1971 and Ford and GM beginning to produce the Taunus and Opel, respectively, in 1974. Thus despite the production of over 3 million vehicles in Argentina between 1959 and 1976, the only models of which more than 100,000 were produced during the period have been the Fiat 600 and the Peugeot 404.

Despite high production costs, foreign firms continued to earn profits throughout the latter part of the 1960s. The situation began to deteriorate in the early 1970s, by 1972 the industry as a whole was declaring a loss, and in 1973 all firms were operating at a loss. These losses were associated with increasing financial costs and exchange losses as a result of the rapid inflation and devaluation of the peso in the early 1970s.

High profit rates in the 1960s were not associated with high rates of capital accumulation after the initial spurt of investment in the period 1960 through 1963 (table 2.6). Subsequently the level of investment in fixed assets has been well below 10 percent of the value of production throughout the period, with the exception of 1970. This factor, when taken together with the relatively high profit rates of the 1960s, implied a considerable outflow of foreign exchange from the industry in the form of remitted earnings. Between 1965 and 1970 the total amount of new foreign investment authorized by the government in the industry came to only $15.5 million.[42] But profit remissions in the period 1968 through 1970 were more than $15 million in each year.[43] Royalties and technical assistance payments to the parent companies should also be included as part of the capital outflow. One estimate puts these at almost $40 million over the period 1968 to 1971 and almost $13 million in 1971 to 1972.[44]

Another estimate based on declarations made by the firms under the Ley de Reconversión de la Industria Automotriz indicated that total royalty payments in 1970 were as much as $26 million, of which $18 million were accounted for by seven terminal firms.[45] Data for 1972 from the Registro Nacional de Contratos de Licencias y Transferencia de Tecnología showed that the motor vehicle industry (both terminal and auxiliary) had royalty charges of $12.7 million and was the most

Table 2.6
Investment in fixed assets as percentage of value of production and in U.S. dollars, 1960–1976

	Production (%)	Investment (millions of U.S. $)
1960	12.6	50.7
1961	10.4	67.4
1962	17.1	94.8
1963	14.4	64.9
1964	4.2	34.5
1965	3.1	32.5
1966	4.3	41.9
1967	3.7	28.5
1968	4.2	33.8
1969	6.9	70.3
1970	11.3	108.0
1971	4.4	49.8
1972	4.7	46.5
1973	5.2	82.2
1974	4.4	91.3
1975	2.1	43.8
1976	1.5	na

Source: Own elaboration from ADEFA data.

important sector in terms of royalty payments, accounting for 16.7 percent of total royalties.[46] Despite the introduction of measures to restrict technology payments, the eight major foreign firms in the industry in 1973 paid more than $18 million in royalties.[47]

Excess payments through overpricing of imported parts and components should also be included in the estimate of profit outflows from the motor vehicle industry. There was ample scope for such payments in the early years of the development of the industry when imports of parts reached well over $100 million in 1961 and 1962. Despite higher domestic content requirements, imports of parts were still significant in the early 1970s, running at over $30 million a year.[48] Total imports by the terminal firms were much higher: almost $300 million over the four-year period 1968 to 1971.[49] Evidence suggests that overpricing of parts was not merely a theoretical possibility during this period. In 1964 it was estimated that Ford earned $1,161,930 in addition to the

$572,000 that the subsidiary reported.[50] In 1974 the Argentine Supreme Court held that a part of deferred payments made by the local Ford subsidiary to the parent company for imported parts represented profit remissions.[51]

The high cost of Argentine cars continued to be passed on to consumers in high prices. Although the industry trade association, ADEFA, claims that car prices relative to other nonagricultural goods had fallen to almost two-fifths of their 1960 level by the early 1970s, this appears to exaggerate the real reduction in price.[52] But even ADEFA recognizes that since 1972 car prices have increased at a faster rate than nonagricultural prices in general.[53] If car prices are calculated in dollar terms, there appears to have been no reduction in price. Between 1965 and 1974 the average price of a car in Argentina increased by 23 percent in dollar terms, which indicates a deterioration compared to car prices in the United States, where over the same period the index of car prices showed only a 16 percent increase.[54]

State Attempts at Restructuring, 1970–1979

Although the economic program of Onganía and Krieger Vassena initially was successful in terms of its objectives—inflation fell and production for most sectors of the economy expanded—the social basis of this strategy was weak, making it dependent on repressive measures. Monopolization of the economy increasingly undermined the position of the petit bourgeoisie, and the control of wages and the attack on working-class gains led to a radicalization of the trade unions, which resulted in the split of the Confederación General de Trabajadores (CGT) in 1968 and the formation of the CGT de los Argentinos in opposition to the government. Moreover the government could not count on the support of the agrarian oligarchy because they had been excluded from the gains of this economic strategy.

The culmination of these trends was the uprising in May 1969 in Rosario and Córdoba in which motor industry workers played an important part. The events led to a national strike, which shook the government.[55] Although Onganía survived this crisis, he was replaced a year later by Roberto Marcelo Levingston. The new government abandoned Onganía's openly pro-foreign capital strategy and adopted a more conciliatory policy toward national capital, granting locally owned firms preference in government procurements and preferential access to credit. Agricultural prices, held down by the previous government, were allowed to rise.

The replacement of Levingston by Alejandro Lanusse in March 1971 did not result in any clear break in terms of economic strategy. The government continued a policy of attempting to gain the support of sectors of national capital and the petit bourgeoisie. A new foreign investment law (no. 19151, July 1971) encouraged association of foreign capital and national capital and required firms to use at least 85 percent Argentine personnel in technical and managerial positions. On fundamental issues like profit repatriation, however, no limitations were imposed.

The Lanusse government attempted to restructure the motor vehicle industry and address some of its problems. The major instrument of this restructuring was the Ley de la Reconversión de la Industria Automotriz, law 18135. The three main objectives of the law were to increase efficiency in the industry, which would permit reductions in prices, to reduce the net outflow of foreign exchange associated with the industry, and to promote national capital and technology.[56]

The government did not engage in a frontal assault on the problem of market fragmentation, attempting instead to prevent further fragmentation by barring new entrants in the terminal sector until after December 30, 1980. Given the initial decision in 1959, which resulted in an excessive number of firms, this was certainly a case of shutting the stable door long after the horse had bolted. The major attempt to improve the situation thus rested on measures to reduce the proliferation of models. The original plan to set minimum quotas for each model and to withdraw from production those that did not meet the quota in any six-month period was weakened under pressure from the industry. The final legislation merely required a firm, before launching a new model, to show that their existing average output per model in production exceeded a certain volume that increased from 15,000 in 1973 to 50,000 after 1980. Moreover the definition of a basic model was left broad to cover vehicles with different engines, transmissions, and two- or four-door, station wagon, and van derivatives of the body. The legislation had no apparent effect on the number of models being produced in the country, which actually increased marginally from 109 in 1970 to 111 in 1976.[57]

In view of the extent of foreign domination of the terminal industry, attempts to strengthen the position of national capital were concentrated on the parts industry. For the first time since the creation of the motor vehicle industry in Argentina, an attempt was made to lay down the conditions for the development of the parts and components industry. The law aimed to prevent the trend toward backward integration by the terminal firms and to provide certain advantages for majority locally owned parts suppliers. These advantages included preferential access to credit, preferential treatment in government purchasing policy, and special tax concessions for exports. But these measures were taken too late, after the terminal firms had already established integrated production and substantial denationalization of the parts industry had taken place.

The measures designed to reduce the sector's balance-of-payments deficit were of similar limited scope. Imports of dies and molds for body stamping were made subject to approval by the Ministry of Industry, Commerce, and Mines, which would usually be granted for new models provided that 90 percent of the total dies and molds were produced locally or at least 50 percent of the production was destined for exports over the next five years. There was also a reduction in the permitted import content to 4 percent of the f.o.b. value for cars and 10 percent for commercial vehicles. Another measure designed to reduce the foreign exchange costs of the industry was the creation of a register of license and technology transfer contracts. Royalty payments were limited to a maximum of 2 percent of the total value of sales, and new contracts could be registered only when they did not contain arbitrary restrictions on the recipient, such as tie-in clauses for equipment or materials and restrictions on exports.[58]

The law also attempted to reduce the balance-of-payments deficit by a 50 percent increase in tax rebates on exported vehicles and parts. These export incentives were further extended in 1972 as part of a general export promotion policy in decree 3764/72 establishing a subsidy of 35 percent of f.o.b. value for cars and 40 percent for commercial vehicles and the repayment of taxes paid on earlier stages of production. The latter was estimated at about 11 percent of the f.o.b. price for cars and over 18 percent for a heavy truck. Taken together with a number of other small incentives, such as those for exporting tires, the repayment of freight and insurance charges, and the incentives for exports to new markets, the total incentive received by an exporting company by 1973 could amount to almost 60 percent of the export price for cars and 75 percent for heavy trucks. In addition the Central Bank provided credit on favorable terms, which could amount to a subsidy of more than

Table 2.7
Exports by Argentine automotive industry, 1965–1977 (thousands of U.S. dollars)

	Completed units		Parts	Total
	Number	Value		
1965	85	189	817	1,006
1966	35	113	3,648	3,761
1967	58	112	6,796	6,908
1968	76	216	6,396	6,612
1969	459	2,675	7,312	9,987
1970	884	3,444	7,405	10,849
1971	601	3,329	13,667	16,996
1972	3,493	17,791	21,014	38,806
1973	11,214	53,300	40,285	93,586
1974	15,132	71,131	60,207	131,339
1975	11,918	82,621	32,628	115,249
1976	13,442	80,335	40,139	120,474
1977	8,013	na	na	na

Source: ADEFA.

5 percent of the vehicle price, and in some cases, such as the much publicized exports to Cuba, exports were financed by government loans.

The measures taken to reduce imports were not successful. Imports of parts by the terminal firms increased from almost $32 million in 1971 to $39 million in 1974.[59] Even when the growth in production over the period is taken into account, this represented an increase in imports from $126 to $136 per vehicle produced.

Where the government did at first glance achieve some success was in promoting exports. The subsidies to exports, when taken together with substantial devaluations in 1971 and 1972, made exporting relatively attractive to the motor manufacturers in this period. The total value of the industry's exports rose from $17 million in 1971 to $39 million in 1972 and $94 million in 1973 (see table 2.7). It has been estimated that the total cost to the government of these exports in subsidies and revenue forgone came to over $5 million in 1971 and almost $13 million in 1972.[60] In general it appears that the rapid growth of the industry's exports did not reflect increasing competitiveness but rather the substantial government subsidies (which in turn contributed to its deficit).[61]

The victory of the coalition of forces that backed Peron in the elections of 1973 can be seen as a new political stage qualitatively different from any other part of the period since 1955. For the first time, what O'Donnell describes as the "defensive alliance" between the nonmonopoly sectors of the urban bourgeoisie (the local bourgeoisie represented by the Confederación General de Economía (CGE) and the popular sectors (working class and unionized middle sectors represented by the CGT) gained power.[62] Thus it could be expected that the new regime would promote stronger measures in favor of national capital and the working class. As far as national capital is concerned, the new foreign investment law, no. 20557, of November 1973 did represent a certain tightening of the conditions for foreign investment. Purchase of shares in nationally owned companies was prohibited, repatriation of profits was limited, and access to domestic credit for terms of more than one year prohibited. No new investments were made under this new law, and no existing foreign companies applied for incorporation under the law, implying that foreign capital at least perceived the legislation as being counter to its interest.

The major policy change for the motor vehicle industry was decree 680/73, which required car manufacturers to increase their exports by relating expansion for the domestic market to the achievement of certain export targets. Firms would be allowed to expand domestic sales by 8 percent per year if they had exports equal to a proportion of 1973 sales, which increased from 15 percent in 1974 to 100 percent by 1978. Firms failing to meet these export targets would have their domestic sales reduced accordingly. The decree was applied only to cars, not to commercial vehicles. In contrast to previous attempts at export promotion that depended entirely on incentives, the element of compulsion in the decree ran the risk of going directly against the interest of the individual firms in the terminal industry, particularly in view of the high production costs of Argentine cars. The legislation could therefore be interpreted as an attempt to make more foreign exchange available for accumulation by local capital through reducing the net balance-of-payments deficit of this group of multinationals.

Although initially, perhaps as much because of subsidies and a favorable exchange rate as of the decree, exports increased to $131 million in 1974, this success was short-lived. Exports fell in succeeding years (see table 2.7), and, despite the decree, in 1977 less than 4 percent of the country's output of vehicles was exported. In 1976 total exports valued at $120 million compared unfavorably with Brazil (exports of

$514 million in the same year) and Mexico, where exports were over $200 million in 1975.[63]

The reason for this failure is largely the recession in the domestic market for vehicles. Decree 680/73 was based on the assumption of a buoyant market for cars in which existing firms would be anxious to expand and therefore be prepared to export in order to maintain their market shares. However, 1973 proved to be a peak year for the industry; car sales to dealers fell from 219,305 to 129,877 in 1976. All producers were manufacturing fewer cars in 1976 than in 1973, and so the pressure to export was absent. This experience, especially when compared to that of Brazil and Mexico, suggests that the internal problems of the industry are also an obstacle to its extension into international markets and that therefore exports cannot be a way of resolving these contradictions. Put another way, the government of Argentina is as anxious to use the motor industry to improve its global balance-of-payments position as is the Brazilian or Mexican government, but it is severely constrained by its inability to guarantee the conditions necessary for capital accumulation in the industry.

The military junta that has been in power since the collapse of the Peronist coalition and the subsequent coup d'état of March 1976 has completely changed the orientation of economic policy, unleashing an attack on the working class and pursuing an aggressive policy of economic liberalization. This has resulted in a sharp reduction in manufacturing output and appears to have benefited mainly the financial and service sectors.

In 1977 there were signs that the government's policy was bringing about a reactivation of the motor vehicle industry, with production figures recovering from the trough of 1976 to almost the same level as in 1975, but this recovery was short-lived; production again fell in 1978 to the lowest level for over a decade (see table 2.1). In 1978 the government abandoned the attempt to restructure the motor industry in the way envisaged in the Ley de la Reconversión Industria Automotriz, which was repealed. As part of the government's overall liberalization policy, the ban on imports of cars and trucks was removed and tariffs reduced to 55 percent for trucks and 45 percent for cars. The restrictions introduced by law 19.135 on production of new parts and models, vertical integration, and ownership by foreign capital were all removed.[64] In February 1979 a new law designed to reduce the costs of car production came into effect. This permits firms to increase import content to 12 percent by 1982 and reduces duties on imports of parts not made locally from a maximum of 45 percent at present to 30 percent in 1984.[65] The new policy is designed to make the Argentine industry more responsive to foreign competition.

The new legislation together with the severe recession and changes in the international motor industry have combined to produce the most drastic restructuring of the industry since the early 1960s. GM, Citroen, and Chrysler have all withdrawn from the industry. GM has decided to concentrate its attention in South America on Brazil and the Andean Pact, especially Venezuela where the domestic market already matches that of Argentina. Chrysler has been taken over by VW, as has the state-owned producer of pickups, IME, and VW is planning to begin production using imported parts from Brazil. Fiat has been concentrating more and more on Brazil where it moved its Latin American head-quarters in the late 1970s. Faced with the competitive threat from VW and Japanese imports, Fiat and Peugeot have established a joint pro-duction and marketing agreement in Argentina. Mercedes-Benz is also reported to be converting its truck plant at Gonzalez Catan into an assembly operation using parts imported from Brazil, and Citroen, as part of the rationalization of the Peugeot-Citroen group, has ceased production.

The drastic rundown of the industry will hit the parts and component producers most severely. Transnational terminal firms will be able to continue making profits either by exporting to Argentina or assembling vehicles using imported parts. The parts producer, however, is often largely dependent on the terminal firm for the greater part of its market and will suffer. This is clearly illustrated by the different positions adopted toward the new legislation by ADEFA (representing the ter-minal firms) and the Consejo Coordinador de la Industria de Autopartes (representing the parts and component industry). While the former sought only to ensure that the rules of the game were not changed too rapidly, the parts producers opposed the new legislation, emphasizing the need to continue with the previous policy, which favored local capital.[66] In the new political situation, there was little prospect of such views receiving government support.

Conclusion

Why has an industry that in the early 1960s appeared to have at least as much potential as the Brazilian or Mexican industries notably failed to expand like the other two countries? It is clearly not enough to refer simply to the more rapid growth of gross domestic product in Brazil and Mexico in explaining this divergence since the motor industry itself has been a major dynamic element in their expansion. On the contrary, an analysis of the stagnation of the Argentine industry may throw light on the lack of growth of the economy as a whole.

The contrast is most marked in a comparison of the development of the Argentine and Brazilian motor industries since the mid-1960s. In 1965 Argentina produced 194,536 vehicles and Brazil, 185,173. Ten years later Argentine production was only 240,036, but Brazil's had increased fivefold to 929,807. In the mid-1960s vehicles produced in both countries were high cost by international standards. In Brazil even the Volkwagen, easily the best-selling car, cost almost twice as much as in Germany, and Argentine cars averaged more than twice the price in the country of origin.[67] Explanations of the high cost of cars in both countries in the mid-1960s emphasized similar factors: small local markets, an excessive number of firms, and a high local content requirements. Nevertheless even at this time costs in Brazil were lower than in Argentina because of a larger domestic market, longer time in operation, permitting capital costs to be written off and suppliers to be developed, quality improved, and costs reduced.[68]

The structure of the industry in the two countries presented marked similarities. In 1965 there were eleven firms operating in Brazil and thirteen in Argentina. Capacity utilization in both countries was running at around 60 percent or less. But in Brazil Volkswagen had already established a clear lead in car production, with an output of more than five times its nearest rival, whereas in Argentina the market was much more evenly divided.[69] Thus although Volkswagen in Brazil continued to suffer from high costs by international standards, it enjoyed a relative cost advantage in comparison to other local producers.

From about 1968 the experiences of the motor vehicle industry in Argentina and Brazil diverge sharply, although the basis for these developments was laid in the immediately preceding period. The period 1965 through 1968 saw the consolidation of foreign control in the terminal industry of both countries, but whereas this involved significant further concentration of production in Brazil where Vemag was taken over by Volkswagen, Willys Overland by Ford, and Simca and International Harvester by Chrysler, there was no increase in concentration in Argentina.[70] In Brazil these changes consolidated the position of VW as market leader with over 50 percent of vehicle output and brought Ford into a clear second place with almost 70,000 vehicles in 1968. In

Table 2.8
Value added and wage and salary payments, 1960–1972

	Value added (millions of pesos ley) (1)	Wages and salaries (millions of pesos ley) (2)	(2)/(1) (%)
1960	129.8	26.0	20.0
1961	216.7	46.0	21.2
1962	162.9	61.0	37.4
1963	262.8	82.0	31.2
1964	397.2	122.0	30.7
1965	615.7	185.1	30.1
1966	802.7	265.6	33.1
1967	1,022.4	331.3	32.4
1968	1,219.9	374.4	30.7
1969	1,305.9	455.1	34.8
1970	1,530.5	514.0	33.6
1971	2,339.8	734.7	31.4
1972	2,786.0	1,115.1	40.0

Source: Own elaboration from ADEFA data. Note: Value added calculated by subtracting imports of parts and local purchases from factory sales at prices to the dealer.

the same year, the Argentine market leaders, Fiat and IKA, each produced only some 40,000 vehicles.

The period of phenomenal growth of the Brazilian industry, from 1966 to 1974, saw almost a doubling of output per worker, whereas productivity in Argentina was virtually stagnant.[71] In two years, between 1969 and 1971, hours worked in the Brazilian industry per vehicle produced fell by over a fifth, whereas in Argentina there was no such reduction.[72] Increased productivity in Brazil was reflected in a fall in the share of wages in value added (calculated as sales minus domestic purchases) from a third in 1965 to just over a fifth in 1972,[73] whereas, as table 2.8 indicates, the share of wages in Argentina actually increased from 30 to 40 percent over the same period.[74]

These increases in productivity and reductions in labor cost reflect a number of factors. In part they may be explained by the economies of scale achieved through the rapid expansion of the Brazilian industry in this period, which were denied to the Argentine industry, although this does not explain the lower labor productivity in Argentina in the mid-1970s compared to the mid-1960s at similar levels of output (see table 2.5). There is also evidence to suggest that increased output per worker in Brazil has been brought about by increases in the intensity of labor through speedups and new standards. In Argentina, on the other hand, workers have been far more successful in resisting such attempts to increase work rates, as in the case of GM in 1973 when the company tried to impose a new standard on its assembly lines in order to produce more cars per shift.[75] The greater strength of the Argentine workers in comparison to those of Brazil was reflected in the involvement of union representatives on the committees concerned with production standards in a number of Argentine firms and on the committees on job evaluation for all firms except one, whereas such representatives were entirely absent in Brazilian firms.[76] It seems reasonable to suppose that union representation in these committees would facilitate resistance to management attempts to increase the intensity of labor.

A third important factor in increasing productivity was the new investments made in the Brazilian industry as excess capacity was exhausted in the early 1970s. In the three years between 1971 and 1973, new investments totaling around $1,000 million were approved in the terminal sector of the Brazilian industry. Over the same period new investments in Argentina amounted to only $179 million, and over the entire history of the Argentine motor vehicle industry from 1960 to 1975, total investment in fixed assets came to less than $950 million (see table 2.6). This low level of investment in Argentina inevitably meant that there was little opportunity for increasing productivity through modernization of existing plant and construction of new and technologically more advanced plants.

The evolution of demand for vehicles in Argentina and Brazil is another important factor. In part the more rapid growth of demand in Brazil reflects the faster overall growth of gross domestic product, which increased twice as rapidly as in Argentina between 1965 and 1974.[77] However, this is only part of the story; the rapid growth of the motor vehicle industry has played an important role in Brazilian expansion generally, and the rate of growth of motor vehicle production was more than four times as fast in Brazil as in Argentina.[78]

The major factor in enabling demand for vehicles, particularly cars, to increase much faster than income in Brazil since 1965, while no such trend is evident in Argentina, must be sought outside the motor industry in overall developments in the two countries since the mid-1960s. Specifically the Brazilian military regime that came to power in

1964 imposed crushing defeats on the working class, which not only enabled real wages to be reduced and productivity increased but also concentrated income at the top of the distribution, bringing about a sharp rise in the purchasing power of potential car buyers.[79] The attempt of the Onganía regime to establish the Brazilian model in Argentina after 1966 collapsed with the mass insurrection in the city of Córdoba in 1969.[80] In Argentina movements in real wages and the share of wages in national income over this period suggest that no concentration of income of the kind seen in Brazil occurred between the mid-1960s and early 1970s, while the Peronist victory in 1973 was accompanied by a progressive redistribution of income.[81] The only available data on the personal distribution of income in the late 1960s indicate a fall of almost 5 percent in the share of the top 20 percent in Argentina compared to an increase of almost 9 percent for the same group in Brazil.[82] At the same time the continued high price of vehicles in Argentina ensured that cars remained a luxury consumer good. In 1973 the average car in Argentina cost three or four times the annual wage of workers on the lowest grades in car factories and almost twice the average wage of the highest paid workers.[83] The situation does not seem to have changed significantly since 1966 when it was reported that the best-selling Argentine car, the Fiat 1500, sold at two and a third times the average annual income of hourly paid workers in the Argentine motor vehicle industry.[84] In 1976 the sharp fall in the real wages following the military coup put cars even further out of reach of those who produce them. According to one report, car workers earned an average income of 12,000 pesos a month ($48).[85] On this basis it would require almost eight years' wages at this level to buy the average Argentine car.

The prolonged crisis of the Argentine motor industry is a reflection of the crisis of Argentine capitalism generally and in particular the failure of the project of monopoly capital from the mid-1960s. The paradox of a strong and well-organized working class and the dependent position of Argentina within the world economy has had a number of consequences. It has meant that neither the market, through concentration and centralization of capital, nor the state, through an upward redistribution of income to provide favorable conditions for the growth of demand and neutralization of the working class, nor the companies themselves, through speedups and increased productivity, have been able to break through the barriers to accumulation in the industry. It remains to be seen whether the brutal repression of the working class and the compression of real wages by the military regime since 1976 will herald a second and more successful attempt at Brazilianization of Argentina or whether there is likely to be a progressive dismantling of the Argentine motor vehicle industry.

Notes

1. ADEFA, *La Industria Automotriz Argentina* (Buenos Aires: Asociación de Fábricas de Automotores, 1969).

2. D. Phelps, *The Migration of Industry to South America* (New York: McGraw-Hill, 1936).

3. CONADE, *La Industria Automotriz (Análisis Preliminar)* (Buenos Aires: Consejo Nacional de Desarrollo, 1966), table 3.

4. M. Wilkins and F. Hill, *American Business Abroad* (Detroit: Wayne State University, 1964).

5. F. G. Donner, *The World Wide Industrial Enterprise: Its Challenge and Promise* (New York: McGraw-Hill, 1967).

6. ECLA, *External Financing in Latin America* (New York: United Nations, 1965), table 127.

7. IMF, *World Automotive Industry* (Frankfurt am Main: International Metalworkers Federation, 1964), table VII.

8. In 1958 new foreign investment (including reinvestment) almost doubled compared to 1957, and in 1959 it doubled again. See ECLA, *External Financing*.

9. M. Kaplan, "50 Años de Historia Argentina: el Laberinto de la Frustración," in P. Gonzalez Casanova, *América Latina: Historia de Medio Siglo* (Mexico City: Siglo XXI, 1977), pp. 55–56.

10. See the statement of R. Frigerio, Frondizi's chief economic adviser, quoted in J. Sourrouille, *The Impact of Transnational Enterprises on Employment and Income: The Case of Argentina* (Geneva: ILO, WEP 2–28, WPT, 1976), p. 12.

11. Ibid., table 9.

12. D. Felix, *Industrialización Substitutava de Importaciones y Exportación Industria en la Argentina* (Buenos Aires: Instituto Torcuato di Tella, 1968), table 12.

13. Sourrouille, *Impact*, table 12.

14. It is relatively easy to achieve a local content of around 35 percent in a vehicle without undertaking any major investment through local assembly and local purchase of parts. See Rhys Jenkins, *Dependent Industrialization in Latin America: The Automotive Industry in Argentina, Chile and Mexico* (New York: Praeger, 1977), pp. 90–91. Add to this the fact that the initial Argentine decree did not specify the way in which local content was to be calculated, and the scope for making high initial profits on a minimal investment is clear. This is

illustrated by the internal rate of return for Ford, GM, and Mercedes-Benz, which was in excess of 100 percent in 1960. See J. Sourrouille, *El Complejo Automotor en Argentina* (Mexico City: ILET, mimeo, 1979), table VI.

15. CONADE, *La Industria Automotriz*, table 32.

16. O. Altimir, H. Santamaria, and J. Sourrouille, "Los Instrumentos de Promoción Industrial en la Post-Guerra" *Desarrollo Económico* 6, no. 21 (1966) pp. 99–105.

17. F. Knickerbocker, *Oligopolistic Reaction and Multinational Enterprise* (Cambridge, Mass.: Harvard Graduate School of Business Administration, 1973).

18. Quoted in Sourrouille, *El Complejo Automotor*, p. 33, my translation.

19. CONADE, *La Industria Automotriz*, p. 49.

20. CIFARA, *Estudio Técnico-Económico de la Industria Nacional del Transporte* (Buenos Aires: Camora Industrial de Fabricantes de Autopiezas de la República Argentina, 1970), p. 126.

21. CICSO, *El Poder Económico en la Argentina* (Buenos Aires: Centro de Investigaciones en Ciencias Sociales, 1971), p. 45.

22. Editorial of *Industria Automotriz*, no. 13–14 (January–April 1959).

23. E. Eshag and R. Thorp, "Economic and Social Consequences of Orthodox Economic Policies in Argentina in the Post War Years," *Bulletin of the Oxford University Institute of Economics and Statistics* 27, no. 1 (1965), table IX.

24. Asociación de Fábricas de Automotores (ADEFA).

25. Interviews with ex-Siam directors.

26. *Motor Business* (April 1964).

27. E. Gastiazoro, *Argentina Hoy* (Buenos Aires, Editorial Emele, 1971), table IX.

28. J. Lenicov, "Algunos Resultados de la Política Desarrolista (1958–64): El Caso de la Industria Automotriz," *Económica* 19, no. 3 (1973): table 4. Lenicov gives a lower figure for the period 1959–1964, but this seems to be an underestimate in view of the data for the period up to 1963 given in CONADE, *La Industria Automotriz*, table 20.

29. Lenicov, "Algunos Resultados," p. 326.

30. N. Schroeder, "Radicación de Capitales Estranjeros: la Experiencia Argentina, 1954–72," *Económica* 22, no. 1 (1976): table 2.

31. See Donner, *World Wide Industrial Enterprise*.

32. ADEFA, *La Industria Automotriz Argentina*, p. 68. Since most investment in the industry was made after 1959, this suggests the widespread use of secondhand equipment.

33. There are no data on the extent of overpricing of machinery.

34. O. Braun, ed., *El Capitalismo Argentino en Crises* (Buenos Aires: Siglo XXI, 1970).

35. D. Aspiazu, C. Bonvecchi, M. Khavisse, and M. Turkich, "Acerca del Desarrollo Industrial Argentino: un Comentario Crítico," *Desarrollo Económico*, no. 60 (1976): 590–591.

36. Sourrouille, *El Complejo Automotor*, table 20. See also R. García Lupo, *Contra la Ocupación Extranjera* (Buenos Aires: Editorial Centro, 1971), chap. 5.

37. ADEFA, *La Industrial Automotriz Argentina*, p. 29.

38. Dirección Nacional de Estudios Industriales, *Situación Actual y Perspectivas de Mercado de Automoviles en la República Argentina* (Buenos Aires: Ministerio de Economía y Trabajo, 1969), p. 6.

39. ADEFA, *La Industria Automotriz Argentina*, p. 73.

40. Lenicov, "Algunos Resultados," table 16.

41. Rhys Jenkins, "International Oligopoly and Dependent Industrialization in the Latin American Motor Industry," Development Studies Discussion Paper No. 13 (Norwich: University of East Anglia, 1976), table 2.

42. Lenicov, "Algunos Resultados," table 4.

43. S. MacDonell and M. Lascano, *La Industria Automotriz: Aspectos Económicos y Fiscales* (Buenos Aires: Dirección General Impositiva, Departamento de Estudios, División Planes, 1974), table 40.

44. Ibid., tables 8, 40.

45. B. Raddavero, "Análises de la Transferencia de la Tecnología Externa a la Industria Argentina: El Caso de la Industria Automotriz," *Económica*, no. 18 (1972): 369.

46. INTI, *Aspectos Económicos de la Importación de Tecnología en la Argentina en 1972* (Buenos Aires: Instituto Nacional de Tecnología Industrial, 1974), table 2.

47. Jenkins, *Dependent Industrialization*, p. 179.

48. ADEFA, *Informe Estadístico*, August 28, 1974, table 10.

49. MacDonell and Lascano, *La Industria Automotriz*, table 40.

50. J. Baranson, Datas and Fontenay, *Industrial Protection of the Automotive and Heavy Equipment Industries in Argentina, 1955–65* (Washington: IBRD, n.d.).

51. *La Opinión*, May 22, 1974.

52. See Dirección Nacional de Estudios Industriales, *Situación Actual*, pp. 1–4, for an alternative index that indicates a fall in relative prices of less than 5 percent 1960 and 1967 compared to 30 percent claimed by ADEFA over the same period.

53. ADEFA, *Informe Estadístico*, November 30, 1976.

54. Calculated from ADEFA data on the value of sales and numbers of cars produced in Argentina converted at current exchange rates and the U.S. consumer price index for new cars.

55. E. Laclau, "Argentina-Imperialist Strategy and the May Crisis," *New Left Review* (1971).

56. The detailed objectives as spelled out in article 2 of the law were: gradual reduction of the price of vehicles in the internal market to enable their acquisition by relatively low-income sectors; concentration of the terminal and parts industries, obtaining a greater productive efficiency with the maximum possible economies of scale; intensive promotion of national design and technology; reduction of the outflow of foreign exchange from the country to import goods or technology for the industry with the consequent increase in national value added; significant and permanent exports of vehicles and parts; and consolidation of national capital with real decision-making powers in the parts industry.

57. ADEFA.

58. Prior to the law, royalty rates well in excess of 2 percent and contractual restrictions were common. See Raddavero, "Análisis de la Transferencia," for details.

59 ADEFA.

60. MacDonell and Lascano, *La Industria Automotriz*, table 37.

61. See M. Lascano, *Crisis de la Política Económica Argentina* (Buenos Aires: Editorial Astrea, 1973), pp. 149–151, for an analysis of the relation between the total value of tax certificates issued and the government deficit. In 1972 certificates issued to the terminal motor industry accounted for 15.1 percent of the total value of all certificates issued. MacDonell and Lascano, *La Industria Automotriz*, table 36.

62. G. O'Donnell, "State and Alliances in Argentina, 1956–1976," *Journal of Development Studies* 15, no. 1 (1978).

63. K. Sharpe and D. Bennett, "Transnational Corporations and the Political Economy of Export Promotion: The Case of the Mexican Automobile Industry," (mimeographed), n.d., table 5.

64. *Latin American Economic Report*, June 9, 1978.

65. *Financial Times*, April 30, 1979.

66. Sourrouille, *El Complejo Automotor*, pp. 56–58.

67. J. Baranson, *Automotive Industries in Developing Countries* (Washington, D.C.: World Bank Staff Occasional Papers, No. 8, 1969), annex table 22.

68. Ibid., p. 39. Insofar as costs are implied to be a function of market size and time in operation, one would have expected some catching up by Argentine producers as a result of the latter factor to offset partly the larger size of the Brazilian market.

69. The leading producer in Argentina, IKA, produced only 40 percent more than its nearest rival, Fiat, in 1965.

70. Jenkins, *Dependent Industrialization*, table 7.1.

71. Vehicles produced per person employed increased from 4.54 in 1966 to 4.99 in 1974. Own elaboration from ADEFA data. For details on man-hours per vehicle produced, see table 2.4.

72. Own elaboration of Asociação Nacional dos Fabricantes de Veículos Automotores (ANFAVEA) data.

73. Calculated from ANFAVEA data.

74. See table 2.8. The figures are not strictly comparable since value added in Argentina was calculated by subtracting both domestic purchases and imports of parts from the value of sales, but in view of the low proportion of imported parts used in Brazil, this difference should not significantly alter the result.

75. J. Torre, "Workers' Struggle and Consciousness," *Latin American Perspectives* 1, no. 3 (1974): 76–77.

76. United Auto Workers, International Affairs and Information Systems Departments, *Survey of Latin American Auto Contracts* (Washington, D.C.: UAW, 1970).

77. The relative figures were 9.3 percent per year in Brazil and 4.6 percent per year in Argentina.

78. Total motor vehicle output in Brazil grew by 19.3 percent per year compared to 4.4 percent per year in Argentina between 1965 and 1974, while car production grew by almost 25 percent per year in Brazil compared to 5.3 percent per year in Argentina over the same period.

79. See M. Tavares and J. Serra, "Beyond Stagnation: A Discussion on the Nature of Recent Developments in Brazil," in J. Petras, ed., *Latin America from Dependence to Revolution* (New York: John Wiley and Sons, 1973), and J. Serra, "The Brazilian 'Economic Miracle,' " in ibid.

80. For a comparison of the success of the Brazilian model and the failure of the Argentine revolution of 1966, see J. Portantiero, "Dominant Classes and Political Crises in Argentina Today," *Latin American Perspectives* 1, no. 3 (1974).

81. P. Gerchunoff and J. Llach, "Capitalismo Industrial, Desarrollo Asociado y Distribución del Ingreso entre los Gobienos Peronistas: 1950–1972," *Desarrollo Económico*, no. 57 (1975); M. Botzman, E. Lifschitz, and M. Renzi, "Argentina: Autoritarismo 'Librecambio' y Crisis en el Process Actual," *Económica de América Latina*, no. 2 (1979).

82. In Argentina the share of the top 20 percent declined from 52 percent in 1961 to 47.4 percent in 1970. Data for 1961 from ECLA, *Economic Development and Income Distribution in Argentina* (New York: United Nations, 1968), table 21, and for 1970 from H. Chenery et al., *Redistribution with Growth* (New York: Oxford University Press, 1974), table 1.1. In Brazil the top 20 percent increased

their share from 54.4 percent in 1960 to 63.3 percent in 1970. Serra, "Brazilian 'Economic Miracle,' " table 10. The figures are not strictly comparable between the two countries since the Argentine data refer to households and the Brazilian to individuals.

83. Rough estimates from data in Evans, Hoeffel, and James in this book on wage rates and ADEFA on car sales.

84. Baranson, *Automotive Industries*, annex table 22.

85. *Latin American Economic Report*, September 17, 1976.

3 Latin America and the World Motor Vehicle Industry: The Turn to Exports

Rich Kronish

The motor vehicle industries of Latin America have entered a period of transition. After two decades of relative isolation, these industries have begun to assume a very different relationship with the world industry as the transnational corporations (TNCs) move to integrate their worldwide subsidiaries more closely. Indeed, under certain circumstances, the TNCs have begun to transform their Latin American operations into important export bases supplying components or finished vehicles, or both, to large sections of the world industry. These developments represent a significant break with the classical division of labor prevailing in both the motor vehicle industry and the world economy as a whole. They challenge the widely held assumption that the TNCs are reluctant to site export production outside the developed countries and demand explanation.

The Latin American Motor Vehicle Industries

TNCs have produced motor vehicles in Latin America for over sixty years. For most of this period production entailed the assembly of imported parts and components. Although the suspension of vehicle imports during World War II did promote the growth of local parts industries, it was only with the passage of the automotive decrees of the 1950s and 1960s that the Latin American industry entered a new stage of development. Providing a complex of sanctions and often highly lucrative incentives, these decrees attempted to induce participating firms to increase domestic vehicle production and sourcing. Although only the Brazilian and Argentine governments effected the installation of true manufacturing facilities, the Mexican government did establish advanced assembly operations, and throughout Latin America levels of domestic production and sourcing jumped.

The national industries producing these vehicles emerged from the automotive decrees with two distinguishing characteristics. First, foreign motor capital remained dominant as it had been during the previous forty years, although the entry of new firms (including Volkswagen, Fiat, Mercedes, Renault, and Kaiser) did undermine the traditional hegemony of the three big U.S. producers. Majority-owned local firms played significant roles initially, although they typically functioned as joint ventures with foreign capital, operating under foreign licenses. They all but disappeared, however, in the last half of the 1960s, often swallowed up by their erstwhile partners. By 1976 the four largest vehicles producers in Latin America were Volkswagen, Ford, General Motors, and Chrysler. Together they accounted for almost 80 percent of total production, with Renault, Fiat, Peugeot-Citroen, Mercedes-Benz, Toyota, Nissan, and American Motors producing most of the remaining vehicles.[1] (See table 3.1.)

The second distinguishing characteristic of the new Latin American vehicle industries was their relative isolation from the rest of the world industry. The TNCs did not significantly integrate the production of their Latin American subsidiaries with the rest of their worldwide operations. Two factors limited integration. On the one hand, the domestic content requirements imposed by the various automotive decrees restricted all automotive imports (both parts and finished vehicles). Indeed in Argentina and Brazil, 95 to 100 percent domestic content requirements practically eliminated all imports. On the other hand, with no Latin American motor vehicle plant (let alone production model) even approaching internationally competitive levels of production until the early 1970s, the Latin American industries failed to realize the economies of scale enjoyed by vehicle plants in the developed capitalist world. Consequently they remained inefficient and uncompetitive, with costs, especially for finished vehicles, far higher than in North America, Western Europe, or Japan.[2] Under these circumstances the TNCs relied on their plants in the developed countries for exports. As late as 1968 exports from Argentina, Brazil, and Mexico together amounted to less than $25 million. By 1972 these figures were still relatively modest: Argentina, $38.8 million; Brazil, $49.4 million; and Mexico, $81.6 million.

A rapid expansion of Latin American motor vehicle exports took place in the 1970s, with totals from Argentina, Brazil, and Mexico topping $500 million in 1974.[3] In the last half of the decade Mexican and Brazilian exports continued to rise. By 1976 Mexican exports stood

Table 3.1
Total vehicle production by firm in Latin America, 1976 (units)

Firm	Argentina	Brazil	Chile	Colombia	Mexico	Peru	Venezuela	Total	% of Latin American market
American Motors					22,669[a]		1,213[a]	23,882	1.4
Chrysler	21,986	27,831		15,336	55,929	11,031	43,355	175,468	10.2
Citroen	15,839		1,764[a]					17,603	1.0
Fiat	44,444	8,350	1,439	4,023			4,510	62,766	3.6
Ford	33,954	171,931			45,497		52,317	303,699	17.7
General Motors	16,195	181,144	960		36,757		30,238	265,294	15.4
Mercedes-Benz	6,682	48,817					2,180	57,679	3.4
Nissan					30,624	5,453	4,856	40,933	2.4
Peugeot	16,121		1,557[b]					17,678	1.0
Renault	30,896		1,307[b]	15,998	36,894[a]		5,266[b]	90,361	5.3
Toyota		1,498				6,609	7,326	15,433	0.9
Volkswagen		529,636			70,398	9,628	3,000	612,662	35.7
Others	7,400	16,262			1,161	1,623	8,471	34,917	2.0
Total	193,517	985,469	7,027	35,357	299,929	34,344	162,732	1,718,375	100.0
Percentage	11.3	57.3	0.4	2.1	17.4	9.5	100.0		

Source: R. N. Gwynne, "The Motor Vehicle Industry in Latin America," *Bank of London and South America Review* 12 (September 1978): 471.
Note: Uruguay, Ecuador, and Costa Rica assemble small numbers of vehicles.
a. Joint ventures with respective governments.
b. One firm produces two different makes.

at \$290 million, and Brazil recorded exports of \$1.2 billion in 1978.[4] Moreover, VW, GM, Ford, Chrysler, Mercedes, Fiat, and others announced plans to expand exports still further in the late 1970s and early 1980s. The most dramatic growth was planned for Mexico and, especially, Brazil.[5] The TNCs also agreed to increase their exports from the smaller Latin American countries, especially in the Andean Pact; for example, VW committed itself to annual exports of approximately \$150 million from Ecuador beginning in the early 1980s.[6]

In attempting to promote export activities, governments relaxed barriers on motor vehicle imports. Brazil reduced its domestic content requirements in the early 1970s (from 98 to 80 percent for trucks and from 99 to 85 percent for cars) provided that imports are balanced by exports.[7] The military government in Argentina eliminated legislation prohibiting manufacturers from importing parts identical to those already produced in the country. At the same time Argentine domestic content requirements were also relaxed, from 90 percent to 75 to 82 percent for commercial vehicles and from 96 percent to 88 percent for cars.[8] With the Mexican government having long pursued a policy linking low content requirements and exports (and with the other Latin American industries having still lower content requirements), the TNCs thus had the opportunity during the latter part of the 1970s to integrate their Latin American subsidiaries with the rest of their worldwide operations.

These developments have broad significance. In the late 1950s and early 1960s the emergence of motor vehicle manufacturing in Latin America marked an important departure from the classical division of labor that defined both the world vehicle industry and the entire world economy. The growth of Latin American motor vehicle exports—and the parallel growth of vehicle exports from other areas outside the developed countries—further transforms this division of labor. However, the present importance of these exports, particularly vis-à-vis the developed countries, should not be exaggerated. Table 3.2 shows that Argentine, Mexican, and Brazilian exports together accounted for only 5 percent of U.S. motor vehicle imports in 1977. Nevertheless the very rapid growth of these exports presages the development of a new international division of labor. As Frobel, Heinrichs, and Kreye have observed, "Fundamental changes are actually taking place in the world economy: the classical international division of labor . . . is being replaced by a *new* international division of labor. For the first time in

Table 3.2
Selected U.S. motor vehicle imports from Argentina, Brazil, and Mexico (millions of dollars)

Year	Argentina	Brazil	Mexico	Three-country total	Total U.S. imports	Three-country total as % of U.S. imports
1971	$0.38	$ 3.9	$ 29.5	$ 33.78	$2,013	1.7
1973	1.2	14.7	83.2	99.1	3,756	2.6
1975	1.3	43.0	120.9	165.2	3,918	4.2
1977	5.0	111.3	208.8	325.1	6,371	5.1

Source: *U.S. General Imports* (1971–1977), Bureau of the Census, U.S. Department of Commerce, table III, schedule A.

centuries [some] underdeveloped countries are becoming [export] sites for manufacturing industry on a vast and growing scale."[9]

The development of export production in both the motor vehicle industry and in manufacturing as a whole coincides with the aims and policies of many Third World governments. In the motor vehicle industry, concern with unemployment and balance-of-payments difficulties (both directly and indirectly exacerbated by motor vehicle production) has led the Latin American and other Third World governments to introduce carrot-and-stick policies designed to encourage the TNCs to develop export production in their respective countries. These policies, which include tax incentives, subsidies, reduction of local content requirements, and market sanctions, have played a major role in explaining the location of vehicle export production in particular countries. They do not provide, however, an adequate explanation for the overall growth of vehicle exports from Latin America and the underdeveloped countries as a whole, as well as other countries outside the traditional vehicle-producing areas, such as in Eastern Europe. Indeed an understanding of this overall growth in exports and, more generally, of the TNCs' efforts to create a new international division of labor in the industry requires a perspective that links these developments to changes in the motor vehicle industries of the developed countries.

Crisis in the Developed Capitalist Countries

The motor vehicle industry is in a period of crisis in the developed capitalist countries. While the rate of growth of new sales in the major

Table 3.3
New registrations in six developed countries (thousands of units)

Country	1973	1975	1977	1978
France	2,016	1,689	2,205	2,244
West Germany	2,169	2,215	2,699	2,820
United Kingdom	1,944	1,443	1,554	1,854
Italy	1,533	1,124	1,332	1,314
Japan	4,915	4,309	4,194	4,682
United States	14,380	10,659	14,217	14,909
Total	26,957	21,439	26,203	27,823

Source: Motor Vehicle Manufacturers Association, *World Motor Vehicle Data—1979 Edition*, p. 17.

markets of the developed world has steadily declined over the past twenty to twenty-five years, it plummeted in the post-1973 period. Total sales in the six leading markets of the capitalist world declined by over 5 million units over the 1973 through 1975 period and failed to regain the 1973 level until 1978 (table 3.3). Furthermore the long-term growth rate seems to have declined to a new level. Estimates suggest that vehicle demand in Japan will stagnate over the 1978–1980 period and then grow at an average rate of 4.7 percent from 1983 to 1990, well below its 1963–1973 performance.[10] Similarly, the rate of growth of the West European automobile market is expected to decline to 3 percent or less during the next five years, while in the United States "a drop in the long-term growth of the automobile industry from its traditional 4 percent to around 1.5 percent seems more than likely."[11]

With labor productivity and profit rates positively correlated with the volume of production, the slowdown in growth has initiated a period of intense competition among the dozen or so giant firms that dominate the industry worldwide. The opening round of this competitive struggle was won by Japanese producers. Despite a decline in the absolute size of their home market, their output increased by over 2 million vehicles between 1973 and 1978. Exports, now accounting for 50 percent of the total output of the Japanese industry, rose by over 2.5 million units, with exports to North America and Europe increasing by over 1.2 million and 340,000 units, respectively.

Despite the expansion of the Japanese firms, some of the West European and North American firms successfully held their ground. With the exception of VW, hard hit by the precipitous decline of its exports to the United States, the French and German industries fared reasonably well. Both recovered in 1976 from the 1973 crisis and registered significant growth between 1976 and 1978. In the U.S. industry, both General Motors and Ford failed to surpass their 1973 output levels until 1977, but they showed significant growth between 1976 and 1978. The remaining firms—Chrysler, American Motors, Fiat, and BL and the rest of the British industry—produced 1.3 million fewer vehicles in 1978 than in 1973. Facing declining output and highly costly but necessary reinvestment, several of these firms threatened to collapse.

These circumstances have heightened the interest of all the major firms in foreign sales. Domestic content requirements in the Third World coupled with fluctuating exchange rates, insufficient dealer outlets, and other nontariff barriers in the developed countries effectively limit, however, the potential growth of new (especially intercontinental) exports. Consequently, the major North American and West European producers—except the two weakest firms, Chrysler and BL—have engaged in significant foreign investments throughout the world since the mid-1970s.[12] It is worth emphasizing the intensity of these firms' efforts to expand in the areas outside the developed countries where market growth rates have frequently exceeded those prevailing in the developed countries. Some of the more prominent of these investment programs are identified in the appendix.

Growing TNC interest in the markets of Eastern and Southern Europe, Asia and the Middle East, and Latin America has implied both increased vehicle production in these locations and increased exports. It has also provided those host governments intent on developing exports with a bargaining chip sufficiently attractive (particularly in conjunction with various financial incentives) to induce the TNCs to acquiesce to demands for export production. Indeed many of the recent investments and agreements entail mounting export production, and it is not unreasonable to suppose—in accordance with Streeten that "the ability of the host country to strike a good bargain" in part reflects "the extent to which the TNC in question is competing with others eager to invest—that in some cases governments did wrest the promise of export production from the TNCs as a concession by threatening particular firms with the loss of a substantial and growing market.[13]

The utility of this bargaining perspective is limited, however. Its underlying assumption—that the TNCs remain reluctant to site exports outside the traditional vehicle-producing areas of the developed countries—is unwarranted in the case of the motor vehicle industry. In fact, as the TNCs have attempted to reduce their production costs in a second strategic response (in addition to the drive for sales) to the intensification of competition, the siting of export production in these areas has become increasingly attractive.

The attraction of siting export production outside the traditional vehicle-producing areas does not reflect simply the intensification of competition in the industry. More precisely it reflects the interplay of this competition with the continuing conflict between capital and labor in the industry in the developed countries. This conflict, like the competitive relationship between the vehicle producers, is endemic to the industry and certainly not of recent origin.[14] Nevertheless this conflict and its costs seem to have intensified, particularly since the 1960s.

Automobile workers' "increasing reluctance . . . to put up with factory conditions" has manifested itself throughout the developed countries in a variety of costly forms, including absenteeism, labor turnover and tardiness, as well as grievances, strikes, and other work stoppages.[15] These actions, representing indexes of labor discontent or militancy, generally rose during the 1960s (especially after 1968), increasing with production itself to a peak in 1973. The U.S. industry, for example, experienced a marked increase in labor discontent and militancy in the 1960s and early 1970s. Labor turnover doubled between 1965 and 1970, increasing to 25 percent at Ford.[16] The absentee rate also doubled and by 1973–1974 stood at 5.4 percent at Ford and 7.09 percent at Chrysler, with some Chrysler plants exceeding 10 percent.[17] Tardiness, arguments with foremen, and complaints about discipline and overtime all increased.[18] The annual number of grievances also increased, rising from 106,000 in 1960 to 307,000 in 1973 at GM alone.[19] Another important indicator of discontent, the number of local demands at issue in national contract negotiations, increased substantially. The "vast increase in local demands and the number of grievances" in turn generated a large number of both official and unofficial strikes, including three important wildcat strikes in Detroit in the summer of 1973 that directly challenged both Chrysler and the UAW leadership.[20]

The available data for the post-1973 period are incomplete. Nevertheless they indicate (in a manner consistent with historical experience) that the decline in vehicle production in the developed countries in 1973—1974 occasioned a general decline in the various indexes of labor discontent and militancy.[21] With increasing production, these indexes have also tended to increase and regain their 1973 levels. Fiat, for example, recorded a 14 percent absenteeism rate in 1978, approximating its 1973 rate.[22] Similarly, GM reported that absenteeism at its U.S. plants increased approximately 30 percent between 1976 and 1979, rising to 5.8 percent during the first six months of 1979. GM also released figures showing that in 1979 the number of written grievances filed against the company regained its 1972 level after falling sharply between 1973 and 1975.[23]

Absenteeism, turnover, and tardiness, as well as strikes and other work stoppages, represent hidden but nevertheless substantial labor costs. Absenteeism at GM's Oldsmobile Division, for example, cost about $50 million in fringe benefits alone in 1971.[24] A British study estimated that scheduled production lost through stoppages represented 11 percent of the British industry's actual production in 1972, and Fiat claims that strikes and absenteeism cost the firm an estimated 200,000 cars in 1979.[25] Poor labor relations have affected labor productivity in the vehicle industries of all developed countries, with the "unsatisfactory state of labor relations" in the British industry often designated as the primary reason for its lower labor productivity compared to other developed countries.[26]

The hidden labor costs arising from labor discontent and militancy have significantly increased total labor costs in the motor vehicle industries of the developed countries. They represent an important addition to a level of compensation (wages and benefits) that is far in excess of prevailing levels outside these countries (see table 3.4). Under these circumstances, the attraction of siting export production outside the developed countries has grown. As the *Economist* observed, "Car workers earn better money and fringe benefits in countries where trade unions are strong, so car companies are always on the look-out for stable [low-wage] countries to invest in where unions are weak."[27]

The Internationalization of the Process of Production

Historically Third World manufacturing has entailed considerably higher labor costs per unit of output than manufacturing in the developed countries. With relatively low levels of productivity, Third World industries have been unable to translate lower labor costs per worker into lower labor costs per unit of output. Indeed with most Third World vehicle producers unable to reach internationally competitive production volumes, the cost of vehicles produced in the Third World continues to exceed comparable costs in the developed countries. What is more,

Table 3.4
Hourly compensation for selected countries, 1977 (U.S. dollars)

United States	$11.59
United Kingdom	3.87
France	6.13
West Germany	9.46
Italy	5.82
Japan	4.61
Sweden	8.92
Brazil	1.97
Mexico	2.73
South Korea	1.08
Spain	3.10

Source: Citibank, *Monthly Economic Letter* (December 1978): 15.
Note: Hourly compensation includes hourly wages, as well as employer contributions to statutory, contractual, and voluntary insurance and to other benefit programs for employees.

the large investments necessary to build up a Third World subsidiary's productive capacity to internationally competitive volumes entail levels of cost and risk unacceptable to the TNCs, especially at a time of market stagnation. With the exception, then, of some of their largest subsidiaries, the TNCs have been unwilling to site the export production of complete vehicles in the Third World despite the attraction of low wages and stable political conditions.

Component production is a very different story. In the first place, with the exception of engines and transmissions, component production requires relatively modest levels of investment compared to the manufacture of whole vehicles. Second, these investments entail little risk. Component sales are relatively predictable for they represent intrafirm transactions rather than consumer purchases. Consequently drawn by low wages and stable political-economic conditions, the TNCs have begun to establish specialized component plants in the Third World (and Eastern Europe) that are internationally competitive and integrated with worldwide operations.

These export-oriented plants represent an important element in an emerging international division of labor within the firm or, to put it somewhat differently, in the internationalization of the production process. At the same time the TNCs' efforts to reorganize their worldwide operations into an increasingly integrated, truly international production process have created a context that has facilitated the growth of these plants. These reorganization efforts now center on the "world car," a group of vehicles sharing a basic design; competing in markets all over the world; and containing a large number of common components (although certainly not all) sourced at centralized locations throughout the world and produced at sufficient volumes to realize enormous economies of scale.[28] The world car thus promises to provide the TNCs with several advantages—including the elimination of duplicative costs (for example, design costs or dealer organizations representing two subsidiaries in third countries) and the pooling of joint resources for increasingly expensive costs (such as research and design) that might otherwise exceed the resources of any particular subsidiary—as well as two developments of both actual and potential significance for the growth of exports from outside the traditional producing areas: the double sourcing of parts, subassemblies, and even whole vehicles, a measure that profoundly undermines the power of any group of national workers to strike and bring the production process to a halt, and the reduction of production costs as the common use and centralized production of components permits the TNCs to increase production runs in all countries to optimal levels.

The world car will militate against the relative isolation that has characterized the vehicle industries of Latin America and indeed the entire Third World. The world car will not, however, stimulate only the growth of exports. In addition the world car and the internationalization of the production process imply increasing vehicle imports. As the TNCs attempt to integrate their worldwide operations—or as the Volkswagen annual report has put it, effect a "close-knit exchange of deliveries and services . . . between the various companies of the VW Group"—the domestic content requirements now limiting parts and component imports have come under severe attack.[29] In fact the TNCs have attempted to link expansion of vehicle exports to the relaxation of import restrictions, promising in some cases to create a net trade surplus.[30] As a GM official stated, "We feel strongly that if developing countries want to take advantage of economies of scale, then they must establish their local-content requirements with the idea in mind to allow certain import-export credits. . . . We would like the governments to give us the responsibility of having our operation provide a balance-of-payments surplus."[31]

Siting Export Production

Changes in the motor vehicle industries of the developed countries have thus led the TNCs to site production outside these countries. Determination of the factors influencing the TNCs' choice of sites requires some understanding of the particular siting pattern prevailing in the motor vehicle industry. The electronics, clothing, and other simple, labor-intensive industries have tended to locate production in poor, very low wage countries.[32] The dominant pattern in the vehicle industry is quite distinct, however. For several reasons vehicle firms have preferred to locate export production in the more developed countries of the Third World. First, these countries have an important chip to bargain with the TNCs. With relatively large existing or potential markets for motor vehicles, they can in effect exchange market access (for example, through market quotas) for export development. Government policies in Brazil, Mexico, and Spain have employed this strategy and have no doubt obtained "a much better deal . . . by tough bargaining."[33] Second, only the more developed Third World countries have the infrastructure necessary to provide the inputs (including skilled labor and raw materials) required by the production of major components like engines and transmissions. Finally, the TNCs have significant, underutilized capacity in many of the more developed countries. Use of these existing plants for export production promises to increase their efficiency and thereby reduce unit costs, as well as limit the costs of new investments.

Among the more developed LDCs (less developed countries) several factors have determined the allocation of export production. In the motor vehicle industry, as in the electronics, clothing, and other labor-intensive industries, political stability—the stability of a state and its commitment to maintain the integrity of foreign investment, regardless of its public ideology—is paramount.[34] Indeed political stability seems to represent a necessary condition for major investment in all these industries. In the motor vehicle industry, the high cost of new investments coupled with the drive to create an integrated, international production process make it extraordinarily unlikely that the TNCs would site export production in any country where the risks of expropriation had not been minimized.

In addition to political stability, four relative factors, all affecting costs, also influence the location of export facilities among the more developed LDCs. These additional factors include labor docility, as Nayyar has put it.[35] The attraction of this factor is that it permits the

TNCs to minimize their total labor costs. With a weak, tightly controlled labor force, the TNCs can minimize wages, impose speedups, and cut employment during periods of market decline while limiting the costs of industrial disputes. While the TNCs thus prefer a more docile labor force, labor docility does not represent the primary or basic factor in the motor vehicle industry that it does in the clothing and electronics industries.[36] The continued development of Spain as an export base, for example, suggests that transnational vehicle producers are willing to operate with moderately strong, independent labor unions as long as the unions do not challenge the firms' ownership and control of their investments or threaten political stability.

The effectiveness of the carrot-and-stick policies of host governments has also influenced the location of export facilities among the more developed LDCs. Government policies have attempted to link the development of export production to access to the domestic market, threatening in effect to limit domestic sales unless exports reach a specified level. In addition host governments have offered incentives to encourage the transnationals to comply with export goals. As governments, driven by the same balance-of-payments and employment difficulties, have begun to vie for the same export facilities, these incentives have become quite substantial. In Brazil, for example, the BEFIEX program offers vehicle exporters tax credits and subsidies that represent 30 to 40 percent of the value of the exports. The program also reduces import restrictions, permitting producers to use cheaper foreign-made parts for up to one-third of the value added in Brazil. Similarly the Spanish government's successful bid for a new GM export-oriented plant contained substantial incentives, including a subsidy of 10 to 20 percent of the plant's costs, plus loans for an additional 25 percent.[37]

Transportation and other distance costs (such as insurance) also play a significant role in the location of export production. Accordingly the TNCs have tended to concentrate the production of components designed for export to the developed countries in nearby areas. In Europe, Spain and Portugal, as well as some East European countries, have become important export bases, while the U.S. industry has tended to rely upon Mexican production. Similarly as some Third World industries (in Brazil, for example) become important centers of production, it seems likely that transportation costs will encourage the siting of component production designed for these industries in adjacent areas.

U.S. and European Economic Community (EEC) tariff policies have accentuated the attraction of nearby countries. The U.S. Tariff Schedule (item 807.0), for example, permits imported components assembled with parts fabricated in the United States to enter the country on special terms. (These components are subject to U.S. duty only on that portion of value added abroad.) The primary importance of this provision and similar policies in the EEC is its general encouragement of the TNCs' efforts to site component production abroad.[38] These tariff policies have also implied, however, a doubling of transportation distances (as U.S. parts are carried to Mexico for assembly and then reimported back into the United States). This doubling has enhanced the attraction of siting export production in nearby countries. These considerations help explain the recent announcements by both GM and Chrysler to establish *maquiladoras*, or industrial plants assemblying U.S.–made components for export back into the United States, just south of the border in Juarez, Mexico.[39]

While transportation and other distance costs apply to the export-oriented production of all components, the TNCs have turned to nearby countries, particularly in the case of relatively heavy and bulky components (while preferring for the same reasons to locate final assembly plants in the intended market itself). By contrast, components "which have high value relative to their bulk, and therefore have transportation costs which make up a very small proportion of their total value," may be suitable for production and export "at greater distances from the final market."[40] Indeed production of these latter components might be located in export platforms in the least developed LDCs, particularly if they incorporate relatively simple, highly labor-intensive operations.

Finally the efficiency of existing production operations affects the location of export production. For two reasons the TNCs have tended to favor Third World countries with production operations that have already achieved an internationally competitive level of efficiency. The more efficient operations provide a flexibility of production that their less-efficient competitors do not. Since they do not require export production to reach efficient volumes of production, they can, for example, produce on an efficient basis components with relatively small export markets. In addition, these operations can serve as regional centers for the production and export of finished vehicles, especially to other Third World countries. While several Third World operations play (or have the potential to play) this role, VW's Brazilian subsidiary with its enormous São Bernardo plant is notable in this regard. Based on a volume of production that at over 500,000 units is internationally competitive, this plant enjoys substantial economies of scale. With relatively low unit costs, it has become a significant exporter of finished vehicles. In 1978 it exported 65,000 vehicles (including complete knockdowns) largely to other Third World countries in Latin America, Africa, and the Middle East.[41]

These factors together explain the pattern or growth of Latin American motor vehicle exports. They suggest further that the TNCs will continue to concentrate their export production in Mexico (with its proximity to the United States and its large and potentially oil-rich market) and especially Brazil (with its large market and efficient existing production operations). This concentration will limit the potential growth of export-oriented production in the other Latin American countries, although those TNCs without large production operations in Brazil and Mexico (such as Renault) may also attempt to develop export bases in Argentina (if labor relations stabilize) and/or Venezuela (with its oil-rich market and membership in the Andean Pact). At the same time the smaller Latin American countries that provide political stability and a favorable mix of the four relative factors will also demonstrate substantial growth in their exports (albeit from very low base levels) as the TNCs restructure their worldwide operations.

Appendix: *TNC Expansion Outside the Developed Countries in the Late 1970s* *

Renault signed a contract with the Portuguese government to invest $400 million in Portugal, obtaining control of the modernization of the Portuguese industry; developed a 40 percent interest in a joint venture with Dina, the government-owned vehicle firm in Mexico; and announced plans to double capacity output in both Turkey and Rumania (to approximately 100,000 and 150,000 vehicles, respectively).

Volkswagen entered the Brazilian truck market for the first time by its acquisition of two-thirds of the stock of Chrysler do Brasil; announced its intention to invest $40 million in a South African engine plant; agreed to its intention to assemble the Rabbit in Ecuador and the Beetle in Egypt (joint venture with the Egyptian government); began negotiations with the Hyundai Motor Company of South Korea concerning

---

Sources: World Business Weekly, Latin American Economic Report, and Ward's Auto World.

the local assembly of VW vehicles; agreed to deliver 10,000 Rabbits in a barter deal with the East German government; and in competition with Peugeot-Citroen began negotiations with the Soviet Union to modernize its auto industry.

While *Peugoet-Citroen* expanded primarily in Western Europe (with Peugeot absorbing Citroen in 1976 and then Chrysler's European operations in 1978), it also attempted to increase its sales outside this area. In addition to its present negotiations with the Soviet Union, Peugeot-Citroen agreed to build a $600 million plant in Rumania designed to produce a new car for the local market; signed a contract with the prerevolutionary Iranian government to produce its 305 model; and began development trials of a new basic utility vehicle it plans to produce and market in Vietnam.

Volvo reached agreement with the Brazilian government on the construction of a $75 million plant designed to produce heavy-duty trucks.

Fiat initiated production in Brazil (selling 93,000 vehicles in 1978, its second year of operation); expanded its controlling share of SEAT, Spain's largest car manufacturer; entered negotiations with the Algerian government on the construction of a 100,000 cars-per-year plant; and signed trade agreements and exchanges with the governments of Poland and Yugoslavia.

Ford reached agreement with the Egyptian government on the construction of a $145 million factory to produce truck and diesel engines for the regional market; discussed, in competition with General Motors, plans to develop sales and production operations in China; announced plans to expand its Taiwan facilities with a $40 million investment; announced plans to expand its Portuguese operation; and invested some $700 million in Spain to produce the Fiesta.

General Motors announced its intention to invest $13 billion outside the United States over the next decade. While subsidiaries in the developed countries will absorb a considerable proportion of this sum, GM will invest $2 billion in new facilities in Spain and Austria and $500 million in Brazil. The company also bought the Chrysler plants in Colombia and Venezuela and agreed to invest several hundred million dollars to double its Mexican vehicle output.

Notes

1. The Renault and American Motors subsidiaries in Mexico are joint ventures, with the Mexican government holding the majority share in both.

2. Jack Baranson, *Automotive Industries in Developing Countries* (Washington, D.C.: International Bank for Reconstruction and Development, 1969), chap. 5.

3. The sources of these data include: for Argentina, Rhys Jenkins, *Dependent Industrialization in Latin America* (New York: Praeger, 1977), p. 213; for Brazil, Kenneth S. Mericle, "The Brazilian Motor Vehicle Industry: Its Role in Brazilian Development and Its Impact on United States Employment" (unpublished manuscript, 1975), p. 58; *Latin American Economic Report*, March 25, 1977; for Mexico, *Mexico-La Industria Automotriz de Mexico en Cifras 1976* (Mexico City: AMIA, 1977); and William Gudger, "The Regulation of Multinational Corporations in the Mexican Automotive Industry" (Ph.D. diss., University of Wisconsin, 1975), p. 331.

4. *Automotive News*, March 26, 1979.

5. Ronald Muller and David Moore, "Case One: Brazilian Bargaining Power Success in Befiex Export Promotion Program with the Transnational Automotive Industry," prepared for the United Nations Centre on Transnational Corporations (January 1978), p. 15A.

6. *Business Latin America*, December 27, 1978, p. 416.

7. *Latin American Economic Report*, December 16, 1977, pp. 244–245.

8. *Business Latin America*, June 14, 1978, pp. 190–192, and February 14, 1979, pp. 52–53.

9. F. Frobel, J. Heinrichs, and O. Kreye, "Export-Oriented Industrializaton of Underdeveloped Countries," *Monthly Review* (November 1978): 23.

10. *Automotive News*, July 17, 1978, p. 48, and "Short Term Prospects for the Japanese Motor Industry," *Motor Business*, no. 99 (third quarter 1979): 12.

11. *Economic Week*, February 28, 1977; *World Business Weekly*, June 18, 1979; "The Prospects for the Automotive Industries in the United States and Canade in 1978," *Motor Business*, no. 93 (1978): 12. See also *World Business Weekly*, June 18, 1979.

12. In major retrenchments dictated by deteriorating financial circumstances, Chrysler and BL have liquidated a considerable portion of their overseas holdings. The Japanese producers have relied quite successfully on exports for foreign sales; however, under a growing protectionist threat, they have entered joint manufacturing ventures with firms in Western Europe and are planning operations in the United States. See *Motor Business*, no. 99. (1979): pp. 1, 6–7; and *World Business Weekly*, February 18, 1980.

13. Paul Streeten, "Bargaining with Multinationals," *World Development* 4, no. 3 (March 1976): 227–228; Muller and Moore, "Case One," p. 17.

14. For example, Ford's introduction of the assembly line from 1910 through 1914 generated enormous discontent. According to one account, "In December of 1912 the turnover rate was 48 percent for the month alone. During the prolonged labor crisis of 1913, the annual rate was 38 percent. To maintain a work force approaching 14,000, Ford hired over 52,000 men. Most of the tens

of thousands who left the factory were not fired. They simply walked out. . . . The managers kept the factory running by taking almost all comers and putting them to work on the increasingly simplified jobs created by rationalization. Some lasted, some did not." Jack Russell, "The Coming of the Line—The Ford Highland Park Plant, 1910–1914," *Radical America* (May–June 1978): 40.

15. Malcolm L. Denise, vice-president of labor relations, Ford, quoted by B. J. Widick, "Work in Auto Plants," in Widick, ed., *Auto Work and Its Discontents* (Baltimore: Johns Hopkins University Press, 1976), pp. 10–11.

16. Harry Braverman, *Labor and Monopoly Capital* (New York: Monthly Review Press, 1974), pp. 32–33, and Judson Gooding, "Blue-Collar Blues on the Assembly Line," *Fortune* (July 1970): 70.

17. Gooding, "Blue-Collar Blues," p. 70; Jim Woodword, "Labor Notes," *Workers' Power*, August 21–September 3, 1975, p. 4.

18. Gooding, "Blue-Collar Blues," p. 70.

19. William Serrin, *The Company and the Union* (New York: Random House, 1970), p. 39; and General Motors statement to the UAW, August 7, 1979, p. 8.

20. Widick, *Auto Work*, pp. 9–10. See also General Motors Corporation, "1979 Bargaining Fact Sheet," p. 16.

21. See, for example, Richard Kronish, "Crisis in the West European Motor Industry: Class Struggle in the British Motor Industry," *Review of Radical Political Economics* 10, no. 2 (1978): 38–41.

22. "Is Fiat Getting Ready to Move?" *Dun's Review* (May 1979): 124.

23. General Motors statement to the UAW, August 7, 1979, pp. 3, 8.

24. Ken Waller, "The Lordstown Struggle and the Real Crisis in Production," *Solidarity Pamphlet 45* (1974), p. 2.

25. National Economic Development Office (UK), *Motors—Industrial Review to 1977* (1973), p. 44; *World Business Weekly*, November 5, 1979.

26. D. T. Jones and S. J. Prais, "Plant-Size and Productivity in the Motor Industry: Some International Comparisons," *Oxford Bulletin of Economics and Statistics* 40, no. 2 (May 1978): 149.

27. *Economist*, June 10, 1978.

28. Edouard Seidler, "Lutz: No World Car in Ford's Plans," *Automotive News*, August 13, 1979; *World Business Weekly*, June 18, 1979.

29. Volkswagen, *Report for the Year 1976*, p. 14.

30. *World Business Weekly*, August 27, 1979; *New York Times*, February 8, 1979.

31. *World Business Weekly*, August 27, 1979.

32. United Nations, "International Subcontracting Arrangements in Electronics between Developed Market-Economy Countries and Developing Countries," report by the secretariat of the United Nations Conference on Trade and De-

velopment (1975), p. 16; G. K. Helleiner, "Manufactured Exports from Less-Developed Countries and Multinational Firms," *Economic Journal* (March 1973): 45–46.

33. Sanjaya Lall, "Less-Developed Countries and Private Foreign Direct Investment: A Review Article," *World Development* 2 (April–May 1974): 47.

34. Deepak Nayyar, "Transnational Corporations and Manufactured Exports from Poor Countries," *Economic Journal* 83 (March 1978): 77.

35. Ibid.

36. Ibid., pp. 74–76.

37. *New York Times*, July 9, 1979; *Economist*, June 16, 1979.

38. United Nations, "International Subcontracting," pp. 21–22.

39. *New York Times*, February 6, 1979; *Automotive News*, March 5, 1979; and *New York Times*, March 3, 1980.

40. Helleiner, "Manufactured Exports," p. 36.

41. Volkswagen, *Report for the Year 1978*, p. 43.

Labor in the Brazilian Motor Vehicle Industry

John Humphrey

The question of workers in multinational corporations in Latin America has been the subject of much speculation but little concrete inquiry. In Brazil, where the motor vehicle industry ranks in the world's top ten, the only published in-plant survey of workers in the automobile sector is based on research carried out in the early 1960s.[1] Such neglect is not confined to either Brazil or the motor industry. In Latin America generally the working class is rarely considered an important political force. If considered at all, it is as an object of political and economic processes, something that is acted upon, created and shaped by forces that originate elsewhere.

Neglect of the working class by academics contrasts sharply with the amount of attention paid to workers and their organizations by governments in Latin America. In North America and Europe the state is supposed to play a relatively minor role in industrial relations, and yet workers and unions, particularly those in the motor industry, are never far from the public eye. Their problems have been analyzed by journalists, academics, and government working parties. In Latin America the opposite is the case. The state plays an interventionist role in labor matters, particularly in Brazil, and a system of repression and control has kept the labor question out of the public eye for long periods. The calm that prevails in the labor field for long periods, however, is neither natural nor unproblematic. Periodic expressions of labor discontent, as seen in the mass strikes of 1978 and 1979 in the motor industry, are a surprise only to those who do not look beneath the surface calm.

In the early period of the development of the motor vehicle industry, labor was not a problem for the employers. Production was small scale, and firms adopted a high-wage policy to attract sufficient workers of suitable quality. Generally the activities of auto workers were overshadowed by those of workers in other industries in the turbulent early 1960s, but this is not to imply that the situation in the motor vehicle plants was quiet. Reports from one of the largest plants at the time, Willys Overland, indicated stoppages for wage increases, boycotts of the canteen to improve the food, and delegations of workers sent to management to discuss shop floor problems. This activity stopped abruptly in 1964 when workers in the motor vehicle industry suffered in the general clampdown on working-class activities, but in the following years auto workers began to become more involved in wider class movements. In 1968 they figured prominently in the strikes and stoppages in São Paulo, and in the early 1970s the union representing most motor vehicle workers came to play a major role in trade union affairs. The rapid growth of the motor vehicle industry from 1968 to 1974 gave these workers a greater weight within the working class as a whole, and the salience of the industry and its importance for the economic life of Brazil has given motor industry workers a strategic importance.

In the 1970s demands for changes in industrial relations practices and in the role of the state in labor affairs have been building up in Brazil. The auto workers have been centrally involved in this movement, and as conditions in the industry deteriorated after 1974, labor protests intensified. At the end of the decade a general crisis in labor policy called into question both the viability of the development strategy pursued in the miracle period and the specific policies used in the motor industry to control labor. Demands for changes in government policies culminated in protests and strikes in 1977, 1978, and 1979. In 1978 plant-level stoppages affected four of the five major firms in the auto manufacturing belt (the São Bernardo area of São Paulo), and in 1979, an all-out strike of 200,000 metalworkers paralyzed the motor vehicle industry in São Paulo. Demands for direct negotiations with the employers, the formation of factory committees, and intermittent stoppages during the year transformed industrial relations in the motor industry and contributed to a wider political crisis.

This chapter provides an account of the situation and demands of workers in the motor vehicle industry based on research in two major auto plants in the São Paulo area conducted in 1975.[2] Combined with information on recent struggles and trade union demands, this analysis is designed to refute certain speculative preconceptions about motor industry workers, assess the significance of demands for reform, and discuss the impact of such reforms on labor relations in the motor industry. I pay particular attention to wages, working conditions, and industrial relations in the plants and the relation of auto workers to other sectors of the working class. The analysis concentrates on the situation of auto workers in the period immediately prior to the major confrontation between these workers and the state in 1978–1979 and discusses the importance of recent developments in the motor vehicle industry for industrial relations in the 1980s.

Modern Industry and Its Workers: Some Misconceptions

The installation of new industries in the major Latin American economies in the 1950s and 1960s produced a sharp transformation of their industrial structures. Foreign capital was encouraged to turn its attention to the manufacturing sector, and there was considerable expansion of the consumer durables and capital goods industries. This development had an especially profound impact on Brazil, where the new industries expanded much more rapidly than the traditional sectors, generating an industrial structure and employment of an apparently distinctive type. Firms in the chemicals, rubber (including tires), paper and cardboard, metalworking, mechanical, transportation equipment, and electrical sectors are disproportionately located in the São Paulo region. They are more likely to be owned by or associated with foreign capital, to be well above the average firm size for industry as a whole, to be in competition with a small number of other large firms, and to pay higher than average wages. Such firms typify oligopolistic, modern, large-scale international capitalist development.

The characteristics of these firms have led some writers to make distinctions between different sectors of the working class according to the type of industries in which they work. For example, Quijano has distinguished hegemonic and competitive sectors of the economy. He argues that workers in the hegemonic sectors form a stable and privileged (because of better wages and working conditions) group, marked off from other sections of the working class by their special skills, training, and cultural and psychological attributes.[3] Similarly Cardoso has suggested that workers in the modern, internationalized sectors of the economy may be more linked to management in those sectors than to the rest of the working class.[4] Other authors have produced a variety of arguments in support of the general notion that workers in the modern sectors, of whom workers in the motor industry are a major part, will tend to have characteristics that mark them off from the rest of the working class in general.[5]

These general statements about workers in the modern, dynamic industries have been reinforced by two important accounts of the situation of workers in the Brazilian motor vehicle industry. The first, by Rodrigues, is based on a study carried out in 1963. Rodrigues provides a detailed account of the attitudes of auto workers, and in spite of occasional reservations and provisos, his main argument is that the upward mobility of the mass of workers from agricultural employment to industry and the specific experience of employment in a high-wage, modern, enlightened firm creates a labor force that is satisfied by and large:

Large firm, auto firm, more agreeable firm, etc., rightly constitute for the workers synonyms for "higher wages" and "better employment opportunities." And it is in the big firms as well that workers believe they can find better chances of promotion. At the same time the firm makes possible better training, a specialization and the acquisition of a skilled trade that often small firms cannot offer. . . . For almost all of the respondents the company amply fulfilled the expectation which accompanied the search for a job.[6]

At the same time, the firm's wage policy and general attitude to industrial relations effectively neutralizes the trade union, and internal promotion offers real advancement possibilities for many workers:

It is obvious that the wages—as well as the other advantages that the workers value—do not appear to the group as being the result of collective pressure or of trade union action. . . . In addition, partly for technical reasons and partly as a result of its human relations policy, the auto firm attempted to promote internally and use its own employees to fill vacancies in the company hierarchy. The more capable and senior workers had, then, effective chances of promotion which did not occur in other industries, and which may not occur in this same sector in other countries. These chances will probably disappear when the Brazilian auto industry reaches maturity.[7]

The proviso at the end is significant, but it does not alter the argument that at the time of the study the workers were reasonably happy with their situation.[8] This view, combined with the fact that workers in the industry earn above-average wages, has produced a stereotype, widespread in Brazil, of the well-paid, privileged, skilled auto worker.

The second account of the situation of workers in the motor vehicle industry is found in the work of Almeida.[9] Drawing on the work of Anibal Pinto and Maria da Conceição Tavares, she argues that the heterogeneity of the industrial structure resulting from the development of modern industry produces a differentiation of workers and a diversity of trade union activity:[10]

The increasing heterogeneity of the industrial structure creates a differentiation of shop floor workers themselves with regard to situation and conditions of work, skill levels and wage opportunities. All this is well known. In terms of the present work it is important to stress that this internal differentiation of factory labor implies a diversification of the problems confronting the distinct groups of workers, their interests and their demands. More than this, it is interesting to note how the rise and the dominance of the large modern firm within the industrial structure makes possible the emergence of new bargaining thematics, new forms of negotiation and trade union organization, and finally new types of trade union action distinct from [populist forms].[11]

The implication here is that workers in industries like the motor vehicle industry will have different interests and priorities from workers in other sectors. In spite of a qualification concerning the heterogeneity of the labor force in the modern sector (an acknowledgment that even in large, modern firms there may be groups of unskilled and semiskilled workers not enjoying stability of employment, high wages, and promotion opportunities),[12] Almeida clearly implies that workers in the modern sector, and more specifically workers in the motor industry, are more likely to be stable and highly paid than other workers and that the nucleus of such workers is large enough to determine the characteristics of unions in this sector of industry and differentiate them from unions in the more traditional sectors.[13]

In her discussion of motor vehicle industry labor markets, Almeida introduces the concepts of primary and secondary labor markets.[14] A primary labor market is defined by high wages, good working conditions, chances of advancement, stability of employment, and equity in the administration of work rules.[15] A secondary labor market lacks these characteristics, and workers employed in it are much less privileged. Based on these concepts, Almeida assumes that high wages paid in the motor vehicle industry indicate that other characteristics of a primary labor market also exist. This procedure is followed in the case of the Mexican motor vehicle industry by Miller and coworkers.[16] The use of this conceptual approach allows a series of largely unsupported generalizations about the nature of employment in the motor vehicle industry to enter the argument. These assumptions are of crucial importance because the definition of a primary labor market is closely related to factors of privilege and security. It is assumed that workers in motor vehicles are protected by a closed, internal labor market that provides job stability, relatively high wages, and good chances of promotion.[17] This picture corresponds closely to the description by Rodrigues. But I argue here that although wages are relatively high in the motor vehicle industry, other aspects of employment are not of the sort defined by the concept of primary labor market. In fact Brazilian auto workers face unstable employment, harsh supervision, limited promotion prospects, and intensive work.

Both Rodrigues and Almeida imply that workers in the motor industry are relatively privileged, stable in their employment, and provided with opportunities for advancement. Quijano makes a similar case for modern-sector workers as a whole. All three believe that these attributes differentiate modern-sector workers from the rest of the labor force. This has two important consequences for industrial relations in the motor vehicle industry and the situation of the working class in general. First, it is implied that workers in the motor industry and other modern sectors will not have a great amount in common with workers in other industries. As Almeida has put it, "The problems confronted by a worker in Volkswagen in the course of his daily work are necessarily different from those which trouble the workers in a small clothing factory in Bom Retiro."[18] The argument is developed into an assertion that workers in the motor industry will pursue their interests independently of other sections of the working class and by different means. They will tend to stand apart from the mass of workers in the traditional industries. Such an argument can imply that auto workers constitute a labor aristocracy, a divisive force that prejudices the interests of the working class as a whole.[19] The most highly developed sector of the working class acts as an elite.[20] Second, if wages, working conditions, and chances for advancement are assumed to be good and workers are generally satisfied, firms in the motor industry will not have serious labor problems because the combination of enlightened management and wage levels sustainable by monopoly profits will be sufficient to defuse discontent and incorporate the mass of the labor force.

The analysis presented by Rodrigues and Almeida cannot explain recent events in the Brazilian motor vehicle industry. The workers in the industry and the union that represents the majority of them have played a dominant part in the opposition to the state and its economic policies, and they have catalyzed workers' militancy that has led other workers to challenge the state. In May 1978 most of the major motor plants stopped work, and in March 1979 all of the plants joined an all-out strike of 200,000 metalworkers. Workers in the motor industry are demanding significantly higher wages, improved working conditions, protection against dismissal and victimization, and the right to form factory committees. The basic premise of the labor aristocracy position, the existence of a primary labor market in the motor vehicle industry, is unfounded. On the contrary conditions in the industry are a significant factor in explaining why its workers have been playing a leading role within the working class in Brazil. This role has implications for the future development of industrial relations both within and without the motor vehicle industry.[21]

Characteristics of Employment in the Brazilian Motor Vehicle Industry

The aspects of motor vehicle employment that are salient in assessing workers' situations are skill levels, recruitment, training and promotion, stability of employment, working conditions, wages, and nonwage benefits. By examining these aspects from interviews with workers at two assembly plants, referred to as AF1 and AF2, it is possible to evaluate conditions in the industry.[22]

Skill

There is little basis for the assumption that auto workers are a highly skilled group, as Quijano and Almeida implied. In the two motor vehicle plants studied, 70 percent of manual workers were classified by the company as either unskilled or semiskilled, a level comparable to other metalworking firms.[23] The ratio of skilled workers may be higher than in some traditional industries, but it is not so high as to suggest that skilled workers are either a majority of the labor force in the industry or the dominant group within it.

Recruitment, training, and promotion: Internal and external labor markets

There are three basic types of skilled workers: toolroom workers, maintenance men, and skilled production workers. Skilled production workers, who constitute about 5 percent of the total labor force in the two plants studied, have skills found only in the metalworking sector. Included in this group are production mechanics, painters, and metal finishers, and they are often trained within the auto plants. The other

Table 4.1
Previous occupational experience of workers in two São Paulo auto plants
(percentage)

Occupation[a]	Previous work experiences						Total number
	Auto industry	Other industry	Other[b]	Direct from agriculture	First job	No responses	
AF1							
Laborer	6	62	25	6			16
Assembler	38	42	8	4	4	4	24
AF2							
Laborer	3	67	20	10			30
Assembler	44	38	13	6			16
Press operator	25	50	20	5			20
Machinist	27	57	7	7	3		30

Source: Interviews.
Notes: Two other small groups of assembly-line workers, welders and metal finishers,
were also interviewed, along with groups of skilled toolroom workers in each plant. The
two groups were too small a sample for general use, but information relating to them
will be advanced when it is illustrative.
a. Laborers are classified by the firm as unskilled; the other categories are semiskilled.
b. Includes commerce, the service sector, small workshops (including mechanical workshops), and self-employment.

skilled workers possess general skills found in many other industries.
The toolroom workers sampled in both factories were hired from a
range of firms, and the managements of both plants were well aware
that they were competing with many other employers, including small
ones. In the case of twenty toolmakers interviewed in AF2, for example,
three had been taken on as apprentices and sent to the state training
school, two had completed courses at night school without company
assistance, and fifteen had been recruited from other firms as toolmakers.
For most skilled jobs, the firm attempted to recruit from the external
labor market. With the exception of the skilled production jobs, semiskilled workers were barred from skilled positions because there was
no training within the firm.

Unskilled and semiskilled workers were also recruited from a wide
range of firms (see table 4.1). In all the job categories sampled, the
majority of workers had not previously worked in the motor vehicle
industry, but most had worked in some form of industrial enterprise.
The workers recruited came from small, medium, and large firms and
from a wide range of industries, including textiles, glassmaking, auto

components, plastics, foundries, furniture, and rubber. Workers who were engaged in nonmanufacturing sectors immediately prior to entering the company came from construction, distribution, public transport, street cleaning, small workshops, and self-employment. This diversity seems to contradict the argument of Quijano and also the more specific claim made by Cimillo and coworkers concerning the segmentation of the labor market between textiles and motors.[24]

Unskilled workers receive little formal training in the plant. The Training Department in AF1 had only three staff, and they concentrated on health and safety work rather than skill training. In each of the semiskilled categories listed in table 4.1, approximately 50 percent of the workers interviewed were hired as semiskilled workers, having either worked in the motor vehicle industry prior to recruitment or gained relevant experience in some other industry. Unskilled workers could expect to be promoted to the semiskilled category after fifteen months or more of employment. There was no general policy of filling semiskilled jobs from the internal labor market and no systematic training to qualify the unskilled for semiskilled positions. In fact it was a common complaint among workers that unskilled labor was paid a lower rate for doing the same work as semiskilled labor.

Many jobs in motor vehicle plants require little training. As Beynon points out, most assembly-line jobs can be learned in a very short time, and it has also been noted that as machine shops become more automated, training times can be reduced to a matter of weeks.[25] This neither implies that there are no training costs nor denies that there is informal training; it is to argue that such training is limited. The distinction between semiskilled and unskilled workers is more likely to be based on practice and specialized knowledge of special production processes than on the acquisition of marketable skills.[26]

In each factory there are elongated lines of promotion whereby an unskilled worker theoretically could reach the level of a top-grade metal finisher in seven or more years of constant incremental promotions; however, there appears to be no functional basis arising from the production process for this elaborate differentiation. A comparison of Argentine and Brazilian motor vehicle employers in 1963 (when the industries were roughly the same size) showed that job structures of the seven major Argentine firms had between five and seven grades, while the five major Brazilian firms had between ten and fourteen grades.[27] It can be argued that lines of promotion, such as exist in Brazil, are means of ameliorating pressure for wage rises, dividing the labor force, and tying long-service workers to the firm.[28]

Closed internal labor markets are characterized by recruitment to the entry-level jobs, followed by training and promotion up job ladders. Once within the system, workers can expect promotion and relatively secure futures. Relatively high training costs encourage stability of labor. In the two factories studied in São Paulo, the situation is very different. No workers (other than in the case of the three small groups of skilled production workers) cross the dividing line between semiskilled and skilled jobs. Workers are recruited from outside the plants to all levels of jobs in the plants. Once workers are at the top of their semiskilled category, their chances of promotion are highly restricted. As Rodrigues predicted, opportunities for promotion have been reduced as the industry has become more mature.

Stability of labor

Training and recruitment are also relevant to the question of stability. Given that internal training is very limited and that potential replacements for workers at all levels can be found outside the plants, management does not need to maintain a stable labor force. In other words the costs of rotation are low. The issue of stability is of considerable importance in Brazil because workers have none of the guarantees found in countries with a more developed trade union movement. After 1966 certain restrictions on the right of employers to dismiss workers were removed, and there is no system of seniority, layoff pay, or recall rights. Most workers can be dismissed (with a lump-sum payment as compensation), and once dismissed, they have no further rights. Data on job tenure and turnover are not generally available, but existing evidence suggests that instability is high.

The demand for motor vehicles and levels of production fluctuate. As the industry has become more competitive, some firms have faced decreasing market shares and volatile production levels accompanied by fluctuating employment levels, an adjustment facilitated by the lack of restrictions on layoffs. In both AF1 and AF2 large-scale dismissals took place at the time of the study, but no attempt to stop overtime or introduce short-time working was made except in the case of toolroom workers. Ease of replacement appears to give employers the freedom to hire and fire at will.

Evidence from different periods confirms that firms not only adjust the level of employment to suit current demand, but they also pursue a simultaneous rotation policy, which further increases labor turnover. Evidence from three different sources at three different times points in the same direction. For 1974 the following information is available: "In 1974 General Motors do Brasil S.A. disclosed that in the first four months of the same year, 1,792 workers had been laid off, while 1,870 new workers had been hired. Volkswagen do Brasil S.A. told the press that 3,930 new workers had been hired and 1,300 laid off in the first three months of 1974."[29] If it is assumed that not more than three-quarters of total employment in each firm is accounted for by blue-collar workers (who are more likely to be affected by dismissals), then the dismissal rates in the two firms were, respectively, 17 percent and 10 percent of blue-collar employment in December 1973.[30]

A similar picture is revealed by table 4.2. In only one of the seven largest motor vehicle firms did less than 14 percent of workers leave between January and June 1977. The dismissal rate for the industry as a whole was 13.8 percent, although new entries meant that the size of the labor force fell by only 3.2 percent. There is clearly a pattern of labor instability, but more information is needed because turnover rates alone do not indicate who leaves and why. Turnover might affect only limited groups of workers, and such workers might leave of their own accord.

Information from the Metalworkers Union of São Bernardo provides a further basis for evaluating whether turnover is voluntary.[31] The figures for five major factories in the São Bernardo area show that for each worker who left employment voluntarily, more than five were dismissed without just cause; they committed no disciplinary offense that would merit dismissal without the right to compensation. (See table 4.3.)The fact that between 7.4 and 16.3 percent of workers were dismissed by the five large firms in the area in 1978, even though they had worked for their employer for more than one year, indicates that longer-service workers are also affected.

Without detailed information it is not possible to provide a definite picture of which workers are prone to dismissal, but it can be shown that even skilled and experienced workers are dismissed. In 1974 there was a wave of dismissals in AF1, affecting mostly the assembly shops, although there were also reductions in subassembly and materials handling (see table 4.4).. In the course of one month the number of workers in the assembly area fell by 27.9 percent, and although the cuts fell

Table 4.2
Entries and exits in the motor industry by firm, January–June 1977

Firm[a]	Number of workers January 1977	Entries in period	%	Exits in period	%	Change in employment	%
Chrysler	3,777	426	11.3	531	14.0	105	− 2.8
FNM	4,377	1,003	23.0	631	14.4	372	+ 8.5
Fiat	5,326	2,614	49.1	871	16.4	1,743	+32.7
Ford	23,071	1,315	5.7	3,603	15.6	2,888	− 9.9
General Motors	19,795	454	2.3	3,552	17.9	3,098	−15.7
Mercedes-Benz	16,460	3,314	20.0	2,558	15.5	756	+ 4.6
Volkswagen	39,057	2,141	5.5	3,698	9.5	1,557	− 4.0
All motor industry	117,900	12,456	10.6	16,226	13.8	3,770	− 3.2

Source: SINE, taken from figures from Asociação Nacional dos Fabricantes de Veículos Automotores.
Note: a. Includes only the larger firms.

Table 4.3
Workers in selected auto plants with at least one year's service notifying union they have left their job, 1978, São Bernardo do Campo

Plant	Number of workers[a]	Reason for Leaving				All dismissals (%)
		Dismissed without just cause[b]	%	Asked to be dismissed	%	
Chrysler	2,112	160	7.6	41	1.9	9.6
Ford	11,339	1,070	9.4	219	1.9	11.3
Mercedes-Benz	15,487	1,467	9.5	197	1.3	10.8
Saab-Scania	2,927	445	15.2	40	1.4	16.6
Volkswagen	32,106	3,046	9.5	604	1.9	11.4
Total motor industry in São Bernardo	63,971	6,188	9.6	1,101	1.7	11.3

Source: Union records.
Notes: a. All workers, including white-collar workers.
b. Means that workers are fired for no disciplinary reason that would affect their right to compensation.

Table 4.4
Reductions in the AF1 labor force, December 1974 (percentage)

Area of factory	Reduction in numbers employed
Quality control	0
Materials handling	14.1
Body and assembly	27.9
Stamping plant	2.1
Subassembly	12.4
Maintenance	2.7
Toolroom	4.6
By job category in body and assembly	
Laborers, unskilled, grade 3	42.2
Assemblers, semiskilled, grade 7	20.8
Welders, semiskilled, grade 8	17.7
Trimmers, semiskilled, grade 9	17.8
Metal finishers, skilled, grade 9	28.6
Production mechanics, skilled, grade 9	23.4
Production painters, skilled, grade 9	29.6

Source: Company records.

disproportionately on the unskilled workers, between 20 and 30 percent of skilled production jobs were also cut. The company has no provision for reclassifying workers and no seniority system, so there are no rules to protect more experienced or skilled workers from dismissal.[32] Protection for workers comes mainly from labor market shortages; skilled workers are protected from mass dismissals by a general shortage of skilled tradesmen in greater São Paulo. However, even skilled workers will be dismissed if they are not cooperative. There were reprisals against workers who took part in the stoppages in 1978, and in the course of the interviews, workers often stressed that they had no problems if, for example, they agreed to overtime when asked and if they carried out their work tasks properly. The threat of dismissal hangs above the heads of all workers, particularly those involved in trade union activity.

Finally, some information about labor stability can be gained from an examination of what workers do when they leave an employment in the motor vehicle industry. Do they find work in another motor plant, or are they forced to seek employment in another industry? In the two plants studied, a sample of 166 semiskilled, skilled, and highly skilled workers was taken. Of this group fifty workers had worked in the motor vehicle industry at some point prior to entering either AF1 or AF2. The average length of stay for each group of workers in their previous motor vehicle employments was under three years. Half of the fifty workers had taken a job outside motor vehicles between their first employment in it and the time of the interviews. Of the thirty-three workers who had moved directly from one auto company to AF1 or AF2 (some had worked in two or more auto firms prior to AF1 or AF2), twenty-one had moved because they had been dismissed. Dismissal is not confined to semiskilled workers; nine of the fourteen toolmakers who had moved directly to AF1 or AF2 from other auto firms had been dismissed. The evidence suggests that workers in the motor vehicle industry are not stable in one firm or permanently employed within the industry.[33]

Working conditions and wages

My focus here is on two issues of particular concern to workers: intensity of work and health and safety. The International Labor Organization ranks Brazil as having one of the highest accident records in the world. In one of the plants the pressure to increase production led to unsafe working conditions because the output demanded of it went beyond the original capacity of the plant. The dangers included component bins left in walkways, dangerously loaded storage areas, and workers and machines put too close together. A report prepared by management on the state of the forklift truck fleet illustrates the general problem.[34] It revealed that cramped facilities provided operators with inadequate room to maneuver. At the same time pressure to increase productivity meant that workers overloaded the forklifts and ran them at unsafe speeds, that the machines were badly maintained, and that the materials handling department was receiving insufficient resources. The report concluded that the safety problems were the result of a systematic pattern of management designed solely to increase output.

The pressure to produce is general in the Brazilian motor vehicle industry. Detailed production and manning figures are not available, although there have been marked increases in output per worker in the industry.[35] An indication of the pressure that can exist is given by this statement from an assembly line foreman in AF1:

They [the workers] are working more now. One doing the job of another. I had to let another two go yesterday, but the work's the same. It's the management that gives the orders. Economies, there's no sense in it. Before, each job was timed, but not any more. Before, if they reduced the work force we got more machines, but not any more. Nothing is altered and the timings for the jobs go on falling. . . . Each manager wants to cut down even more. Time Study lowered the time allowed for each chassis, and the management then did the same. [To prove his point the foreman goes to his desk and gets out two sheets of paper. He explains the figures. On one sheet are the times allowed for the complete set of operations for a particular type of vehicle on his section of the line, as prepared by Time Study and operative for the current month and four months ahead. On the other sheet are the times allocated by the plant management for the same operations.] Look, here's the time allowed by Time Study, and here's the time from management: the management want . . . [a 5% reduction in time on the assembly of one model, and 4% on another]. *And* they expect us to work at 102% efficiency.

A similar situation prevailed at AF2.[36]

The degree of intensity of labor best explains the high wage policies of the Brazilian auto firms. The high wages of the industry are the starting point for theories of labor market segmentation and internal labor markets. Starting from neoclassical economic theory, these theories assume that high wages must reflect either monopoly power (hence labor market segmentation), or higher marginal productivity (greater education or training or skill), or attempts by firms to offset training costs by reducing turnover. None of these theories seems to account for the high wages of motor industry workers in Brazil. Indeed those who receive the highest differential over their potential earnings in other industries, the assemblers, are among the least skilled, trained, and stable of all of the workers in the industry. A statement by Henry Ford provides a solution to this paradox: "One frequently hears that wages have to be cut because of competition, but competition is never really met by lowering wages. Cutting wages does not reduce costs— it increases them. The only way to get a low cost product is to pay a high price for a high grade of human service and see to it through management that you get that service."[37]

The motor industry pays higher wages and then recoups the cost through control of the labor process. The high grade of human service that Ford refers to is not skilled labor but rather workers who will work hard and well. When Ford introduced the "five dollar day" in 1915, turnover at the Rouge plant in Detroit had risen to 300 percent per annum, but the introduction of high wages did not stabilize work in the motor industry.[38] It remained a notorious hire-and-fire industry until at least World War II.[39] However, higher wages did enable Ford to have a large supply of workers from which to choose his labor force. He could determine who was to enter the Rouge and stay there. This power is important in maintaining high levels of productivity. In neo-classical terms marginal productivity is attributable not only to skill, education, or some other attribute that the worker possesses as an individual but also to the capitalist control of the production process viewed as a social relation involving domination.

The relationship between high wages and the discipline and intensity of work was not lost on either workers or foremen in the Brazilian firms. A few workers in both plants commented on intensity of work without prompting when asked about wage levels, and two former workers from AF2, interviewed while working as foremen at a small-components plant, commented on the difficulties of imposing discipline in a low-wage plant. In the high-wage auto plants the disciplinary threat is the potential wage loss in the event of dismissal. High rates of turnover and the possibility of not finding work in other auto plants make this threat real. Following this line of thought, one would expect wages in the auto industry to move according to the same basic pattern as the general wage level—that is, auto wages would have been squeezed along with wages in general.

There is little direct information available on this point; however, the assessments of workers in the two plants point to a narrowing of differentials between motor industry wages and wages for industry in general, particularly for skilled workers.[40] Although this could be the result of the leveling up of other firms to motor industry rates (given the expansion of modern industry in the fifteen years before the in-terviews), the company's wages planning department declared itself to be following a policy of paying the market rate for the job. In 1973, for example, the wage structure of AF1 was reorganized strictly in accordance with demand and supply of different types of workers. If it is reasonable to assume that wages in the motor industry moved roughly in line with wages in other industries between 1964 and the mid-1970s and in particular in line with the wages of workers in large firms in the center-south of Brazil, the following would have happened: wages would have fallen immediately after the coup in 1964, remained stable (if government inflation indices are accepted) for unskilled and semiskilled workers and risen slowly for skilled workers between 1966 and 1972, and then fallen after 1972 because of rising inflation and manipulation of the inflation index.[41] Between 1973 and 1975 wages

Table 4.5
Comparisons of wage rates for 1974

Job category	
AF1	
Laborer, 3–6 months service[a]	205
Laborer, average rate	224
Assembler, 3–9 months service	300
Assembler, average rate	354
Construction[b]	
Laborer	137
Painter	256
Installer	282

Source: AF1 company records.
Notes: Minimum wage = 100. The figure taken for the minimum wage is the average level of the minimum wage in São Paulo from November 1973 to October 1974. The minimum wage is published as an hourly rate in the *Anuário Estatístico*.
a. Wage rates for AF1 are those prevailing in November 1974, adjusted to take into account the rise of that month and an anticipation of that rise of 10 percent granted approximately six months before. In other words the rates are a rough average of rates for the period November 1973 to October 1974.
b. The construction rate is the average for each job category for the year 1974 in São Paulo.

for unskilled and semiskilled workers in the two plants seemed to have risen in line with the trade union settlements, which lagged behind the true rate of inflation, while skilled workers managed larger rises, which probably offset the gap between the settlements and price rises in the period.[42]

Overall, wages in the motor industry are well above the minimum wage. In 1975 unskilled workers in AF2 were being paid an hourly rate over twice the minimum wage, and machinists on average were earning over four times the minimum.[43] However, it would be mistaken to think that such wages put auto workers well above workers in other sectors. Bacha's study of earnings in large firms in the center-south of Brazil indicated that earnings in these firms were at a level comparable with those found in AF2 for similar occupations, and even in such a traditionally low-wage sector as construction, average wage rates are well above the minimum (see table 4.5). In the São Paulo construction industry in 1974, only laborers would have been likely to earn less than a laborer in the motor industry. While motor industry workers do receive well above average wages, it should be remembered that for most workers in the industry, the national wage policy has contained incomes since 1964.

Industrial Relations in the Motor Industry

Workers in the motor industry in Brazil have grievances on wage levels, wage structures, intensity of work, job security, fringe benefits, and working conditions.[44] There are three levels at which these grievances could be handled: government and legislation, negotiations in the official machinery, and direct negotiations at plant level.

At the national level the trade unions appear to have virtually no influence on government policy. Since 1964 a large amount of legislation generally considered prejudicial by trade unionists has been passed, including restriction of the right to strike, state determination of wage increases, and a new law on employment protection. All union protests about these laws, and others, have been ignored. Furthermore existing protective labor legislation is not effectively enforced—for example, in the areas of health and safety, excessive overtime, Sunday work, and wage indexation.[45] Military governments have been largely isolated from working-class pressure, making this approach to negotiations almost completely ineffective.

The second line of activity by the unions involves using the annual negotiations between employers and unions as a forum for airing grievances and suggesting new proposals. The scope of possible discussions can be gauged from the list of demands presented by the Metalworkers of São Bernardo, the union representing most auto workers at a union assembly prior to the 1977 claim:

1. No rise in the cost of fringe benefits in the life of the contract.

2. An eight-hour day with two hours overtime maximum, except when twelve-hour shifts are absolutely necessary.

3. A substitute clause such that workers hired to take the place of dismissed workers cannot be taken on at a lower rate.

4. Priority to dismissed workers when the firm rehires.

5. Formalization and regulation of disciplinary procedures.

6. Inclusion of habitual overtime in the calculations for holiday pay, the thirteenth-month bonus, dismissal compensation, and rest days.

7. Provision of day-care facilities on factory premises or within one kilometer in firms of more than fifteen employees aged sixteen or over.

8. Factory representatives with protection against layoff in all firms, with the number proportional to the size of the firm.

Clearly the union thinks there is plenty to negotiate about. The Metalworkers' list illustrates the preoccupations of workers in the motor industry. In some cases the demands are direct substitutes for new legislation (item 3), in others they are attempts to reinforce ineffective laws (item 2), and in still others, they address long-running disputes (item 6 has been the subject of protracted litigation). In most cases large firms are as lacking as small firms in their observance of the practices demanded by the union.

The items listed represent one-fourth of a list of thirty-two demands discussed by the union in advance of the 1977 negotiations. They express serious grievances found within the metalworking industries of the area, but many probably are shared by workers in other sectors. The unions have not had the means to force serious negotiations with employers. The power of the unions is restricted by the state, leaving employers free to ignore their demands. The unions continue to make claims at the time of the annual negotiations in order to publicize their demands among the rank and file and to familiarize the labor courts with them on the theory that the arbitration decisions of the courts will eventually favor the unions. In the 1970s the annual negotiations were an exercise in formal procedure: the unions put forward demands, the management rejected them, and the labor courts arbitrated in favor of the owners. Almeida has pointed out that the negotiations are also ineffective as a means of settling plant-level disputes because the owners argue that only matters affecting workers as a whole can be discussed in them.[46]

The third arena in which bargaining could take place would be inside the factory itself, between plant management and workers' representatives, who might be the official union leadership from outside or workers' leaders from the plant. In 1974–1975 there was no formal consultative procedure in either of the two plants studied. The only committee with management and worker participation was the Internal Accident Prevention Committee, required by law. Union requests for joint worker-management committees in the metalworking industries have been turned down by management at the annual negotiations, and management will discuss matters collectively with workers only under duress. Plant negotiations are definitely categorized as abnormal by management. If workers have grievances, they either communicate them to the foremen, or they undertake some form of collective action to make their feelings known. In AF1 workers in the toolroom worked without enthusiasm in 1973 in order to press home the point that wage levels were too low. They reinforced their views by bringing in advertisements from other firms offering better rates for toolroom workers. In AF1 workers in the toolroom and the machine shops organized short work stoppages in 1974 in order to force management to take notice of their claims. In other factories there have been slowdowns, "good work movements" (workers devote such care to each piece of work that output levels fall dramatically), overtime bans, and petitions. In some cases concessions were won but only when workers were not immediately cajoled by management into returning to normal work. Even when successes were registered, they were generally limited to small concessions over wages. Until 1978 at least, managements in the motor vehicle industry saw little reason to enter into plant negotiations.

The Brazilian system of industrial relations as practiced in the motor industry depends on certain conditions for its functioning. By suppressing grievances rather than attempting to resolve them and by excluding the unions rather than negotiating with them, employers implicitly rely on force and intimidation. For this to be successful, the work forces of the auto plants have to be sufficiently disorganized to permit management dominance. This is the reason for hostility to the unions and their attempts to organize. This system relies on the help of the state in the harassment and curtailment of union activities. Within the plants management can look to the informal help of the state through arrest, and worse, of rank-and-file activists by the security forces, as well as the formal use of the police or the army against workers.[47] The following newspaper report provides an example:

Yesterday troops of the Army Police occupied the installations of the General Electric factory in the Rua Miguel Angelo in Maria da Graça. The movement of the forces of the Army Police was part of maneuvers for industrial security. There were 52 cases of intoxication by tear gas among local people who watched the exercise.[48]

Management's main weapon is intimidation by the threat of dismissal. The threat is made real by the absence of legal protection of job security, the inability of the unions to oppose dismissals effectively, and the existence of an adequate supply of job seekers attracted by high wages. Management has great discretion over who remains in work and who is forced to leave their factories. The impact of this fact is illustrated by comments of workers in AF2 who were asked why they had not joined other workers in a stoppage in 1974: "Some men in the Press

Shop wanted to, but others didn't. They were scared. If everyone stopped, they wouldn't sack anyone, but they're still scared." "In our section we weren't united. But, on the other hand, I think it was fear that did it. The sack. That's why I didn't stop." The threat of dismissal is a regular theme. Those who will not do regular overtime, those who are getting too old for heavy work, those who are late or often absent, those whose names come at the top of petitions, those who try to organize, and those who take on union office are prime targets.[49]

This pattern of management dominance depends on authoritarian government. Without the heavy hand of the state to contain the unions and wider social movements, work places would not remain so disorganized, unions might be able to force more serious negotiations, and new political forces more sympathetic to labor problems might alter the balance of the statute book and state agencies. The future of labor relations in the industry is uncertain at present because the future of authoritarianism is uncertain. Ironically it has been the attitude of the major employers in the industry that has encouraged the mobilization of the trade union movement behind demands for sweeping reforms and produced major labor unrest. The repressive system that worked so well after the military coup is now under attack.

The Motor Industry in 1978–1979: Workers, Management, and the State

Trade union leaders in Brazil, particularly those in the dynamic sectors, have been demanding reforms in the union structure and the state's role in industrial relations for some time. The issue of union reform has taken on renewed significance after the stoppages and strike movements in 1978 and the battle over the metalworkers' negotiations in 1979.

In May 1978 a series of stoppages spread from the Saab-Scania factory in São Bernardo to much of the motor industry. Organized from within the plants, the immediate goal of the stoppages was a wage increase of 15 to 20 percent to compensate for previous losses of real income, in particular losses due to the government's deliberate underestimation of inflation by almost 13 percent in the administration of its wage-setting formula in 1973–1974. In Saab-Scania and Mercedes workers returned when management promised raises but resumed their stoppages when only 6.5 percent was offered. At Ford a stoppage lasting over a week affected the entire plant, and the Chrysler factory was paralyzed. Only at the giant Volkswagen plant was strike action prevented when management dismissed twenty-eight toolmakers and sent the rest home before the stoppage could spread.[50] Stoppages and work interruptions spread to many components and general engineering firms in São Bernardo. At the end of the stoppages, the major auto employers agreed to pay two increases: an 11 percent raise to compensate for the underestimation of the previous inflation and a 13.5 percent increase in anticipation of the 1979 settlement. Both increases were paid in stages. A show of strength by the rank and file, ably assisted by the union, was able to secure wage raises and force direct negotiations between firms and their employees.

This demonstration of workers' power provoked a general period of labor unrest. Stoppages spread to other large firms in the metal-mechanical sector, such as Phillips, Pirelli, and General Electric, and then to smaller firms and other sectors, such as chemicals, textiles, ceramics, and petroleum. In the months following the first stoppages in the motor industry, labor unrest affected nonindustrial areas too as workers in schools, hospitals, banks, and public service attempted to recoup some of the losses sustained in the previous decade. It is estimated that in the first four months of the strike wave, 280,000 workers in over 250 firms struck and that an estimated 1 million workers were affected directly or indirectly by wage settlements negotiated as a result of such stoppages.[51] The movement lasted over six months and spread far beyond the motor industry.

This rapid rise in labor unrest was possible only because of a changing political climate in which the outgoing government of President Ernesto Geisel made a commitment to relax state repression and control and to begin a process of controlled liberalization and democratization that would continue during the administration of General João Figueiredo scheduled to begin in March 1979.[52] Given the government's continued commitment to controlled democratization, the way was made clear for a period of turbulent and ill-defined relations between the labor movement on the one hand and the employers and the state on the other. The state was unwilling to allow the unions a completely free hand to resolve their problems, but it was unable or unwilling to impose the kind of discipline on workers and unions that had secured their subordination in the earlier part of the decade. While all preexisting labor legislation remained intact, there was a period of experiment and struggle to define just how much of it would actually remain operative.

The struggle was fierce in the motor industry where labor was stronger and better organized.

The 1978 stoppages marked the first stage in a long-running conflict between the Metalworkers Union of São Bernardo and the major employers in the area. As the conflict continued, the state played an increasingly important role, shifting from its position of nonparticipation in 1978 to complete control of events in 1980. Following the 1978 strike both management and unions were anxious to make gains during the negotiations for the April 1979 wage settlement. The union, having gained a significant propaganda victory in May 1978, wanted to consolidate its position and translate the direct negotiations that settled that dispute into a permanent form of collective bargaining, thereby suspending the operation of the legal channels laid down for union-employer settlements. Among the employers, however, a strong current of opinion favored a quick reversal of the union's 1978 successes by means of a hard line in 1979.

The 1979 wage negotiations led to a bitter two-week strike ended by the intervention of the state. But in spite of the apparent success of the employers in forcing a strike and then getting the state to defeat the union, the result was only a partial victory. In the negotiations leading up to the strike, the employers presented a package that discounted most of the gains made in May 1978. This was accepted by the *pelegos* controlling the less active unions, but it was completely unacceptable to the workers and unions in the southern industrial belt of São Paulo, who had been most involved in the 1978 strikes.[53] These unions were forced to take strike action in isolation from the other thirty-one unions that accepted the settlement.[54] Managements in the major firms expected the strike to fail. After nearly two weeks with the union still not accepting the original terms, the Ministry of Labor took control of the three unions involved and dismissed their directors.

At this moment the strike appeared to be a failure, and some employers were jubilant about the dismissal of the union leaders. Following the ministry's action, however, the situation appeared to get out of hand, with no immediate return to work and serious clashes between strikers and the security forces appearing probable. Calm was restored only by an agreement between the contending parties that returned the union to the elected officers in exchange for further negotiations and a resumption of work.[55] The employers expected that no concessions would be necessary during these negotiations since the workers would be back in the plants, but when a further stoppage took place at Ford early in May, the motor industry employers conceded a further 3 percent rise to most workers.[56]

This episode amply illustrated the problem facing the motor employers. They were extremely concerned about the increasing strength of the union and wished to contain and control it. One way of doing this was to use the state against it. But, the methods that had been effective earlier did not appear to work in the new situation. State intervention had not stopped the strike, and there was a danger that elimination of the union would create many more problems than it would resolve. Among the employers, there was a split between the Europeans, led by Volkswagen, who favored an all-out attack on the union and shop floor militants, and the Americans, led by Ford, who were more inclined to accept and negotiate with the new union power.

After May 1979 both sides prepared for the following year. The employers were confident that a firmer line from the government on strikes, combined with changes in the wages policy, would be sufficient to demobilze workers, while the union prepared for a longer strike that could be sustained without the involvement of its leaders (who might be imprisoned) or the use of its own headquarters (which might be taken over). In April 1980 negotiations finally broke down over the issue of guarantees of stability of labor. A forty-one day strike ensued, which ended in defeat only after the union had been taken over again and many union leaders imprisoned. This time the victory of the employer group appeared to be complete. After a return to work without any concessions, they (with the exception of Ford) began to dismiss the militants most involved with the union. Volkswagen set the seal on its strategy later in the year by creating a system of employee representation that was specifically designed to substitute and marginalize the union.[57]

The deposed union leadership, however, did not accept defeat and marginalization, and in the case of the Volkswagen representation plan, they obtained a large, write-in protest vote for the union's mascot in the elections. As the 1981 negotiations approached, some employers felt that the deposed leadership was the only authentic voice of the majority of workers in the area. In recognition of this, the Ministry of Labor removed its official and established an interim committee composed of workers openly sympathetic to the deposed leadership. The failure of the hard-line strategy was further revealed during a week-long strike in July 1981 in opposition to the dismissal of 400 workers. The company displayed a very conciliatory line. The police were not called, the company's premises were used for meetings, and the deposed union president, Luís Inácio da Silva, conducted the events. As part of a negotiated compromise, the company recognized a factory committee of fourteen workers, guaranteed no further dismissals for four months, and promised to give priority in rehiring to the fired workers.[58] Once more the union had successfully established direct negotiations with employers.

The turbulent events in the motor industry indicate that workers' organization is strong enough in some large firms for management to prefer some recognition rather than attempt to manage in outright opposition to it; however, the implementation of generalized reforms in industrial relations and collective bargaining would require a much broader challenge to both the *pelego* elements in the unions and the legally constituted system of industrial relations.

The strength of the *pelegos* lies in their control of the federations and confederations. In order to break this strength, it is necessary to mobilize the smaller unions by extending the campaigns out from the major industrial concentrations; however, a fundamental attack on *peleguismo* must involve an attack on the bases of their power, which lie in the structure of the trade union movement itself. Demands for reform of the trade union movement have been voiced by a growing group of union leaders, called authentic unionists, who seek a major overhaul of the corporatist structure ranging from ending the Ministry of Labor's right to intervene in unions and control their affairs to demands for abolition of the ministry's right to recognize unions and collect finances for them. The latter would permit plural unionism, imply the abolition of the federations and confederations, leave the way open for horizontal interunion contacts, and force unions to survive on membership dues and their ability to attract support in work places.

The nature of collective bargaining will also need to be transformed if unions are to be able to carry on negotiations directly with major employers and pursue grievances through industrial action. Necessary changes would include an end to restrictions on the right to strike, protection for union delegates in the factories, the right to settle with one firm or group of firms (or to enter supplementary agreements with selected employers after a general contract has been negotiated), termination of the legally binding arbitration in the labor courts, and the abandonment of the state's wage policy.

This list of potential changes demonstrates the degree to which the current union situation is above all a political question. It can be argued that the current wave of disputes has taken place within a specific political situation and that it forms one part of a wider social movement against the military regime that has included rural workers, urban protest movements, protests against the cost of living, opposition to political repression, and dissatisfaction within the ranks of formerly progovernment groups. The political space and general climate within which the mobilizations have taken place are a precondition for its further development. If the unions have failed to obtain even minimal concessions from the military regime in the past and if they have been faced with harassment and intervention after 1978 as their members attempt to secure the elementary rights of direct negotiations and a living wage, what hope is there that more fundamental reforms can be expected from a military government? The president of the Metalworkers of São Bernardo has expressed the link between union reform and democratization succinctly: "It is impossible to imagine any change of behavior in the current, or in any political structure, if the right to resolve its own problems is not conferred on the working class. . . . To demand the rule of law [as opposed to military rule] is the fundamental question, because that will give birth to trade union freedom."[59]

Democratization will open up the possibility of reforms because a democratic government will be more responsive to workers' demands, and democratic rule will allow unions and workers a much greater area of freedom within which to organize and act. It is in the context of the struggle for democratization that the union leaders linked to the authentic current launched a new political party in 1979. The aim of forming the Workers party (Partido dos Trabalhadores) was to create a vehicle that would allow a political mobilization of workers without subordinating the authentic current to outside political agencies. The rapid growth of the party between 1979 and 1981 was proof of its ability to mobilize support not only among the workers in the main industrial concentrations but also among small town and rural workers.[60]

The rapid union and political development in Brazil after 1978 shows considerable unrest within the working class. The demands of the workers and unions in the most dynamic sectors of industry have been capable of mobilizing workers in many other sectors as well. In many unions and in many parts of the country, the *pelego* leadership has been challenged by more rank-and-file elements, and although the labor movement is far from unified, most sections now at least verbally support demands for union reform and greater freedom of organization. The rapid development of the unions and the Workers party casts serious doubts on theoretical analyses that portray auto workers as a privileged and self-interested labor aristocracy in relation to the rest of the working class. Auto workers have acted as a class vanguard by raising political demands that would transform Brazilian industrial relations in a manner consistent with the interests of the working class as a whole and by opposing and defying repressive policies of the employers and the state.[61] In pursuit of their demands, workers in the motor vehicle industry have provided workers in many other industries with an example that they have not been slow to follow. Insofar as the adequate resolution of their grievances implies major changes in the nature of trade unionism and political life, one can expect auto workers to continue to play a vanguard role. There will be disagreement within the ranks about strategies, but the crucial factor is that insofar as mass movements develop that provide a serious challenge to the state, one can expect auto workers to play a major role.

Industrial Relations in a Democratic Period

It is not possible to predict the future of politics in Brazil; however, the impact of a return to democracy on the situation in the motor industry deserves discussion since the current state of the industry depends on specific labor controls exercised by the state, which would be undermined by any move in a democratic direction.

In terms of the general changes in economic policy that a democratically elected government might make, two issues potentially are important: a shift in emphasis from private cars to trucks, buses, and nonroad transport and a redistribution of income. The effects of both policies should not be overestimated. Passenger car production has been out of favor since the oil crisis in 1974–1975, and the state has been much stricter in requiring exports. Growth in vehicle production (in unit terms) dropped from an average of 20.7 percent per annum from 1969 to 1974 to only 4.5 percent per annum between 1974 and 1979. In 1980 and 1981 vehicle sales were hit by measures taken to control spiraling inflation and serious balance-of-payments problems. Even before democratization, the auto companies faced serious problems.[62] The effect of income redistribution, were a new government willing and able to force a change in distribution patterns, need not be a threat. It can be argued that a limited redistribution of income will not have much impact on auto sales.[63] More important would be the effect on costs of rising real wages.

Real wage gains by workers in industry in general, and in particular in the motor industry, would cut into profit margins if price rises were contained, and there is some possibility of this occurring. As Brazil-based producers compete more aggressively for the home market and also export increasing quantities, competition will become more acute, especially with the arrival of Fiat in the car sector and the entry of Volkswagen into the larger car, small truck, and medium truck markets after the takeover of Chrysler. With Volvo starting production of heavy trucks in 1980, the major producers may be less profitable.[64] Things are likely to get worse for the industry before they get better. This will be the case irrespective of the transition to democracy. A relaxation of authoritarian rule will have its main impact on the motor industry in the field of plant organization and the activities of unions.

Possibly a democratic government will not be as effective as an authoritarian regime in controlling the working class and intimidating the unions, but the range of possible variation is great. A new populist regime could result in pressure to verticalize the union movement and replace independent leaders in major unions, as occurred in Argentina during the Peronist regime in the 1970s.[65] It is also possible that union leaders will retain their independence and use the democratic period to push forward with demands for reforms. Irrespective of who gains power, democratization is likely to lead to a short-term upsurge in rank-and-file activity, as occurred in Argentina in 1973.[66] In the longer term, the results of this upsurge will depend on who gains control of the unions and how much control they are able to exercise over the rank and file.

In this new situation management will have to develop new tactics and strategies for dealing with workers. It will no longer be possible to ignore workers' grievances. Industrial peace will no longer be guaranteed by the repressive apparatus of the state backed up by company discipline. What will be management's response to this new situation?

In the first place, the bourgeoisie will attempt to limit any concessions made on union and workers' rights. Already industrialists are opposing a complete relaxation of state control over union activity. Even the more liberal industrialists seem to be wary: "I'm in favor of open government, democracy, but with authority. At the present time the Brazilian worker is not prepared to have an instrument such as the strike in his hands because he doesn't know how to use it."[67] The same *Veja* report said that a majority of industrialists favored some restrictions on union activities. A second strategy might be to encourage splits within the labor movement. This scenario is most likely under a populist leader who would probably cause as much confusion in the trade union movement as among political forces. It should not be assumed, however, that there is a clear basis for a split between unions in the modern and traditional sectors.[68]

A third major strategy that will probably be employed by industrialists is centralized bargaining. If management is to minimize the effects of either legal sanctioning of direct bargaining or the incapacity of the Ministry of Labor to enforce legally established practices, then a shift in bargaining from the shop floor to the boardroom and union offices will be necessary. If motor industry employers wish to minimize the effects of union autonomy and the reduced level of intimidation applicable on the shop floor, they will try to keep bargaining units as large as possible. This can be seen as the UAW solution, as opposed to the bargaining patterns found in the British motor industry in the past. Management will attempt to isolate the union leadership from the rank and file by centralizing negotiations and offering in return full bargaining rights and other privileges that might be difficult to achieve without management cooperation. Management will try to use the union as a means of control over the rank and file since more direct methods will lose effectiveness. Whether union leaders could deliver the rank and file would depend on the degree of democracy within the unions and the concessions that employers could offer to workers.[69]

Although employers will be forced to ameliorate working conditions in response to the increased effectiveness of workers' organizations, major concession seems unlikely. The difficulties experienced by the auto industry in 1980 and 1981 would seem to indicate that conflicts between employers and unions will intensify as job instability increases further as a result of the economic recession. In 1981 the auto industry experienced its first strike solely concerned with stability of employment when the Ford Motor Company dismissed 400 workers in July. Management faces a possible transition to a new labor relations regime in a period of great economic difficulty. In addition they face the transition following a fairly protracted period in which the unions and the rank and file have been faced by intransigent employers and government. The legacy of workers' struggles from 1978 onward will make it more difficult for management to shift its emphasis toward co-optation of unions.[70]

Management strategies and attitudes of workers and unions toward them are uncertain, but it can be said that management will have to pay more attention to labor matters and that it will face much greater challenges to its authority than in the past. Management may not have the free rein to organize production that it enjoyed in the past, but it is not possible to quantify the effects of such changes or predict their precise form. The outcome will depend on struggles in government, in the unions, and on the shop floor, struggles likely to be characterized by conflicts, repression, victimization, and political disagreements.

Conclusion

Auto industry workers cannot be considered a stable, satisfied, and privileged elite; in the present period they have acted as a class vanguard. One of the implications of this role for industrial relations is that management in the motor industry will be forced to change its practices in the new period.

These findings have certain implications for the development of the motor industry in Brazil. There seems little doubt that workers will be more assertive and less susceptible to management control in a democratic period and that this would have some effect on flexibility and productivity. Profits might suffer as a result. However, the future of the motor industry probably depends much more on the overall performance of the Brazilian economy than on the specific conditions of production in the major auto firms. One significant aspect of the overall performance of the economy is the effect of democratization on bourgeois domination. During a period of democratization, serious instability might occur, posing problems for capitalist accumulation. The longer and harder the working class has to struggle for its democratic rights, the more likely such a challenge to bourgeois rule will occur. If this is the case, the future of the motor vehicle industry, and the situation of auto workers, will depend on the working class in general, not on workers in the motor industry alone.

Notes

1. Leôncio M. Rodrigues, *Industrialização e Atitudes Operárias* (São Paulo: DIFEL, 1970).

2. The materials on motor vehicle plants presented here were collected in Brazil in 1974 and 1975. Workers in two large assembly plants owned by a major transnational vehicle producer were interviewed.

3. Anibal Quijano, "The Marginal Pole of the Economy and the Marginalised Labor Force," *Economy and Society* 3, no. 4 (1974): 407–408, 419.

4. Fernando H. Cardoso, "Dependent Capitalist Development in Latin America," *New Left Review*, no. 74 (1972): 93.

5. Some authors have noted wage differences and differences in political attitudes and union behavior but have not made specific statements about skills and labor market segmentation—for example, Monica P. Ramos, *Etapas de Acumulación y Alianzas de Clases en la Argentina (1930-1970)* (Buenos Aires: Siglo XXI, 1973), in the case of Argentina—while Elsa Cimillo et al., *Acumulación y Centralización del Capital en la Industria Argentina* (Buenos Aires: Tiempos Contemporáneos, 1973), pp. 145-146, argue that labor markets are segmented. Richard U. Miller, "The Relevance of Surplus Labor Theory to the Urban Labor Markets of Latin America," *International Institute for Labor Studies Bulletin* (1971): 227, argues that firms in the modern sector recruit from a narrow section of the labor market because of the qualifications they require, the use of internal training, and the lack of knowledge of job opportunities among the mass of workers. Adriana Marshall, "Mercado de Trabajo y Crecimiento de los Salarios en la Argentina," *Desarrollo Económico* 15, no. 59 (1975): 392, on the other hand, explains wage differences by references to union power and ability of certain types of firms to grant rises.

6. Rodrigues, *Industrialização e Atitudes Operárias*, p. 45.

7. Ibid., pp. 101-102.

8. Rodrigues is, in fact, ambiguous to the point of contradiction. At two points, ibid., pp. 38, 84, he argues that he can demonstrate only that workers in the motor vehicle industry will not adopt a revolutionary or socialist perspective, but he proceeds to argue much more than this. For example, he argues that the firm's policy of small, frequent rises in wages could explain the absence of strikes in the factory.

9. Maria H. T. de Almeida, "O Sindicato no Brasil: Novos Problemas, Velhas Estruturas," *Debate e Crítica*, no. 6 (1975); "A Autonomia Sindical," *Movimento*, July 18, 1977; "Desenvolvimento Capitalista e Ação Sindical" (unpublished paper, 1977). The third paper was published in *Revista Mexicana de Sociología* 55, no. 2 (1978).

10. Maria da Conceição Tavares, "Relações entre Distribuição de Renda, Acumulação e Padrão de Desenvolvimento" (unpublished paper, 1973); Anibal Pinto, "La Concentración del Progreso Tecnico y de sus Frutos en el Desarrollo Latinoamericano," *Trimestre Económico*, no. 125 (1965).

11. Almeida, "Desenvolvimento Capitalista," p. 19.

12. Ibid., p. 23.

13. Ibid., p. 25.

14. These concepts come from Peter Doeringer and Michael J. Piore, *Internal Labor Markets and Manpower Analysis* (Lexington, Mass.: D. C. Heath, Lexington Books, 1971).

15. Almeida, "Desenvolvimento Capitalista," pp. 22-23.

16. Richard U. Miller, Mahmood Zaidi, and John Lund, "Modern Sector Internal Labor Market Structure and Urban Occupational Mobility: The Case of the Automobile Industry of Mexico" (paper for the Fourth World Congress of the International Industrial Relations Association, Geneva, September 1976), p. 17.

17. For the distinction between closed and open internal labor markets, see Doeringer and Piore, *Internal Labor Markets*, pp. 33–34. The authors define an internal labor market as "an administrative unit . . . within which the pricing and allocation of labor is governed by a set of administrative rules and procedures" (pp. 1–2). The implications of this definition are often ignored when the term is applied to Latin America. The authors tend to reduce the possible forms of internal labor market to two: where there is entry at the bottom of the job hierarchy and filling of all higher posts by promotion within the firm, and where jobs are filled from the outside according to some nonmarket allocation criterion (for example, union card). The existence of any barriers to the hiring or firing of workers in an enterprise is then often taken as an indication of the first type of internal labor market whereby workers are protected from external market pressures once admitted to a firm. The main problem for workers is to gain admittance initially, and once this is obtained the workers gain stability, good working conditions, good wages, and promotion.

18. Almeida, "A Autonomia Sindical," p. 18.

19. This is general conclusion of Almeida's 1975 article, but it is modified significantly in the 1977 papers. Ramos, *Etapas de Acumulación y Alianzas de Clases*, on the other hand, sees motor vehicle workers in Argentina as only a potential labor aristocracy.

20. For a similar linking of the most developed sector of the working class to the notion of privileged group, see Henry A. Landsberger, "The Labor Elite: Is It Revolutionary?" in Seymour M. Lipset and Aldo Solari, eds., *Elites in Latin America* (New York: Oxford University Press, 1967), p. 209.

21. Attention will be concentrated on workers in the assembly sector of the motor vehicle industry in greater São Paulo; however, many of the conclusions can be extended to workers in other major metalworking firms who also took part in the stoppages in 1978 and 1979.

22. The source material for this section was collected during fieldwork in 1974–1975.

23. This skill distribution is common to the motor vehicle industry in general. It is noted by Rodrigues, *Industrialização e Atitudes Operárias*, pp. xviii–xix, for example. For the United States, Widdick gives the following skill distribution for blue-collar workers in General Motors in 1974: 21 percent skilled, 71 percent semiskilled, 4 percent unskilled laborers, and 4 percent service workers. B. J. Widdick, "Work in Auto Plants, Then and Now," in Widdick, ed., *Auto Work and Its Discontents* (Baltimore: John Hopkins University Press, 1976), p. 8. A survey of one parts firm in greater São Paulo gave figures of 18 percent unskilled, 64 percent semiskilled, and 21 percent skilled, *Veja*, March 8, 1978.

24. Cimillo *et al.*, *Acumulación y Centralización del Capital*, pp. 145–146.

25. Huw Beynon, *Working for Ford* (Harmondsworth: Penguin, 1973), p. 118; H. A. Turner, Garfield Clack, and Geoffrey Roberts, *Labour Relations in the Motor Industry* (London: George Allen and Unwin, 1967), p. 89.

26. See Doeringer and Piore, *Internal Labor Markets*, p. 15.

27. John R. Erikkson, "Wage Structures in Economic Development in Selected Latin American Countries: A Comparative Analysis" (Ph.D. diss., University of California, Berkeley, 1966), p. 141.

28. For a further discussion of this question, see John Humphrey, "The Development of Industry and the Bases for Trade Unionism: A Case Study of Car Workers in São Paulo, Brazil" (D.Phil. diss., University of Sussex, 1977), chap. 6.

29. Marcos Arruda, Herbert de Souza, and Carlos Affonso, *Multinationals and Brazil: The Impact of Multinational Corporations in Contemporary Brazil* (Toronto: Brazilian Studies, Latin American Research Unit, n.d.).

30. The employment figures for the two firms are taken from *Quem é Quem na Economia Brasileira* for 1974.

31. I am grateful to Werner Wurtele of the Latin American Institute at the Free University in Berlin for making this information available to me.

32. It is not easy to measure dismissal incidence by length of employment within job categories. It can be said that in AF1 and AF2 workers with shorter periods of employment in the firm are more likely to be dismissed than long-term workers, but even those with relatively long service were not immune from dismissal. Seniority did not carry with it any rights in either factory.

33. Nun's analysis for workers dismissed from two motor vehicle firms in Argentina in the late 1960s shows that over half of the workers dismissed had more than three years of service. After a period of over eighteen months, one-third of those dismissed were self-employed, 12 percent were in service industries, and 10 percent were unemployed. Over half of the remainder, who found industrial employment, went to work in firms employing fewer than twenty-five people, and at the time of the survey, 39 percent still worked in such firms. José Nun, "Despidos en la Industrial Automotriz Argentina: Estudio de un Caso de Superpoblación Flotante," *Revista Mexicana de Sociología* 55, no. 1 (1978).

34. This report was prepared by part of junior management in one of the two plants studied after interviews with workers in the forklift section had been undertaken as part of the background preparation for health and safety courses.

35. Kenneth S. Mericle, "The Brazilian Motor Vehicle Industry: Its Role in Brazilian Development and Its Impact on United States Employment (unpublished manuscript, 1975), p. 96.

36. Speedup is found not only on the assembly lines. In AF1 workers were asked if they had experienced any increase in work load since entering the plant. The numbers answering yes were machine shop laborers, 20 percent;

machinists, 33 percent; press operators, 37 percent; assembly line laborers, 40 percent; and assemblers, 50 percent.

37. Henry Ford, *Today and Tomorrow* (London: Heinemann, 1926), p. 43.

38. Harry Braverman, *Labor and Monopoly Capital* (New York: Monthly Review, 1975), pp. 146–150.

39. William H. MacPherson, *Labor Relations in the Automobile Industry* (Washington, D.C.: Brookings, 1940), p. 3.

40. Humphrey, "Development of Industry," pp. 102–104.

41. Edmar L. Bacha, "Hierarquia e Remuneração Gerencial," in Ricardo Tolipan and A. C. Tinelli, eds., *A Controvérsia sôbre a Distribuição da Renda e Desenvolvimento* (Rio de Janeiro: Zaher, 1975), p. 140.

42. Fringe benefits were not noticeably better in AF1 and AF2 than in two motor vehicle parts firms also surveyed in 1974–1975. The cost at which such benefits were paid by the company were a source of friction between workers and management.

43. See Humphrey, "Development of Industry," p. 58, for a fuller analysis of this issue.

44. Ibid., chap. 4.

45. For an analysis of the wages policy and the manipulation of the inflation index, see Departmento Intersindical de Estatística e Estúdios Sócio Econômicos, *Dez Anos da Política Salárial* (São Paulo: DIEESE, 1975).

46. Almeida, "O Sindicato," pp. 65–66.

47. Manoel Filho, whose death under torture at the DOI/CODI headquarters in the Rua Tutoia in São Paulo led to the dismissal of the commander of the Second Army, was a metalworker. *Latin America*, January 30, 1976. Less horrific are the routine intimidations: "They [bus operators in São Paulo] are so dissatisfied that they have not yet given wage rises to the majority of their 25,000 drivers and conductors. Ten of these drivers, who work for Viação Intercontinental, all failed to turn up for work on one day last week. . . . By the end of the morning these drivers were taken to the *Delegacia de Ordem Política e Social* [a mixture of detective and political police] to help with inquiries, according to an official of the transport department." *Jornal da Tarde*, June 3, 1974.

48. *Jornal do Brasil*, April 13, 1976.

49. This is not a theme limited to Brazil. Resistance to unionization in parts of the United States, particularly the South, takes the same form.

50. For a firm-by-firm account of the stoppages, see the newspaper of the metalworking union in the area, *Tribuna Metalúrgica*, for June 1978.

51. *Veja*, September 20, 1978.

52. A good analysis of the political transformation can be found in Fernando Henrique Cardoso, "Os Impasses do Regime Autoritário: o Caso Brasileiro," *Estudos CEBRAP*, no. 26 (1980).

53. A *pelego* is a union official closely linked to the Ministry of Labor. The degree of accommodation of such officials to the state is notorious.

54. In the April negotiations thirty-four unions and the Metalworkers Federation take part. Prior to the 1979 negotiations, they had agreed on a common platform.

55. See *Latin American Political Report*, March 30, 1979, and *Financial Times*, March 29, 1979.

56. *Isto E*, May 16, 1979.

57. There are many accounts of the Volkswagen scheme, its implementation, and the reactions of workers to it. See, for example, *Movimento*, September 15, 1980, and *Isto E*, November 26, 1980.

58. Many Brazilian newspapers carried extensive reports of this strike. In English there is a short but incisive evaluation of it in *Latin American Weekly Report*, July 24, 1981.

59. Luís Inácio da Silva, reported in *Jornal do Brasil*, September 4, 1977.

60. Support by the Catholic church of the Workers party has aided its expansion in rural areas.

61. Divisions in the labor movement over the Workers party do not fall along lines of dynamic versus traditional industries or large versus small firms. Support for the party comes from all sectors, as does opposition.

62. Between January and July 1981 employment in the assembly sector fell by 14,500 due to tough anti-inflation policy. *O Estado de São Paulo*, July 18, 1981.

63. A more substantial redistribution of income could have a more significant effect. Automobile ownership is still concentrated in the higher income strata, and new sales must be even more concentrated.

64. *Economist*, February 3, 1979.

65. See Elizabeth Jelin, "Conflictos Laborales en la Argentina, 1973–76," *Revista Mexicana de Sociología* 55, no. 2 (1978).

66. See Juan Carlos Torre, "Workers' Struggles and Consciousness," *Latin American Perspectives* 1, no. 3 (1974).

67. Maurício Roscoe, President of the Construction Employers of Belo Horizonte, reported in *Veja*, September 14, 1977.

68. See John Humphrey, "The State and Labor in Brazil: Accumulation of Capital and Class Struggle" (paper for CEDLA Conference on Industrialization and the State in Latin America, Amsterdam, November 1978), pp. 13–14.

69. No one type of union organization guarantees reliable long-term management control. Intimidation at work or through state repression can produce worker passivity, weak unions, and employer domination of bargaining. Corruption is another means of extending management control. For example, the 1978 Goodyear proxy report revealed a number of bribes of trade union officials in Latin America made in order to secure wage settlements and avoid strikes.

However, weak unions can also lose control of their membership, leaving management faced by rank-and-file resistance out of control of the union. Similarly differences exist over the relationship between union size and managerial control. Large unions may be more powerful, but smaller unions are less susceptible to external pressure and are more easily controlled by radical workers. For example, auto workers in Argentina were put into the small and weak mechanics union, SMATA, in the late 1950s, which emerged as a radical force in Córdoba in the late 1960s, outside of the control of any central union.

70. The unions will be forced to make some accommodation to the state and the employers at some point. They will be pressured by their own members to do so. They are not revolutionary organizations, although they can play important political roles at certain times. For a discussion of the unions' role in political mobilization, see I. M. Roldan, *Sindicatos y Protesta Social en la Argentina* (Amsterdam: CEDLA, 1978).

5 Reflections on Argentine Auto Workers and Their Unions

Judith Evans, Paul Heath Hoeffel, and Daniel James

Argentine auto workers have become synonymous over the last decade with a high level of both political and trade union consciousness. They have consistently challenged the economic and social policies of the various political and military forces that have assumed power in Argentina, and on the factory floor they have developed a high level of militancy defending their interests. In addition they have fostered the development of forms of rank-and-file activism that have directly challenged the dominant style of Peronist trade unionism. Yet despite the widespread recognition of the auto workers' "rebellious reality," there has been surprisingly little empirical research into precisely what factors created this reality. Research has tended to focus on the peaks of militancy, which had the most evident political repercussions at the expense of more mundane issues, such as the nature of work conditions, shop floor organization, the specific nature of the auto workers' unions, and the dominant grievances expressed by the workers. Thus the specific conditions surrounding auto workers as a social force struggling to determine the conditions of the reproduction of its labor power within an accumulation process have been neglected, and the political manifestations of this struggle have consequently tended to be analyzed in isolation from its social context. At worst this approach has conceived auto workers as uniquely militant, possessing some unspecified virtue that provides a peculiar receptivity to radical political ideologies. We attempt to provide an alternative to this approach by examining the general social context within which auto workers emerged as a social and political force.

The 1955–1973 Period

The expansion of the automobile industry and the consequent growth of the auto workers as a powerful force within the Argentine working

class dates essentially from the presidency of Arturo Frondizi
(1958–1962). Prior to this period vehicle production had been extremely
limited. The only foreign company that had set up production facilities
in Argentina was Kaiser, which had opened its Cordoba plant in 1955
after being forced out of the North American market. Some other foreign
companies, like Mercedes Benz and Fiat, had made limited investments,
but the industry as a whole remained embryonic with production growing from 108 vehicles in 1951 to 6,391 in 1955. Frondizi's develop-
mentalist policies provided a massive influx of foreign capital, and one
of the favored areas of investment was the automobile industry. The
industry's growth was dramatic; output more than quadrupled between
1959 and 1961. By the mid-1960s the industry had consolidated its
position and was dominated by eight large foreign producers: Mercedes,
Peugeot, General Motors, Chrysler, Ford, Citroen, and Fiat in Buenos
Aires and IKA-Renault and Fiat in Cordoba. In addition a large network
of other industries had grown up to service the terminal plants. It was
calculated that in 1966 the jobs of one in nineteen Argentines were
tied directly or indirectly to vehicle production.[1]

   The first stage in the industry's growth and consolidation lasted
roughly until 1965 or 1966 and was characterized by generally tranquil
labor relations. Tranquility seems to have reflected two basic factors.
First, it resulted from relatively high wages and relatively full employment. By the mid-1960s the automobile industry stood well at the
top of the industrial wage scale together with other members of the
dynamic sector, such as the chemical industry and certain sectors of
metallurgy.[2] The gap between wages in these dynamic industries and
those of the traditional sectors grew consistently in these years. Similarly
the employment situation in the industry was favorable. As the industry
expanded more or less consistently in the first half of the 1960s to
meet the large, unsatisfied demand for trucks and cars, the size of the
labor force grew substantially.[3] The extent to which this expansion in
production and the labor force represented stability in employment is,
of course, problematic. Some firms, including Fiat, were already making
large-scale periodic firings in the early 1960s.[4] Nevertheless given the
favorable market situation and the absence of articulated labor protest
over layoffs (which emerged as a major issue in the changed market
situation after 1966), it would seem safe to assume that relative employment stability was characteristic of this period.

   The second factor affecting the relative tranquility of labor relations
was the industry's early pattern of unionization. From its inception,

jurisdiction over the industry had been a matter of contention between the Metalworkers' Union (Union Obrera Metalurgical—UOM) and the Motor Mechanics' Union (Sindicato de Mecanicos y Afines del Transporte Automotor—SMATA). With the industry's great expansion after 1959, the issue was decided decisively in SMATA's favor by the Ministry of Labor.[5] This decision coincided with the wishes and needs of the large companies. While the UOM dominated the entire metalworking sector and was the most powerful Argentine union, SMATA was a weak union that had emerged in 1946. Composed largely of garage workers, SMATA was isolated and had little national influence. It was also apolitical in the sense that it was not involved in the power politicking among Peronist unions (led by the UOM), governments, and the military. Thus the likelihood of pure business unionism in the auto industry was far greater with SMATA than with UOM. Indeed SMATA's failure to participate in either the reestablishment of the CGT in 1963 or the factory occupations of the 1964 *Plan de Lucha* seemed to demonstrate precisely this point.[6]

Two other government decisions also affected the industry's pattern of unionization and the relative tranquility of labor relations. In the early 1960s the Ministry of Labor authorized the creation of plant unions at the Fiat factories and the introduction of company agreements in the industry as a whole. These twin developments represented a break with the prevailing labor structure, which dated from the Peronist era. This structure was based on unions *per rama de industria*—one union with bargaining rights for the whole of an industrial activity. It further entailed industry-wide contracts negotiated at a national level and applicable to all firms within that industry.[7] With these two decisions the Ministry of Labor thus permitted the fragmentation of bargaining and hindered development of a unified workers' response on wages and conditions.

By 1966–1967 the tranquil period was coming to an end. The period of seemingly limitless expansion of the auto market was reaching its limits. Car ownership had increased rapidly, lowering the ratio of cars to people from one in twenty-four in 1959 to one in twelve in 1966.[8] At the same time the fragmentation of the Argentine industry (excessive firms and models) heightened the unit cost of Argentine-produced vehicles and thereby limited the extension of the market to new sectors of the population. The recession induced by the economic plan of the new military government further tightened market conditions and led the companies to rationalize their operations. Mass firings and suspensions of work now became a dominant feature of the industry. In addition the military government's new wage control policy undercut the relatively high wages of the auto workers. While their wages remained above average, the auto workers lost more heavily in comparison with lower paid workers.[9] The effect of these changes was to erode the basic conditions underlying the docility of the labor force in the pre-1965–1966 period, and the typical grievances associated with the automotive labor process came more to the fore, exacerbated now by company speedup and rationalization in response to sharpened competition.

Concomitant with the erosion of favorable economic conditions within the industry was the consolidation of the auto workers as a trade union force of considerable potential. By the mid-late 1960s SMATA had achieved the formal organization of a respectable portion of the work force. Membership figures for 1973 in the main plants (excluding Fiat) show 19,603 union members, or 56 percent of the work force. Among production workers alone, the rate of unionization was considerably higher. At both the Ford and Citroen plants, for example, where white-collar workers were not unionized at all, 73 percent of Ford production workers and 81 percent of Citroen production workers were unionized.[10]

The auto workers' organizational consolidation in the late 1960s reflected the logic of the industrial relations system, which guaranteed a recognized union in an industry sole bargaining rights for that industry. The Fiat plant unions represented the only exception to this pattern in the industry. Consequently in all other plants, SMATA, once it had gained recognition, was for all practical purposes the only feasible bargaining agent for the workers. Recognition meant that SMATA received not only the membership dues from its affiliates but also the worker and employer contributions for its social welfare fund. The sums of money involved were large with assets approximating $3.8 million in 1974.[11] This enabled the union to offer its membership a wide variety of social and medical services.[12]

It also may be suggested plausibly that as the tranquil period came to an end, so too did workers' dreams of individually achieved mobility and status, which had been fostered by the initial boom conditions, SMATA's initial weakness as a union, and the often overtly paternalistic ideology of automobile management.[13] Thus workers' perception of their situation was increasingly directed toward the need for a collective organizational solution to the increasing problem they faced in the plants from the mid-1960s.[14] In this context, it was not coincidental that at this time there began a movement among Fiat workers for the right to affiliate with SMATA and abandon their plant unions.

The concrete manifestation of these factors was the high level of conflict between 1965 and 1972, in both Cordoba and Buenos Aires. Examination of these conflicts suggests several conclusions. First, it is clear that while the conflicts involving the IKA-Renault and Fiat Cordoba workers displayed the most radical method, such as plant occupations, and had the greatest political impact, the Cordoba workers were not isolated. Workers in the Buenos Aires plants also took part in a considerable number of struggles. Second, an increasing number of these disputes were led, especially after 1968, by internal commissions of shop floor delegates. The majority of these delegates were hostile to both the military government and their own union leaders.

Under the military government of General Ongania, the traditional union leaderships in Argentina found themselves in a very difficult position. By postponing indefinitely the operation of pluralistic party politics, as well as by imposing tight government limits on wage increases and suspending normal collective bargaining, Ongania undermined the two basic sources of trade union bargaining power in Argentina. At the same time the government's economic policy showed a radical shift in the accumulation process based on the redistribution of income away from the working class through a reduction of real wages and an increase in labor productivity.[15] This policy created a dilemma for the union leaderships. Should they resist the new policies, they faced a military government prepared to intervene and remove them from their positions. On the other hand, their credibility was constantly eroded as their members experienced the effects of government policy.

The first sign of the internal crisis this situation provoked in the traditional, mainly Peronist union leadership was the split of the CGT into two bodies at the March 1968 conference. The CGT de los Argentinos (CGTA) emerged representing that section of the leadership advocating a policy of outright opposition to the military regime.[16] This body provided a focus for the growing rank-and-file discontent with government policy and union leadership inactivity in 1968–1969. Automobile workers were in the vanguard of this reawakening of the labor movement with mobilizations of IKA-Renault workers in Cordoba and conflicts over rationalization and layoffs in most of the Buenos Aires plants. Most of the plant committees who led these conflicts supported the CGT de los Argentinos. By contrast SMATA's national leadership favored the more conservative CGT Azopardo, although it officially expressed its neutrality in the dispute. The conflict within the CGT also echoed directly within SMATA as activists from the main Buenos Aires plants organized a rival opposition grouping, Movimiento de Renovacion y Encuentro de SMATA, in September 1968. Delegates from Mercedes, General Motors, Chrysler, Ford, Fiat (Buenos Aires), and Citroen plants, as well as the main components companies, overwhelmingly voted in favor of SMATA's affiliation to the CGTA.[17]

Despite the collapse of the CGTA—as a result of repression, internal Peronist pressures, and its own internal incoherence, the auto workers continued to search for ways to articulate their grievances and show discontent with the union leadership. They increasingly supported radical, often non-Peronist, alternatives, primarily in Cordoba but also in Buenos Aires plants. Left-wing groupings of militants, such as the Tendencia Activista Mecanica (TAM), were a strong influence in the Citroen, Peugeot, and Chrysler plants by 1968 and at General Motors after 1970. Even the more traditionally backward plants, such as Ford and Mercedes, were backing the main opposition grouping to the national SMATA leadership by 1970.

In order to assess the nature and limits of the growing rank-and-file militancy of the auto workers, it is necessary to examine the context that shaped its emergence and development. First, the specific nature of SMATA's leadership needs to be considered. SMATA had a reputation among militants as a soft bureaucracy with relatively limited control over its membership compared to the UOM. In part this reputation reflected the leadership style of the group that won the union elections of 1968 on a platform of increasing internal democracy. The new secretary-general, Dirk Kloosterman, was strongly influenced by the AFL-CIO–backed Instituto Americano para el Desarrollo del Sindicalismo Libre. Kloosterman advocated a style of union *caudillismo* with its attendant features of power politicking and rigorous repression of internal dissidence. Kloosterman's ideal was an efficient, responsible business unionism purged of the intra-Peronist political maneuverings typical of other unions.

SMATA's reputation also reflected the actual situation in the auto plants. The SMATA leadership lacked the long-established internal apparatus of control that existed in the UOM, as well as the construction and textile unions. SMATA was a relative newcomer and did not consolidate its presence in the auto plants until the mid-1960s. Moreover its internal structure permitted a degree of autonomy—particularly for those plants outside Buenos Aires—that was in sharp contrast to other unions. For example, article 107 of SMATA's bylaws in its *Estatuto Social* provided the sections or locals with a measure of autonomy and internal democracy in running elections that was unthinkable in the UOM. With each contending group having a representative on the section's electoral committee, it was difficult for incumbents to steal elections through open fraud, increasing the chances of opposition groups' replacing discredited leaderships as occurred in Cordoba in 1972.

Thus SMATA's structure and leadership aided the articulation and organization of rank-and-file discontent. Kloosterman, for example, suffered constant defeats in plenary meetings of delegates in 1968, which would have been inconceivable for a leader like Vandor in the UOM. The SMATA national leadership certainly did take counter-measures, adopting antidemocratic procedures to maintain their positions. Perhaps most significant was their impugning of opposition electoral lists. In the 1970 and 1972 national SMATA elections, the membership was provided with only the official list for which to vote. Nevertheless at most of the main plants, absenteeism generally outran support for the official list, while in Cordoba write-ins exceeded it.[18] Similarly in 1968 the national leadership instituted a new electoral provision requiring 2,000 members' signatures before a list of candidates could be presented in an election. While these and other measures were sufficient to ensure permanence in power for the union leadership at the national level, its power in individual plants remained limited.

Another feature affecting the emergence of rank-and-file militancy in the auto plants was the collective bargaining system used in the industry. While plant bargaining fragmented the unity of the auto workers, it also had a more positive implication. The determination of conditions and wages at the plant level provided a concrete focus for plant activity. This focus was missing in factories in the metalworking industry, for example, where these issues were determined at the national level by national negotiators and then handed down to the localities. By contrast the auto workers could hope to influence and even to determine issues of crucial importance to their working lives; their own activity, their own choice of shop floor representatives, could have *some* impact on their wages and conditions. The role of the national leadership in these negotiations could be limited. A militant negotiating committee could hold out successfully for wages and conditions beyond what the national union leadership would have accepted.[19]

Although these factors undoubtedly contributed to the emergence and development of rank-and-file activism in the auto industry, it is also necesary to consider countervailing tendencies. Rank-and-file organizing in the industry occurred in a context of state and employer repression and union leadership vigilance. A militant in the Chrysler plant in Buenos Aires, a member of TAM, explained the painstaking process that radical opposition groupings had to follow to organize effectively:

Two years ago, at the beginning of 1970, we won part of the internal commission and from then on we carried out a work of organization with constant assemblies. . . . We combined a legal organization with a parallel clandestine activity to organize activists, to have people ready to take over. . . . Clandestine organization was fundamental to our winning the factory leadership, with constant meetings of activists to take our policies to the mass of workers. When the vote for the wage committees arrived we had a chance to see what force we had; we won and formed the majority. . . . Once we got on the wage committee, the bureaucratic part of the union began to act—trying to undermine our standing in every way.[20]

Thus militant organization in the industry was characterized by difficulties and vulnerable to a variety of pressures despite the relative weakness of the internal apparatus of control. Indeed at the same Chrysler plant, a strike in May 1971—provoked by the management before the militants of TAM could consolidate their factory work—was defeated, with many militants victimized.

A final crucial factor must be examined in order to understand the context conditioning the possibilities of rank-and-file organization in the auto industry at this time: the impact of the specific production cycle in autos on the development of rank-and-file activism. After 1966 the vehicle market became prone to overproduction, and this tendency manifested itself in drastic short-term fluctuations. For example, vehicle production in January 1966 represented a 19.8 percent decline from the January 1965 level. A year later in January 1967 production had increased by 48.7 percent, only to decline again by 31.5 percent in January 1968 and climb again by 76.2 percent in January 1969.[21]

These production fluctuations carried with them considerable employment instability. At General Motors' Buenos Aires plant, compared to 1964, employment increased 6 percent in 1965, fell by 4 percent in 1966, regained 1964 levels in 1967, and then declined 2 percent in 1968. Employment at Fiat's Buenos Aires plant swung more wildly, increasing in 1966 to a measure of 214 (1964 = 100) before falling to

167 in 1968.[22] In addition these annual comparisons do not take into account labor turnover within each period, which, according to José Nun, averaged 15 to 20 percent of the personnel in these plants in each of the years between 1960 and 1968.[23]

Fluctuations in employment had implications for the development of militant union organizations in the auto plants. According to Nun only a small proportion of the workers dismissed from the four Buenos Aires plants succeeded in regaining employment in the dynamic sector of the economy, and even fewer returned to the auto industry or the plants where they had worked previously. The majority entered the more traditional sectors, the tertiary sector, or set up businesses on their own. Nun concludes that periodic layoffs in the auto industry thus implied a process of "proletarian fragmentation" that "not only weakens the objective possibilities workers have to accumulate more or less common experiences vis-à-vis the bosses but also seriously erodes their capacity for organization."[24]

Our own investigations suggest a modification of this general picture, at least in relation to rank-and-file organization in the auto industry. The short-term cycle in the industry seems to have had more ambiguous implications in practice than Nun's general argument suggests. During the cycle's upturn, employers hired workers rather indiscriminately in order to expand production rapidly. Militants seem to have used these occasions to return to the industry. At Chrysler, for example, "there are people who have been dismissed three times and have been taken on again each time, and there are people who have worked their way through every shop in the plant."[25] This passing in and out of several shops and/or plants by militants—particularly those involved with radical political groupings who ascribed a strategic significance to organizing in the industry—was common in the industry.[26] It meant that militant experience built up in one factory or one shop could be transmitted and widened. Moreover the influx of new workers, following an upturn, promised to have a regenerative effect. For example, after the defeated strike in Citroen in 1965, morale became low and the plant organization moribund. The upturn of late 1966 and the consequent influx of several hundred new workers yielded militants who won the internal elections and led the successful strike of May 1967.[27]

There was another side to this coin; with the downturn of the cycle, the rank-and-file organization was endangered. Large-scale firings threatened to remove key activists from the plant, as well as undermine general plant morale and organization. Rank-and-file organization in the industry was thus often precarious. Nevertheless many of the most active militants were not completely lost to the industry but reentered the plants during the following upturn. And on the more general level the short-term nature of the cycle meant that the capacity of the auto workers to organize and accumulate experience was not fundamentally undermined. Short-term layoffs were sufficient to create deep grievances among the auto workers but did not produce the devastating effects that long-term structural unemployment did. In the textile industry and the more traditional sectors of metalworking, long-term unemployment profoundly debilitated rank-and-file organization and militancy. By contrast layoffs in the auto industry were only temporary. They permitted the auto companies to undermine militant organization but not to destroy its long-term capacity to recover.

The Cordoba Auto Workers, 1955–1973

The Cordoba auto workers have a somewhat distinctive history that merits special examination.[28] The motor vehicle industry began in Cordoba in 1955. At that time, Kaiser established Industrias Kaiser de Argentina (IKA), a joint venture with Renault and American Motors. (In 1967 Renault acquired the majority holding in IKA.) The other major auto producer in the area was Fiat, which began operations in 1954 with the acquisition of the tractor facility of the state-owned Industrias Aerotecnicas y Mecanicas del Estado (IAME). Fiat later established two additional plants in Cordoba in 1957 and 1961.

The auto companies chose Cordoba for several reasons. In part their choice reflected government policy to decentralize the industrial concentration in grand Buenos Aires by providing tax exemptions and subsidies on plant construction. In addition the companies found the city's low rate of unionization and relative isolation from the central Peronist union apparatus in Buenos Aires attractive. More traditional employer concerns, including the availability and cost of labor, were not primary factors and were offset by the existence of an energy source and the city's infrastructiral facilities.[29]

The initial phase of the industry in Cordoba followed the contours of Buenos Aires auto development. Harmonious labor relations accompanied a process of industrial consolidation. By 1965 Fiat employed some 5,665 workers in its three Cordoba plants, and IKA had over 7,000 in its Santa Isabel and Perdriel plants. The difference in unionization between the two companies was considerable; the three Fiat plants had weak plant unions, while by 1966 SMATA had organized a large majority of the IKA workers.

The end of the initial period of relative industrial peace in Cordoba, as in Buenos Aires, coincided with growing market difficulties for the companies. In 1965 both Fiat and IKA initiated production suspensions and layoffs, which led to a strike and occupation at the Fiat plants in July. The Fiat plants remained quiescent for the following four years, but the attempts of IKA management to resolve its problems through layoffs and rationalizations provided a constant focus for militant organization and activity among its work force in the years 1965 to the Cordobazo and beyond.[30] IKA's problems were essentially the same as those of the Buenos Aires companies, although IKA complained that specific factors worsened its situation. These factors included higher transport and energy costs, as well as more modest tax exemptions than operating in Buenos Aires. In addition IKA complained of the existence of *sabado ingles*, a tradition in Cordoba in which workers were paid for a full day on Saturday although they worked only half the day.

Suspensions of production were common at IKA after 1965. In August 1966 SMATA complained to the governor of Cordoba of two days' suspension in May, four in June, five in July, and eight in August.[31] In the first half of 1968 suspensions cost IKA workers twenty-three days of work. In June the company's plan to suspend production for another seven days provoked a strike.[32] Periodic large-scale firings were also common, and by 1968 the company was talking of the need to prune its work force by 500. The choice, according to the company, was one of "rationalizing or dying."[33] Rationalizing implied intensified production speeds and an attack on concessions, such as *sabado inglés*, which provoked a strike in November 1968.

The leadership of SMATA in Cordoba belonged to the Vandorist wing of the Peronist union movement. Its secretary-general, Elpidio Torres, was an astute exponent of typical Vandorist trade union tactics. Prone to negotiate and compromise where possible but also capable of mobilizing his membership, Torres walked the fine line between accommodating pragmatism and militant confrontation. At the same time that the union led its members in the violent strike of June 1968, the company's personnel manager could talk of the "very cordial" relations between company and union.[34] In fact, the space available for this sort of traditional union maneuvering was increasingly restricted, both by the military government's policy and by the company's determination to rationalize production.

Although Torres was reelected in March 1968 against a candidate backed by the national leadership, he was subject to growing pressure from his rank and file. More radical groups, such as the CGTA and non-Peronist leftists, had growing support inside IKA-Renault. In October 1968 Torres managed to maintain control over the Internal Commission by sixty-five votes to fifty, but he had to adopt a far more militant stance in order to maintain his hold on a membership angered by government and employer policy. In fact with his own margin for negotiation virtually nonexistent, Torres had little option but to put himself at the head of the IKA-Renault workers' struggle.

In May 1969 the national government abolished *sabado ingles*. On May 14 at a mass meeting, 5,000 SMATA members decided to initiate a forty-eight-hour protest strike. As they left the meeting, they were attacked by the police. Working-class reaction throughout the city was immediate, and the forty-eight-hour stoppage was turned by the local CGT into a city-wide strike that focused on a wide spectrum of grievances felt by different sections of the working class. The main demands were for an end to the government's wage freeze, the restoration of *sabado ingles*, and modification of rationalization plans in the auto industry. The Cordoba CGT called another forty-eight-hour strike for May 29 and 30. It was this strike that became known as the Cordobazo as workers and other sectors of the population took over 150 blocks of the center of the city and battled first the police and then the army.

While analysis of the specific factors that came together to create the explosive conjuncture known as the Cordobazo is crucial, it is also necessary to consider the underlying reasons for the Cordobazo. For the auto workers, their participation and indeed their role as major protagonist was a culmination of several years of mobilizations over the concrete problems they faced in the plants. Although the Cordobazo was unprecedented in the extent of its mobilization, in its impact on the working class as a whole, and in the militancy of its tactics, the fundamental issues were those that had generated consistent struggles during the previous years.

The Cordobazo inaugurated a period of working-class militancy nationally and particularly in Cordoba. Between 1969 and 1971 there was a wave of general strikes and work stoppages in Cordoba in opposition to both government policy and the national leadership of various unions. Inside SMATA the growing strength of radical opposition groups in

Cordoba challenged Torres's position. By 1970 he had lost control of the section's Body of Delegates. Torres then seems to have attempted to weaken his opposition by supporting the company's attempt to transfer four newly elected opposition delegates from the Perdriel IKA plant to another plant. In response the Perdriel workers occupied their plant and forced the abandonment of the attempted transfer.[35] A month later Torres swung in the opposite direction and launched the occupation of most of the Cordoba plants in an attempt to regain his prestige with the increasingly radical rank and file and to respond to the pressures of the hostile delegates. In the end these occupations were not successful and exposed many militants to company reprisal. Over 700 workers, including the most active militants, were dismissed. The failure of these occupations was a crucial blow to Torres's prestige, and he soon retired, leaving his successor with an impossible task of restoring the prestige of the leadership group. In 1971 delegates from various left-wing groups of both radical Peronist and Marxist orientations organized the Movimiento de Recuperacion Sindical and won the March 1972 union elections. The new SMATA secretary-general in Cordoba was Rene Salamanca, a non-Peronist with Maoist sympathies.[36]

Too frequently it is assumed that there was a sharp contrast between the radically militant auto workers of Cordoba and their quiescent Buenos Aires counterparts. This was not the case. The auto workers of both cities confronted the same problems—rationalization, layoffs, and wage control—which generated intense struggles in both locations. Similarly it is not the case that Cordoba auto workers were intrinsically more susceptible to radical ideologies. Radical activists, both Peronist and non-Peronist, were active in Buenos Aires and successfully challenged the union leadership's control of several plants there. Nevertheless there were significant differences between the two groups of auto workers involving methods of struggle and the impact of these struggles. Factory occupations and work stoppages were far more frequent in Cordoba than in Buenos Aires. And occupations and work stoppages in Cordoba frequently had major significance, transforming a limited union struggle into a political confrontation at the provincial and national levels.

Several factors help explain these differences, including SMATA's internal structure, which provided the Cordoba section with a significant degree of financial and operational independence from the national union leadership. While in most Argentine unions dues flowed directly to the central leadership which controlled their distribution, a very different practice prevailed in SMATA. Article 78 of SMATA's Estatuto Social granted that 90 percent of basic union dues went to the section from whose members they had been collected; only the remaining 10 percent went to the national leadership. There was, however, an important restriction: all dues collected within the federal capital or a radius of 60 kilometers from the capital were to go directly to the Consejo Directivo Nacional (CDN). Thus the Cordoba section but not the Buenos Aires plants enjoyed relative financial independence, which gave it the capacity to resist financial pressures used in most other Argentine unions to control dissident sections. For example, the social services of SMATA Cordoba were immune from national leadership attack by the withdrawal of central funds. Interestingly the Cordoba Light and Power workers enjoyed the same financial immunity from the Luz y Fuerza national control and were, along with SMATA Cordoba, the other major union to develop an independent progressive leadership.

In addition SMATA's statutes provide the sections with authority to initiate independent actions that again contrasted with the centralized practice of most other unions. Article 128(b) gave the leadership of the sections the authority to determine measures of direct action for their sections as a whole, as well as in particular plants within their sections. Here again, however, a crucial caveat was inserted that distinguished Cordoba and Buenos Aires: all actions, such as strikes and slowdowns, within plants in greater Buenos Aires and the federal capital were to be decreed by the CDN.

We are not suggesting that a more centralized formal union structure could have controlled or eliminated activity on its own. The ability and willingness of the national union leadership to use its formal power in fact depended on a number of other factors, including the militancy and political consciousness of the membership. Thus, in theory, the national leadership of SMATA had the authority to intervene in the Cordoba section at any time. Nevertheless it did not act to remove Salamanca for two years because the political cost was too high given the upsurge of the Cordoba workers' movement in those years. What we are suggesting, however, is that the issue of union structure was important. While SMATA's structure generally militated against the development of independent oppositional activity, several distinctive elements did facilitate the possibility of the growth of this activity in Cordoba.

Another important factor explaining the differences was the significance of the auto industry in the two cities. The vehicle industry in Cordoba had a far greater social weight within the wider context of the city and its society than its Buenos Aires counterpart. The Fiat and IKA-Renault plants were the basis of Cordoba's economy, and whatever happened in these plants had an immediate city-wide impact, which was not the case in Buenos Aires. Thus the actions of 7,000 IKA-Renault workers had a far greater potential social impact than the actions of 7,000 Ford workers. In addition the social space within which the Fiat and IKA-Renault workers acted was relatively integrated and compact. With many of these workers living close to the plants in communities dominated by auto workers, a close integration between the plants and the wider working-class community developed. This integration inevitably contributed to the wider impact of factory struggle and also meant that collective organization and confidence built up at the point of production was not broken down when the worker entered the anomic urban world beyond the factory. It implied too a strong community legitimation for actions within the plants. The contrast with Buenos Aires is clear. Not only were the auto plants situated on the periphery of greater Buenos Aires at widely differing points, but the workers traveled far to work from numerous points in the working-class suburbs. Inevitably grievances and collective consciousness formed at the point of production were diluted within the huge urban conglomeration of the metropolis.[37]

Cordoba auto workers were clearly aware of their crucial position in the city. This is illustrated in Elpidio Torres's warning to the company in 1968 after the June confrontation over layoffs: "Let nobody forget that here in Cordoba the auto workers have the numbers, the experience and the unity, and that if anyone is going to do something here, that anyone is us."[38] The Cordoba auto workers also recognized that paralyzing the city was often the most efficacious way to do something about their grievances. We found in conversations with auto militants a common perception that to be effective, a strike had to gain the attention of either the provincial or national authorities immediately.[39] No less common was the perception that the decision-making centers capable of resolving workers' problems were located well outside Cordoba and that the workers had to shout loudly and aggressively to make themselves heard.[40]

Militant action was often effective in Cordoba. The provincial government frequently intervened, for example, to get company plans for layoffs revoked, albeit temporarily, after the workers had taken militant action. Confirmed by experience, these tactics then had their own internal dynamic. As one author has written about the 1965 Fiat occupation, "The consciousness of being able to overturn and paralyze the fragile economic mechanism centered on monoproduction . . . had in the course of the following years a multiplying effect on the level of class consciousness of these sectors."[41] Immediate militant collective action was almost the normally expected response of the Cordoba auto workers. Legitimized by past experience, plant occupations and confrontations with authorities became an accepted part of working-class culture, particularly during the extraordinary wave of factory occupations and work stoppages in 1971 and 1972. Confidence in future actions was enhanced by the perception among auto workers that they were not isolated. They could expect support and solidarity from both the wider working-class community and other social sectors. As early as 1965 during the Fiat strike, individual unions had provided active support, and the local CGT had called for sympathy strikes. Moreover by the late 1960s, there was a tradition of student solidarity with plant occupations and clashes with the authorities.

The contrast with the situation in Buenos Aires is clearly revealed in the Chrysler strike in May 1971. Like the Cordoba auto workers, the Chrysler workers demonstrated a militant consciousness, electing a radical socialist plant leadership and enduring a fifteen-day strike. The Chrysler workers acted, however, in a different context and with different confidence in the feasibility of militant tactics. They rejected the idea of a plant occupation. As an activist explained:

We didn't discount the possibility [of an occupation] but we thought that in Fiat when they took the plant there was a specific internal situation and a specific Cordoba experience which made it possible. . . . Our experience of occupations is different. We had a sad experience here a year ago in GM. The factory was occupied . . . but the reality didn't fit and it failed. This shows you that you can't be mechanical with factory occupations. Here in Chrysler we didn't have the possibility of taking the plant, there wasn't the atmosphere to even start to prepare one . . . and there was an even stronger argument here in Chrysler; the last defeat we experienced six years ago was over a 3-day factory occupation; this experience was very influential.[42]

The same worker also observed that the Chrysler workers had considerable difficulty gaining support from other auto plants and other workers in the district. Thus although conflicts arose, the context and working-class experience in the Buenos Aires plants implied a different perception on the part of workers concerning the actions they might take.

SITRAM-SITRAC and *Clasismo*

Clasismo, as a distinct revolutionary current in the Argentine workers' movement, is associated with the radical unions established in the Cordoba Fiat plants. In the mid-1960s Fiat operated three plants in Cordoba, as well as its main terminal operation in greater Buenos Aires: Fiat Concord (established 1954; products: industrial motors, tractors, and auto engines; work force: production workers, 2,492, white-collar workers, 1,182); Fiat Materfer (established 1961; products: railroad rolling stock, diesel buses, intercity coaches, trolleys, electric underground stock; work force: production workers, 975, white-collar workers, 705); and Grandes Motores Diesel (established 1957; products: heavy diesel engines for industrial use and railroad use; work force: production workers, 408, white-collar workers, 303).[43]

In the late 1960s plant unions represented the workers of these three plants. In 1965 they represented the following percentages of workers: SITRAC (Sindicato de Trabajadores de Concord), 20 percent; SITRAM (Sindicato de Trabajadores de Materfer), 10 percent; and SGM (Sindicato de Grandes Motores), 50 percent.[44] The company pursued a consciously paternalistic policy and crushed any attempt at organizing an independent union, resorting to mass firings when necessary. After the strike and occupation of Concord and Grandes Motores in 1965, company appointees took control over SITRAC and SITRAM.

The Fiat workers, however, could not be isolated from the rising tide of militancy affecting Cordoba auto workers. In May 1970 both Concord and Materfer workers occupied their plants, demanding the removal of their union leaders and calling for new elections. The company, pressured by local and national governments anxious to avoid another major confrontation in an already tense situation, gave way, and in the subsequent elections new radical leaderships were elected in both plants. The new leaderships represented a wide spectrum of left tendencies from Peronismo de base to the Maoists of the Partido Comunista Revolucionaria, with the non-Peronist Marxist Left predominating.[45] From the election of this leadership to the forcible closing of the two unions by the army in October 1971, SITRAC and SITRAM engaged in a process of constant mobilization, including several plant occupations on issues of working conditions and wages. Outside the plants they became a major political protagonist of the military government, developing a revolutionary current of union groupings known as *clasistas*. The high points of these struggles included the Fiat workers' mass occupation of the Fiat plants in January 1971, their leadership in the second Cordobazo (or Viborazo) of March 1971,[46] and their organization of a National Meeting of Combative Unions, Clasista Groups and Revolutionary Workers in August 1971.[47]

Ideologically *clasismo* called for the overthrow of capitalism and the creation of a socialist society by the working class. The program of SITRAC-SITRAM of May 1971 proposed massive nationalization of the means of production and workers' control of industry. While distinguishing between the role of a trade union and a revolutionary party, SITRAC-SITRAM stressed the need for the unions to act in a highly class-conscious and combative fashion. As one leader put it, "The supporters of a clasista union orientation are perfectly aware of the natural incompatibility between their own class interests and those of the dominant classes."[48] In rejecting class harmony and in supporting working-class political organization independent of any bourgeois alliance, SITRAC-SITRAM stood in sharp contrast to the key tenets of Peronist ideology. As a result SITRAM-SITRAC opposed the Peronist Gran Acuerdo Nacional in 1971 and called for "neither coup nor election" but "Revolución."[49]

Clasismo also has another less specifically political connotation. It rejected the bureaucratic, semioligarchic model of trade unionism associated with the dominant Peronist union leadership. In its place it attempted to create a democratic model of rank-and-file trade unionism based on hostility to the employers, the mobilization of union members, and the development of a permanent interchange between the rank · and file and the leadership. This model of trade unionism and its combative defense of the membership's interests—rather than the leadership's ideology—created widespread support for SITRAC-SITRAM and other militant groups within the auto industry. Faced with concerted management and government attack and a traditional union leadership undergoing a crisis of credibility, auto workers supported plant activists who offered militant, democratic leadership. As the Chrysler militant quoted above stated, the auto workers supported "whoever defends them. . . . At Chrysler . . . it mattered little if we were *guerrillas* or communists, what was important was that we defended them, and so they defended us. . . . the rank and file don't respond to an ideology, they respond to honest leadership, nothing else."[50]

The development of this "honest" leadership at SITRAM-SITRAC had a profound impact. A worker at Fiat Materfer described it:

Those 15 months of union democracy left an enormous legacy for Fiat workers. . . . we showed what we could do to better our working conditions when we organize and the leaderships we elect authentically carry out the mandate of the rank and file. . . . We got wage increases, upgrading of categories, improvements in the canteen, in medical attention. We stopped arbitrary firings. But more important than all this was the total change in life in the plants. Delegates defended us from the foremen in all the problems which arose at work. We controlled production speed which had previously been terrible. We eliminated the oppressive climate which existed in the factory and we could claim our rights as human beings.[51]

Even more than the political program of SITRAC-SITRAM, these developments represented the heart of *clasismo* and led the government in October 1971 to dissolve the unions and imprison their leaders. The government hoped to suffocate any lingering impact of SITRAC-SITRAM, and in October 1972 Concord and Materfer were placed under the UOM's jurisdiction by government decree. In November a plebiscite held in Concord showed 1,399 workers in favor of joining SMATA against 177 for the UOM. Thugs from the UOM prevented a similar plebiscite taking place in Materfer.

Auto Workers from Peronist Government to Military Coup, 1973–1980

The end of military rule and the election of a popular Peronist government in 1973 initiated a new and increasingly conflictual stage of class relations in Argentina. With the *Pacto Social* (the formal agreement among employers, unions, and government) officially removing wage bargaining from the legitimate area of worker-employer negotiation, conflicts focused on issues such as working conditions and the reinstatement of dismissed workers.[52] In a favorable political and economic conjuncture, workers sought to resolve long-held grievances in these areas. Many of these struggles were led by internal commissions whose capacity to mobilize was aided by the generally flexible attitude adopted by the union leaderships and the new Ministry of Labor.

The favorable new conjuncture increased the combativeness of the auto workers. A typical conflict of the period occurred at General Motors in June 1973 over a company attempt to increase the speed of the production line. The workers refused to accept the new standards, and

GM fired the entire internal commission. With Ministry of Labor intervention and the maintenance of work force solidarity, the firings were rescinded and line speeds drastically modified.[53]

By the end of 1973, with the ascent of Peron to the presidency, relative tolerance for nonofficial working-class mobilization came to an end. Peron moved to reconcentrate control of the workers' movement within the formal hierarchical structures of the CGT and national union leaderships. The new Law of Professional Associations of November 1973 greatly increased the powers of these bodies to intervene in local sections, increased their financial powers, and extended their mandates from two to four years. The effect of Peron's attempt to restrict rank-and-file initiatives was apparent in the auto industry. In early 1974, for example, a plant occupation at Mercedes Benz led by neoclasistas was crushed as the Ministry of Labor declared the action illegal; thugs beat up the militants, and SMATA replaced the plant leadership with its own officials. Similar events occurred at Ford.

The chief concern of the SMATA leadership and the Ministry of Labor was to crush the power of SMATA Cordoba. Kloosterman's attempted intervention with officials from Buenos Aires misfired as auto workers mobilized to defend their elected leaders and expel the would-be intervenors. The issue became even more important for the national leadership with the drift of events in the Fiat plants. There, despite the former minister's decision to place them within the UOM's jurisdiction and the Peronist minister's indecision in regard to their fate, workers at the three Fiat plants affiliated in effect with SMATA. Assemblies of workers voted overwhelmingly in favor of joining SMATA, and their elected delegates joined the *Cuerpo de Delegados* of SMATA Cordoba, collecting dues from their members and handing the money over to SMATA. This affiliation meant that SMATA Cordoba represented over 13,000 auto workers in the two companies, making it by far the strongest single section within SMATA.

In July 1974 the Cordoba section sought a wage increase well above the government norm and backed its demand with a slowdown that severely cut production. IKA Renault issued suspension notices to over 2,000 workers. At this juncture the Ministry of Labor declared the SMATA Cordoba action illegal and warned the national leadership that the next step would be to withdraw legal recognition from the union at the national level. Using this threat, the national leadership pushed through the expulsion of the Cordoba section leaders and appointed their own intervenor. The union also obtained, with ministry approval, a wage increase from IKA Renault that was well above the norm. After two months of conflict, isolated from any national support, the majority of IKA Renault workers returned to work without the reinstatement of their deposed leaders. When Salamanca proposed to continue the strike to gain reinstatement of the expelled committee, he was defeated in a mass meeting.[54] Soon afterward warrants were issued for the arrest of the former leaders.

The crushing of the independent leadership in SMATA Cordoba and similar events in Luz y Fuerza Cordoba and the Buenos Aires Print-workers were key stages in the reassertion of centralized control over the union movement by the Peronist union hierarchy.[55] Activists who challenged government policy increasingly were subject to officially backed terrorism and intimidation. The control of the hierarchy was, however, based on unsound foundations. As the Argentine economy entered a profound crisis in mid-1974, the union leadership saw its prestige increasingly eroded by its intimate involvement with the Peronist government. It was forced to take up the growing mobilizations of its members against attempted government austerity plans. These mobilizations had considerable success in forcing modifications of the austerity plans, and the union leadership found itself the real power in the Peronist government without being able to offer any coherent policy that would resolve the economic crisis in its members' interests. In effect it got the worst of two worlds: weakening the government of which it was the centerpiece without reestablishing its credibility with its membership.

Developments in the auto industry reflected this general process. It soon became clear, for example, that the national leadership's ability to control the Cordoba section was more formal than real. Although intensive repression of militants temporarily cowed IKA Renault, in other companies the major internal commissions remained faithful to their old leaders. Spontaneous walkouts occurred when warrants were issued for the arrest of Salamanca and others. By early 1975 the intervenors increasingly were confined to the union office and kept away from the shop floor.[56] In Buenos Aires, too, the work force became restive as their salaries were hurt by inflation. Auto workers in the plants in San Justo, General Pacheco, and San Martin, as well as those in Cordoba, were among the first to abandon their work in response to the economic package introduced in July 1975 by Celestino Rodrigues. This action, later known as the Rodrigazo, snowballed into a spontaneous general strike paralyzing Argentine industry for a week. With the CGT obliged to take up its demands, the strike led the government to abandon the economic package and grant a large wage increase.

While the strike's successful outcome temporarily strengthened the union leadership, the deepening economic crisis weakened the leadership's control over the working class. Within SMATA the weakness of the national leadership was increasingly evident. By mid-1975 IKA Renault was ignoring the official Cordoba leadership and negotiating directly with the unofficial plant committees. In Fiat there was a similar situation, and in October 1975 the company closed its Materfer plant, saying that it would remain closed "until the conditions of civilized coexistence are secured." Management officials had been seized by union leaders and held hostage. The company added that in the previous months, "it has been impossible to reestablish order, authority, safety and production rhythms" and that go-slows had cut production to one-third of normal.[57] In Mercedes Benz there was also a militant strike led by a rank-and-file committee.[58] Another indication of the relative weakness of the national union leaderships was the formation of coordinating committees in various zones of Buenos Aires and Cordoba. These committees originally arose during the July 1975 general strike as informal assemblies of militants. They then reemerged toward the end of the year and grew in influence as the crisis deepened and the hold of the CGT on its membership began to disintegrate. Their function seems to have been to act as informal structures, linking workers and militants from different plants and unions to discuss working-class needs and strategies. Current information suggests that the auto workers played an important role in the coordinating committees to the north and west of Buenos Aires, which were the most active committees. In Cordoba the committee was centered on the industry and seems to have formed virtually a parallel organizational structure to the formal unions.[59]

The situation of the auto work force since the coup of 1976 can be ascertained only approximately. The military government's economic policy of monetary liberalism and its ruthless repression of labor activity have led to spiraling inflation and a severe cut in real wages. The auto industry is experiencing a long-postponed structural crisis and reorganization. Vehicle production in 1978 was nearly 110,000 units below the 1975 figures. The attempt to resolve the long-term structural problems of the industry has resulted in the merging of Fiat and Peugeot and of Volkswagen and Chrysler, as well as the shutting down of General Motors and Citroen.

The joint impact of government repression and terror, government economic policy, and the industry's structural crisis and reorganization on labor activity within the plants seems fairly clear, although precise information is not available. With unions intervened, strikes illegal, and activists persecuted, the level of activity has inevitably declined. Nevertheless resistance has persisted. In late 1976 reports of drastic cuts in production due to slowdowns and sabotage filtered into the press. These job actions seem to have occurred on a broad front. General Liendo, the minister of labor, went with troops to the General Motors Barracas plant and installed troops inside the plant to ensure that production speed picked up. It would seem clear that given the general situation, production slowdowns was the most viable tactic. Capacity to engage in these actions also seems to have depended on the particular plant. For instance, in 1978 Mercedes Benz workers were able to pressure management to concede cost-of-living-related increases. This success seems to have been possible at Mercedes because it produced for the truck and bus market, which remained buoyant compared to the car market. Thus the economic conditions were more favorable toward pressure for higher wages than in other plants. This success, however, must be placed within the general context of fierce repression, which limited how far even the Mercedes workers could pressure the management.[60]

Concluding Remarks

We have attempted to establish a historical context within which to place an analysis of the development of the auto workers as a social and political force within Argentine society. Within this general concern we have been particularly interested in examining the factors influencing the emergence of unionization among the auto work force, the nature of that unionization, and the political implications within the wider Argentine society. We have sought in particular to establish the importance of studying the activity and organization of rank-and-file auto workers both on a wider political level and on the more immediate shop floor level if any adequate analysis of the unionization of the automobile labor force is to be achieved.

We have also suggested some of the variables that have determined the nature and extent of the auto workers' union militancy and the limits of its effectiveness. It is clear that in the decade up to the coup of March 1976, the Argentine auto workers emerged as a militant social force that challenged government policies in dramatic fashion and consistently opposed the auto companies' efforts to increase productivity. Indeed they developed a level of militant organization and consciousness that blocked the successful implementation of the companies' efforts. Yet if we are to go beyond a simple celebration of the heights of political consciousness and combativity of militant organization achieved, we must pay more attention to variables that lie primarily in the social context of both the auto plants and the wider working class community within which the auto workers live and mold their organizations.

It is clear that our efforts are only a tentative first step in this direction, establishing some of the basic parameters within which future research could take place. We lack in-depth case studies available for other Latin American countries. Only such studies will permit the examination of the feasibility of some of the hypotheses presented here and the analysis of the variables determining the emergence and functioning of rank-and-file organization in particular and unionization in general in the Argentine auto industry.

Notes

1. José Nun, "Despidos en la Industria Automotriz Argentina: Estudio de un Caso de Superpoblacion Flotante," *Revista Mexicana de Sociologia*, no. 1 (1978).

2. For an analysis of intersectoral differences, see P. Gerchunoff and J. Llach, "Capitalismo Industrial, Desarrollo Asociado y Distribucion del Ingreso entre dos Gobiernos Peronistas, 1950–72," *Desarrollo Economico*, no. 57 (April–June 1975).

3. See Nun, "Despidos en la Industria Automotriz Argentina."

4. "Informe Preliminar sobre el Conflicto en FIAT," *Pasado y Presente* (la Epoca), no. 9 (1965).

5. Legal jurisdiction is crucial to Argentine unions since it grants sole bergaining rights in the industry.

6. The *Plan de Lucha* was a multistaged mobilization organized by Peronist unions that culminated in the mass occupation of factories in June 1964. The plan was directed by Augusto Vandor, the leader of the UOM. It involved strong Peronist political opposition to the radical government of Arturo Illia.

7. The unions apparently accepted the growing number of plant contracts provided that they maintained ultimate control over negotiations. This was preferable to the individual plant unions such as those set up in Fiat.

8. *CGT*, August 22, 1968.

9. See Monica Peralta Ramos, *Estapas de Acumulacion y Alianzas de Clase en la Argentina, 1930–1970* (Buenos Aires, 1972).

10. SMATA, Buenos Aires, 1974.

11. SMATA, *Memoria y Balance* (1975), p. 155.

12. For examples of other, less social uses of these funds, see Jorge Correa, *Los Jerarcas Sindicales* (Buenos Aires, 1972).

13. The paternalistic ideology was most clearly revealed at Fiat. See "Informe Preliminar sobre el Conflicto en FIAT."

14. One could also cite the tradition of strong state-backed unionization and the post-1955 role of unions as the only legitimate representatives of the political aspirations of the majority of Argentine workers.

15. For the general nature of the military government's economic policies, see Monica Peralta Ramos, *Etapas de Acumulacion y Alianzas de Clase en la Argentina* (Buenos Aires, 1973).

16. The CGT de los Argentinos was led by Raimundo Ongaro, the leader of the Buenos Aires Printworkers. CGT Azopardo represented most of the traditional Peronist unions and was led by Augusto Vandor of the Metalworkers.

17. *CGT*, September 12, 1968.

18. *La Verdad*, March 23, 1970. *La Verdad* was the paper of a Trotskyist group with influence among auto militants. The election claims were backed up by detailed figures in the opposition press and can be taken to be generally reliable.

19. The leadership could attach assessors to negotiating committees and had the right to ratify any final agreement. There was a clear perception that increases above the norm were a direct function of rank-and-file militancy. For example, in 1969 Mercedes' increase of 10 percent higher than Chrysler and General Motors was generally attributed to greater rank-and-file pressure. *CGT*, April 4, 1969.

20. *Avanzada Socialista* (January 1972).

21. ADEFA data quoted in *Voz de SMATA* (March 1969).

22. Nun, "Despidos en la Industria Automotriz Argentina."

23. Ibid.

24. Ibid.

25. *Ya!* December 28, 1973.

26. Interviews with activists from Buenos Aires plants, August 1973, February 1974.

27. *La Verdad*, May 29, 1967.

28. We do not intend to provide an account of the Cordobazo but rather to sketch the development of the auto workers in Cordoba in the period up to 1973. For studies of the Cordobazo, see Beba Balve et al., *Lucha de Calles, Lucha de Clases* (Buenos Aires, 1974); Francisco Delich, *Crisis y Protesta Social: Cordoba, Mayo, 1969* (Buenos Aires, 1970); and Roberto Massari, "Le 'Cordobazo'." *Sociologie du Travail*, no. 2 (1975).

29. Fernando Ferrero, *Localisation Industrial en la Provincia de Cordoba* (Universidad Nacional de Cordoba, 1964), quoted in Massari, "Le 'Cordobazo'. "

30. FIAT's quiescence may be partly due to its wider product range, which was not so severely hit by fluctuations in the auto market.

31. *La Voz de SMATA* (August 1966).

32. *Electrum* (paper of Luz y Fuerza, Cordoba), June 7, 1968.

33. *Analisis*, June 17, 1968.

34. Ibid.

35. *Noticias*, March 1, 1974.

36. Salamanca generally claimed to be independent of party affiliations, but it seems clear that he was influenced by the Maoist *Partido Comunista Revolucionario*. No one tendency dominated the leadership.

37. Kerr and Siegel argue that workers with a lower propensity to strike "are more likely to live in multi industry communities, to associate with people with quite different working experiences than their own and to belong to associations with heterogeneous membership. In these communities their individual grievances are less likely to coalesce into a mass grievance." Their theory may be of relevance to the Cordoba-Buenos Aires contrast, with the proviso that Cordoba represents a city-wide working-class community centered around one industry, in contrast to the Kerr and Siegel prototype of a group of workers isolated from other workers and the wider community. See Clark Kerr and Abraham Siegel, "The Inter Industry Propensity to Strike—an International Comparison," in Arthur Kornhauser et al., *Industrial Conflict* (New York 1954).

38. *Analisis*, June 17, 1968.

39. Interviews by authors with auto militants, August 1973, Cordoba.

40. Workers were also aware that the market difficulties of the companies, with resulting layoffs, involved wider priorities of government policy. They realized that unemployment could not be resolved simply at the enterprise level. There was thus an element of inherent politicization in the issue of layoffs and suspensions, which was enhanced by the military government's centralization of decision making.

41. Massari, "Le 'Cordobazo'. "

42. *Avanzada Socialista* (January 1972).

43. *Pasado y Presente* (Primera Epoca), no. 9 (1965).

44. Ibid.

45. A wide variety of Marxist groups had some influence in the plants. The PCR and Vanguardia Comunista were Maoist groups that had split from the Communist party in the early 1960s. Young militants from the student Left

generally defined themselves as independent Marxists rejecting both Chinese and Soviet models.

46. The *viborazo* was directed against the governor, a hard-line right winger who had affirmed that he would root out subversives. The mobilization, led by SITRAM-SITRAC workers, was in many ways more militant than the Cordobazo and resulted in the removal of the governor.

47. For an analysis of the SITRAC-SITRAM experience, see *Los Libros*, no. 3 (1971). See also Elisabeth Jelin, "Spontaneite et Organisation dans la Mouvement Ouvrier: le Cas de l'Argentine, du Bresil et du Mexique," *Sociologie du Travail*, no. 2 (1976).

48. Interview with SITRAC-SITRAM leader published in *Los Libros*, no. 3 (1971).

49. There were great differences between various Left groups within SITRAC-SITRAM as to actual political strategy and the precise road to socialism.

50. *Avanzada Socialista* (January 1972).

51. *Nuevo Hombre*, March 29, 1972.

52. For an analysis of the submergence of these issues in the post-1955 period, see Daniel James, "Rationalisation and Working Class Response: The Context and Limits of Factory Floor Activity in Argentina," *Journal of Latin American Studies* (November 1981). For their reemergence in 1973, see Juan Carlos Torre, "The Meaning of Current Workers' Struggles," *Latin American Perspectives* 1, no. 3 (1974).

53. See Torre, "Meaning of Current Workers' Struggles." Also see Elisabeth Jelin, "Labour Conflicts under the Second Peronist Regime, 1973–76," *Development and Change* 10 (1979).

54. For details of the IKA conflict, see Jelin, "Labour Conflicts."

55. In 1974 Ongaro, leader of the Printworkers, was displaced and arrested. Luz y Fuerza was intervened by the central leadership with army help.

56. *No Transar*, February 19, 1975.

57. *Buenos Aires Herald*, October 26, 1975.

58. See Werner Wurtele, "International Trade Union Solidarity and the Internationalisation of Capital—the Role of the International Metalworkers' Federation in Latin America" (The Hague: Institute of Social Studies, 1977).

59. A detailed study of this development has not been done. Our information came from conversations with militants.

60. *Politica Obrera*, July 8, 1978. There was a keen debate in the plant between those who wanted to escalate the conflict and those who argued that given the threat of repression, it would be wiser to accept the offer and consolidate factory organization. This more realistic line prevailed.

6   Labor in the Mexican Motor Vehicle Industry

Ian Roxborough

The automobile industry in Mexico is an important and dynamic part of the economy. In terms of both its own importance and its possible repercussions throughout other sectors of the economy, union behavior in the automobile industry can have a major impact on national wage policy, strike propensity, and the political support given by the union movement to the government. The auto industry has also been the scene for a number of important struggles within the union movement. These struggles have crystalized over the demands by the rank and file to break free of the tutelage of the government-affiliated Confederación de trabajadores de México (CTM) and organize independent unions. In these struggles, the auto workers have played a vanguard role in recent Mexican labor conflict, often without a clear consciousness of doing so. To understand how this has occurred, it is necessary to place the automobile workers in their context within the working class as a whole.

The National Context

Throughout the postwar period the Mexican economy has grown at the impressive annual average rate of 6 percent.[1] This economic miracle has been accompanied by a degree of political stability unusual in Latin America. There have been few major challenges to the dominant party, the Partido Revolucionario Institucional (PRI), and there has been an orderly transfer of power from one president to another. Some analysts believe that an important part of the explanation of this coincidence of rapid economic growth and political stability is to be sought in the organization of the labor movement under the aegis of the CTM.[2] They see a direct connection between control of the labor movement by the government-affiliated CTM, low strike levels, slow growth in real wages, low levels of inflation, and rapid and sustained economic growth.[3] In this argument the potential discontent of the rank and file of organized labor has been headed off by the leadership of the official union apparatus, linked closely to the state.

This dominance of the official union movement was not the only factor in the Mexican miracle. The effects of the agrarian reform, efficient capital markets, the manner in which the Mexican bourgeoisie was largely dependent on the state, and proximity to the United States are all obvious and important contributions to Mexico's economic growth and political stability.[4] Within this general panorama the labor stability brought about by the official union bureaucracy played a central role. Dominating the official union apparatus is the CTM.

In 1936 the previously fragmented and weak Mexican trade union movement was brought together into a single union confederation, the CTM, as a result of the initiatives of President Lázaro Cárdenas, a progressive. The reforming presidency of Cárdenas came to a close in 1940, and he was succeeded by a series of conservative presidents, committed to import substitution industrialization. In the push toward industrialization, real wages were kept down. Under the cover of national unity, real wages of Mexican workers dropped dramatically during the war and in the immediate postwar years.

Before the union movement could fully recover from the dramatic wage cut imposed on it during the war, a series of changes in the CTM leadership ensured that a conservative clique of union bureaucrats would actively prevent the rank and file of the labor movement from disturbing industrial harmony.[5] In a series of purges and organizational splits, the Communists and the independent leftists around Vincente Lombardo Toledano were pushed out of the CTM, and the Fidel Velázquez group took over. Attempts by the radical group to set up a rival union confederation failed when the government refused to grant it legal recognition.[6]

As a result, at a national level, the CTM came to exercise an effective monopoly over organized labor. There were a number of other rival union confederations, but these were not able to challenge the CTM's hegemony and favored political position. Nor were the rank and file of the CTM in much of a position to challenge the leadership. There was a steady series of insurgent attempts throughout the postwar period, but as long as the government supported the official union leadership, the insurgent movements had little chance of prospering. If they seemed to be taking over the union, the government would intervene in union elections to ensure that its preferred candidates were successful.[7] Day-to-day union administration involved more routine methods for controlling the rank and file. A typical device was the use of the closed shop provision of the labor law to ensure that troublesome workers lost their jobs.[8] The offending workers were removed from union membership using some vaguely worded clause in the union constitution referring to appropriate conduct, the employer would then have no option but to dismiss them. In an economy with chronically high levels of unemployment, this closed shop provision was a powerful weapon in the hands of the union bureaucracy.

This complex of irregular union practices came to be known as *charrismo* and the leaders as *charros*. It became the dominant style of Mexican unionism in the postwar period, though there were always exceptions and variations. The effect of this structure of trade union control was to ensure that strikes were infrequent and predictable (occurring almost entirely over wages during contract revisions) and that wages rose slowly and in line with other prices and costs. *Charro* control over the labor movement became one of the pillars of Mexico's postwar economic expansion and political stability and a keystone of the Mexican miracle.

Emergence of Independent Unionism

The domination of the official union bureaucracies over the labor movement did not go unchallenged, however. A number of insurgent movements in the postwar period, notably in the electrical industry, on the railways, and among teachers, usually involving attempts to take over the union leadership from within, met with various degrees of success.[9] In the late 1960s and early 1970s a form of parallel unionism began to emerge, usually company based and unaffiliated with any of the union confederations linked to the government. Some of the independent unions formed their own coalition, the Unidad-Obrera-Independiente (UOI). By the early 1970s more than a hundred independent unions existed in various industries.[10]

At the political level this sudden surge of union militancy was quite clearly sparked by the initial attempts of the incoming president, Luis Echeverría, to distance himself from the CTM leadership. In this context it is important to recall that Echeverría took office immediately after the student protests of 1968, which had led to the massacre of hundreds of demonstrators by the army.[11] The leadership of the PRI clearly felt a need to reestablish political legitimacy, and the concrete expression this took was Echeverría's so-called democratic opening. As part of his attempt to incorporate these potentially destabilizing dissident movements, Echeverría distanced himself from the old union bureaucracy and encouraged the new independent unions.[12]

At the economic level the reasons for the upsurge of indendent unionism are much less clear. It has been suggested that these independent movements were located predominantly in the more dynamic and modern sectors of industry, frequently dominated by transnationals.[13] (The automobile industry fits into this category.) The logic of the argument is that wage costs are relevant in these industries only in relation to productivity and that it is not against the interests of these firms to have a high wage and militant labor force, providing that high productivity can be achieved. There is, therefore, no reason for the firms to support a *charro* leadership that cannot control its own rank and file. As a consequence such firms will not actively oppose the development of independent unionism. This is not, in fact, an accurate reflection of the position of the automobile manufacturers. And in any case, the evidence that these insurgent movements occur primarily in the new and dynamic sectors of industry is far from conclusive.[14]

Another possible explanation has to do with the strength of the CTM bureaucracy at a regional level. Many of the new plants were set up outside Mexico City proper, in adjacent states. The CTM bureaucracy in these states—Puebla, Morelos, and Hidalgo—was not particularly powerful. In the case of Puebla, an old textile center, rival union confederations (the CGT and the CROM) existed to dispute the hegemony of the CTM, and neither Hidalgo nor Morelos was an industrial center.[15] But the industrial city of Toluca in the state of Mexico was a quite different situation. The city was firmly controlled by the CTM, and it is not surprising that attempts at rank-and-file revolts there met with determined opposition. In the late 1970s, as some companies were thinking of expanding, they frequently chose to locate in Toluca so as to reap the benefits of the CTM's dominance there.[16]

Unionism in the Automobile Industry

Mexican labor law allows for the formation of a variety of types of unions.[17] Of the kinds that are of relevance here, unions may be formed at the level of the plant, the enterprise, or the industry. The unions in the Mexican automobile industry are a mixture of plant and enterprise unions. Each union has exclusive jurisdiction.

Table 6.1
Union affiliation in the Mexican automobile industry, 1978

Company	Number of workers	Location of plants	Union affiliation
VW	9,500	Puebla	Unidad Obrera Independiente (UOI)
Nissan	2,750	Cuernavaca	UOI
		Toluca	Confederación de Trabajadores de Mexico (CTM)
Dina	7,000	Ciudad Sahagún	UOI
Ford	4,700	Mexico City (three plants)	CTM (one union)
General Motors	5,500	Mexico City	Confederación Revolucionaria de Obreros y Campesinos (CROC)
		Toluca	CTM
VAM	2,200	Mexico City	Confederación Obrera Revolucionaria (COR)
		Toluca	COR
Chrysler	5,650	Mexico City	CTM
		Toluca	CTM

When the Mexican government tried to induce the automobile companies to expand their operations and move from the assembly phase to manufacturing, the automobile industry was characterized by conservative unions to which the label of *charro* would not be inappropriate. With the exception of General Motors, which had always had a remarkably democratic union, affiliated with the CROC, the unions were affiliated with the CTM and controlled by distant and self-perpetuating leaderships.[18] When the new plants were set up in the mid-1960s, they also came under the control of the CTM.[19]

There were, however, signs of change. A successful struggle was waged in the state-owned Dina plant in 1962 to break away from the CTM and form an independent union.[20] In 1972 the Nissan and VW plants followed suit. There were also unsuccessful movements in Ford and Chrysler. The result, by the late 1970s, was a complex and diverse panorama. Table 6.1 outlines the structure of unionism in the Mexican automobile industry in 1978.[21]

Trends in the Automobile Industry

The diversity of forms of union organization in the Mexican automobile industry and its modern and dynamic nature (typical of industries likely to increase in importance) make it a useful test case of trends of organized labor as a whole. Moreover because the automobile industry has a relatively homogeneous technology and produces a relatively homogeneous product, it can be used as a kind of controlled experiment in order to assess the relative importance of possible factors affecting the development of different kinds of unionism. In particular it provides a test case of both independent and official unions.

The recent emergence of independent unions has attracted considerable attention in Mexico, which can be simplified and restated as contrasting positions. One position argues that the independent unions are militant, democratic, and potential challengers of the status quo. This might be labeled the optimistic hypothesis. A more pessimistic view of the independent unions would see them as highly susceptible to co-optation or repression, or both. Both the nature of the Mexican political system and the operation of Michels's iron law of oligarchy would ensure that, over time, the independent unions increasingly would resemble the established and conservative CTM unions.[22] The Mexican political system, it has been argued, is characterized by a tendency to co-opt dissident movements and incorporate them in the ruling consensus, a process facilitated by the revolutionary rhetoric of the dominant party and the widespread corruption of political leaders. This process is given additional impetus by the inherent tendency of trade unions to be governed by leaderships that are increasingly oligarchic. Michels argued that because the mass of rank-and-file union members could not be expected to participate actively in union activity, power would devolve on a small group of leaders who would grow increasingly distant from the rank and file and form a self-perpetuating oligarchy. Such an oligarchy would have a vested interest in maintaining the status quo and would oppose militant actions by the membership. This might be called the pessimistic or neo-*charro* hypothesis.

The logic of this position would indicate a comparison between the three unions affiliated with the Unidad Obrera Independiente (the independent unions) and the rest (the official unions). The empirical lineup, however, turns out to be rather different. On the measures used, there is indeed a clear distinction between the various unions, but this line of division does not run between the three independent unions and the six official unions. Rather it runs between the three UOI unions plus the General Motors union in the Mexico City plant and the union in Ford versus the rest. (In the following discussion, we refer to the post-1977 Ford union.)

The three areas on which we compare the various unions are the frequency of industrial conflict, the types of demands raised by the unions, and the degree of democracy in internal union government. Specifically the optimistic hypothesis would suggest that the independent unions would experience higher levels of conflict with management and go beyond wage demands to demands concerning job control and that the union leaderships would be more responsive to to membership.

Frequency of Conflict

Conflict, however measured, is low, both nationally and in the automobile industry. Officially recorded strikes in the automobile industry have been infrequent and have occurred mainly during the renegotiations of collective contracts every two years (see table 6.2).[23]

Because of the legal constraints on strikes and the weakness of shop floor organizations in Mexico, there appear to have been almost no unofficial or wildcat strikes. Data on other forms of industrial action are almost nonexistent. Our use of strikes as a measure of levels of industrial conflict has a number of problems, but it is the only easily available indicator. The frequency of strikes in the auto industry appears to have risen in the 1970s, though whether this will be a long-term trend is another matter.

It is true that the three UOI unions have gone on strike more than the CTM unions, as the optimistic hypothesis would suggest, but two important qualifications need to be made. The GM union in Mexico City has a strike propensity as high as any other union, and this appears to be a well-established trend. Second, there was a movement in 1976–1977 to make the Ford union independent of the CTM. The result was an important reorganization of the union in 1977, giving it considerable autonomy within the CTM. Since this period the Ford union appears to have maintained a reasonably high level of militancy.

Types of Demands

All unions placed demands for higher wages at the top of their list of priorities. (Payment is by hourly wage, with few incentive or productivity

Table 6.2
Strikes and duration in days, 1970–1980

	1970	1971	1972	1973	1974	1975	1976	1977	1978	1979	1980	Total strikes
Nissan-Cuernavaca			1	1	21		46	1	1			6
Dina					14		1	6	3	1		5
VW					7		8	1	15			4
Ford							30		1		12	3
GM-DF				1+6[a]		30		62		22	106	6
GM-Toluca												0
Chrysler						2[b]						0
VAM	32[b]											0
Nissan-Toluca										6[b]		0

a. There were two strikes that year in GM-DF: one of one day and one of six days.
b. Unofficial strikes against union leaderships.

schemes and very little overtime.) Wage data are highly complex and not particularly reliable. Some comparative data for 1976 are given in table 6.3. However, since differences in absolute levels of wages are due to a variety of factors, such as capital-labor ratios, average wage costs in the region where the plant is located, seniority, and skill levels, a more interesting measure is change in wages over time. According to the optimistic hypothesis, wage increases ought to be greater in the independent unions. Data published by the Ford Motor Company suggest that this is indeed the case. Taking 1975 as 100, wages increased as show in table 6.4. (Unfortunately Dina was not included.) Basically there appear to be only minor differences between the companies. Nevertheless such differences as exist suggest that the three independent unions, together with Ford, have obtained higher wage increases.

The next most important set of demands concerned fringe benefits.[24] Currently these seem to be worth about another 40 to 60 percent on top of the basic weekly wage. Information on fringe benefits is not very reliable, but there do seem to be substantial differences between companies. In addition to their purely economic significance, many of these fringe benefits are awarded selectively by the union, and the allocation of fringe benefits is clearly a potential power resource for leadership vis-à-vis the rank and file.

Following on from these economic demands are a number of job security issues involving clauses in the contracts stipulating preferential hiring of family members and clauses increasing the percentage of the work force covered by *planta* contracts. Mexican labor law recognizes two kinds of employment contract: *de planta*, an indefinite contract with no stipulated termination date, and *obreros eventuales*. These *eventuales* may be hired for *obra determinada* (for example, during the production of cars numbered X_n to X_m or for *tiempo determinado* (a stipulated period varying from one week to eleven months). The importance of the distinction consists primarily in the legal provisions for compensation subsequent to dismissal. A dismissed *planta* worker must be given the equivalent of three months' pay plus twenty days' pay for every year worked in the company. When the *eventual* is dismissed at the end of the contract, the employer has no further legal obligations. Obviously if substantial layoffs are anticipated, it is in the employer's interest to ensure that they fall on the *eventuales*. The use of *eventuales* does not imply a high rate of turnover in the industry. The general tendency is for firms to rehire *eventuales* for subsequent periods and, after some

Table 6.3
Wages and fringe benefits, 1976

	Wages (millions of pesos)	Salaries (millions of pesos)	Fringe benefits (millions of pesos)	Workers	Total labor costs (millions of pesos)	Total cost per worker (pesos)	Wages and salaries per worker (pesos)	Fringe benefits per worker (pesos)	Fringes as % of wages and salaries
Ford	222	193	436	4,944	851	172,127	83,940	88,188	105.06
GM	155	311	209	5,043	675	133,849	92,405	41,444	44.85
VW	137	362	280	9,379	779	83,058	53,204	29,854	56.11
Dina	406	536	n.d.[a]	7,911	n.d.	119,075	n.d.	n.d.	n.d.
Chrysler	206	218	221	5,018	645	128,537	84,496	44,041	52.12
Nissan	91	143	54	2,959	288	97,330	79,081	18,249	23.08
VAM	78	58	22	1,964	158	80,448	69,246	11,202	16.18

Source: José Othon Quiroz Trejo, *Proceso de Trabajo en la Industria Automotriz Terminal*, Cuaderno 40 (Mexico: Centro de Estudios Latinoamericanos, UNAM, 1980).
a. n.d. = no data.

Table 6.4
Increase in wage rates

	1976	1977	1978	1979	1980
Nissan (Cuernavaca)	148	165	188	222	274
VW	148	165	192	226	281
Ford	145	167	194	229	293
GM (CROC)	140	154	174	204	251
GM (Toluca)	141	156	177	208	255
Chrysler	141	156	176	207	253
VAM	138	152	173	199	248

Source: Ford Motor Company, *Proyección*, no. 14 (May 1981).
Note: 1975 = 100.

years, promote them to *planta* status. Each firm tends to have its own distinct reserve pool of aspirant workers.

Both of these job security issues have become more salient since the mid-1970s. The preferential hiring clause has not met with much apparent resistance from management, largely because it appears to be in management's short-run interest. The increase in the percentage of workers on *planta* contracts has met with more sustained opposition from management, and unions have differed greatly in their success with these demands. Since the Mexican auto industry is subject to considerable fluctuations in output, managements generally have preferred to have a substantial proportion of their work force in the *eventual* category, where the cost of layoff is lower.[25] In this area of conflict, both Dina and Nissan have been very successful in raising the percentage of workers on *planta* contracts to something like 90 percent of the total. They have been followed closely by GM-CROC, VW, and Ford.[26] Chrysler stands out at the other extreme as the company that makes most use of *eventuales* and uses shorter *eventual* contracts than is the rule elsewhere in the industry.[27]

There have also been a number of struggles over job mobility within the plants, both horizontally (from one department to another) and vertically (promotions and upgrading). The more militant unions have insisted on making promotions automatic (*escalafón ciego*) and on reducing management's right to move labor freely within the plant. Throughout the industry management has fought to maintain control of the deployment of labor. On this issue the sharpest division lies between the UOI unions plus GM-CROC and Ford on the one side and the rest. The union with the strongest job control is Dina. There seem to be three possible reasons for this.

Management claims that the principal reason is Dina's status as a nationalized industry, which subjects it to political pressure to give way to the workers and to appoint managers on the basis of political considerations. This explanation (offered by the industrial relations managers who had recently come to Dina from private enterprise) is part of a general critique of Dina's inability to operate profitably.[28]

Anthropologist Augusto Urteaga argues that the social background of the work force has contributed to a high degree of work place cohesion, which has led to a high level of job control by the work force.[29] Dina was set up in the 1950s as a new industrial town in the middle of the countryside, some sixty miles from Mexico City. The work force was recruited from the impoverished peasants of the area, and according to Urteaga, initial alignments in the union tended to follow family and neighborhood lines. Over a period of twenty years these social networks have been reinforced rather than eroded. Hence job control issues have a high salience for the work force, which is in a good position to bargain successfully on these issues.

Third, the union in Dina became independent of the CTM in 1962, several years before Nissan and VW left the CTM.

Struggles more directly related to control over the work process itself have been much less frequent in the Mexican auto industry. Historically management seems to have taken the initiative in determining working conditions, and the union has concerned itself almost exclusively with wage determination and issues around hiring procedures. There are, of course, recorded instances of shop floor conflict over working conditions in GM-CROC and Ford dating back to the 1940s; nevertheless, the weakness or absence of shop floor organizations has been a central feature of the Mexican auto industry.[30]

This situation appears to be changing in recent years. In 1977 the Ford union threatened a strike over speedup, claiming that the company had violated the collective contract.[31] Seemingly this is the first time this has happened in the Mexican auto industry. The company quickly gave in. In the other unions there also seems to be an increasing concern over these issues. By 1978 Nissan, Dina, Ford, GM (Mexico City), and VAM all had clauses in their contracts stipulating some form of control over work speeds. The remaining unions either did not have such clauses or had language specifying that control over work processes was a management prerogative. Once again, with the exceptions of

VW and VAM, the same pattern is visible: the independents, GM (Mexico City) and Ford, are more likely to have some measure of control over work processes than the other unions.

The reason is not entirely clear. It may be that, as the percentage of workers on *planta* contracts increases (to something like 90 percent in some unions), management feels pressure to increase efficiency in the manning and allocation of work. Second, the ten years' expansion of the industry after 1965 must have provided a relatively good climate for industrial relations. The industry was expanding rapidly, most companies had recently opened new plants, and the work force was relatively inexperienced. (This set of factors led to a very specific series of conflicts, mainly revolving around attempts at breaking free of CTM control. These conflicts are not likely to be repeated.) After 1975 this situation changed, and the industry had to face a serious contraction, which may have altered managerial strategy toward labor.[32] The days of unlimited expansion were over, and management would now have to be quite careful about taking on extra labor, particularly workers with *planta* status. This, however, must remain a somewhat speculative conjecture.

The increasing salience of conflicts over working conditions seems to be closely related to another recent development, the increasing importance of *delegados departmentales*.[33] This is a very sensitive subject since the difference between the formal existence and powers of the *delegados* and their actual or real power may vary considerably. For example, VAM has *delegados*, but any shop floor incident is dealt with directly by the general secretary of the union. The *delegados* exist only on paper. All unions now have *delegados*, and GM-CROC, Ford, Chrysler, and Dina have had *delegados* for many years. One indicator of the differences between the various unions in terms of the strength of shop floor union representation is the number of full-time union officials whose salaries are paid by the company. The numbers for 1978 are: Nissan-Cuernavaca, four; Dina, eight; VW, nine; Ford, four; GM-CROC, nine; GM-Toluca, five; and Chrysler, VAM, and Nissan-Toluca, none.[34]

This is by no means an infallible measure since the data could indicate an increasingly complex apparatus used by management to control the rank and file. It should be noted that these are small unions and that the increases in number of union officials have been correlated with militancy, not with increasing conservatism. The real question is how union officials and *delegados* actually behave on the shop floor. This question cannot be answered with any confidence, but the situation appears to be as follows.[35]

In Ford the *delegados* play a considerable role in the management of day-to-day conflicts, and since the union leadership is an uneasy coalition of diverging political tendencies, they also play an important role in determining union strategy.[36] In Nissan and VW the *delegados* are important in day-to-day conflicts but do not directly influence union policy since the union leaderships there tend to be fairly homogeneous groups. In Nissan, at least, the relationships between the *delegados* and the union officers are strained, and it is not infrequent for the general secretary of the union to have to resolve shop floor conflicts. In GM-CROC and in Dina the *delegados* appear to be the organizational and leadership nuclei of the internal political groups in the union. They tend to be highly involved in shop floor issues, but their relationships with the union leadership depend on whether they belong to the same political faction. This is slightly different from the situation in Nissan and VW where the *delegados* do not appear to be so directly involved in internal union politics. In Chrysler the *delegados* appear to have quite a lot of importance on the shop floor. They are, however, lieutenants of the general secretary and form part of his political clientele and are appointed by him.[37]

To summarize, there are general trends in the Mexican auto industry that some unions (UOI, Ford, and GM-CROC) tend to lead and the others (Chrysler, VAM, GM-CTM, Nissan-CTM) follow reluctantly. It appears that the unions that are more militant in terms of strike propensity also tend to lead the industry in terms of the percentage of the work force with *planta* contracts, the number and importance of shop floor union officers, and success in obtaining explicit acceptance that they should have at least some voice in matters relating to work loads and line speeds.

Although the correlations along these dimensions are not perfect, they are strikingly consistent. Moreover the line of demarcation is not one that divides the independent unions from the official unions, as both the optimistic and the neo-*charro* hypotheses imply. Rather the line of division is between the three independent unions together with two of the official unions versus the rest. This strongly suggests that the key factor distinguishing one type of union from another is not whether it is independent or belongs to a government-affiliated union confederation but some other factor.

Union Government

Trade union government is often discussed in terms of democracy and oligarchy, with the general (Michelian) assumption being that the oligarchic forces are greater than the democratic.[38] The importance of the discussion about union democracy arises from the presumed conflict of interest between the rank and file and the trade union bureaucracy. A general assumption is that the trade union bureaucracy is interested in maintaining stable and nonconflictual relationships with management; hence the greater the extent of rank-and-file pressure on the leadership, the more militant that leadership will be. If we accept this as a working hypothesis, then we may expect a positive correlation between union democracy and militancy. Note that union democracy is implicitly defined in this context as the ability of the rank and file to bring pressure to bear on the leadership to take specific actions. As such, democracy is a continuum.

Four main indicators of democracy are used: rotation of leaders, contested elections, closeness of voting in elections, and the existence of permanent and organized opposition. These are by no means infallible indicators and should be used with caution.

Despite considerable similarity of technology, working conditions, and wages in the automobile industry, there is considerable variation in union behavior from one firm to another. The unions discussed here represent a range of behavior from extreme oligarchy (Chrysler) to considerable degrees of democracy (GM and Dina), though even in the same union, there may be considerable changes over time, as illustrated by the GM union.

The Chrysler union was formed in 1938, and when Chrysler opened its new plant in Toluca, the union covered the workers in both plants. By 1970 there was considerable discontent among the Toluca workers, and in January 1970, a strike broke out over a claim that the Toluca workers were being paid less than the workers in Mexico City.[39]

In the course of the strike, the executive committee was changed. Meanwhile the company organized a meeting in Mexico City, and a different executive committee was elected.[40] Thus two executive committees claimed to speak for the workers. The Ministry of Labor recognized the committee elected in Mexico City, headed by the production manager in the Toluca plant. This executive committee was reelected for another six years without opposition when its term of office expired in 1976. There is considerable circumstantial evidence to suggest that in the 1970 election, the majority of the Toluca workers did not favor the person eventually recognized as general secretary of the union. After the strike a substantial part of the work force was fired, and the closed shop provision was used against a number of workers.

There was another rank-and-file revolt by Chrysler workers in 1975, leading to a brief strike.[41] Once again the insurgents lost, large numbers of workers were dismissed, and the closed shop provision was widely used to purge the union of dissidents. In their submission of evidence to federal labor courts, several workers who entered claims of unjust dismissal as a result of these incidents asserted that they had been dismissed on the direct orders of the general secretary of the Chrysler union and that physical violence had been used to intimidate them.[42] In any case, with the exception of the original meeting in 1970, which had forced the executive committee to step down, the four other elections were uncontested. The existence of serious internal conflict in the union suggests that the absence of opposition does not necessarily indicate mass support for the trade union leadership.

In Nissan, there were nine elections for the post of secretary-general in the eleven-year period between 1966 and 1977 compared with five in a twelve-year period in Chrysler. Moreover not once in Nissan was an incumbent reelected, though two men served twice. Not only have elections in Nissan been more frequent, but they have always been contested by two or three slates, corresponding to definite political tendencies. There is a militant Christian Democratic group (Frente Auténtico del Trabajo), a dominant and slightly less militant group (Unidad Obrera Independiente), and a rather conservative, pro-CTM group. There is a high degree of awareness among the work force of what voting for these tendencies means in terms of factory-level politics and collective bargaining since each has held union office.[43] In contrast to Chrysler where it appears that a leadership clique divorced from the membership has consciously attempted to retain power by any means, no self-perpetuating oligarchy has been able to form in Nissan. Instead there has been considerable rotation of the union leadership. But neither rotation nor contested elections in themselves are sufficient measures of democracy. One of the key tests is the ability of the membership to vote an incumbent out of office.

Clearly even in the most oligarchic union (Chrysler), the work force was able to organize a mass meeting and depose the incumbent union leadership. However, in the face of determined managerial opposition and apparent support for management from the federal labor courts, the mass of the workers were not able to ensure that their victory was more than fleeting.

In the other unions there are clear examples of the membership's voting incumbents out of office. In Nissan CTM affiliation was changed to UOI affiliation, and more recently the previously popular FAT-affiliated leadership was replaced by the more moderate UOI. In GM and Dina there are a number of unambiguous examples of such leadership change. Incumbents were defeated on at least three occasions in Dina and on seven occasions in GM. Incumbents have also been re-elected in these unions, however, though continuity in office is less frequent in these unions than rotation.

Not all changes of office holders have been smooth and constitutional. The troubles in Chrysler in 1970 had their counterparts in Nissan, Dina, and GM. In the elections in Nissan in 1969, the closed shop provision (*claúsula de exclusión*) was applied to twenty workers, of whom seven appeared on the slate that won the election the following day. The defeated general secretary wrote to the local labor court demanding that the election be declared invalid on the grounds that the twenty expelled members had voted in the elections. The court ignored his request. The new executive committee was scarcely a group of committed democrats. When they lost the following year's election, a court order was necessary to force the defeated general secretary to hand over the union premises to the new administration.[44]

In the other unions formal complaints to the Ministry of Labor claiming electoral fraud or malpractice were more frequent. In addition to the one complaint in Nissan, there were two complaints in Chrysler, three in GM, four in Dina.[45] Complaints do not automatically indicate a lack of democracy. On the contrary, they suggest that opposition groups within the union believe in the legitimacy of elections and believe that they have some chance of persuading the Ministry of Labor to intervene to call new elections in which their chance of winning will be high. And indeed the scattered evidence tends to support this interpretation. In both GM and Dina, the Ministry of Labor intervened to supervise new elections, which resulted in reversals of the previous results.[46]

Some of the events that gave rise to accusations of electoral misconduct in Dina involved strong scenes with rival groups occupying the union headquarters and fistfights breaking out.

Although the GM union never experienced the bitterness that arose in some of the conflicts in Dina, it too had troubles. The GM union was formed in 1937.[47] The original constitution specified that meetings were to be held every two weeks, and the executive committee was to be elected every six months. An elaborate procedure was set up whereby candidates for union office would have their qualifications discussed by speakers for and against. Then the number of candidates would be reduced to two by acclamation, followed by a secret ballot. Each post was considered in turn, and unsuccessful candidates could, and did, run for other positions. In the 1930s the total membership was about 300, so this sort of informal democracy was perhaps feasible. Elections soon became yearly, however, and meetings were held monthly.

By the early 1940s although union membership had dropped to about 150, the electoral process had become more formal, with slates being organized for elections. In 1945 the statutes were once more reformed to give the executive committee a two-year period of office with half the officers being elected each year. The slates, however, still bore traces of the kind of informal and personality-oriented democracy that prevailed. For example, in the election of 1947, four offices were up for election, and five slates were presented. There were, however, only fourteen candidates in all since some candidates appeared on more than one slate.

There existed the real possibility of a lapse into anarchy, which occurred in the election of 1950. Four offices were to be filled. Nine slates were presented with a total of only eighteen candidates. There were also a number of independent candidates: two for one post, four for another, and five for a third post. This chaotic situation lasted until 1955 when the slates became more organized and stable and began to have names. As table 6.5 shows, after 1955 a limited number of slates continued to contest elections with considerable regularity.

Unlike the situation in Nissan, however, it is not possible to identify these slates directly with political tendencies. Throughout this period the unions faced no major problems; there were high turnouts to the monthly meetings and a frequent rotation of union officers. As table 6.6 shows, attendance was consistently high from 1947 to 1965, followed by a period of erratic attendance. But even at its lowest, turnout at GM's union meetings still is very high by international standards.[48]

Meetings appear to have been somewhat boisterous (there were occasional difficulties in obtaining a hall to meet in since the owners frequently complained about the damage caused by the GM workers).[49] By the early 1970s the relatively stable two-party democracy had once again degenerated into a collection of short-lived electoral alliances.

Table 6.5
Principal slates contesting elections in GM union

Year	Names of principal slates	Total number of slates
1955	Blanca *Verde*	2
1957	Blanca *Azul*	6
1958	*Circulo-Verde* Azul	2
1959	*Circulo-Verde* Azul	4
1960	Circulo-Verde *Azul*	2
1961	*Circulo-Verde* Unificación	2
1962	*Circulo-Verde* Unificación	2
1963	Unificación *Democrático*	4
1964	*Circulo-Verde* Azul Unificación	4
1965	Circulo-Verde Azul *Unificación*	6
1966	Coalición *Unificación*[a]	2
1967	*Coalición* Unificación	3
1968	*Coalición* Unificación	2
1969	Acción Coalición *Unificación*	5
1970	Acción Coalición Unificación *FUT*	2
1971[c]	Acción Unificación FUT	4
1972	Acción Renovación-sindical *Unificación* FUT[b]	6
1973	Acción *Renovación-sindical* Unificación FUT	9
1974[c]	Acción Unificación FUT	5
1975[c]	Acción Renovación-sindical Unificación	13
1976[c]	Acción Renovación-sindical Unificación	9
1977[c]	Acción Renovación-sindical Unificación	13

Source: Union minutes.
Notes: Winners are italicized.
a. Circulo-Verde and Azul joined to form Coalición.
b. Coalición changed its name to Renovación-sindical.
c. No single slate won.

Table 6.6
Attendance at GM union meetings

Year	Membership	Number of meetings	% attendance (yearly average)
1947	882	8	83.5
1948	790	3	86.5
1949	808	4	95.0
1950	902	3	66.8
1951	1,361	5	91.2
1952	1,302	1	86.6
1953	1,511	4	56.6
1954	964	8	88.8
1955	977	6	84.9
1956	1,028	9	82.5
1957	1,174	9	80.1
1958	1,109	7	66.9
1959	1,176	13	67.8
1960	1,132	9	61.8
1961	1,167	10	66.2
1962	1,231	5	70.5
1963	1,455	5	68.8
1964	1,547	8	73.6
1965	1,626	13	96.7
1966	2,261	9	69.8
1967	3,430	4	33.8
1968		11	

The 1977 elections were fought between no fewer than twelve slates, often with overlapping candidates.

What conclusions can be drawn from GM's long and torturous history? First, GM has never fallen into a really solidified oligarchy. The tendency, in fact, has been toward the opposite extreme of undisciplined libertarianism. Oligarchic tendencies have always been present, but each time a particular group appeared to be gathering power for its own private uses, a storm of protest from the rank and file forced it to desist, or overthrew it. The successful operation of this veto power seems to be a result of continuing permanent factions within the union.[50]

The absence of permanent and organized opposition may explain the ease with which the insurgent movement in Chrysler in 1970 was crushed and a procompany leadership elected. By contrast the continued division of Nissan workers between FAT and UOI may explain the continuation of democracy in that union.

According to anthropological research on Dina, the formation of groups and factions in the union stems in large part from the politics of locality and kinship groups.[51] To what extent this will continue to be the case must remain a matter for speculation. The situation in the other unions is less well known, but in general they appear to fall within the range defined by General Motors at one end and Chrysler at the other.

The notion of a single continuum with democracy as one pole and oligarchy as the other is perhaps misleading. A more complex typology is required to do justice to the range of variation of union government.[52] The aim here has been more limited, to indicate the existence of a wide range of forms of union government in the Mexican automobile industry. This is important in view of a widespread tendency to view most Mexican unions as oligarchic or *charro*.[53] It has been argued that the term *charro* is devoid of analytic utility and no satisfactory definitions exist.[54] One consequence is that all the oligarchic forms of union government tend to be reduced to a single, undifferentiated notion. However, just as it seems useful to explore the notion of union democracy in more detail, so, too, does it seem worthwhile to examine briefly the different forms of oligarchic control. The example in the auto industry that comes closest to the standard image of *charrismo* is the Chrysler union, characterized by electoral fraud, government and management connivance, mass firings, expulsions from the union, absence of internal democracy, and wages that lag behind other firms in the industry.

The three other *charro* unions have not had to resort to such obviously antiworker measures. There seems, in fact, to be general support in the factory for VAM's general secretary, and the fact that that union is basically promanagement can be explained by the nature of the work force rather than by the imposition of a union bureaucracy.[55] VAM is a small and older company that did not undergo the same rapid expansion as the rest of the firms in the second half of the 1960s. Although it is a subsidiary of American Motors, two-thirds of its capital comes from the state.[56]

Both GM-CTM and Ford (before 1977) were clear examples of the operation of CTM bureaucracies. The control of the CTM in the GM plant in Toluca has to be seen in the context of the CTM in Toluca as a whole. The CTM office in Toluca is run by four brothers. One is the legal adviser for the CTM; a second is a state deputy; a third is secretary-general of at least three industrial unions with statewide jurisdiction; and the fourth is the secretary of the GM branch of the metallurgical union and a town counselor. Together they form a kind of local power elite. Clearly anyone at the GM plant in Toluca who runs afoul of the union is not going to get another job in a CTM-organized factory anywhere else in Toluca. And that, given the close relationship between *desarrollista* PRI politicians who run Toluca and the CTM, means no job at all.

In Mexico City (despite the fact that it is one of CTM's strongholds), it is not so easy for the CTM to control the situation.[57] Here in the Ford plants the CTM controlled the union through a two-tier structure.[58] Prior to its 1977 reorganization, the Ford union was a branch of a metallurgical union whose general secretary was a PRI senator. He was always elected unopposed at meetings of the delegates from the various branches. In turn, the delegate in Ford acted as a liaison between the general secretary and management. The general secretary never set foot in the plant, and the delegate handled all the day-to-day problems directly with management.[59] But negotiation of the collective contract was carried out by the general secretary. This meant that management, delegate, and general secretary were each able to deny responsibility and defuse any incipient worker protest.[60]

The situations in both Ford and in GM-Toluca seem to be typical of CTM control mechanisms. Certainly the leaders in both cases were genuine Fidelistas. The leader of the Chrysler union did not start out as a Fidelista but entered the CTM from outside (he came from middle management) in the middle of a crisis. These factors seem to account for the higher levels of overt repression in Chrysler, which seems to be atypical of the CTM as a whole.

If we reexamine these cases in terms of mechanisms of control and co-optation, it will be apparent that the emphasis placed on coercion by some analysts of Mexican politics seems somewhat one-sided. Rather than simply talking about oligarchies, *charro*, or co-opted unions, a somewhat more complex typology of union government is necessary. Tentatively the following might be suggested: both types of union rule, democracy and oligarchy, may be subdivided into three forms. Structured democracy corresponds to a situation with stable, competing parties or caucuses. Caesarist democracy is a situation where a dominant party, caucus, or clique controls the union leadership but can be voted out of office by a rank-and-file revolt. Personalist democracy corresponds to a situation where leaders do not belong to organized factions and are elected on personal merit. Turnover of office, however, is high. In this typology Nissan, Dina, and GM (for some periods) would be structured democracies. In some periods the GM union would more closely resemble a caesarist or a personalist democracy.

Similarly one could subdivide oligarchic rule into bureaucratic where a leadership group retains control through manipulating formal organizations (a two-tier system of elections would be typical); repressive where a leadership group retains control principally through coercion and intimidation; and paternalist where the rank and file are not politicized and a leadership clique is reelected through inertia and apathy. The GM union in Toluca and the Ford unions before the 1977 reorganization fit the bureaucratic model, the Chrysler union is an obvious candidate for the repressive model, and the VAM union seems to fit the paternalist model.

This typology is merely a preliminary and tentative effort to illustrate the complexity of the situation. If we simply retain a democracy-oligarchy dichotomy, then it seems reasonable to describe the following unions as democratic: Nissan (Cuernavaca), Dina, Ford, GM-CROC. The VW union is an ambiguous case, and the other unions (GM-Toluca, Chrysler, VAM, and Nissan-Toluca) clearly are run by oligarchies.

Mechanisms of Control and Co-optation

Physical coercion and intimidation are used against workers in the Mexican auto industry, usually by union leadership. This seems to be largely confined to the case of Chrysler, however, which in many ways is an exceptional one. The manipulation of elections is more frequent, though the evidence suggests much higher levels of union democracy than might be expected. One frequent mechanism of control is the closed shop provision, which union leaderships use to expel workers from the union and hence from their employment. Of a sample of individual grievances brought to the Junta Federal de Conciliación y Arbitraje, 89 percent concerned claims of unjust dismissal.[61] Of these eighty-nine cases, there is evidence that forty directly involve the union. Of these forty cases, the union was codefendant with the employer in twenty-nine, and in eleven cases, the union was involved by providing legal aid or some other form of support for the worker.

The bulk of the twenty-nine cases citing the union as codefendant were in Chrysler (twenty-five), with two in Ford, one in VW, and one in GM-CROC. Of the eleven cases involving union support for the worker, ten were in Nissan (Cuernavaca) and one was in GM-CROC. These data are reproduced in table 6.7, with a plus sign indicating union support for the worker and a minus sign indicating that the union was a codefendant. The overall pattern among the various auto unions is presented in table 6.7.

The Market for Labor

Before companies (and union leaderships) resort to firing workers, they have at their disposal the hiring process. One of the effects of the *eventual* system was to put the worker on a lengthy period of probation before being given *planta* status. The union was involved in constant discussions with management over upgrading, and it is clearly important for workers to have support from union officeholders if they are to be given *planta* status. Probably the same holds true for promotions within the permanent labor force. Here again is displayed the importance of rank-and-file demands to end the discretionary power of management and union leadership and replace it with strict seniority provisions.

In terms of hiring, all managers interviewed insisted that they were reluctant to hire workers from other companies (with the exception of highly skilled workers). In effect each company has its own labor market. The evidence from a sample of workers at Ford tends to confirm this; very few Ford workers in this sample had worked previously in other auto firms.[62]

The entire hiring and promotion process seems to be one of the central factors in the development of styles of unionism in the Mexican

Table 6.7
Summary: Patterns of union activity in the Mexican automobile industry

Union	Location	Affiliation	Number of strikes, 1970–1980	Democratic	Number of union officials	Court cases[a]	Control over work processes	Wage increase, 1975–1980[b]
Nissan	Cuernavaca	UOI	6	Yes	4	10+	Yes	274
Dina	Cuidad Sahagún	UOI	5	Yes	8	0	Yes	n.d.
VW	Puebla	UOI	4	?	9	−1	No	281
Ford	Mexico City	CTM	3	Yes	4	−2	Yes	293
GM	Mexico City	CROC	6	Yes	9	−1/1+	Yes	251
GM	Toluca	CTM	0	No	5	0	No	255
Chrysler	Toluca and Mexico City	CTM	0	No	0	−25	No	253
VAM	Toluca and Mexico City	COR	0	No	0	0	Yes	248
Nissan	Toluca	CTM	0	No	0	0	No	n.d.

Note: Data are for 1978 unless otherwise indicated.
a. A plus sign indicates union support for the griever; a minus sign indicates that union was cited as codefendant.
b. 1975 = 100; n.d. = no data; source, Ford Motor Company, *Proyección*, no. 14 (May 1981).

auto industry (and presumably in other industries as well) and deserves closer examination.

Turning to co-optation, what seems important is that the unions have a certain discretionary power over the allocation of fringe benefits, of which cheap housing is perhaps the most important. This inclusionary form of corporatism gives union leaderships considerable potential power over the rank and file.[63] Finally, it should be stressed that the unions in the Mexican automobile industry have successfully negotiated wage increases. Real wages in the industry have risen steadily during most of the postwar period.[64]

Generalizing from Automobiles

The automobile industry does not appear to be markedly atypical of Mexican industry as a whole. The general trend has been toward slowly expanding employment, low labor turnover, rising real wages, and few and predictable strikes. The Mexican miracle does not depend on absolutely low levels of real wages. After the wartime shock, all that was necessary was that wages not rise more rapidly than the rate of growth of the economy as a whole so that an increasing proportion of national resources could be channeled into capital accumulation and increased consumption for the higher income brackets. Thirty years of rising real wages no doubt is a contributory factor in explaining the relative passivity of the Mexican working class in the postwar period. It would be a mistake to attribute the passivity of organized labor solely to the machinations of the union bureaucracy (though this has played a very important role).

The crucial factor in the success of the Mexican model has been the predictability of strikes and wage settlements. In moments of crisis the official union bureaucracy has usually been able to count on the unconditional backing of the state. Only in the unusual conjuncture of the late 1960s and early 1970s was this no longer the case, and then the rise of the independent unions demonstrated quite clearly the problems that might arise from the development of mass rank-and-file activity.

Trends and Countertrends

The labor force in the Mexican auto industry is relatively new. It is quite young (though this varies from plant to plant), and turnover rates are very low.[65] For these reasons the question of the previous experience of the work force and the trends in recruitment are important. It is widely believed that the location of many of the newer plants in small industrial towns near Mexico City (Toluca, Puebla, Cuernavaca) has meant the recruitment of peasants. This seems to have been the case in Dina, but the evidence from Nissan in Cuernavaca suggests caution in generalizing from the experience of Dina. One study reports the previous job experience of Nissan workers as follows: peasant, 8.8 percent; services, 44.3 percent; workers (*obreros*), 33.0 percent; construction, 5.8 percent; no experience, 7.4 percent; and others, 3.6 percent.[66] These data should be treated with considerable caution.[67] Nevertheless the fact that a third of the labor force claimed to have previously worked as *obreros* is important.[68]

It is perhaps too early to speculate on the possible long-run effects of patterns of recruitment to the industry. However, the notion that the labor force is composed of peasants in any simple sense must be discarded. The workers in the factories located in the major urban centers appear to come, as might be expected, from families settled in those places rather than from recent migrants.[69] In the factories located in less urbanized areas, previous occupational experience seems to be in the direction of nonagricultural employment. Even in the case of the Dina plant, the result of preferential hiring provisions means that many new workers are the sons of older workers and, once again, it seems unwise to think of these people as peasants in any straightforward sense. It seems reasonable to expect the labor force in the industry to become increasingly homogeneous and proletarian in origin. The effect of this change on work force solidarity and on industrial conflict is uncertain.

At the same time that the work force is becoming more homogeneous, we are seeing, perhaps, a shift of power away from the union bureaucracy toward the shop floor due to the increasing salience of job control issues and the increasing role of the *delegados departmentales*. These factors operate irrespective of whether the union is official or independent.

The pattern of causality that we hypothesize runs as follows. Certain conditions (a weak regional CTM and the starting up conflicts of new plants) give rise to union democracy. Irrespective of the factors that initially gave rise to the existence of union democracy, once in place a democratic union will be more militant, will tend to increase the number of workers on *planta* contracts, and will increase the number of union officers. As the percentage of workers on *planta* contracts increases, conflict over work processes will increase. This will increase militancy and by raising the salience of the union for rank-and-file workers will generate an interest in maintaining democracy.

Hypotheses Examined

Neither the optimistic hypothesis nor the neo-*charro* hypothesis appears to describe the situation adequately, for two reasons: (1) the line of division is not UOI versus the rest, but UOI plus GM-CROC and Ford (after 1977) versus the rest, and (2) it may be true that the militant unions appear to be becoming less militant and less democratic, but there are also powerful forces at work forcing all the official unions to pay more attention to the rank and file. These pressures are most obvious in Ford and GM-CROC but also at work in the more oligarchic unions as well.

The pressures on the official unions to be more militant do not stem solely from factors internal to the auto industry; there are also national political factors concerning the role of the CTM in national politics. For most of the postwar period labor tranquility has been assured with the close alliance between the major official union organization, the CTM, and the dominant party, the PRI. The CTM has been run by an oligarchic clique centered around Fidel Velázquez who, as the undisputed national leader, has ruled the CTM with an iron hand. As Velázquez's possible retirement approaches, there is a lot of maneuvering going on to choose a successor and to unify the independents and the official unions in a new union confederation. The result is likely to be an increasing convergence of the two styles of unionism at a national level. As the Mexican auto industry is inserted into this complex process of restructuring the political alliances of organized labor, its immediate future is likely to be affected by these maneuvers. Whether these factors will have a long-run influence is unknown.

The Mexican labor movement as a whole is in a state of flux; it may be some years before the trends of development become clear, although substantial changes are likely to occur throughout the union movement. This does not necessarily mean that the CTM will lose its place, though a renegotiation of its position vis-à-vis the government is quite likely. On the other hand, the independent unions are now facing a difficult economic situation, slower growth than in the early 1970s, and more government and employer hostility.

The implications for the automobile industry are not clear. The likelihood of a single, UAW-style industrial union being formed is distant. We suggest that, given this fragmentation, there will be a slow evolution to a common style of bargaining and union organization in the industry. As questions of productivity become more salient, we hypothesize that *delegados departmentales* will play an increasingly important role and more conflicts will revolve around work-related issues. This will, in turn, provide the basis for rank-and-file opposition and will force even the most conservative leadership to respond to this potential threat.

The ways in which such a potential threat might be confronted are various, ranging from an increase in repression of the membership at one extreme to more militant and democratic unionism at the other. One important background factor will be the composition of the labor force. In marked contrast to the situation in Argentina and Brazil, the labor force in the Mexican automobile industry has an extremely low turnover rate.[70] The possible effect of this low rate and of the increasing amount of internal recruitment of friends and relatives has ambiguous consequences for the behavior of these unions. They may increasingly come to form a privileged sector of the industrial labor force. Whether this means that they will be a conservative labor aristocracy or use their position of relative privilege to press forward as a labor vanguard remains to be seen.

At the moment the Mexican automobile industry is in a phase of expansion. New investments are being undertaken. But despite the vast reserves of oil recently discovered in Mexico, there are a number of signs that the economy may be on the edge of a serious economic crisis. In the context of world recession and considerable reorganization of the international automobile industry, it would be unwise to assume that the Mexican automobile industry will continue to be in a position to make concessions to its workers. Given this uncertainty, the hypotheses we have put forward concerning the likely trends and countertrends in industrial relations in the Mexican automobile industry must be regarded as highly provisional. The outcome will depend very much on the consciousness and action of the auto workers themselves.

Notes

Financial support for the research presented in this chapter came from the Social Science Research Council and the Institutes of Latin American Studies at the Universities of Glasgow and London. I thank the participants in the

SSRC automobile industry seminar; my colleagues at Glasgow and the London School of Economics, in particular David Stansfield, Keith Bradley, and Keith Thurley; Mark Thompson, Ken Coleman, Francisco Zapata, and José Luis Reyna at the Colegio de México; and my research assistant, Miguel Zenker. Without the generosity and courtesy of many people in the Mexican automobile industry, this study would have been impossible.

1. Clark Reynolds, *The Mexican Economy* (London: Yale University Press, 1970). The Mexican economy experienced a downturn in the mid-1970s that undoubtedly affected the context in which the research was carried out.

2. See Pablo Gonzalez-Casanova, *Democracy in Mexico* (New York: Oxford University Press, 1970); Judith Adler Hellman, *Mexico in Crisis* (New York: Holmes and Meier, 1978); Roger Hansen, *The Politics of Mexican Development* (London: Johns Hopkins, 1970).

3. The mean number of strikes per year from 1940 up to the mid-1960s was 256. James Wilkie, *The Mexican Revolution* (London: University of California Press, 1967). These data refer only to strikes reported by the Secretaría de Trabajo y Previsión Social and are therefore probably an underestimate. It is, nevertheless, an extremely low figure.

4. F. Chevalier, "The Ejido and Political Stability in Mexico," in C. Veliz, ed., *The Politics of Conformity in Latin America* (London: Oxford University Press, London, 1967); D. Bennett and K. Sharpe, "The State as Banker and Entrepreneur," *Comparative Politics* 12, no. 2 (January 1980).

5. J. Bortz, "El Salario Obrero en el Distrito Federal, 1939–1975," *Investigación Económica*, no. 4 (October–December 1977).

6. For a brief history of Mexican labor, see Raul Trejo Delarbe, "The Mexican Labor Movement," *Latin American Perspectives* 3, no. 1 (1976).

7. Well-known cases include the petroleum and railway workers' unions. Antonio Alonso, *El Movimiento Ferrocarrilero en México* (Mexico: Era, 1972).

8. *Nueva Ley Federal del Trabajo Reformada* (Mexico: Porrúa, 1976), art. 371. The *clausula de exclusión* was used in an internal faction fight at Nissan in 1969 in an attempt to rig the elections for the union's executive committee. Secretaría de Trabajo y Previsión Social, Registro de Asociaciones, Archive.

9. Silvia Gomez Tagle and Marcelo Miquet, "Integración o democracia sindical: el caso de los electrecistas," in José Luís Reyna et al., *Tres Estudios Sobre el Movimiento Obrero en México* (Mexico: El Colegio de México, 1976); Alonso, *El Movimiento Ferrocarrilero*; Evelyn Stevens, *Protest and Response in Mexico* (London: MIT Press, 1974); Stevens, *Protest and Response*; Rogelio Luna Jurado, "Los Maestros y la Democracia Sindical," *Cuadernos Politicos*, no. 14 (October–December 1977).

10. Leopoldo Alafita Méndez, "Sindicalismo Independiente en México," *Memoria del Primer Coloquio Regional de Historia Obrero* (Mexico: CEHSMO, 1977).

11. Elena Poniatowska, *La Noche de Tlatelolco* (Mexico: Era, 1971); Sergio Zermeño, *México: Una Democracia Utopica* (Mexico: Siglo XXI, 1978).

12. Magdelena Galindo, "El Movimiento Obrero en el Sexenio Echeverrista," *Investigación Económica*, no. 4 (October–December 1977).

13. E. Contreras and C. Silva, "Los Recientes Movimientos Obreros Mexicanos Pro Independencia Sindical y el Reformismo Obrero," *Revista Mexicana de Sociología* 34, nos. 3–4 (July–December 1972).

14. Railways, textiles, secondary education, and electrical supply have seen the development of some of the more important independence movements.

15. CGT (Confederación General de Trabajadores) was founded in 1921 as an anarchosyndicalist organization. CROM (Confederación Regional Obrera Mexicana), founded in 1918 under the leadership of Luis Morones, was closely associated with the governments of Calles and Obregón in the 1920s. Both organizations experienced a rapid demise in the late 1920s but still retain some support in their original stronghold in the textile industry.

16. This was certainly one of the factors that induced Nissan to set up its second plant in Toluca rather than near its first plant in the troubled city of Cuernavaca. Interview with Nissan executive, April 13, 1978.

17. F. Zapata, "Afiliación y organización sindical en México," in Reyna, *Tres Estudios Sobre el Movimiento Obrero en México*.

18. The CROC (Confederación Revolucionaria de Obreros y Campesinos) was formed in 1952 and affiliated with the PRI, though it remained outside the CTM. The GM union's affiliation with CROC does not explain its democratic history.

19. New plants included Nissan in Cuernavaca, Morelos, VW in Puebla, Ford in the northern industrial belt of Mexico City (Cuautitlán and Tlanepantla), and VAM, Chrysler, and GM in Toluca, Mexico.

20. At the time of this research, Dina was producing Renault cars under license. See Victor Villaseñor, *Memorias de un Hombre de Izquierda* (Mexico: Grijalbo, Mexico, 1976); Victoria Novelo and Augusto Urteaga, *La Industria en Los Magueyales* (Mexico: Nueva Imagen, 1979).

21. The information in this table differs somewhat from that in Francisco Javier Aguilar, "El Sindicalismo del Sector Automotriz," *Cuadernos Políticos*, no. 16 (April–June 1978). In part this is due to differences in defining the universe. Our data refer only to companies producing passenger cars. In addition Aguilar's information for GM and VAM is incorrect.

22. For a classic statement on control and co-optation, see B. Anderson and J. Cockcroft, "Control and Co-optation in Mexican Politics," in J. Cockcroft et al., eds., *Dependence and Underdevelopment* (Garden City, N.Y.: Doubleday Anchor, 1972);. R. Michels, *Political Parties* (New York: Collier Books, 1962).

23. After 1976 collective contracts were renewed annually.

24. Fringe benefits usually include health care and insurance, sickness and accident benefits, paid vacations, access to subsidized housing, scholarships for dependents, and subsidized meals.

25. An impression of the amount of variation in monthly output may be gathered from the following data. The first number indicates mean monthly production in units and the second standard deviation for the period 1970–1977: Chrysler (2,514, 876), Ford (2,221, 806), GM (1,368, 552), Nissan (1,638, 542), VAM (1,401, 521), VW (5,568, 2563), Dina (1,414, 466). AMIA, Boletin no. 145 (January 1978).

26. It was not possible to obtain reliable data on the distribution of the work force between *planta* and *eventual* status for all companies. Moreover the data must be used with caution since short-term reductions in employment can (since the workers who are laid off are mainly *eventuales*) increase the *planta-eventual* ratio rapidly.

27. Interview with Chrysler management, August 2, 1978.

28. Cf. Villaseñor, *Memorias de un Hombre de Izquierda*.

29. Novelo and Urteaga, *La Industria en Los Magueyales*; and Augusto Urteaga, "Los Sindicatos de Sahagún" (master's thesis, Escuela Nacional de Antropología e Historia, 1977).

30. Secretaría de Trabajo y Previsión Social, Registro de Asociaciones, Archive; Sindicato de Obreros de la Planta de Montaje de la General Motors de México, Minutes.

31. This was repeated in the following year. *Uno Más Uno*, April 11, 1978.

32. This contraction was short-lived though quite severe. Since fieldwork was carried on during the phase of contraction, some of the conclusions of this chapter may have been influenced by this fact.

33. The *delegados departmentales* (department delegates) are somewhat akin to British shop stewards though with greatly reduced powers and privileges.

34. Sources are the various union contracts.

35. The following statements are based on a series of interviews with union leaders and industrial relations managers in the automobile companies in 1978.

36. The fact that three geographically separate plants are formed into a single union may be an explanatory factor. For the differences among the plants, see Aguilar, "El Sindicalismo del Sector Automotriz."

37. Interview with general secretary, Chrysler union, August 16, 1978.

38. This appears to be an unreasonable assumption. Seymour Lipset et al., *Union Democracy* (Glencoe, Ill.: Free Press, 1956), start from the assumption that union democracy is the exception rather than the rule. In fact, as J. Edelstein and M. Warner, *Comparative Union Democracy* (London: Allen and Unwin, 1975) suggest, union democracy is empirically more widespread than the Michels thesis would indicate. This seems also to be the case in Mexico.

39. Angel Fojo, "Estudio de un Conflicto Industrial: el caso Automex," unpublished manuscript (Mexico, 1973).

40. *Solidaridad*, March 31, 1970.

41. Aguilar, "El Sindicalismo del Sector Automotriz."

42. Junta Federal de Conciliación y Arbitraje, Archive.

43. Lucía Bazan, "Sindicalismo Independiente: El Caso de Nissan Mexicana," unpublished manuscript (Mexico, 1977).

44. Secretaría de Trabajo y Previsión Social, Registro de Asociaciones, Archive.

45. Ibid.

46. A number of works appear to assume that the Ministry of Labor will generally intervene to support entrenched union bureaucracies (for example, Alonso, *El Movimiento Ferrocarrilero en México*). On the basis of the fragmentary data on the automobile industry, it is not possible to say if this is a realistic assumption. The existence of contradictory evidence does suggest, however, that such interpretations of the behavior of the ministry may be somewhat one-sided.

47. This section is based on the Registro de Asociaciones archive and on a collection of union minutes.

48. A question arises about the validity of the data presented here. Union minutes indicate that, on several occasions, the meetings were delayed while workers arrived. It also seems that workers would be paid for attending.

49. Minutes.

50. These factions seem to be of a personalistic nature and sometimes owe their origin to particular sections of the work force. How this affects union politics is unclear.

51. Novelo and Urteaga, *La Industria en Los Magueyales*; Urteaga, *Los Sindicatos de Sahagún*.

52. See Edelstein and Warner, *Comparative Union Democracy*.

53. *Uno Más Uno*, May 23, 1978.

54. Ian Roxborough and Francisco Zapata, "Algunos Mitos Sobre el Sindicalismo en México," *Dialogos* 14 (November–December 1978).

55. VAM is run paternalistically. Interview with management, February 27, 1978.

56. State participation may have some effect on the conduct of industrial relations, though it is not clear what this might be.

57. The reason for the CTM's inability to control the situation in the auto plants in Mexico City remains a matter for speculation.

58. This two-tier system, common in the CTM, removes the top leadership from direct contact with, and accountability to, the membership.

59. Interview with Ford management, May 16, 1978.

60. As an illustration of what this situation meant, it may be noted that none of the Ford workers had access to copies of the collective contract. Interview with Ford management, May 16, 1978. This is no longer the case.

61. A sample of 100 individual grievances in the automobile industry presented to the Junta Federal de Conciliación y Arbitraje was analyzed.

62. A sample of 250 workers at one of the Ford plants indicated that 13.6 percent had previous experience in another automobile firm. The data were drawn from job applications in the industrial relations office at the plant.

63. For a distinction between inclusionary and exclusionary corporatism, see Alfred Stepan, *The State and Society* (Princeton: Princeton University Press, 1978). This implies a major difference in the power union leaders have vis-à-vis their members and also vis-à-vis the state between countries of inclusionary corporatism like Mexico and countries like Brazil and Argentina characterized by a form of exclusionary corporatism.

64. Bortz, "El Salario Obrero en el Distrito Federal, 1939–1975."

65. In Nissan in 1971 87 percent of the workers were twenty-nine years old or younger. Bazan, "Sindicalismo Independiente: El Caso de Nissan Mexicana." In the Ford sample taken in 1978, only 41 percent were under thirty. Thirty-nine percent were between thirty and forty years old, and 19 percent were over forty. Interviews with management suggested that voluntary quits were infrequent and that, because (in part) of the costs of firing workers with *planta* status, company policy was to hoard labor during recessions wherever feasible.

66. Juana Valenti, "Empresa, Sindicato y Conflicto: El Caso de Nissan," thesis, FLACSO, Mexico, 1978, pp. 83–84.

67. The figure for construction seems very low, and the meaning attached to *obrero* is open to debate.

68. The evidence from the Ford sample tends to support the conclusions of the Nissan data. Only 1 percent of the sample had previously worked in agriculture, and 28 percent had worked previously in large industrial establishments.

69. Fifty-four percent of the Ford sample had been born in Mexico City.

70. J. Humphrey, "Operários da Indústria Automobilística," *Estudos Cebrap*, no. 23 (1979); J. Nún, "La Industria Automotriz Argentina," *Revista Mexicana de Sociología* 4, no. 1 (January–March 1978).

7

Agenda Setting and Bargaining Power: The Mexican State versus Transnational Automobile Corporations

Douglas Bennett and Kenneth Sharpe

When the administration of Adolfo López Mateos took office in December 1958, there was no significant autombile manufacturing activity in Mexico.[1] Cars sold in Mexico were imported whole or as CKD (completely knocked down) kits needing only assembly. The new government saw the industry as an important candidate for import substitution policy, one that could help reinvigorate a growth strategy. With the automobile firms in Mexico showing no inclination to increase the scope of their operations, the López Mateos government sought to use state power to compel the manufacture of a substantial percentage of each vehicle in Mexico. Given the size of the Mexican automobile market and the prevailing economies of scale in the industry, this move to local manufacture could be accomplished efficiently only if the domestic industry were limited to a very few firms. This was a key point in the government's initial proposals. Because of the intense competition for new markets in the international automobile industry, however, this issue of limiting the number of firms—an issue of industry structure—became a particularly contentious one in the bargaining that ensued between the Mexican government and the major transnational automobile firms. A variety of other proposals put forward by the Mexican government, among them certain restrictions on the behavior of the firms that would constitute the industry and on the ownership of these firms, also became issues of contention because they were seen as threatening the firms' global strategies. Other proposals were not so contentious, however. The transnational firms (TNCs) sought to

Douglas C. Bennett and Kenneth E. Sharpe, "Agenda Setting and Bargaining Power: The Mexican State versus Transnational Automobile Corporations," *World Politics* 32, no. 1 (October 1979). Copyright © 1979 by Princeton University Press. Reprinted by permission of Princeton University Press.

mobilize their power to resist the more uncongenial proposals, and on some issues, including the key issue of limiting the number of firms, they succeeded.

In what has become the classic formulation, Charles Kindleberger conceptualized such relationships between TNCs and host country governments with regard to direct investment as one of bilateral monopoly—one buyer and one seller of a foreign investment project. "In a typical situation, a company earns more abroad than the minimum it would accept and a country's net social benefits from the company's presence are greater than the minimum *it* would accept . . . with a wide gap between the maximum and minimum demands by the two parties."[2] Thus viewed, economic theory could locate the outside limits of acceptability, but the precise terms of the investment would be a function of the relative bargaining strengths of the two parties. Equilibrium analysis must give way to power analysis, economics to political science.

This balance of bargaining power approach has proved a useful conceptualization in studies of TNC-host country government relations, but it is marred by certain recurrent weaknesses, which show its kinship with the pluralist approach to power in U.S. political science.[3] Our attention here is focused on two key issues. (1) Studies using the balance of bargaining power framework have tended to take as given the agenda of bargaining. They have concentrated solely on issues that happen to be topics of conflict and have failed to ask how this agenda was set. Which actors and which interests have been included in the bargaining, and which have been excluded? Why are some issues and not others contested by the parties to the bargaining? (2) There are weaknesses as well in explaining the outcomes of bargaining encounters. Sometimes there is a failure to distinguish between potential power and actual power, and thus a failure to explore obstacles to the full utilization of potential power in the determination of outcomes. Of equal importance is a tendency to conceptualize (potential) power as consisting simply in the possession of certain resources by each actor, an approach that gives little consideration to what relationships or circumstances allow something to serve as a source of potential power.

Agenda Setting

Like the behavioral-pluralist approach to the study of power to which they owe perhaps unwitting allegiance, studies of bargaining conflicts between TNCs and less developed country (LDC) host governments have tended to overlook questions of agenda setting. Consideration has been accorded solely to overt, visible conflicts, and the question of why some issues and not others become subjects of bargaining and conflict have been ignored. Peter Bachrach and Morton Baratz's discussion of the "other face of power" first called the attention of political science to such questions of agenda setting. Their concern was with the use of power to prevent some issues from ever forming part of the bargaining agenda.[4] There are other considerations in agenda setting that are equally important, however. Instead of excluding certain issues from the bargaining agenda, some key actors may be excluded. Denied access to the bargaining table, their particular concerns and interests may not be articulated unless some other actor has reason to put them forward. Particularly when the state is involved in a bargaining encounter, it may, for reasons concerning the state's social foundations, speak for certain class interests. In Mexico, for example, labor and national entrepreneurs had interests that were deeply affected by the shape of policy toward the automobile industry. Nevertheless the bargaining over that policy principally involved only the Mexican government and certain of the major transnational automobile firms (the U.S.-based ones). Labor voices were completely excluded, and national entrepreneurs played only a minor role. The exclusion of these actors did not necessarily entail the exclusion of their interest, however; in the bargaining the Mexican state articulated some interests of the national bourgeoisie, though the interests of labor went largely unrepresented.

Noting how and why certain actors and their interests are excluded from the bargaining provides one kind of insight into the formation of the bargaining agenda, but there is a further important point to be made about agenda setting. In focusing strictly on overt, visible conflicts, in taking these issues as the given agenda of bargaining, studies using the balance of bargaining power approach have tended to understate the areas of agreement between TNCs and LDC host country governments. In concentrating solely on points over which there is conflict, the two actors are presented as if they were antagonists across the board. The bargaining agenda can be more fully and deeply understood only if we attend to areas of agreement (over which there is little or no need to bargain), as well as to areas of disagreement, and this can best be accomplished by explaining the interests of the actors included in the bargaining in order to locate points of conflict and of convergence of interest among them.

In so proceeding we are taking interests as having an objective (or real) basis. Thus a careful consideration of the goals and circumstances of each actor will reveal its fundamental interests. This procedure diverges from the standard pluralist approach to power, which takes interests as merely subjective; an actor's interests are whatever it says they are, and no further deeper analysis or explication is possible.[5] In basic outline, the interests of our two central actors seem straightforward. The auto TNCs wanted to maximize broad international earnings; the Mexican government sought to promote industrial growth. That there were a number of strategies by which each could have pursued its central goal means that subjective considerations entered into the formation of these interests as well. Which strategies were adopted was not a matter of purely voluntaristic choice of actors, however, but rather something shaped in and by the national and international contexts in which the actors found themselves. Thus an examination of the bases of the interests of these actors will allow us not only to locate the points at which their interests converge and conflict (constituting a bargaining agenda) but also to anticipate how changes in their contexts of action prompt changes of strategy and interest.

TNC interests and the international automobile industry

Two central characteristics of the international automobile industry in the late 1950s and early 1960s were its high (and increasing) concentration and the internationalization of competition among the surviving firms.

The very earliest years of the automobile industry saw hundreds of firms producing cars in the United States, Great Britain, France, Germany, and other industrialized countries. The assembly line and other scale of production economies, however, coupled with the substantial degree of risk in the industry, served to promote steadily increasing concentration.[6] In the United States the number of firms in the automobile industry dropped from nine to four in the two decades following World War II. In Europe a similar process of concentration was taking place, tending toward a situation in which each major producing country had one national firm, which competed against a number of smaller foreign (usually American) subsidiaries.[7] The Japanese automobile industry was later in developing, coming to maturity only very late in the 1950s; but here too four firms accounted for 82 percent of automobile production by 1961, and further concentration was being actively promoted by the government. By 1973 this process of concentration had reached the point where two firms (GM and Ford) were responsible for over 40 percent of total world automobile sales and the largest eight for about 85 percent.[8]

Changes in the shape of competition among the major automobile producers have been both a cause and a consequence of this increasing concentration. Prior to World War II and extending into the 1950s firms sought to take advantage of scale economies through longer production runs to lower costs. In the post–World War II period nonprice forms of competition have predominated. In the United States particularly annual model changes and the need to supply a full range of models have been important factors in increasing concentration.[9] Until the mid-1950s the prevailing pattern was for the major producers to enjoy a well-protected market in their home base and to compete internationally only to the extent of exporting assembled vehicles to LDCs. The American firms with a less protected home market and with substantial foreign assembly and manufacturing operations (particularly in Europe) constituted a significant exception to this pattern. Since the mid-1950s, when there was a return of a buyer's market, however, there has been a substantial interpenetration of markets among the leading producing countries, facilitated in Europe by the European Economic Community but evidenced in the United States as well by the invasion of the market by European and Japanese small cars.

In the developing countries this internationalization of competition meant the end of the geographic division of markets among the major producers (the U.S. firms having concentrated on Latin America, the French and British firms on their foreign colonies, and so on). The slowdown in growth of the major industrialized markets led first the European firms (spearheaded by Volkswagen) and later the Japanese firms to begin a worldwide export drive. U.S. hegemony in Latin America was threatened, and this area "became a battleground in the competitive struggle within the automobile industry."[10]

The internationalization of competition in the industry—the new interest of European and Japanese firms in Latin America—coincided with the decision of a number of Latin American governments, Mexico included, to impel domestic automobile manufacturing.

The state's interests and the Mexican political economy

The problem of the interests of the state is particularly difficult conceptually, especially in view of the prevailing tendency (following

Weber) to identify the state in terms of means rather than of purposes. What is needed is a theory of the state or at least the outlines of one. Very briefly we view the state as having distinct and discernible interests but ones that must be seen as having been filled in or taken on by the manner in which a state comes to rest on particular social class foundations and by the manner in which it institutionalizes solutions to problems that are thrown up for it by the domestic and international political economy.[11] What, then, were the outlines of the Mexican state's interests?

By 1958 import substitution industrialization was firmly entrenched as the centerpiece of Mexico's strategy of economic growth. The country had insulated its domestic market during the Depression and World War II, and following the war a policy apparatus (import licenses, tariffs) was implanted to maintain the protection of the domestic market. Between 1940 and 1960 GNP increased at an annual rate of 6.3 percent, with the manufacturing sector (at an average annual growth rate of 7.7 percent) pacing the way.

The particular character of Mexico's import substitution strategy was conditioned by the changing social foundations of the Mexican regime. Of note here are the orientations of the state toward the Mexican private sector, labor, and foreign investment. Despite the strains of social radicalism in the Mexican revolution, primary reliance for investments for economic growth was placed on the private sector following that conflict. In the lack of a national bourgeoisie that could undertake the necessary entrepreneurial activities, the state set about creating such a class, one that became increasingly capable of influencing governmental policy as it grew.[12] State policy encouraged private investment in a number of ways: corporate and personal income taxes were kept low; an orthodox monetary policy (*desarrollo establizador*) adopted in 1954 allowed the government to finance its expenditures in an essentially noninflationary manner through the use of complex reserve requirements and selective credit controls applied to the private banking system; the state provided long-term, low interest loans through state investment banks and made investments in infrastructure and basic industries (steel, petroleum refining); and government policies allowed for the emergence of a skewed pattern of income distribution, which allowed an affluent managerial and professional class of sufficient size to spur the import-substituted consumer goods industries despite low per capita income. "Labor peace" was maintained politically through the corporatist organization of the ruling Partido Revolucionario Institucional (PRI), co-optation of labor leaders, and occasional repression. The resulting low wages and relative docility of urban and rural workers helped to encourage continued high rates of investment.[13] Thus while the national bourgeoisie was becoming an increasingly important actor whose interests had to be taken into account by the state, labor and its interests were most often excluded; this pattern was to characterize the bargaining in the auto industry in the early 1960s.

The Mexican state served domestic business interests in another important way: the revolutionary heritage made economic nationalism a hallmark of government policy for more than fifty years. In some sectors, among them natural resources, banking, insurance, transportation, and communications, foreign investment was excluded altogether. Such was not the case in manufacturing where import substitution, particularly as it moved into more sophisticated goods (such as automobiles), has required the technology, management capabilities, and marketing skills of TNCs. Increasingly since 1950 the policy emphasis in manufacturing toward foreign investment has been toward Mexicanization, the requirement that foreign investment be associated in a firm with majority Mexican capital, a policy that allows the participation of TNCs in the economy while preserving a role for the national bourgeoisie.[14]

The Mexican State and the Auto TNCs: Convergence and Conflict of Interest

The reliance on private investment, the political control of labor, and the expanding managerial and professional class proved attractive to foreign investment, Mexicanization notwithstanding. After World War II, as import substitution policy coincided with the expansionary thrust of U.S. TNCs, direct foreign investment in manufacturing increased rapidly, from $32 million to $602 million between 1940 and 1960. In automobiles and in other manufacturing industries, there was a particularly strong convergence of interests between government economic policy and the corporate strategies of the TNCs.

The government's initial intention, as early as 1925, was to encourage the assembly of vehicles from imported CKD kits. Ford took advantage of the modest tariff reductions offered and began assembly in 1926; General Motors followed suit in 1937; and a Mexican firm, Fábricas Auto-Mex, started assembling Chryslers in 1938. When import substitution was adopted as a conscious strategy after World War II, import quotas and additional tariff advantages impelled the creation of a number of other assembly operations. There was little conflict of interest here: the sending of parts in CKD kits still allowed TNCs the longer production runs and lower per unit costs in their home country plants that stiffened international competition required. In auto manufacture economies of scale are very much lower in assembly operations than they are in the fabrication of motors or in body stamping operations. In addition domestic assembly effected some economies in transportation costs.[15] When government policy moved from a concern with assembly toward an interest in inducing vehicle manufacture, however, the convergence of interest between the state and the transnational automobile firms began to disintegrate. How and why did the policy change?

When the López Mateos administration came to power in December 1958, the growth miracle that had been sustained for nearly twenty years faced serious difficulties. The easy phase of import substitution was facing exhaustion. Mexico had already initiated the domestic manufacture of many simple consumer goods, and investments were needed in certain industrial sectors if growth were to be sustained on this strategy. The attention of economic policymakers focused on a number of candidate industries, the automobile industry among them.

The Mexican automobile industry in 1958 consisted of eleven firms operating assembly plants. A small number of already assembled vehicles were imported by a number of other firms. The Mexican consumer could choose from among 44 makes and 117 models. Ford, GM, and Fábricas Auto-Mex were by far the dominant firms, accounting for three-quarters of the automobiles sold. Ford and GM were 100 percent foreign-owned subsidiaries; Fábricas Auto-Mex, long wholly owned by the Azcárraga family, sold one-third of its equity to Chrysler in 1959. The other assembly plants were smaller and wholly Mexican owned, assembling under license from foreign manufacturers.

A number of considerations recommended the automobile industry as a candidate for policy. Domestic manufacture of automobiles (as opposed to their mere assembly) would stimulate a broad array of other industries through backward and forward linkage effects. Automobile manufacturing would create a large number of new jobs. There would be foreign exchange savings: imports of parts and finished vehicles accounted for around 11 percent of Mexico's total import bill during the 1950s, and foreign ownership of the major firms (with resultant profit remittances) tended to exacerbate this problem. Argentina and Brazil had already moved to impel automobile manufacture, and if this set up an example, it also constituted a threat; if Mexico did not follow suit, these countries could pressure Mexico to open its markets to their auto exports under the terms of the Latin American Free Trade Area agreements.[16]

The initial planning was done by the Committee for Planning and Development of the Automobile Industry, an interministerial technical committee constituted in 1959 and headed by the principal state development bank, Nacional Financiera (NAFIN). On it were represented the Ministry of Finance, the Ministry of Industry and Commerce, and the Bank of Mexico. Final responsibility for formulating and administering the policy was given to the Ministry of Industry and Commerce.

On the basis of considerable staff research and visits to a number of countries (including several that had recently initiated automobile manufacture) but without much consultation with the transnational automobile firms (the bargaining came later), a report was prepared and approved by the Committee.[17] The emphasis in the report was quite consistent with the basic national industrialization goals followed by Mexico since 1940. It constituted the initial position of the government's highest economic *técnicos*.

The proposals embodied in this report can be divided into three areas concerning the structure of the industry, the behavior or conduct of the firms comprising the industry, and the ownership of the firms.[18]

Proposals concerning industry structure

Limitation of the number of firms in the terminal industry (the industry producing finished vehicles) to three to five firms.

Limitation of the terminal firms to motor machining and final assembly (other manufacturing to be reserved for a supplier or auto parts industry).

Creation of a central body stamping plant.

Proposals concerning firm behavior

Production of at least 60 percent of the content of vehicles (measured by direct cost of production) in Mexico.

Limitations on the number of acceptable makes and models produced by each firm.

Limitations on frequency of model changes (freezing of model years).

Standardization of certain parts.

Proposals concerning ownership

Majority Mexican ownership of firms in the terminal industry.

Majority Mexican ownership of firms in the supplier industry.

Table 7.1
Chronology

December 1958	Adolfo López Mateos becomes president of Mexico
1959	Ministry of Industry and Commerce reorganized
1960[a]	Nacional Financiera Report
April 1960[a]	Ford report
August 1962[a]	Automobile decree promulgated
December 1962–January 1963[b]	Approval of applications from automobiles firms
July 1963	Granting of tax incentives to firms
September 1964	Official deadline for compliance with the 1962 decree
Late 1964	Nissan application approved
November 1964	López Mateos administration leaves office

a. Stage 1.
b. Stage 2.

These proposals followed from the government's conception of what was required to sustain economic growth, but the transnational automobile firms saw a number of the proposals as threatening their corporate strategies. The bargaining that followed the emergence of this conflict of interests unfolded in two stages. The first stage encompassed the various discussions between the firms and the Ministry of Industry and Commerce prior to the promulgation of the August 1962 manufacturing decree and concerned the terms of the decree; the second stage concerned the submission and approval of applications by various firms to manufacture under the terms of the decree. Ownership and firm behavior issues were contested in the first stage. Ford, GM, and Fábricas Auto-Mex were the major TNC actors; they were the only transnational auto firms in Mexico with substantial capital already invested, and together they dominated the Mexican market. The number of firms to be permitted—the principal issue of industry structure—was negotiated through both stages; consequently all firms applying for entry (U.S. based and non-U.S. based) participated in this bargaining. (See table 7.1.)

The bargaining focused on four closely related issues.

1. The requirement of 60 percent local content. The government's interest here was clear; it was this requirement that was to move the auto industry from assembly to manufacture and thus to stimulate further import substitution industrialization.

The TNCs, however, were not eager to begin manufacturing operations. These would require new investments far greater than those in assembly plants (and the TNCs that merely licensed Mexican-owned assembly operations had yet to commit any capital investment to Mexico). The Mexican market was still quite small; it produced only 65,000 autos and trucks in 1962. Manufacturing in Mexico would mean surrendering important scale economies. And finally there were serious difficulties of supply; the existing auto parts industry was limited mainly to the manufacture of simple replacement parts. The creation of an adequate parts industry would be a substantial undertaking, one involving considerations of quality and availability, as well as of cost. In some cases necessary raw materials were not available at acceptable prices or at acceptable levels of quality.

Surprisingly, however, the firms did not take a position in bargaining that was foursquare against auto manufacturing in Mexico; the explanation lies in the emergent dynamics of internationalized competition among the firms in the world automobile oligopoly. As Knickerbocker has shown, direct foreign investment in competitive, product pioneering manufacturing oligopolies tends to conform to a follow-the-leader pattern of defensive investment. "Rival firms in an industry composed of a few large firms counter one another's moves by making similar moves themselves," seeing this as a risk-minimizing strategy.[19] When one firm in the oligopoly makes an investment, other firms defend their positions by making similar investments. The Mexican government (rather than an independent investment decision by one of the firms) triggered the process in the case at hand, but as soon as one of the firms agreed— early in the policy-making process Ford had expressed a willingness to commence manufacturing under the right conditions—the other firms were quick to follow. Eighteen firms submitted applications when the final decree stipulating automobile manufacturing was promulgated in August 1962.[20] Thus while it may not have been in the interests of the firms taken individually to commence manufacturing operations in Mexico, they were prepared to do so rather than risk the possibility of that market being conceded to a competitor.

Consequently the issue of local manufacture, the requirement that on average 60 percent of each vehicle be manufactured in Mexico, never became an issue of contention in the bargaining between the Mexican state and the transnational automobile firms.[21]

2. Limiting the number of firms—the central issue of industry structure. Structurally limiting the number of firms to no more than five

was a key provision of the Nacional Financiera Report's proposals, and this issue became the most important one in the bargaining. The Mexican government was attempting to learn from the mistakes of unrestricted entry of auto manufacturers in Brazil (eleven) and Argentina (twenty-one). The Mexican market was not expected to exceed a few hundred thousand vehicles annually within the next decade. Allowing the market to become fragmented among many firms, each with a multiplicity of makes and models, would result in overcapitalization and excess capacity in the industry and would lead to higher consumer prices and thus lower demand. Only a limitation on the number of firms would allow the industry to achieve the significant scale economies available in automobile manufacture.[22]

In view of the efficiency gains, probably none of the automobile firms opposed in principle such a limitation on the number of firms, though perhaps the American firms were made uncomfortable by a governmental stipulation of this sort. What troubled each of them was the prospect that it might be one of the firms excluded. This prospect particularly worried the American firms since they already had a major stake in the Mexican market. If the Mexican government were to provide a place for its state-owned auto firm (Diesel Nacional), favor producers of small autos, attempt to diversify the country sources of foreign investment, and give preference to Mexican-owned firms—all measures the government had indicated it was inclined to pursue—then a limitation on the number of firms would surely spell exclusion for one or more of the American auto producers. Consequently the issue of exclusion became a highly contentious one in the bargaining. In the first stage the American firms lobbied to have removed from the Decree any specific limit on the number of firms that would be permitted. In the second stage a large number of firms took steps to ensure that they would not be excluded.

3. The issues of firm behavior: standardization of parts, freezing of models, and limitations on acceptable makes and models. Like the proposed limitation on the number of firms, these various measures were proposed in the Nacional Financiera report to ensure greater efficiency in production; each measure would increase the volume of each part or unit manufactured and thus permit greater economies of scale. They became contentious issues in the first stage of the bargaining, in the writing of the decree when the U.S. firms were the major voices heard, because they threatened the dominant competitive strategies of these firms. In comparison with European and Japanese firms, the U.S.

firms favored a strategy of product differentiation based on annual model changes and stressing the performance characteristics of their motors (a leading candidate for standardization).

4. The ownership issue. The proposal of the Nacional Financiera report that all firms have majority Mexican ownership reflected the long-standing nationalist orientation of the Mexican state and its desire to encourage and protect Mexican private investment. Furthermore participation of Mexican investors might help ensure that the interests of the TNC subsidiary in Mexico would not be continually sacrificed to the global rationality of the parent when the two conflicted.[23] This issue, too, was negotiated in the first stage and became a sharp issue because it threatened a key article of operating procedure of the U.S. firms, particularly Ford and GM: 100 percent ownership of foreign subsidiaries. These two firms had adopted worldwide policies of not entering into joint ventures; an exception in Mexico could lead to a similar insistence on joint venture status in other developing countries.

While technically an issue of industry structure, the proposed restrictions on vertical integration of the terminal firms (limiting them to assembly operations, machining of engine blocks, and any manufacturing operations in which they had been engaged prior to the decree) were also aimed partly at ownership. Such a restriction would reserve a place for the national bourgeoisie in the manufacture of auto parts, particularly important if the American TNCs prevailed on the Mexicanization issue.[24] The TNCs opposed this limitation as well, though with much less vehemence. It would make them dependent on the quality, price, and availability of Mexican-made parts but did not threaten their entrenched worldwide competitive strategies. The proposed requirement would limit them to nearly the same array of activities in which they had come to be engaged in the United States (where, because of risk-sharing considerations, a large number of parts are supplied by independent parts suppliers).

The interests of the TNCs and the Mexican state conflicted most sharply over proposals concerning limiting the number of firms, certain issues of firm behavior (standardization of parts and model freezing), and ownership restrictions. Consequently these issues formed the major items on the bargaining agenda. Who prevailed, and why? Answering these questions requires attention to the bases of potential power and to the factors that influence an actor's ability to use fully its potential power in a particular contest. In considering these, we focus attention on the issue of limiting the number of firms. Not only was this the issue on which the interests of the actors diverged most sharply; it was also the issue that would most seriously affect the course of the industry and the success of future government regulatory policy.

Bargaining Power

When the Automobile Manufacturing Decree was promulgated in August 1962, it was evident that the bargaining of the U.S. TNCs had succeeded in changing rather considerably the proposals first being put forward in the Nacional Financiera report.[25] Automobile firms producing for the Mexican market would be required to incorporate at least 60 percent locally manufactured content in their vehicles, and limits were placed on the vertical integration of the firms. The Decree required nothing in the way of Mexicanization of the terminal firms, and the other proposals regarding firm behavior had been dropped. Most important, the Decree set no limit on the number of firms that would be allowed; ten of the eighteen firms that applied were approved. (For the ten firms that were approved, see table 7.2.)

Sources of potential power

The relative power of actors ought not to be gauged merely from the outcome of a conflict. Such a post hoc analysis of power tends to exclude any meaningful analysis of why a particular outcome occurred and surely forecloses the possibility that one actor had potential power it did not exercise.[26] The standard manner of conceptualizing potential power in the pluralist approach to power sees it as consisting in the actors' possession of certain resources. This passage from a distinguished work in the balance of bargaining power literature well illustrates the approach: "The foreign investor offers capital, know-how (technological and managerial), some opportunities of commercialization, and, among other possibilities, that of a certain structure of industrial development. The host country offers access to the home market (particularly in the manufacturing sector), access to natural resources (as in extractive industries), and access to special comparative advantages (such as cheap labour)."[27]

Variations in these resources explain differences in bargaining power. In the Mexican case the automobile companies had capital, technology, and administrative and marketing know-how; the government controlled access to the domestic market and could (through tax policy,

Agenda Setting and Bargaining Power

Table 7.2
Mexican auto industry

Firm and date of first approval	Makes	Ownership at time of first approval	Subsequent changes in status
Diesel National (DINA), December 1962	Renault	100% domestic (government)	1978: 40% equity sold to Renault; renamed Renault Mexicana; DINA continues as truck manufacturer
Fábricas Auto-Mex, December 1962	Chrysler	33% foreign, 67% domestic	1968: Chrysler increases equity to 45% 1971: Chrysler increases equity to 99%; renamed Chrysler de Mexico
Ford Motor Co., December 1962	Ford	100% foreign	None
General Motors de Mexico, December 1962	GM	100% foreign	None
Promexa, December 1962	VW	100% domestic	1963: 100% equity sold to Volkswagen; renamed Volkswagen de Mexico
Vehiculos Automotores Mexicanos (VAM), December 1962	American Motors	100% domestic	1963: 40% equity sold to American Motors; remaining 60% acquired by Mexican government 1977: Mexican government share rises to 94%
Impulsora Mexicana Automotriz, January 1963	Borgward	100% domestic	1963: renamed Fábrica Nacional de Automoviles (FANASA) 1969: ceased operations
Reo de Mexico, January 1963	Toyota	100% domestic	1963: ceased operations
Representaciones Delta, mid-1963	D.K.W.	100% domestic	1964: ceased operations
Nissan Mexicana, late 1964	Datsun	100% foreign	None

control of the labor force, and other means) influence the costliness of various factors of production. An additional resource that strengthened the hand of the government was its increasing technical expertise which it had gained by careful study of automobile manufacturing in a number of other countries.[28]

Conceiving of potential power simply in terms of the possession of certain resources, however, is not an adequate approach. Needed as well is an understanding of how an actor's potential power is shaped by the complex web of relationships—relationships with actors not directly party to the bargaining—in which each actor is enmeshed.[29] The relationships in which we are interested here are conceptualized somewhat differently by world system theory, by dependency theory, and by models of the international power structure and of "international organization," to mention a few of the more prominent contemporary analyses.[30] There are important issues separating these approaches, particularly with regard to how asymmetries in global relationships are conceptualized and made subject to empirical analysis. We intend to avoid entering the lists on behalf of any one approach by limiting our attention to the particular set of international and transnational relationships that bear on the case at hand. We focus especially on the relationships among the TNCs in the international automobile industry; the relationships of these TNCs to domestic firms in Mexico; the relationships between the Mexican state and the home country governments of the TNCs; the relationships between the Mexican state and certain domestic social classes (especially the national bourgeoisie); and the relationships among various ministries and agencies of the Mexican state. We will argue that it is the structure of these relationships that defines what constitutes a power resource; determines when such resources can be employed or withheld; and determines the potential for the entry of new actors into the conflict as allies or as enemies.

1. The structure of relationships defines what constitutes a power resource. One danger of a conceptualization that sees potential power as consisting simply in the possession of certain resources is its tendency to an easy but dangerously misleading supposition that power resources are "fungible," that the possession of power resources gives one a "generalized capacity" that can be employed whenever and wherever one pleases.[31] Power resources are not so interchangeable from context to context and from contest to contest. What serves as a basis of power in one situation may be worthless, perhaps even a liability, in another. This lack of fungibility of power resources is commonly paid due obei-

sance; what constitutes a power resource depends on the context, on who is trying to get whom to do what; the scope and domain must be specified.[32] Quite obviously the TNCs' control over automotive technology gave them only potential power in a context where it was desired that automotive products be domestically manufactured. But it is not sufficient (and power discussions rarely go further) merely to stipulate the context dependency of power resources. Rather than delimiting the appropriate context by fiat, we need an analysis that shows how and why certain resources come to serve as bases of power in particular circumstances. A central feature of such an analysis will have to be a specification of relationships of dependency and interdependency in which the actors are enmeshed and which serve to constitute certain resources as base of power.

If we say that Mexico's need for automotive technology made the TNCs' possession of such technology a basis of power, we need to ask the further question how and why such a need arose; it must not be taken for granted. Over several decades the Mexican state had committed itself to rapid economic growth, the continued provision of which had become a central basis of regime legitimacy. Import substitution industrialization, once adopted as the growth strategy, had requisites of its own. The threatened exhaustion of this strategy in the late 1950s had led to the targeting of the automobile sector for domestic manufacture. These are important features of the context, but they do not explain why technology and investments from TNCs were needed. A functional, if simple and inelegant, car of Mexican design was probably not beyond the bounds of feasibility.[33] What further is required to understand Mexico's need for the technology of the automobile TNCs is an understanding of the class structure that had evolved under import substitution and particularly the relationship between the Mexican state and the national bourgeoisie. For thirty years a national bourgeoisie had been nurtured to pace economic growth, and its increasing size, power and centrality to the growth project made it a key social foundation of the state. Import substitution had been propelled by burgeoning consumer demand—the demand of this national bourgeoisie and of the middle classes that had been spawned with it. These classes, however, had become accustomed to modern U.S.-style products; they would not have accepted a Mexican car. The relationship of the Mexican state to its national bourgeoisie thus stipulated that Mexico needed the sort of automobile industry that only the TNCs could provide.

If the context established Mexico's need for the technology of the automobile TNCs, a further question should be asked: how easily could the Mexican state have changed those features of the context that defined the need and thus constituted the technology as a power resource? Clearly, not very easily; it would have required fundamental changes in the strategy of economic growth and in the domestic class structure.[34]

2. The structure of relationships determines when power resources can be employed or withheld. Relationships of dependence and inter-dependence in which the actors are enmeshed shape which of their possessions and attributes may serve as power resources in a particular conflict, but other relationships may serve to limit the actors' freedom to commit or to withhold their resources as they please. A structure of relationships defining Mexico's place in the world political economy and the Mexican state's relationship to the domestic class structure defined a need for a certain kind of automobile industry and thus constituted the resources of the transnational automobile firms as sources of potential power; but the pattern of competitive relationships among these transnational automobile firms (in their worldwide competition) served to constrain sharply the potential for the individual firms de-ploying these resources to their own best advantages in the bargaining with the Mexican state. More precisely the follow-the-leader pattern of defensive investment that made the firms so eager to be allowed to produce for the Mexican market weakened their potential to withhold their participation if conditions and terms were not precisely to their liking. Knickerbocker had called the proclivity to defensive investment of TNCs a "trump card for the LDC": "When one member of the club makes a move, the others pant to follow; and by realizing this, the LDC is in a position to demand a high entrance fee."[35] Since the move to auto manufacture in Mexico coincided with heightened international competition, the potential power of the Mexican state was enhanced as the ability of the TNCs to withhold their resources was weakened. Had the industry been differently organized—had it, for example, been characterized by collusion and mutual forbearance strategies—the Mexican government would not have had such substantial potential power.

Given the pattern of international automobile competition, the Mex-ican state's control over access to the Mexican market was the most potent power resource available to either side in the bargaining, but it should be recognized that certain relationships constrained somewhat the Mexican state's ability to deploy this advantage to the fullest extent.

Most important, in its pursuit of industrial development along an import substitution route, Mexico had come to be dependent on certain industrialized countries, particularly the United States, for trade and capital inflows. These relationships shaped a set of needs for continued flows of trade and capital in a number of sectors that served to limit what the state could do in the automobile sector; a favorable investment climate had to be maintained if growth was to be assured. The Mexican government was forcefully reminded of this in 1960 and 1961, as it was formulating its automobile policy, when its relations with the United States deteriorated. Mexico's refusal to submit to U.S. pressure to support the trade sanctions against the Castro regime led the U.S. government and press to criticize what it called the left-wing tendencies of the López Mateos government. This perception was reinforced by a variety of new policies toward foreign investment—since taking power the López Mateos administration had nationalized the electric power industry and implemented important new policies in the petrochemical and mining sectors—which were branded by certain TNCs and conservative Mexican business interests as socialist. The effect was felt in a flight of capital of about $200 million between 1960 and 1961.[36] in this context the Mexican government had to be cautious in its treatment of the foreign (especially U.S.) auto corporations, lest policy in this sector threaten the wider growth strategy.

The Mexican state's relationship with its own national bourgeoisie also served to limit its ability to play this trump card of market access to fullest advantage. The Mexican state was committed to the development of a national bourgeoisie, and this class had become a key social foundation of the state. Especially if wholly foreign-owned firms were to be approved, it would have been politically disquieting not to show a measure of favoritism to some domestically owned firms.

3. The structure of relationships determines the potential for the entry of new actors into the conflict as allies or as antagonists. Having already established themselves in the Mexican market through their assembly operations, the three major U.S.-based firms (Ford, GM, and Fábricas Auto-Mex) could draw on support from their consumers and employees and, more important, from their distributors and parts suppliers (supplies of replacement parts and what few parts were procured in Mexico for original equipment). In bargaining, these major U.S. firms could (and did) call attention to the disruption that would attend their exclusion: Mexican owners would find replacement parts and service hard to find, the value of these vehicles would decline, their distributors would be

put out of business, and their Mexican employees would be put out of work. The distributors and parts supply firms made separate representations of these same points, but these were not powerful allies; they were weak and disorganized. No wider alliance between the TNCs and the national bourgeoisie—for example, depicting the attempt to exclude certain TNCs from the market as a general attack on private investment—was possible. This has been an effective strategy in other cases of LDC-TNC bargaining, but the Mexican state's clear intention to accord its national bourgeoisie special treatment in the automobile industry through the proposals for Mexicanization and for reservation of the supplier industry forestalled such an alliance.[37]

A more formidable set of allies on which the TNCs drew were their home country governments.[38] The potential power of these home country governments resided in their ability to influence the trade and capital flows between Mexico and these industrialized countries on which Mexico had become dependent. To grasp the potential power of these home country governments, we must return to the first two points: a set of interdependent relationships in which Mexico was enmeshed defined a need for resources over which the home country governments had a measure of control, thus constituting these resources as bases of potential power; and the asymmetric character of these trade and investment (inter-) dependencies meant that the home country governments were likely to be freer to commit or to withhold those resources than the Mexican government was to do or to do without them.

From potential power to actual power

How did the two major actors—the TNCs and the Mexican government—transform (or fail to transform) their potential power into actual power? As Keohane and Nye point out, "Political bargaining is the usual means of translating potential into effects, and a lot is often lost in translation."[39] Our concern will remain focused on the central issue of industry structure: how did the firms prevail over the government's efforts to limit severely the number of firms in the industry?

The mobilization of corporate power

The U.S. firms began early their efforts to mobilize their power to influence the terms of the decree. As the NAFIN committee was preparing its report, Ford was already preparing a detailed, two-volume proposal of its own. In frequent discussions with officials in SIC, the firms attempted to use their superior know-how to convince policy planners of the unreasonableness or impracticality of their proposals. On the issues of exclusion and ownership (mandatory Mexicanization would have been tantamount to exclusion for Ford and GM) and even on certain questions of firm behavior, the government *técnicos* were, however, unmoved.[40] TNC mobilization of support from distributors and parts suppliers also provided little leverage. Instead a major key to their success was the support they could mobilize from the U.S. government.

The Minister of Industry and Commerce was informed by the U.S. Ambassador that the Department of State would look unfavorably on the exclusion of the U.S. firms. Other high officials of the ministry were told that any such exclusion would be viewed as a "not very friendly act."[41] Precisely what was said, however, is not so important as how anything said on this issue by the U.S. government would be understood. The explicit backing given by the U.S. government to the interests of these TNCs in the bargaining conflict meant that auto policy would be linked with and would affect what happened in other spheres of the bilateral relationship and that sanctions might be employed beyond those strictly under the control of the three firms.[42] The particular context of the strained relations over Cuba and the recent capital flight meant that the president, ministers, and other officials of the Mexican government needed to be particularly sensitive to what was said during visits of high corporate executives and U.S. government officials.

Pressure may also have been forthcoming from the German government to ensure that a manufacturer of at least one German make was approved, but the Minister of Industry and Commerce's desire to include at least one manufacturer of a small, inexpensive car, (*auto popular*), his unwillingness to rely wholly on the state-owned Diesel Nacional (Renault) for this purpose, and the Mexican ownership of Promexa (Volkswagen) at the time of approval (the Mexicans sold out to the German parent a few months later) were probably sufficient in themselves to ensure the approval of the Volkswagen licensee.

The acceptance of Nissan's application two years after the legal deadline for approval, however, can be explained only by looking at another TNC–home country government alliance.[43] Nissan's relationship with its home country government made possible the utilization of an additional and unlikely power resource to gain its acceptance: cotton.

In 1963 cotton was the most important source of foreign exchange for Mexico, accounting for foreign exchange earnings of $196 million, over 20 percent of the total.[44] In addition taxes on cotton exports steadily earned the government about $15 million.[45] About 70 percent of these cotton exports went to Japan, Mexico's most important trade partner after the United States. The trade balance between the two countries ran strongly in Mexico's favor, however. In 1962, for example, while Mexico's exports to Japan valued $127.8 million, Mexico's imports from Japan totaled only $22.6 million. For a number of years the Japanese government had been pressuring Mexico to import more, even offering a loan of $100 million if there were some improvement in this regard.

The Japanese government used its position as Mexico's major cotton buyer as a lever to support Nissan: it threatened to cut cotton imports if the Nissan proposal were not approved. The threat proved successful.

Because of its historical commitment to the national bourgeoisie, the Mexican state's capitulation in approving some wholly foreign-owned firms weakened its ability, and perhaps its resolve, to turn down applications from some wholly or majority Mexican-owned firms. State-owned DINA had been assured of a place in the industry from the beginning. VAM was a well-established venture of Sociedad Mexicana de Credito Industrial, one of the country's largest industrial development banks. Fábricas Auto-Mex's hand was strengthened by its being majority owned by a wealthy and well-connected Mexican family. In the cases of Impulsora Mexicana Automotriz, Reo, and Representaciones Delta (all private firms, 100 percent Mexican owned), political favoritism and perhaps bribes rather than technical competence or financial clout were responsible for their being approved when other domestically owned ventures were rejected.

In total ten firms were approved to manufacture in Mexico, far more than the NAFIN report had recommended and far more than the size of the Mexican market warranted. When the government saw that it would not prevail in limiting the number of firms, it pinned its hopes on competition to winnow down the industry over the next few years. To a large extent this was a vain hope; the NAFIN report had correctly assessed that competition would not serve to drive out subsidiaries of the TNCs because of the ability of these firms to cross-subsidize their various international operations. Further since both wholly domestically and wholly foreign-owned firms had been approved, steps were taken to protect the national firms (both public and private) from the size and superior resources of the foreign firms. A system of production quotas was introduced which limited the production of each firm and thus ensured a market share for the Mexican firms.

On some issues the Mexican government succeeded in accomplishing its goals. The firms that had been approved would be required to manufacture 60 percent of each vehicle in Mexico. Further these firms would be limited to the machining of the motor and the final assembly of vehicles. Other manufacturing activities would be reserved for a supplier industry that needed to be created, and the onus would fall squarely on the TNCs in the terminal industry to assist in this development.[46]

The opposition of the American firms and their allies proved sufficient to have removed from the auto decree the other key requirements concerning product differentiation: freezing of models, standardization of parts, and limits on the number of acceptable makes and models. The question of the exclusion of these firms had been a particularly sharp issue in the bargaining, and when they prevailed on this, they won as well the right to manufacture automobiles in their accustomed manner, with product differentiation and annual model changes.

Organizational constraints on the exercise of state power
On certain fundamental issues—the number of firms, the ownership of the terminal industry, product differentiation—government proposals for rationalizing the auto industry were undermined. Looking at the potential power of the state, it is important to ask why the state's trump card—the pattern of oligopolistic competition in the automobile industry—was largely unplayed or underplayed.

At first glance there seems to be a simple and plausible answer: certain characteristics of the structure of dependence, particularly political and economic relations with the United States and Japan, allowed the TNCs to muster home government allies and change the game to one where Mexico's card was no longer trump. But it is possible that the Mexican state could have acted differently. There were alternative strategies, ones recognized by at least some high officials at the time, it might have pursued to take better advantage of its potential power.

In the case of the U.S. firms, a divide-and-rule strategy could have been tried, playing Ford and Chrysler, or both, against the remaining one(s). Alternatively the government could have yielded on the question of limiting the number of firms while insisting that these firms submit to much stiffer regulations of firm behavior (for example, limits on product differentiation) and on ownership. In the Nissan case the state might have responded to Japanese government pressure by negotiating for the entrance of substantial Japanese investment in some other industrial structure or even by calling its bluff; as some Mexican officials were aware, particularly in the Finance Ministry, Japan could not easily have found suitable alternatives for the long-fibered Mexican cotton needed for its textile industry.

The point is not to argue that these strategies would have succeeded but rather that the Mexican state had potential power and alternative courses of action that it did not employ. When an actor in a power conflict is a collectivity rather than a person, there may be organizational constraints on the use of potential power. For internal reasons the actor may not be able to draw on all of the potential power that theoretically is available. With a complex entity like the state, such internal constraints may stem from a lack of the organizational coordination necessary to wield its potential power to full effectiveness. To understand the internal constraints on the exercise of power in the case at hand, we need to consider the relations among specific agencies and departments and the bureaucratic politics of policy formation inside the Mexican government.[47]

Not only did the two ministries most centrally concerned with industrial policy, the very powerful Finance Ministry and the Ministry of Industry and Commerce, fail to coordinate in the making of automobile policy, they were seriously at odds during much of this period. Prior to the López Mateos administration, the Finance Ministry had control of the two principal policy instruments for industrial planning: tax policy and import tariffs and quotas. Such steps as were taken to encourage greater local content in the automobile industry were the work of the Finance Ministry's capable Department of Financial Studies. When the Ministry of Industry and Commerce was reorganized in 1959, it was given control over import tariffs and quotas; questions of automobile policy became principally its concern. The Finance Ministry resisted the diminution of its control over import policy, however, and the conflict between the two ministries became quite sharp, at times requiring presidential mediation. The Director of the Department of Financial Studies, who had been in his post a number of years and had considerable experience with the automobile industry, supported a much stronger automobile policy, along the lines of the original NAFIN report. Had there been effective coordination between these two ministries, Industry and Commerce could have had powerful support for taking a tougher line. But it proceeded alone, using import controls as its only tool. (Tax policy toward the industry was not negotiated until after the 1962 decree, and the Finance Ministry refused to grant the firms any fiscal incentives over which it had discretionary authority.) The making and implementing of automobile policy became a means by which Industry and Commerce established a sphere of autonomy, but the cost was a diminution of the state's effective power.[48]

Second, inside the Ministry of Industry and Commerce there were serious divisions. The Director and Subdirector of Industries had been deeply involved in the technical studies that preceded the bargaining (the NAFIN report, trips to other countries). Like those in the Department of Financial Studies (with whom they had developed close informal relationships; the antagonism was greater at the ministerial level), they believed that a much stronger policy could be successfully carried forward. Their superiors, however, the Secretary and the Assistant Secretary, felt that moderation and compromise with the companies was necessary. Why these top officials were reluctant to take a tougher position is difficult to know with certainty, but interviews with officials in and out of the ministry indicate that several factors were important. For one there was a difference of goals. While there was broad agreement in the ministry that limiting the number of firms was an important policy goal, these top officials also placed a high priority on diversification of the sources of foreign investment and hence were more inclined to look favorably on the applications of (for example) Promexa (Volkswagen) and Nissan.

The political situations of the Secretary and Assistant Secretary made their assuming a tougher position in the face of corporate pressure somewhat difficult. In the Mexican political system, the change of President every six years brings with it changes in all major policy-making posts. Although a person is unlikely to retain the same position, many do move to new positions of importance.[49] Cabinet Secretaries typically are the strongest precandidates for selection as the next president. Among other factors a politician's future will depend on the immediate political consequences of decisions he has made in the previous sexennial—the friends and enemies made, the controversies in which he had been involved. The incentive to pursue risk-minimizing strategies and to judge policies narrowly in terms of their short-run political consequences is strong. Since the deleterious effects of admitting too many firms to the industry would not be felt immediately, it would have taken an unusual person to chance a full-scale confrontation with

Ford, General Motors, and the U.S. government or with the Japanese government unless he had the support of the President.

Finally, there was close connection between Ford and the Minister of Industry and Commerce. This was not simply a personal relationship between the Director of Ford and the Minister. From the beginning of the López Mateos administration, Ford had taken a position openly supportive of Industry and Commerce's goal of moving toward automotive manufacturing. Following a strategy it had employed elsewhere in Mexico, the Ford director, newly arrived from Argentina, immediately put Ford's staff to work on a lengthy feasibility report and an accompanying proposal of what Ford itself would be willing to do in Mexico. Ford reckoned, quite rightly it developed, that such early cooperation would give Ford an inside track on approval and policy input that would result in a policy much closer to what Ford would find amenable. How much Ford's influence was responsible for the divisions within Industry and Commerce and how much it was made possible by divisions already there is difficult to determine.

Given the centralization of power in the hands of the President, lack of coordination and unity among the various ministries is not a necessary characteristic of the Mexican political system. It is possible that explicit direction and firm support from the President could have forged the interministerial and intraministerial unity necessary to act forcefully but tactfully in putting forward a stronger automobile policy. Indeed there is evidence from the interviews not only that a lack of direction left key officials on their own (and thus made it rational for them to pursue risk-minimizing strategies) but also that specific directives to ease up on the TNCs and to give favorable consideration to applications from certain Mexican-owned firms filtered down from the President himself at crucial points in the bargaining. In the context of the Mexican political system, only resolute guidance from the President could have made likely the execution of the steps necessary to fend off the pressures that had been brought to bear, and this guidance was not forthcoming.

Conclusion

The bargaining conflict between the Mexican state and the automobile TNCs between 1960 and 1964 was only the first round of what has proved to be an ongoing conflict. Policy has been renegotiated a number of times, most importantly in 1968–1969 and again in 1976–1977, but

○

this first round was the most crucial bargaining encounter because it set the terms within which the subsequent bargaining has ensued.

In natural resource industries, which have been the far more common subject of bargaining power studies, it has been asserted that the power of the state is lowest at the time of initial bargaining because of uncertainties about the amount, quality, and costs of extraction of the natural resources. Once the large initial investments have been made, however, the balance of power swings dramatically in favor of the state because the uncertainties are reduced and the fixed investments are hostage in the LDC.[50]

The situation is the reverse in a high technology, consumer goods manufacturing sector, such as the automobile industry. Here access to the domestic market is the state's principal basis of bargaining power, and that trump card can be played effectively only at the point of initial investment. Once the large initial investments have been made, the firms entrench themselves in the host country through their relationships with suppliers, distributors, labor, and consumers. Because such manufacturing enterprises are integrated into the local economy to a far higher degree than are resource extraction concerns, they establish relationships within the host country that significantly enhance their bargaining power, both by reinforcing the host country's needs for their kind of production and products and by laying the basis for mobilizing domestic allies. And as long as the industry is dependent on external sources of technology, the possibility of seizure of firms by the host country government is not a credible threat.

Other things being equal, then, the balance of bargaining power in such a manufacturing industry will tend to shift toward the TNCs rather than toward the LDC host country government. In such terms we can understand the paramount importance of the first bargaining encounter between the Mexican state and the automobile TNCs; this is when the structure of the industry was first laid down, the state might not again have the power to restructure the industry, and each subsequent renegotiation of policy has occurred within the bounds of the industry structure set down as a consequence of the first bargaining encounter. Both problems and alternative possibilities are defined within this structure.

The theoretical approach we have taken could be employed in the analysis of these subsequent bargaining encounters in the Mexican automobile industry or in the analysis of bargaining between TNCs and LDC host country governments in other countries and in other industries. We have been concerned with two central issues: agenda setting and bargaining power.

Agenda setting

Understanding the bargaining agenda requires understanding which actors or interests obtain access to the bargaining arena and which are excluded. The historically shaped character of Mexico's political institutions explains not only the exclusion of labor from the bargaining but also the articulation of certain interests of the national bourgeoisie by the Mexican state (despite the rather small role played directly by Mexican entrepreneurs in the bargaining). Once it is clear which actors and interests are to be included in the bargaining, understanding which issues become contested requires an analysis of the points of conflict and of convergence of interest among the major actors. By no means should it be supposed that the interests of TNCs and LDC governments conflict across the board; points of convergence of interests simply do not become bargaining issues. In Mexico, following World War II, an import substitution strategy laid the basis for substantial convergence of interest among the government and TNCs in a range of manufacturing industries. The convergence of interest in the auto industry, given the dynamics of competition in the world industry, went no farther than assembly operations, however. The exercise of state power was necessary to induce the auto firms to commence domestic manufacture. The requirement that these firms incorporate a minimum level of local content was not the most contentious proposal, however, because it merely propelled the firms further along a competitive trajectory on which the firms were already engaged worldwide. Other proposals—a strict limitation on the number of firms, ownership restrictions, and constraints on produce differentiation—did become major points of conflict in the bargaining because they threatened the established competitive strategies of the firms in the industry (particularly of the U.S.-based firms, the firms most active in the bargaining because of their prior market penetration).

Bargaining power

The potential power available to each actor to settle the contested issues cannot be understood as consisting simply in their possession of certain resources. Whether a resource can serve as a source of potential power depends on the context, particularly the structure of domestic and international relationships in which each actor is enmeshed. Such relationships help in defining which resources can serve as base of potential power. It was, for example, the relationship between the Mexican state and certain domestic classes that established Mexico's need for a domestic automobile industry and thus allowed the TNCs control over auto technology to serve as a power resource. That such relationships also serve to determine when power resources can be employed or withheld can be seen in the manner in which the pattern of competitive relationships in the world automobile oligopoly made each firm particularly eager to gain access to the Mexican market. Finally, such relationships define the potential for the entry of new actors into the conflict as allies, as with the firms' mobilization of domestic suppliers and distributors and of their home country governments.

Potential power must be carefully distinguished from actual power. An actor may have sources of power on which it does not draw effectively. In this conflict the TNCs drew more effectively on their potential power than did the Mexican state. The potential power that accrued to the Mexican state from the pattern of oligopolistic competition in the world automobile industry was a trump card substantially underplayed. Understanding why the state did not fully use its potential power requires that this host government not be treated as a single unified entity. Conflicts within and especially between various agencies and the lack of central direction from the president weakened the Mexican state's ability to draw fully on its potential power.

Notes

We would like to acknowledge the useful critical comments we received from Morris Blachman, Susan Eckstein, Michael Fleet, Louis Goodman, Rhys Jenkins, Rich Kronish, Ken Mericle, David Moore, and Miguel Wionczek. Funding from the following foundations made possible the larger research project of which this chapter is a part: the Tinker Foundation, the Social Science Research Council, the Carnegie Endowment for International Peace, and the Doherty Foundation. We are particularly grateful to the SSRC's Working Group on Latin America in the International System—Multinational Corporations in Latin America.

1. Many of the data are drawn from personal interviews with automobile industry executives and with government officials (in Nacional Financiera, Banco de Mexico, and the Ministries of Finance and of Industry and Commerce) active in the bargaining during this period. Our concern here is only with automobile and not truck policy, although the latter raises similar considerations and in

some cases was regulated by the same policy. A number of the issues discussed here will be more fully discussed in a larger work now in progress.

2. Charles Kindleberger and Bruce Herrick, *Economic Development*, 3d ed. (New York: McGraw-Hill, Inc., 1977), p. 320.

3. Among recent literature on this subject, see Theodore H. Moran, "Multinational Corporations and Dependency: A Dialogue for Dependentistas and Non-Dependentistas," *International Organization* (Winter 1978): 79–100; Theodore H. Moran, *Multinational Corporations and the Politics of Dependence: Copper in Chile* (Princeton: Princeton University Press, 1974); Edith T. Penrose, *The Larger International Firm in Developing Countries: The International Petroleum Industry* (London: Allen and Unwin, 1968); Raymond Vernon, *Sovereignty at Bay: The Multinational Spread of U.S. Enterprises* (New York: Basic Books, 1971), chap. 3; and Raymond F. Mikesell, ed., *Foreign Investment in the Petroleum and Mineral Industries: Case Studies of Investor-Host Country Relations* (Baltimore: Johns Hopkins Press, 1971), chap. 2. For one of the few other case studies of a manufacturing industry, see Gary Gereffi, "Drug Firms and Dependency in Mexico: The Case of the Steroid Hormone Industry," *International Organization* (Winter 1978): 237–286.

4. Peter Bachrach and Morton Baratz, "The Two Faces of Power," *American Political Science Review* 56 (1962): 947–952.

5. For a discussion of the place of the concept of interest in analyses of power and a critique of purely subjective conceptions, see Steven Lukes, *Power: A Radical View* (London: Macmillan Press, 1974).

6. On the role that risk plays in the automobile industry, see Lawrence J. White, *The Automobile Industry since 1945* (Cambridge: Harvard University Press, 1971), pp. 7–9, 44–49.

7. Rhys Owen Jenkins, *Dependent Industrialization in Latin America: The Automotive Industry in Argentina, Chile and Mexico* (New York: Praeger Publishers, 1977), p. 20.

8. The largest eight, in order, were GM, Ford, Chrysler, Fiat, Volkswagen, Toyota, Nissan, and Renault. "New Strategies for a World Auto Market," *Business Week*, November 24, 1973, p. 38.

9. White, *Automobile Industry*. See also J. A. Menge, "Style Change Costs as a Market Weapon," *Quarterly Economic Journal* 76 (1962): 632–647.

10. Jenkins, *Dependent Industrialization*, p. 49.

11. For a fuller elaboration of this view, see Douglas Bennett and Kenneth Sharpe, "The State as Banker and as Entrepreneur: The Last Resort Character of the Mexican State's Economic Interventions, 1917–1970," *Comparative Politics* 12 (1980): 165–189.

12. For a more detailed discussion, see Bennett and Sharpe, "State as Banker."

13. Details on these aspects of the Mexican context are provided by Roger D. Hansen, *The Politics of Mexican Development* (Baltimore: Johns Hopkins Uni-

versity Press, 1971); Susan Eckstein, *Poverty of Revolution* (Princeton: Princeton University Press, 1977); William P. Glade, Jr., and Charles Anderson, *The Political Economy of Mexico* (Madison: University of Wisconsin Press, 1968).

14. On Mexican policy toward foreign investment, see Harry K. Wright, *Foreign Enterprise in Mexico* (Chapel Hill: University of North Carolina Press, 1971); and Douglas Bennett, Morris Blachman, and Kenneth Sharpe, "Mexico and Multinational Corporations: An Explanation of State Action," in Joseph Grunwald, ed., *Latin America and World Economy: A Changing International Order* (Beverly Hills: Sage Publications, 1978).

15. Jenkins, *Dependent Industrialization*, pp. 39–40.

16. On these goals, see the statement of López Mateos's secretary of industry and commerce, Raúl Salinas Lozano, in *Comercio Exterior* (August 1964): 547–548, and his introduction to Hector Vazquez Tercero, *Una Década de Política Sobre la Industria Automotriz* (Mexico: Editorial Tecnos, 1975), pp. 5–10. In interview a number of officials of the Ministry of Commerce argued that the balance of payments was not a primary concern (since domestic manufacture would create its own imports, for machinery and raw materials). In their view industrial growth and employment were the principal concerns.

17. Nacional Financiera, *Elementos para Una Politica de Desarrollo de la Fabricacion de Vehiculos Automotrices en Mexico* (Mexico, D.F.: Nacional Financiera, 1960).

18. The notions of industry structure and firm behavior are drawn from industrial organization theory. See Joe S. Bain, *Industrial Organization* (New York: John Wiley, 1959). The presumption underlying industrial organization theory is that structure affects behavior and behavior in turn leads to a performance (the sorts of contributions that an industry makes to the well-functioning of an economy) that can be judged against certain standards. Like economic theory more generally, it takes ownership to be irrelevant, posting a rational actor to be at the direction of the firm. A different presumption has underlain the policies of the Mexican government (among others) toward direct foreign investment—a presumption that the nationality of ownership of firms does make a difference for firm behavior and thus industry performance. Industry performance can be seen from a variety of perspectives that may not be compatible. Performance standards may attend (traditionally) to the contributions of the industry to aggregate growth and stability, or they may be concerned with the distribution of benefits within the economy, the satisfaction of the basic needs of the poorer segments of the populace.

19. Frederick T. Knickerbocker, *Oligopolistic Reaction and Multinational Enterprise* (Boston: Harvard University School of Business Administration, 1973), p. 1. Cf. Jenkins, *Dependent Industrialization*, pp. 40–42. For a discussion of oligopolistic reaction in another industry in Mexico, see Gereffi, "Drug Firms and Dependency in Mexico," pp. 271–272.

20. The same pattern of oligopolistic reaction is apparent all over Latin America. When Brazil imposed its manufacturing requirements in 1956, eleven firms commenced manufacturing operations; when Argentina announced its policy

in 1959, twenty-two firms made the necessary investments; in Chile, twenty; in Venezuela, sixteen; in Peru, thirteen. Jenkins, *Dependent Industrialization,* p. 56.

21. This requirement was made more palatable by its being considerably lower than the mandatory levels of local content that had been required by Brazil and Argentina a few years before and by certain attractive tax exemptions. On these tax exemptions, see ibid., pp. 54–55. Jenkins takes pains to argue, however, that these tax incentives themselves were not responsible for a large number of firms being willing to commence manufacturing. With regard to the 60 percent level of local content, it was the intention of the Mexican policymakers to start at this lower level in order to minimize the inflationary consequences of the transition to domestic manufacture (low inflation being a key goal of government policy). As the industry grew in size and efficiency, they conceived of a gradual increase to higher levels.

22. On these economies of scale, see White, *Automobile Industry,* pp. 38–53, and Jenkins, *Dependent Industrialization,* pp. 265–271. Even such otherwise staunch defenders of free trade as I. M. D. Little, Tibor Scitovsky, and Maurice Scott advocate the use of investment controls by developing countries to limit the number of firms in an industry with significant scale economies, and they single out automobiles as an example; see their *Industry and Trade in Some Developing Countries: A Comparative Study* (London: Oxford University Press, 1970), p. 342. Another proposal put forward in the Nacional Financiera report, the establishment of a single, central body stamping plant, was aimed at this same goal. The plant, to be developed by Altos Hornos, the state steel firm, would make it possible for all manufacturers to use the same body stamping presses, only the stamping dies needing to be changed for each firm. And if models were extended for several years each, these dies could be used to nearly full efficiency.

23. On the sometimes dubious logic of equity participation as a means to control TNC behavior, see Douglas Bennett and Kenneth Sharpe, "El Control de las Multinacionals: Las Contradicciones de la Mexicanización," *Foro Internacional* 21, no. 4 (April–June 1981).

24. Such restrictions on vertical integration would have two other effects as well: they would encourage economies of scale by avoiding the duplication of parts manufacture in each terminal firm, and they would allow better regulation of the 60 percent local content requirement by making it more difficult for the terminal industry to manipulate percentages through transfer pricing.

25. For the full text of the decree, see *Diario Oficial de la Federacion,* August 25, 1962.

26. For a recent employment of these concepts of potential and actual power in a general approach to international relations, see Robert O. Keohane and Joseph S. Nye, *Power and Interdependence: World Politics in Transition* (Boston: Little, Brown, 1977), pp. 11, 53, and passim.

27. Constantine V. Vaitsos, *Intercountry Income Distribution and Transnational Enterprises* (Oxford: Clarendon Press, 1974), p. 119.

28. This resource was different in kind from the other resources since it could not (as the other resources could) be used or withheld as a sanction. It was an infraresource rather than an instrumental resource; it allowed other resources to be used to better advantage. On this notion of infraresources, see Mary F. Rogers, "Instrumental and Infra-Resources: The Bases of Power," *American Journal of Sociology* 79, no. 6 (May 1974): 1418–1433.

29. This myopia arises partly from the strictly diadic character of the standard pluralist conception of power. Such an approach abstracts the actors from all other significant relationships in which they are engaged and thus seeks to locate potential power apart from these other significant relationships.

30. See Immanuel Wallerstein, *The Modern World System* (New York: Academic Press, 1974) for the world system theory. Among a voluminous literature on dependency theory, see Theotonio do Santos, "The Structure of Dependence," *American Economic Review* (1970): 231–236, and Fernando Henrique Cardoso and Enzo Faletto, *Dependency and Development in Latin America* (Berkeley: University of California Press, 1969, 1979). On the international aspect, see Keohane and Nye, *Power and Interdependence*, pp. 42–49, 54–58.

31. From Talcott Parsons whose suggestion that power be seen on the analogy of money particularly leads to the erroneous supposition of the fungibility of power. See Talcott Parsons, "On the Concept of Political Power," in *Sociological Theory and Modern Society* (New York: Free Press, 1967). For a necessary corrective, see David Baldwin, "Money and Power," *Journal of Politics* 33 (August 1971): 578–614.

32. Thus, for example, Robert Dahl: "The domain of an actor's influence consists of the other actors influenced by him. The scope of an actor's influence refers to the matters on which he can influence them. . . . Any statement about influence that does not clearly indicate the domain and scope it refers to verges on being meaningless." *Modern Political Analysis*, 3d ed. (Englewood Cliffs, N. J.: Prentice-Hall, 1976), p. 33. For a recent and thorough review of the power literature that pays particular attention to the questions of the fungibility and context dependency of power resources, see David Baldwin, "Power Analysis and World Politics: New Trends vs. Old Tendencies," *World Politics* (January 1979).

33. The state-owned Diesel Nacional S.A. had already begun work on a medium truck of its own design. It embodied some imported components, some components manufactured under license, and the consulting services of a Detroit engineering firm, but it was nonetheless a Mexican truck and proved to be a successful venture.

34. Thus in Keohane and Nye's terminology, Mexico was both "sensitive" and "vulnerable" to this power resource of the TNCs. "Sensitivity involves degrees of responsiveness within a policy framework" or context, and vulnerability refers to the "relative availability and costliness of the alternatives the various actors face"—that is, this second question of how easily a context or policy framework can be altered. Keohane and Nye, *Power and Interdependence*, pp. 12–13.

35. Knickerbocker, *Oligopolistic Reaction*, pp. 197–198.

36. Miguel Wionczek, *El Nacionalisimo y la Invérsion Extranjera* (Mexico, D.F.: Siglo Veintiuno Editores, 1967), pp. 240–241.

37. For such an alliance in the bargaining over copper concessions in Chile, see Moran, *Multinational Corporations*, pp. 190–197, and for such an alliance in Venezuela in the bargaining over oil concessions, see Franklin Tugwell, *The Politics of Oil in Venezuela* (Stanford: Stanford University Press, 1975). For a general discussion of the conditions under which such alliance between TNCs and the national bourgeoisie may form, see Moran, "Multinational Corporations and Dependency," pp. 93–95.

38. For one discussion of the relationships between TNC automobile firms and their home country governments that especially attends to European automobile firms, see Louis T. Wells, "Automobiles," in Raymond Vernon, ed., *Big Business and the State* (Cambridge, Mass.: Harvard University Press, 1974). For a discussion that illuminates certain aspects of the relationship of the U.S. and Japanese governments toward their own automobile industries, see William Chandler Duncan, *U.S.–Japan Automobile Diplomacy* (Cambridge, Mass.: Ballinger Publishing Co., 1973).

39. Keohane and Nye, *Power and Interdependence*, p. 11. See Moran, *Multinational Corporations*, pp. 169–215.

40. It does seem, however, that they did not fully appreciate how much the pattern of oligopolistic competition strengthened their hand or how zealously the firms would press their cases in their eagerness to be included.

41. Though it was majority Mexican owned, a well-publicized (and rather unusual) visit by U.S. Ambassador Thomas Mann to the Fábricas Auto-Mex plant in August 1961 made it clear that the United States was interested in the treatment of this firm, as well as of Ford and GM's wholly owned subsidiaries.

42. Another documented case of U.S. government intervention on the part of Ford, GM, and Chrysler over somewhat similar issues is well documented in Duncan, *U.S.–Japan Automobile Diplomacy*.

43. An application from a wholly Mexican-owned venture to manufacture Datsuns had been turned down during the normal period of application, though the approval of Reo allowed the manufacture of one Japanese make (Toyota). With Reo's failure in the first year, however, no Japanese makes were included in the Mexican market.

44. Raúl Salinas Lozano, *Memoria de Labores, 1963* (Mexico, D.F.: Secretaria de Industria y Comercio, 1963), pp. 136–137; *Comercio Exterior* (May 1961): 287.

45. *Comercio Exterior* (March 1963): 167.

46. In later bargaining some of the terminal firms have secured approval for more vertical integration; for example, a number of firms now have approval to cast their own engine blocks, and Volkswagen is permitted to make its own body stampings.

47. See the discussion of divisions within the Mexican state as weakening its bargaining position vis-à-vis foreign drug companies in Gereffi, "Drug Firms and Dependency," pp. 279–284. Considerations of the organizational constraints within the TNCs themselves are similarly important to a full analysis of the transformation of potential into actual power. See ibid. for a broad general discussion, see also Alfred D. Chandler, Jr., *Strategy and Structure: Chapters in the History of the American Industrial Enterprise* (Cambridge, Mass.: MIT Press, 1962).

48. Parallel to this lack of coordination was the failure of Industry and Commerce to make any use of the state's own automobile firm, Diesel Nacional, nominal control over which lay with yet a third ministry—National Properties. Dina could have been a valuable source of technical and financial information about automobile manufacturing, and it could have been allotted a place in the industry that would have made it a tool of industrial policy (a competitive check on the other firms). Dina's earlier troubles hardly inspired confidence.

49. Peter Smith, "Does Mexico Have a Power Elite?" in Richard S. Weinert and Jose Luis Reyna, eds., *Authoritarianism in Mexico* (Philadelphia: ISHI Publications, 1977).

50. On this argument, see Moran, *Multinational Corporations*, pp. 157–162.

8

Bargaining Relations in the Colombian Motor Vehicle Industry

Michael Fleet

This chapter analyzes the Colombian motor vehicle industry in terms of host country–transnational (TNC) bargaining relations, placing its somewhat halting development to date in the context of interacting governmental, transnational, and domestic forces and interests. It is specifically concerned with how the Colombians were able to exploit their relatively modest appeal in the initial negotiations with TNCs and why they have been unable to enforce fulfillment of these contracts.

The Colombian case is not easily judged in terms of host country success or failure. In general Colombian governments have failed to provide the incentives and ultimatums necessary to structure the industry as they had hoped. Their efforts have been undermined by a lack of policy consistency and continuity, by the cross-cutting pressures of domestic economic groups, and by the adaptive and retaliatory power of the TNCs. This failure to enforce contract compliance may not be evidence of either weakness or defeat, however. Expansion of the industry entails relatively high social costs, and it could be argued that the state has prevailed over transnational and domestic firms that sought rapid growth by restraining this expansion. In the analysis that follows, I argue that this is not the case. Neither domestic nor transnational interests presumably committed to expansion have suffered hardship or even relative deprivation, and both have been quite happy to move slowly at this stage.

Too often bargaining analysts focus only on the perceived or defined interests of the parties and simply conclude that those who got what they initially appeared to want did so because of superior leverage or power. They do not evaluate the agreement itself to determine whose objective interests it favors or to explain how and why it was reached.

The bargaining approach used here differs from this conventional version in several important respects. First, it considers much of the ostensible or visible bargaining between governments and corporations to be staged for political purposes and hence potentially misleading as far as the real interests and intentions of both parties are concerned. Second, it in no way assumes either wholly or even largely conflicting interests on the part of the bargaining partners. In fact it argues that broad agreement often exists on key issues that are never placed on the bargaining agenda, that these constitute the parameters within which actual bargaining occurs. Third, it evaluates bargaining relationships as ongoing processes encompassing not just the negotiation of agreements but their implementation as well. And finally, it attempts to treat both the state and the TNCs as complex entities containing contradictory forces and impulses, affected by changing contexts, and influenced by other parties (including labor unions, rival TNCs, domestic industrial and financial interests, and political allies).

Colombian Motor Vehicle Industry

During the mid- and late 1960s, Colombia was an unevenly developed country with a low per capita income and an extremely unequal income distribution. Its economy was largely agricultural, although light industrialization had begun as early as the 1920s. The agricultural sector was divided between relatively efficient, and often export-oriented, coffee, cotton, sugar, and rice producers on the one hand and subsistence plot holders and inefficient landed aristocrats on the other. The aristocrats' economic and political fortunes had declined steadily since the late 1940s. The emerging industrial sector included textiles, leather goods, food processing and beverages, and other light industrial activities, although more recently it had expanded into petrochemicals, pharmaceuticals, and other industries in which foreign capital and technology were dominant and domestic value added generally low.

The rivalry and conflict that in other countries developed between agriculture and industry were mitigated in Colombia by the fact that it was often agricultural interests who initiated the industrial undertakings, providing both entrepreneurial talent and financing. Financing usually was provided by one of the country's five major financial groups through which commercial agricultural interests had initially entered the profitable banking and insurance areas. An important consequence of this was a certain fusion of commercial agricultural and industrial interests, with emphasis being placed on one and/or the other in keeping with market conditions and opportunities.[1]

The country's political parties, while important in terms of local (provincial) economic interests and national electoral campaigns (in which clientilistic politics predominated), do not play much of a role in economic planning or policymaking. Instead interested and affected parties (individuals and associational groups) approach the president and the executive branch directly, using both personal ties and institutionalized consultation to press their concerns.

Groups like FEDECAFE (the national federation of coffee growers), ANDI (the national association of manufacturers), and FENALCO (the national merchants association) are among the more important organized interests and are regarded as extremely influential politically.[2] All three were early supporters on the National Front arrangement that brought an end to the years of virtual civil war between 1946 and 1953. Although it was a political success, the National Front was unable to resolve economic and social problems created by general stagnation, continuing mechanization of agriculture, and the resulting influx of jobless rural émigrés into already burgeoning cities.

In 1966 these groups joined liberals and conservatives in support of the *desarrollista* strategy of the Carlos Lleras government (1966–1970), which promised both economic growth and enough social progress (jobs, social services, agrarian reform) to ensure stabilization of the existing socioeconomic order. Lleras's program combined export diversification with general industrial development in which a domestic automobile industry, and hence metallurgical and metalworking industries, would play prominent roles.

Motor vehicle assembly facilities had been established in the country in 1960. Colmotores, which produced Austin (and would later produce Chrysler) cars and trucks, and Leonidas Lara e Hijos, which assembled Willys jeeps and International trucks, began operations that year. Neither was able to maintain regular production schedules, however, and as late as 1967 their combined output was fewer than 2,700 units.[3]

The industry's consolidation came with its restructuring under Lleras. In terms of then prevailing (late 1960s, early 1970s) auto industry contracts, the Colombian government struck relatively favorable bargains. First and perhaps most important, it succeeded in limiting the number of firms operating assembly plants. Initially there was to be a single producer of small cars, although subsequently the two firms already assembling larger cars (Chrysler Colmotores and Lara) were permitted to introduce competing models. Second, the contracts with two of the three (Renault and Fiat) called for joint ventures with Colombian government, with the Renault operation to be financed entirely by French investments and credits. And finally, all three contained provisions requiring the progressive incorporation of domestically produced parts and components and not simply the assembly of parts produced elsewhere. In addition, instead of the concession of autonomy and tariff and tax exemptions that characterized some Latin American contracts, there were provisions establishing export commitments (to compensate for increasing imports) and production quotas (requiring production of certain numbers of buses, trucks, taxis, and economy cars in line with national transportation needs).

The first contract was signed with Renault in 1969 after several years of intense bargaining and negotiations. The French firm, an autonomous state enterprise, was awarded production rights for small passenger cars in a joint venture with the Colombian government's Industrial Development Institute (IFI). In addition to setting up assembly operations, Renault agreed to install and equip a motor plant producing 20,000 units a year (of which 5,000 would be exported) to guarantee additional annual purchases of Colombian exports (including auto parts) equal to the amount of French components and parts (CKD) shipped to Colombia, to offer low interest (3.5 percent, 6 percent, and 8 percent) short- and long-term credits for the purchase of machinery and CKD packs, to incorporate those locally produced parts and pieces indicated by the government and/or available in the required amounts with the necessary technical specifications and at a reasonable cost, and finally, through credits from the French government, to finance both its own and IFI's initial capital outlay ($4 million). In addition to a 50 percent share in the assembly operation (SOFASA), the Colombians would hold 70 percent of the stock in the motor plant (SOCOFAM) and 30 percent in the retailing division (Renault de Colombia).[4]

In 1970 when the assembly licenses of Chrysler Colmotores and Leonidas Lara e Hijos expired, the government used the Renault contract as a precedent for demanding similar terms in negotiating their renewal. It insisted that both firms make better use of locally produced parts than they had been (a minimal 19 percent). Chrysler was permitted to remain under majority foreign ownership for the time being, but the rest of its contract was quite similar to that with Renault. Instead of a motor plant and export obligations, however, Chrysler was asked to commit $10 million in financial and technical assistance over the next ten years to promote the national auto parts industry.[5]

Lara, a locally owned family business assembling Peugeots, Yugo-
slavian Fiats, Jeeps, and International trucks under licensing agreements,
received special treatment. But in 1972 it was forced to merge with IFI
and Fiat to form the Compañía Colombiana Automotriz (CCA), which
would produce Fiat trucks and automobiles under much the same terms
(except for the financing) agreed to by Chrysler and Renault. Moreover
Fiat agreed to take charge of the country's bankrupt and long-idle forge
works, Forjas de Colombia, refinancing it and finding domestic and
international markets for its auto-related products.[6]

These provisions compared favorably with those negotiated by governments of larger and presumably more powerful countries. The limited
number of assembly plants, the financial arrangements (with Renault),
the insistence on compensatory exports, and the joint-venture participation of the government were provisions that Brazil, Argentina, and
Mexico had either not yet achieved or had done so only after years of
less favorable arrangements.[7]

Explanation of these relatively favorable terms requires a closer look
at the bargaining process. In general host country–TNC bargaining
relations depend on how the parties understand and define their interests
and on the leverage each has at its disposal for pursuing them. Such
leverage is a function of their respective resources, the structure and
stage of development of the international auto industry, the extent to
which the needs, interests, and strategies of particular TNCs are fulfilled
or served by the host country (or other countries), and the relationships
between the host government and key domestic economic and political
interests.

The Colombian contract terms were the result of a number of factors
and forces. The first of these was the government's relatively restrictive
demands, a position based at least partly on a critical reading of the
experience of other auto industries. Economic nationalism also played
a role. A number of Latin American governments had recently expro-
priated foreign holdings in oil, copper, and other minerals and were
discussing the idea of a common, and more restrictive, foreign investment policy. President Lleras was a major instigator in these moves,
and his government had already adopted restrictive foreign exchange
regulations (decree 444) in 1967.

Helping the Colombians impose these restrictive conditions were
two additional factors: the interest of European auto firms in gaining
initial or additional footholds in Latin America and governmental skill
in playing the TNCs off against one another during the negotiations.

European interest

The restructuring of the Colombian auto industry roughly coincided with growing European interest in both expansion and Latin America. In 1959 Volkswagen and Renault began assembling cars in Brazil, and Fiat set up operations in Argentina (to go with those established earlier in Spain and Yugoslavia). Somewhat later French producers established new assembly plants in several non-French union countries, increasing the number of French cars assembled abroad fourfold (to over 148,000) between 1956 and 1966.[8]

Several factors contributed to this interest in expansion and in Latin America. Rapid and highly profitable growth between 1946 and 1960 gave the Europeans the financial and administrative capability to launch major international operations. And although Latin America was not as attractive as European and North American markets, it held considerable appeal as a vehicle market, especially as economies developed and already substantial populations continued to grow. Over the long run it would be a major arena of international competition, one that might well determine the success or demise of European firms. Furthermore the region shared a number of topographical, cultural, and socioeconomic characteristics with postwar European societies and might therefore be better suited and more favorably disposed to the smaller, more economical European cars than to the larger, more expensive American models.[9]

Within Latin America, moreover, the Colombian market, although small, had considerable appeal to firms anxious to gain entry to the region and to catch up with North American and European rivals already established in Mexico, Brazil, and Argentina. Colombia's more than 20 million people gave its market long-term potential, even if existing income distribution limited the size of the current car-consuming public.[10] In the shorter run establishment in the country would almost certainly mean privileged access to the emerging Andean common market whose total population would exceed 72 million. And finally the Colombian market appeared ripe for the taking. Chrysler had only a small assembly operation, neither Ford nor General Motors seemed interested, and the Colombian government was willing to grant exclusive small-car production rights to a single firm.

The European industry also had important internal reasons for seeking to expand. By the early 1960s Fiat, Renault, Citroen, Peugeot, and Volkswagen had all but exhausted the rapid growth potentials of their respective national markets, in terms of both size and rate of demand expansion. Between 1955 and 1966 cars-per-person ratios had dropped from 16 to 5.5 in France and from 64 to 9.6 in Italy. Partly as a result of such saturation, annual growth rates in production in France had fallen off considerably, dropping from an average of over 16 percent during the years 1955 through 1960 to 9 percent between 1960 and 1964.[11]

Moreover continued prosperity in Europe had led most of the firms to produce a wider range of models in an effort to retain upwardly mobile clients. Renault and Fiat were pioneers in this regard and by the late 1960s were producing seven and nine models, respectively. Renault's introduction of the R6, R16, and R12 coincided with the decline in R4 sales in France and Europe, as did Fiat's introduction of more expensive models with the fall in sales of its 500 and 850 models. Under the circumstances both were interested in developing new markets for these more economical models.[12]

Bargaining process

Another major factor in the Colombian government's relative success was its ability to exploit this European interest in the course of the negotiations. Colombian government officials were clearly interested in Renault from the beginning; they were impressed by the R4's general performance and by its contribution to the French auto industry and economy in the 1950s and early 1960s. And yet they managed to create the aura of an open bidding process. Indeed before assembly rights were granted to Renault, several years of intense bargaining ensued in which twenty-two firms submitted formal proposals, eight made offers actually meeting the government's general guidelines, and several actively lobbied and bargained with Colombian officials on a one-to-one basis.

The process itself was the object of substantial controversy. Critics charged that the government was in fact committed to Renault as early as 1967 when IFI director Miguel Fadul announced in Paris an "agreement in principle" whereby Renault would manufacture parts and assemble cars in Colombia.[13] They further charged that a seemingly open bidding process was later devised to conceal this but that other firms had not been informed of the criteria by which offers would be assessed and could not effectively compete.[14] Rumors also circulated to the effect that some firms (mostly clearly Chrysler) were seeking to have the idea of a single monopoly assembler of small cars set aside.

The confusion surrounding these matters was reinforced by divisions within the Lleras government. Lleras himself was an early advocate of Andean integration and saw the auto industry as playing an important role in that process. Within the administration, however, opinion varied regarding proper shape and structure of the industry and appropriate demands and expectations vis-à-vis the TNCs. In general the differences reflected conflicting theories and strategies of development, as well as diverse personal and economic ties with the interested firms.

From the beginning the Ministry of Development stressed the need to award exclusive small-cars production rights to a single TNC with which the government would enter into a joint venture. The most explicit opposition to this idea came from the High Level Committee (CAN). Appointed by President Lleras and charged with reviewing and assessing the proposals, the committee was composed of three former ministers and/or leading political figures, Joaquín Vallejo, Armando Puyana, and Manuel Carvajal.

In its final report the committee opposed granting exclusive assembly rights to a single, vertically integrated firm like Renault and instead urged the confinement of assembly operations to a single plant in which several firms would assemble cars and emphasis on large-scale production of parts and components for both export and inclusion in domestic production.[15] This position was based in part on a fear of potentially adverse quality and price effects of even a state-monitored monopoly, as well as the dependency on a single firm that might be eclipsed by unforeseen developments. It also reflected an explicit preference for a horizontal structure in which assembly firms would use standardized parts and components produced in quantities large enough to permit effective economies of scale rather than a vertical structure in which a single firm produced nontransferable parts and components for its own cars.

Among its other recommendations the committee also suggested linking a firm's import licenses to the amount of foreign exchange it earned through export activities, specifying the level and pace of a firm's incorporation of domestically produced parts, and searching for an effective means of controlling transfer pricing of imported parts (majority shareholding status by the Colombian government was perceived as insufficient in this regard).

These recommendations were encouraged, endorsed, invoked, and generally exploited by various interested groups. The most visible was Chrysler Colmotores, a majority-owned (77 percent) subsidiary acquired by Chrysler International in 1965 that had been producing between 1,000 and 2,000 cars annually. Chrysler Colmotores had not participated in the bidding itself and stood to benefit from the abandonment of the single-firm provision and (as an American firm) the adoption of a horizontal struture. The company promoted its interests through a massive public relations campaign, citing its many contributions to the Colombian economy, and through frequent, high-level contacts with government officials.[16]

Other interested parties included domestic industrialists active in ANDI (the national association of manufacturers, which included Chrysler and a number of other firms with ties to U.S. TNCs), FEDEMETAL (which represented largely national firms in the metallurgical and metalworking fields), ACOLFA (the national association of auto-parts' manufacturers, most of them small-scale producers), and ACOPI (the national association of small industrialists, some of whose products would be sold to the assemblers). Each was concerned with promoting the domestic parts industry and favored use of standardized parts in order to increase production scales and lower costs.[17] They did not have equal political and economic strength, however, nor were they equally interested in the industry's development. Many of the firms represented in ANDI, and to a lesser extent FEDEMETAL, were either not directly involved in auto-related production or less exclusively involved than firms belonging to ACOLFA or ACOPI.

Although membership lists for these organizations are not readily available, we do know that most (82 percent) of the country's auto-parts firms were small or medium sized (employing fewer than one hundred workers each) and therefore more likely to be members of ACOLFA or ACOPI. We also know that their financial resources were limited (they had a total capital investment of $28.4 million in 1975) and that they were more dependent on auto-parts production (over one-third of them did virtually no other kind of work, and taken together, 74 percent of their production was devoted to auto parts). The larger firms (those more likely to be members of either ANDI or FEDEMETAL) were both more powerful (their total capital investment in 1975 was $142 million) and more likely to be involved in other economic activities (only 53 percent of their overall production was in auto parts).[18] Not surprisingly, then, firms affiliated with ACOLFA and

ACOPI were more inclined to be economic nationalists and to protect and promote a domestic auto parts industry at virtually all costs. Those represented in ANDI and FEDEMETAL, on the other hand, were more concerned with the need to rationalize the industry and to maintain close and harmonious working relations with auto TNCs, both of which required restraint of overly protective or autarchic impulses in terms of component parts. All four organizations made periodic public statements expressing their concerns and pressed them in normal contacts and consultations with government officials as well.[19]

The impact of these arguments, forces, and developments was to alter the positions of both the government and Renault. They produced a compromise in which virtually all interests and concerns were at least partially satisfied. The government rejected committee proposals for a single multimake assembly operation and horizontal structuring of the industry. It entered formal negotiations with Renault and ultimately awarded it a license to establish assembly and motor plants. On the other hand the government did incorporate a number of the committee's specific suggestions, two of them the idea of a compensated exchange agreement and the establishment of obligatory levels of integration. Moreover it also decided to permit Chrysler to begin immediate assembly of its Spanish-produced Simca 1000 in competition with the Renault 4.

This reversal on a major point in the government's initial position was apparently the fruit of Chrysler's continuing pressure and advocacy during negotiations, although the government also wanted both to alleviate fears regarding the effects of monopoly and to ensure an adequate supply of affordable cars until Renault began production. Whatever the mix of factors, Chrysler's ability to resolve government concerns clerly redounded to its advantage and thus underscores the additional leverage accruing to TNCs whose facilities are in place and operational.

Following the release of the committee's report and under the threat of possible government discussions with Fiat, Renault made concessions of its own. The most obvious was its willingness to share the small-car market with Chrysler's Simca. But it was also during this period that the French first offered to supply initial capital outlay credits, to move quickly to high (60 percent) levels of integration, and to purchase Colombian exports equal to CKD shipments from France.[20] The agreement with Renault set the tone for subsequent negotiations and agreements with Chrysler, Lara, and Fiat. By 1972 the structure of Colombian automobile industry was fairly well defined along the lines of the initial contract with Renault.

It seems clear that government leverage vis-à-vis Renault was strengthened by the latter's desire to gain a strategic foothold in Latin America, by the counteroffers tended by other TNCs, and by the established presence and influence of Chrysler. Regarding the government's concessions, it is difficult to know the extent to which they reflectd autonomous changes in its own views versus external influence and pressure. Common sense suggests a great convergence between certain committee views and corporate interests, but there is little evidence of any causal connection in this regard. Indeed it is difficult to imagine a position that would not have been to the advantage, and thus the result of the influence, of at least one of the interested parties.

One should also resist the conclusion that any of the firms made concessions they were genuinely loathe to make or that the Colombians had thus successfully imposed themselves on the TNCs. Such concessions as there were should be placed in the context of other issues on which the government and the TNCs were in complete agreement and were never the objects of contention although they well might have been. There was never any question, for example, that only a limited number of TNCs would be permitted to produce for the Colombian market, that they would enjoy long-term high tariff protection from external competition, that the Colombians would move only gradually toward full national integration, or that production levels and model changes would ultimately be dictated by corporate rather than country-need considerations.

One would also do well to note the vague terms in which some of the concessions were made and the difficulties that would likely be encountered in enforcing them. What was crucial to each of the firms was its establishment within the Colombian market. This meant acquiring a consumer following, developing a network of spare parts and service facilities, and cultivating organizational and technological dependency among domestic parts producers. Such footholds would provide valuable additional leverage in ongoing relations with the government, and as conditions and developments evolved, earlier commitments might well prove unenforceable.[23]

Ongoing Fulfillment

While faring relatively well in initial bargaining, the Colombians have been unable to obtain fulfillment of contractual commitments. Because of this, the motor vehicle industry has expanded steadily since reactivation but has not had the hoped-for spillover effects or met the country's basic transportation needs.

Since 1969 it has experienced steady growth in passenger car production and sales but much less progress in truck, bus, and taxi production. Auto production and sales, except for 1975 through 1977, have risen annually by at least 25 percent, surpassing 32,000 in 1978. The market is dominated (71 percent in 1978) by Renault, with Chrysler, now GM, and Fiat sharing the truck, bus, and remaining car markets.[21] Truck, chassis (bus), and taxi production, on the other hand, has been uneven, reaching 8,400 in 1971 but falling to an average of 6,000 between 1972 and 1975 before rising to 11,800 in 1978. Because of this, Colombia has had to rely on imports to supplement domestic output.[22]

The auto parts industry, although predating the establishment of the assembly plants, has been stimulated by them. In 1975 it had sales totaling $125 million compared to $177 million for the assembly plants. In terms of actual linkage effects, however, only 37.7 percent (approximately $47 million) of the total went to the assemblers. The rest was sold for export (4.7 percent) or as replacement parts (57.6 percent) and cannot be attributed to the assembly industry since it would be needed wherever the cars were produced.[23]

The $47 million should be reduced even further since that figure includes portions of articles produced elsewhere. In fact the vast majority (85 percent) of products actually produced (and not merely assembled or processed) in the country consist of technologically simple parts whose unit value is less than $7. Under the circumstances it is difficult to speak of any substantial linkage effects generated by the motor vehicle industry.

The limited development of the parts sector reflects the assembly character of motor vehicle production in Colombia. Despite repeated government efforts to enforce the inclusion of locally produced parts and components, the industry remains largely in the easy phase of integration, with levels varying from 10 percent to 45 percent. Renault, whose motor plant machines and assembles motors and U-joints, can claim levels only between 43 and 45 percent while Fiat and Chrysler fall between 10 and 36 percent, depending on the model.[24]

The companies publicly claim levels of over 50 percent, and the government Superintendencia de Producción y Comercio's annual integration lists and percentage quotas are now also in this range; however, these figures are based on the total value of locally produced parts (even though the domestic value added may be virtually nil). Further they fail to include the royalty payments on the imported CKD parts and components, thus undervaluing those still being used, and generally overvalue the completely assembled unit against which the locally produced portion is measured.[25]

In reality the assemblers continue to import virtually all technologically complex components (such as transmissions, differentials, motor blocks, and stampings) from parent or affiliate firms. And with many of the components purchased locally (brakes, clutches, and shock absorbers, among others), they insist on the inclusion of imported parts and materials.

The modest value added contributed by assembly operations is reflected in the limited number of jobs generated. A 1975 survey commissioned by the National Planning Department reported a total of 4,500 persons employed by the assembly plants themselves and another 5,000 by auto parts producers that sell to them. The total of 9,500 represents 1.4 percent of the work force in the manufacturing sector.[26] By 1980 the number of assembly plant employees reached 6,000, but the total of those working in related parts manufacture does not appear to have changed.

The industry's productive efficiency is somewhat mixed. In 1975 the overprice (the percentage difference between the pretax selling price in the country and that for the same model f.o.b. in the country of original production) ran from 12 and 33 percent for the Simca 1300 and Renault 4 to 71 percent for Fiat 125, 75 percent for the Renault 12B, and 118 percent for the Dodge Dart.[27] Normally overprice in Third World industries is attributed to lower production levels and less efficient technologies, particularly in parts and component production. In Colombia, however, overprice has been least in those cars (Simca and Renault 4) with the greatest degree of integration and thus would seem more a reflection of the degree of market competition and overall protection.[28] Although international comparisons are difficult, Colombian government officials insist that the industry's overprice levels are higher than in other Latin American industries when they were at similar levels of production and integration.[29]

Finally corporate performance in meeting the country's basic transportation needs has not been good either, although it improved between 1974 and 1976. Large numbers of taxis and bus chassis had to be imported in 1971, 1974, and 1975 to make up for insufficient production.

In general the TNCs have preferred the more lucrative private passenger car market to that for taxis, trucks, or buses. Annual production quotas for the latter are almost never met, although Chrysler's record has been better than that of the other two.[30]

Under the López government (1974–1978) the production of collective transport vehicles increased substantially, accounting for 30 percent of total production in 1975 and 35 percent in 1976 (compared to 20 percent in 1973). A major factor in this shift was the 35 percent sales tax placed on passenger cars in 1974. This restricted the car market and helped push Chrysler, and to a lesser extent Fiat, into taxi, truck, and bus chassis production on which no sales tax was levied and for which prices were permitted to rise.[31] A less positive trend was a concomitant increase in the production of more expensive and higher profit luxury cars, for which demand seems to be significantly price inelastic. Apparently an agreement was reached allowing firms to produce and sell as many of these cars as they were able (at a price of their own fixing) as long as they met quotas for less expensive cars and/or taxis, trucks, and buses.[32]

In addition to failing to meet general goals, none of the TNCs has fulfilled its specific commitments. Chrysler, for example, was to have established a $10 million fund for financial and technological assistance to the domestic auto parts industry. Its actual contribution has been far less. Annual reports claim substantial contributions and company representatives invariably refer to the fund when citing the firm's contribution to the Colombian economy, but no one seems to know to whom the money has been given, and Superintendencia Bancaria records indicate that only a fraction of the amount to be distributed has actually been processed.[33]

Fiat, on the other hand, was to take over the Forjas de Colombia plant, helping its products find markets within Colombia and abroad. To date, production levels are up, and the plant is operating at about 60 percent of its industrial capacity, against a level of 20 percent for the years preceding Fiat's involvement. Exports remained insignificant at least through 1975, however, and with Fiat's substantial investment in component manufacturing facilities in Brazil in 1976, they are not likely to increase soon.[34]

In the case of Renault the government's principal concern had been the strain on its balance of payments resulting from increased CKD imports. To avoid this, it required the French to purchase additional Colombian exports in compensation.[35] Since 1970, however, Colombia has had a substantial though declining trade deficit with France, a major portion of which is attributable to increased CKD imports.[36] The French have not sufficiently increased their purchases of either traditional Colombian exports (coffee, textiles, textile fibers, leather, and precious stones) or automobile parts. The latter amounted to only $3.5 million in 1975 and $2.5 million in 1976.[37]

The balance-of-payments record of the other TNCs has been even worse. They were not formally bound by any compensatory agreements and have continued to ship ever larger amounts of CKD packs and parts. As a result, Colombia's trade deficit in the transport equipment area rose from $90.9 million in 1973 to over $186.8 million in 1976.[38]

On balance the motor vehicle industry has contributed little to Colombia's social and economic development. It has remained an assembly operation, with the TNCs unwilling to incorporate significant amounts of locally produced parts and components. It is easy to see why they are not eager to do so. The manufacture in country of technologically complex components and the development of basic metalworking capabilities would entail heavy capital investments without assurance of proportionately additional returns. Such investments would cut into the profitable market for parent and affiliate production of these same parts and components. This, of course, was a major factor in Renault's and Fiat's coming to Colombia in the first place and was a particularly important consideration with models such as the R4 and R6 and the Fiat 125, which were no longer as attractive in more developed markets.[39] Finally TNCs with operations in Brazil or Mexico may well be obliged to export certain amounts of their production and might be dependent on their Colombian operation to absorb some of this.

TNCs have good reasons to resist a move beyond assembly, but it remains unclear why they have not been compelled to do so by Colombian governments. Perhaps the most determined and imaginative government efforts have simply been circumvented or resisted by the superior power or guile of the TNCs. But possibly the Colombians did not really try, their commitments to other socioeconomic objectives undercut their attempts in this regard, or they were constrained by domestic socioeconomic and political pressures. To explore these various possibilities (which need not be mutually exclusive), one must consider the specific measures the government used to influence production and integration levels.

Special policy measures

Production and integration quotas, graduated tariffs, and special taxes have been among the more prominent measures that the government has used to influence auto industry performance. Each year, for example, the Superintendencia de Producción y Comercio fixes production schedules (how many of each make and model of car, taxi, truck, and bus chassis) for each assembler. The schedules generally conform to the firms' own proposals, however, and are often adjusted downward during the year. Moreover even these revised quotas are seldom met, and the companies accordingly have been liable to fines, although apparently none have been levied.

Colombian governments have also attempted to influence vehicle production through the use of variable tariffs on imported CKD packs. Tariffs of 10 percent and 30 percent have been levied on packs valued at under $1,000 and $1,500, respectively (presumably those for smaller, more economical cars and taxis), while a rate of 115 percent was applied to those valued at more than $1,500 (those for larger, more expensive cars). In response, however, the companies have taken to removing components from the CKD packs and bringing them in individually at special tariff rates in order to bring its value under the $1,000 or $1,500 limit and qualify for reduction to either 10 percent or 30 percent. As a result of such technological contraband, corporate tariff payments in recent years have averaged about 11 percent, with only marginal differences between lower- and higher-priced models.[40] Also a 1974 decision to permit assemblers to fix their own prices (they were previously controlled) allowed them to pass the cost of higher tariffs along to the consumer. Under the circumstances tariffs had little or no effect on production.

An additional tactic used to stimulate greater production of taxis, trucks, and bus chassis has been the threatened importation of already assembled units. This was attempted under Pastrana in 1972 and again in 1974 and 1975 under López. Results were disappointing in the first instance and only partially satisfactory in the second. In 1972 the government had to abandon its plan because of widespread opposition from domestic and international interests.[41] Unfortunately during the same period (1971–1973), domestic production of trucks and buses declined steadily, while that of taxis remained low. Under López imports rose substantially, but although taxi production increased dramatically, the number of trucks and buses produced locally remained virtually the same.[42]

The impact of importation as such is difficult to assess for a number of reasons.[43] The government has been limited in pressuring transnational assemblers by the dependent relationships that had developed between these and supplier firms. Ironically the same groups that were the intended beneficiaries of government efforts to promote domestic industry actively opposed them and were instrumental in their defeat. Apparently they saw their own long-term interests as dependent on the willingness of transnational producers to share technology and information, although they also believed that the companies would win any tug-of-war with the government and ultimately would dictate the terms of production and cooperation in any case.[44] They therefore concluded that their interests were better served by the continued operation of the assembly plants, despite their disappointing levels of production, than by attempts to force those plants to do what they did not want to do.

Government efforts to promote greater integration of locally produced parts and components have been similarly unsuccessful. A number of strategies have been tried, but none has worked well. Between 1970 and 1975, for example, companies were required to obtain a certain percentage (by value) of local parts if they were available in sufficient quantities, with the required technical specifications, and at a reasonable price (no more than 40 percent higher than the home factory price).[45] This required the local supplier to produce efficiently and competitively, although assemblers could undermine their efforts in a number of ways.

For one, the establishment of minimum percentage (of value) levels of integration did not prevent the TNCs from alternating the components included from year to year, thus upsetting local supplier calculations and preventing them from rationalizing their production costs and becoming competitive. Further the assembler could (and SOFASA often did) refuse to provide potential suppliers with the necessary technical specifications, prompt evaluations of prototypes, or plausible justifications for rejecting them. And finally an assembler could ask its parent to underprice certain of its imported components in order to discourage or prevent domestic suppliers from producing the same articles.[46]

Tax and tariff policies designed for other purposes also adversely affected efforts to raise integration levels. The 35 percent sales tax on passenger cars, for example, had the desired effect of curtailing passenger car demand and increasing taxi, truck, and bus chassis production. But since the integration levels for trucks and buses were substantially less than those for passenger cars, the relative shift toward the former made the raising of overall levels more difficult to compel or justify.

Tariff policy has involved another set of competing or conflicting considerations, this time between consumer prices and integration levels. Under the Lleras government a standard 115 percent tariff was placed on all imported CKD parts, thus increasing production costs and sales prices. In doing so the government showed greater concern for promoting the parts sector than for reducing costs for the car public, a position clung to despite continual appeals and pressure from the assemblers and from ANDI and FEDEMETAL. The latter apparently reasoned that lower tariffs would mean lower prices, greater demand and sales, higher levels of production, and therefore greater purchases of domestic parts in overall totals, if not in amount, per car.[47] By holding its ground, the Lleras government won the support and gratitude of ACOLFA and ACOPI members, although their support was probably less decisive than the fact that ANDI and FEDEMETAL affiliates had other commitments and concerns with which to console themselves.

Moreover, their patience was soon rewarded as the Pastrana administration (1970–1974) introduced reduced tariffs of 10 percent and 30 percent soon after taking office, in order to lower prices and fulfill a campaign pledge to place a family car within the reach of most middle-class Colombians.[48] The immediate impact of this move was to increase the demand for cars and to that extent for domestically produced auto parts as well (as ANDI and FEDEMETAL had previously argued). But these tended to be relatively simple parts, whereas domestic firms interested in producing more sophisticated components were priced out of competition. The net result was greater domestic sales in auto parts but unchanged levels of national integration.

Pastrana's tariff policy was continued under the subsequent López government. To reduce demand for passenger cars, López imposed a sales tax and deregulated prices. He could have achieved the same effect by raising tariffs on imported CKD parts, but this would have encouraged integration while cutting into company profits. Instead the increased costs were covered by the retail consumer, and domestic parts suppliers continued to suffer.

General development policy

While the ability of TNCs to resist or circumvent these various efforts at control is partially a function of their technological and organizational resources, it is also due to the lack of clear and consistent governmental commitment to develop Colombia's motor vehicle industry. Since 1970 Colombian governments have not had an automobile policy as such and have dealt with issues inconsistently and often ineffectively.

The lack of any real policy was particularly marked under the López administration, the result of both bureaucratic rivalries and genuine policy ambivalence. As had Lleras earlier, López stressed the auto industry's importance as a means of expanding the country's metallurgical and metalworking sectors. But his government also stressed the need to limit public investment, and the auto industry was not identified as a priority area.[49] Moreover a significant segment of the administration was openly skeptical of import substitution industrialization generally, and several ministries, including Treasury, were hostile to the auto industry in particular.[50] Other agencies and departments were more supportive but were unable to secure commitments of either financial or institutional support. In general rhetorical support for the industry was rather strong, but actual commitment was weak under López.

The administration no doubt would have liked to increase local value added but refused to permit the necessary expansion of the domestic passenger car market because of the substantial infrastructural expenses required. It also refused to absorb (through higher consumer prices) the increased production costs that greater use of domestic production would have entailed. It was unwilling to finance the expansion and technological upgrading of the national parts industry. And finally, it refused to provide credit for financing passenger car purchases by the general public despite repeated corporate requests. This service, apparently essential to market expansion in most Third World countries, had to be assumed by private finance companies and by the TNCs themselves.[51]

The adverse effects of the López government's policies can be readily seen in the following example. In 1975 in order to undermine TNC resistance to further national integration, the López government introduced detailed lists of specific domestic parts to be incorporated by the companies. The lists were cumulative, so the parts could not be included one year and not the next. According to the timetable for the next several years, all three assemblers were required to source 60 percent of their components domestically.[52] This goal was not reached, nor was its attainment ever very likely. Some of the components required specialized casting and machine work, and thus the acquisition of technology and machinery not currently available in the country. But potential domestic producers lacked the financial resources necessary for these investments and received little or no help from either the companies or the government. Given its overall strategy and priorities, the government was unwilling to invest large amounts of money in such activities. In practice, if not by conscious choice, it had concluded that raising integration levels would be overly expensive in financial and developmental terms.

This is not to say that post-Lleras governments could not have done more than they did. They could easily have enforced existing regulations more effectively and could have raised CKD tariffs, controlled the production and prices of luxury cars, and obliged assemblers to produce more taxis, bus chassis, and economy cars.[53] These were all bargaining issues within existing levels of commitment and priority and would have benefited both the industry and the overall economy. Whatever its overall propriety, the policy confined the auto industry to a relatively modest level of expansion and development and in effect assured the TNCs a fairly free hand. Furthermore the government's overall development strategy was a major obstacle to the achievement of further integration and additional linkage effects.

Bargaining Relationships in the Motor Vehicle Industry

This review of initial success, subsequent failure, and possibly ultimate vindication has several implications for host country–TNC bargaining relations. First, it strongly suggests that a government's resources are principally, though not exclusively, legal and political and that they are more likely to be decisive in public confrontations in which formal relationships are defined and a government's image and authority are at stake. A TNC's resources, on the other hand, are more generally material and economic and tend to assert themselves in the interactions falling between these political moments. Indeed the ultimately decisive strength of a TNC is its material capacity for escaping or neutralizing commitments made during political confrontations.

Until recently TNCs could expect to win these struggles. They seldom faced direct competition from other firms, and the governments with which they dealt rarely had defined strategies of development or were bound by or beholden to nationalist sentiment or interests. These conditions no longer prevail as widely as they once did, however, and unless TNCs are able to recruit allies from among politically influential domestic interests, increasingly they may be obliged to make substantial initial concessions to host governments.[54]

In the auto industry, however, the bargaining relationship changes once a firm establishes itself within a market. At this point its technological, financial, and organizational resources give it effective control over day-to-day operations and decisions. Its control over product development and quality, its power over the shipment of parts and components, the establishment of production schedules, and the character and rate of technological changes permit it to resist virtually any use of its resources or operations it wishes to.

This fact affects both initial negotiations and the long-term outcome of host country–TNC relations. The host country initially is driven to define very specific commitments and enforcement mechanisms, while the firms attempt to reject these but are willing to enter into agreements they later hope to adjust. As we have seen, they do just that once they have established themselves within the country. In some instances the government's efforts at ongoing control are easily resisted or circumvented. In others it is unable or unwilling to sustain such efforts because of opposition or lack of support from domestic economic and political groups.

Governmental leverage, of course, is not solely formal or political; the state possesses or allocates substantial economic resources of its own and certainly can and does use them to influence TNC behavior. Their use is conditioned, however, by complex political and economic relations with both domestic and international forces and is rarely something over which discretionary control can be exercised.

Finally, the government can always suspend, or threaten to suspend, a firm's operating license, reverting the relationship to its initial political moment in which the state was less disadvantaged. While always a possibility, however, a number of factors limit the viability of such a tactic. To be credible, the threat of suspension would have to be used in a limited number of instances and areas and would not be available as an ongoing tactic. Further, the costs of actual withdrawal might well be as high for the host country as for the firm. Consumer allegiance, the development of a spare parts and service sector, and working relationships with local parts producers might be as valuable to the country (which would have to replace them) as to the firm that helped build them up.

Given the limitations of its largely political leverage, the Colombian government has been unable to enforce fulfillment of the apparently

favorable contracts it negotiated. It is not clear, however, that the Colombians have therefore failed in their dealings with the TNCs. It is
true that the assemblers continue the profitable use of parent- or affiliate-
produced parts, to the detriment of the country's industrial development.
And yet Colombia has thus far avoided the socially costly market and
industrial expansion that auto TNCs have actively sought in most other
Third World countries. Although the Colombian state has failed to
obtain contract compliance, it has thereby avoided commitments and
courses of action whose social utility is questionable. Having done so,
it could be considered "relatively autonomous" vis-à-vis corporate interests committed to an expansion of the industry.[55]

This interpretation is not implausible given the Colombian state's
control over financial resources. As of 1968 it held 45 percent of the
total assets of the country's financial institutions and in the years since
has been the recipient of massive international credits ($1,000 million
in 1977 and $770 million in 1978) to finance development projects.[56]
These resources might or might not be spent on roads, gas imports,
consumer credit, supplier industry development, and so on and clearly
could affect the context, terms, and considerations of private economic
decisions. To the extent that they do, they may provide a foundation
for relative state autonomy.

Ultimately, however, the argument for state imposition and autonomy
rests on the questionable assumption that the TNCs are committed to
a much larger market and industry. It fails to consider that they may
be unwilling to risk their foothold in the current market to achieve
such expansion or that they might actually prefer that foothold for the
time being. These possibilities paint somewhat distinct scenarios, but
each implies only very limited autonomy to the Colombian state.

If one considers the current state of the industry as even relatively
frustrating to the TNCs, it would hardly seem enough to resort to as
drastic a move as withdrawal or threatened withdrawal. While hurting
the Colombians in various ways, withdrawal would almost certainly
cost the TNCs more than would remaining under current terms. The
stakes most have in their large assembly operations are limited and
fairly mobile, but their commercial and organizational investments (in
parts and service networks and consumer allegiance, for example) cannot
be as easily or painlessly uprooted and may require endurance of temporary hardship. To the extent that the state can thus force a TNC to
restrain immediate aspirations to further longer-term interests, it is

imposing its terms and itself, although hardly in a manner truly detrimental.

A more plausible characterization is that the TNCs do not want an expanded market and industry at this time and that they are supported in this regard by most of the country's powerful economic interests. The TNCs, although to differing extents, have sold large amounts of home country or affiliate parts in Colombia. They have enjoyed a high ratio of profits to fixed assets.[57] Larger profits might be forthcoming with expanded production and sales but would require additional investments (for new component manufacturing facilities) that might be even larger, at least in the short run.

Renault is the only auto TNC to have made any long-term capital commitment. Apparently it is looking ahead to the Andean common market and an integrated Latin American production system at least partially based in Colombia and is willing to settle for initially smaller returns on its investment. Chrysler and Fiat have made no permanent commitments, and Fiat made investments in Brazil in 1976 that appear to rule out the development of significant manufacturing capabilities in Colombia. Both, in effect, have preferred to run essentially commercial operations for components manufactured elsewhere in their international structure, and there seems to be no reason for them to alter their strategies at this time.

None of the firms, moreover, would seem to risk much by going slow or holding off from developing manufacturing capabilities. Occasionally the firms express concern over the more rapid pace of auto industry development in neighboring Venezuela. But Renault's own experience in Colombia has shown that an entire production facility (its motor machining plant) can be constructed, operationalized, and integrated within a transnational production structure in as few as eighteen months, and the development of manufacturing capabilities can thus be safely postponed until the Andean auto production and market structures are more clearly defined.

The TNCs have been supported and sustained in these attitudes by most of the country's important economic interests. Domestic industrialists confront the same small market constraints as do the TNCs, and given their smaller capital bases, they are even less likely to risk their own money in major expansion at the present time. Moreover even if they were willing and able to do so, they could do little without the technological assistance and authorization of either the parent firms or transnational parts manufacturers currently supplying the assemblers from abroad.[58]

Another critical factor in this regard was the decline in enthusiasm for import substitution industrialization among domestic financial and industrial groups. Beginning in 1970 capital began to shift away from high technology consumer durables and toward chemicals, textiles, food and beverages, commercial agriculture, and building materials (cement and lumber, for example).[59] ANDI, FEDEMETAL, and FENALCO occasionally were critical of the government's lack of commitment to industrial development, but many of the interests belonging to these groups themselves made large investments in light industry and commercial agriculture.[60]

Such moves were consistent with both the integrated character of the country's economic elite and its traditional practice of moving money in response to current opportunities. In this particular instance they were also responding in part to inducements or initiatives from the government (for example, the Pastrana administration's housing construction and loan program) and in part to price movements for cash crops on the international market.

Most of the country's influential economic groups were thus either steered into or consoled by alternate opportunities and concerns. As a result they offered little or no resistance to the government's relative neglect of auto industry development. Colombian governments have had good reasons of their own for not making large-scale investments in the industry, although it is hard to imagine either Pastrana or López persisting in their stances were there no attractive opportunities available to domestic or transnational groups. In view of this, it is neither warranted nor particularly helpful to speak of the relative autonomy of the Colombian state. A more fitting characterization would be that of a conventional regime whose orientation contained both neoconservative and liberal elements and whose policies were generally agreeable to, and reflective of, all domestic and international capital interests.

Notes

1. Cf. Fabio Hernan Gómez, *Concentración del Poder Económico en Colombia* (CINEP, Bogotá); Carlos Castillo Cardona, "Elite y Desarrollo en Colombia," in Rodrigo Parra Sandoval, ed., *Dependencia Externa y Desarrollo Político en Colombia* (Bogotá, 1972), pp. 129–153; and Robert Dix, *Colombia: The Political Dimensions of Change* (New Haven: Yale University Press, 1967), pp. 402–403.

2. Cf. Edwin Corr, *The Political Process in Colombia* (Denver: Graduate School of International Studies, University of Denver, 1972), pp. 77–80, and Dix, *Colombia*, pp. 322–330.

3. Departamento Administrativo Nacional de Estadística, "La Industria Automotriz en Colombia," *Boletín Mensual de Estadística*, nos. 280–281 (November–December 1974): 121.

4. The contract is reproduced in ibid., pp. 175–178. These varying equity arrangements were made uniform (Colombia, 51 percent; Renault, 49 percent) in 1971 in response to Colombian fears that they might be manipulated to French advantage.

5. Between 1965 and 1979, 77 percent of the stock in Chrysler Colmotores remained in foreign hands, the largest block (50 percent) held by Chrysler International, the corporation's Swiss-based holding company. In 1979 Chrysler sold its assembly facility to General Motors as part of its worldwide retrenchment.

6. Earlier Chrysler had expressed an interest in assuming responsibility for Forjas, but negotiations with the government ultimately broke down.

7. None of these countries was able to restrict producing firms to less than eight, none received as generous financial arrangements, none was successful in resisting the entry of wholly foreign-owned subsidiaries, and finally, the export obligations imposed by Mexico and Brazil came only in 1972.

8. B. Hake and P. M. Lynch, *The Market for Automotive Parts in Germany, France, and Italy* (Ann Arbor: Institute for International Commerce, Graduate School of Business, University of Michigan, 1970), p. 11.

9. Volkswagen's success in Brazil (sales leader from its introduction in 1959) was no doubt a source of encouragement and optimism in this regard.

10. A Renault spokesman was quoted as estimating an absorptive capacity of about 50,000 cars annually.

11. Hake and Lynch, *Market for Automotive Parts*, p. 10, and Edouard Mahler, *L'Industrie Automobile et ses perspectives d'avenir dans le nouvel equilibre europeen et mondiale* (Paris: Lausann, 1966), p. 66.

12. Renault had recently (1965 and 1966) made major investment in new manufacturing facilities for the R4 just prior to bringing out a series of new models. See James Ensor, *The Motor Industry* (London: Longman, 1971), pp. 164–166. French, Italian, and German auto producers were again to enjoy high rates of growth in the late 1960s and early 1970s, apparently based on the introduction of several higher-priced models. This turn of events may have taken the car makers by surprise, however, and in any case did not make it any less important to develop new overseas markets for one's economy models.

13. *El Tiempo* (Bogotá), October 3, 1967, covered the agreement.

14. According to conservative critic Raimundo Emiliani, *El Caso Renault ante el Senado* (Bogotá, 1969), p. 13, the data specifically requested were extremely

general and could not be used for comparison or evaluation. The High Level Committee itself admitted as much in its report.

15. Ibid., p. 63.

16. During the period of evaluation of proposals, international and Latin American division executives of the Chrysler Corporation were frequent visitors to Bogotá. Seldom a week went by without a press conference being called by Chrysler Colmotores to announce an increase in production, sales, investments, or employment or plans for reactivating Forjas, or for developing export markets within the United States for Colombian parts, for example.

17. Standardized parts would not appear to be in the interests of small-scale producers since the fragmentation that would otherwise prevail would discourage TNCs from entering, thus leaving the market to less-efficient, less well-capitalized domestic producers.

18. These figures are extrapolated from data provided in *La Industria de Autopartes en Colombia* (Bogotá: Instituto de Investigaciones Technológicas, 1977), pp. 25–27.

19. See, for example, *El Tiempo,* August 3, 1968, p. 11.

20. After having selected Renault for a final round of negotiations, the government (through its Comité Técnico) periodically threatened to resume talks with Fiat and other interested parties unless satisfactory progress was made. See ibid., February 6, March 19, 1969.

21. *Boletín de Información Comercial* (Bogotá: Sofasa, November 1978), pp. 2–4.

22. Departamento Nacional de Planeación, "La Industria Automotriz," *Revista de Planeación y Desarrollo* (Bogotá) 9, no. 3 (1977): 158.

23. *Industria de Autopartes,* pp. 46–67.

24. These figures were provided by technical personnel in the National Planning Department and Foreign Trade Institute (INCOMEX) in May 1977. Little, if any, additional integration seems to have taken place since then. A major factor in this regard is the fact that 50 percent of the materials (particularly metals) used in the domestic production of parts and components are imported. See *La Industria Automotriz* 9, no. 3 (1977): 174.

25. These various means of inflating integration levels were described to me by the government officials. The formula most commonly used to calculate the level of integration is $GIN = 1 - (total CKD/CBU)$ in which CKD represents all imported parts and components and CBU the value of a completely assembled model f.o.b.

26. Chrysler claimed to have created an additional thirty-five jobs for every person it employed directly in its assembly operations. Other assemblers used the more modest but similarly exaggerated ratio of fourteen to one. One reason for the exaggeration is that assemblers include the total number of employees of an auto parts firm even though only a small part of that firm's total production

was actually devoted to producing goods sold to the assembler (the rest going to replacement parts or entirely different industries).

27. *La Industria Automotriz* 9, no. 3 (1977): 200.

28. The overcost is lowest for those models (Simca and R4) that were (1971–1976) directly competitive with one another and tends to be highest for expensive models (Dodge Dart, Fiat 125 and 128, and Renault 12) with price inelastic demand.

29. *La Industria Automotriz* 9, no. 3 (1977): 202.

30. In 1971 4,100 taxis were to have been built, but only 661 were produced. At least 1,000 taxis were imported in early 1972 to help fill this gap. In 1974 at least 700 buses and 1,400 taxis were imported. See *El Tiempo*, June 18, 1974, p. 12a, December 13, 1974, p. 1, and March 15, 1975, p. 10a. From 1971 through 1974 Chrysler fulfilled 29 percent of its taxi commitments, 85 percent of its bus commitments, 88 percent of its automobile commitments, and 66 percent of its truck commitments. Lara e Hijos fulfilled 0 percent, 41 percent, 59 percent, and 72 percent of its commitments in these areas, and Renault fulfilled 10 percent of its taxi and 76 percent of its automobile commitments. See Luis Jorge Garay, *La Industria Automotriz en Colombia* (Departamento Nacional de Planeación, 1974).

31. Chrysler's large profits for 1976, a year in which the firm produced more trucks and buses than passenger cars, suggests that under certain conditions, collective vehicle production can be lucrative. See Michael Fleet, "Host Country Multinational Relations in the Colombian Automobile Industry," *Inter American Economic Affairs* 32, no. 1 (Summer 1978): 9.

32. Several assembly firm officials with whom I spoke acknowledged indirectly the existence of such an agreement and argued that a large portion of their profits depended on these models.

33. Information provided by a technical analyst in the National planning Department.

34. For export and import figures, see yearly editions of the *World Trade Annual*. One former high-level officer of the CCA stated in an interveiw with me that since its decision to move into Brazil, Fiat has regarded its Colombian car operation as a strictly commercial one.

35. For this provision of the initial contract, see *Boletín Mensual de Estadística*, nos. 280–281, p. 176.

36. The proportion of CKD parts to overall imports from France (according to *World Trade Annual* figures) rose from 10 percent in 1970 to 41 percent in 1974 before falling to 35 percent in 1975. Since Renault is the only French automaker exporting to Colombia, these amounts can be reasonably attributed to it.

37. In 1974 Colombian auto exports to France totaled $363,000. *Supplement to World Trade Annual* (1974), p. II-308 (1975), p. II-301, and (1976), p. II-302.

38. Ibid. (1973), pp. II-282, 301, and (1976), pp. 302, 321. The figures given by the *Yearbook of International Trade Statistics* (1977), pp. 291, 293 are 102 million and 199 million.

39. In 1973 Renault sold more CKD parts to Colombia ($22 million) than to any other Latin American country except Mexico, which purchased $23 million. See the *United Nations Yearbook of International Trade Statistics* (1975), p. 271.

40. This figure was supplied by automotive industry experts in both the National Planning Department and INCOMEX.

41. See *El Tiempo*, February 5, 1972, p. 6b, February 7, 1972, p. 14, and February 11, 1972.

42. The following figures indicate the number of units produced and imported, by vehicle, between 1971 and 1976.

		Produced	Imported
1971	Trucks	4,176	2,582
	Buses	4,244	994
	Taxis	315	
1972	Trucks	3,341	354
	Buses	2,767	525
	Taxis	854	
1973	Trucks	2,908	368
	Buses	2,260	598
	Taxis	426	
1974	Trucks	4,084	3,305
	Buses	2,646	1,866
	Taxis	836	
1975	Trucks	3,260	3,719
	Buses	3,213	6,907
	Taxis	2,832	
1976	Trucks	3,213	4,290
	Buses	4,803	1,281
	Taxis	3,517	

La Industria Automotriz 9, no. 3 (1977): 166–169, and *Boletín de Información Comercial* (November 1978): 4.

43. Among these are the lack of reliable data on taxi imports (see note 29 for fragmentary data), the influence of the industry-wide recession (1974–1975) and the 35 percent sales tax, and the difficulty in knowing whether to treat the imported vehicles as dependent or independent variables.

44. Although virtually all of the larger domestic auto parts suppliers were locally owned (95 percent of all foreign investment in the auto parts industry was in either rubber, 77 percent, or the Renault motor plant, 17 percent), most of them were dependent on TNCs for licensing, technological assistance, and production materials. See Instituto de Investigaciones Technologicas, *La Industria de Autopartes en Colombia*, p. 29.

45. This was one important instance of vagueness in the initial contracts. While the price stipulation was fairly clear, considerations of availability (particularly timing) and quality were much more susceptible to interested interpretation.

46. This practice was cited by a high-ranking official of SOFASA who wanted to prove that when Renault did resort to "dirty tricks," they were of a sophisticated nature.

47. See El Tiempo, November 4, 1970, p. 15.

48. No doubt Pastrana was partly motivated by a desire to minimize his difficulties with ANDI and FEDEMETAL, particularly since he (as was Lleras) was determined to resist their efforts to undermine the Andean Pact and decision 24, although just as clearly he was already inclining in this direction for reasons of overall political calculus.

49. According to one account (El Tiempo, November 6, 1974, p. 6a), the government's investment program was broken down in the following manner: agricultural development (credit, extension services, and social and welfare services, for example), 23 percent; primary and secondary education, 29 percent; urban construction, 8 percent; export promotion, 24 percent; small and medium-sized industry development, 3 percent; and housing subsidies, 1.7 percent.

50. Both Rodrigo Botero (López's first treasury minister) and Miguel Urrutia (formerly head of National Planning and later minister of mining) were skeptical of import substitution industrialization and were hostile to the automobile industry. Urrutia once stated publicly that Colombians should ride bicycles and not drive cars.

51. In contrast with the situation in other countries, assemblers in Colombia were compelled to use their own funds for consumer credit. These funds (over $1 million for Renault and even more for Chrysler) became a major part of the TNCs' overall investment and account for the unusually large amount of total assets claimed vis-à-vis fixed assets. See Fleet, "Host Country Multinational Relations," pp. 8–9.

52. Superintendencia de Industria y Comercio, resolución 1278 del diciembre, 1975, "Por la Cual se Fija el programa mínimo de integración para 1976 de la fábrica Chrysler Colombian de Automotores, S.A."

53. For example, the government could have ensured more faithful fulfillment of production quotas (of taxis, small cars, and trucks) by refusing to grant import licenses for CKD materials for other models until these commitments were met.

54. They were able to do this, for example, in connection with their opposition to the controversial Andean Group Statute on Foreign Investment, which was opposed strenuously, and for a while successfully, by ANDI, FEDEMETAL, the Associación Bancaria, and other groups.

55. The term was first used by Marxist Nicos Poulantzas to characterize a state's ability to serve the interests of capital or capitalist development as a whole at the expense of individual firms or interests.

56. Cf. Raul Fernández's unpublished study, "Foreign Capital in the Economy of Colombia," p. 9.

57. See Fleet, "Host Country Multinational Relations," pp. 9–11.

58. See *La Industria de Autopartes en Colombia* and *La Industria Automotriz* for information on the licensing and financial ties between domestic auto parts firms and transnational corporations.

59. Cf. Homero Cuevas, "La Estructura Industrial en Colombia," in *Controversia sobre la Economía Colombiana* (Bogotá: Universidad Externada de Colombia, 1976), p. 149.

60. A case in point is ANDI's investment in the Corporación del Valle de Cauca (an export-oriented agricultural enterprise) in 1973.

9

The Development of the Latin American Motor Vehicle Industry, 1900–1980: A Class Analysis

Rich Kronish and
Kenneth S. Mericle

The motor vehicle industries that have emerged in Latin America since the mid-1950s have grown dramatically. In 1955 production in all of Latin America totaled some 61,000 vehicles.[1] By 1978 total production had climbed to 1,883,960 vehicles, a more than thirty-fold increase, corresponding to an average growth rate of 13 percent.[2] Chile, Colombia, Bolivia, Peru, Uruguay, Venezuela, and other countries now have motor vehicle industries, but production is concentrated in Argentina, Mexico, and, above all, Brazil. This chapter focuses on the development of these three industries, which in 1978 accounted for approximately 86 percent of the total Latin America production, with the Brazilian industry—the world's ninth largest—alone accounting for over half of total production.[3] (See table 9.1.)

Perhaps even more significant than the actual growth in vehicle output in Latin America has been its form. Unlike many of the other industries in less developed countries (LDCs), the vehicle industries of the larger Latin American countries are not merely assembly operations. Assembly operations did dominate vehicle production in the 1950s, but by 1975 advanced manufacturing operations, representing production with more than 90 percent local content, comprised the bulk of total production, particularly in the larger countries.[4] Similarly, and again unlike many other LDC expanding industries, the vehicle industries of Argentina, Brazil, and Mexico are not simply enclaves of industrial production. Like their counterparts in the developed capitalist countries, the Latin American vehicle industries occupy central roles in their respective national economies. In Brazil the major terminal producers (as distinct from the parts producers) accounted for 4.3 percent of Gross Domestic Product (GDP) in 1973 as compared with 3.8 percent in the United States.[5] The Brazilian industry as a whole represented 5.5 percent of GDP and over 12 percent of industrial production in the

Table 9.1
Production of motor vehicles in Latin America

Year	Brazil	Argentina	Mexico	Latin American total (thousands)
1957	30,542	15,635	N.A.	102.2
1958	60,983	27,834	N.A.	144.2
1959	96,114	32,952	N.A.	197.0
1960	133,041	89,338	49,807	289.2
1961	145,584	136,188	62,563	359.7
1962	191,194	129,880	66,637	405.7
1963	174,191	104,899	69,135	377.9
1964	183,707	166,483	90,842	494.3
1965	185,187	194,536	96,396	534.0
1966	224,609	179,453	117,900	595.9
1967	225,487	175,318	124,500	601.1
1968	279,715	180,976	156,777	716.5
1969	353,700	218,590	161,831	816.8
1970	416,040	219,599	187,306	954.6
1971	516,067	253,237	210,833	1,143.5
1972	609,470	268,593	229,766	1,277.3
1973	729,386	293,742	286,045	1,369.1
1974	905,103[a]	286,312	350,750	1,739.7
1975	929,807	240,036	356,624	1,740.5
1976	985,469	193,517	324,979	1,743.8
1977	919,864	235,356	280,820	1,674.6
1978	1,062,197	179,875	384,127	1,884.0
1979	1,029,347			
1980	1,162,403			

Sources: Brazil, ANFAVEA; Argentina, ADEFA; Mexico, 1960–62, *Motor Business*, no. 66 (April 1971): 44, and 1963–1978, U.S. Department of Commerce; Latin American total, 1957–1962, Rhys Jenkins, *Dependent Industrialization in Latin America* (New York: Praeger, 1977), p. 279; Latin American total, 1963–1978, U.S. Department of Commerce.
a. Total includes 46,727 complete knockdown kits that were exported.

mid-1970s.[6] Despite a five-year period of decline and stagnation, the Argentine motor vehicle industry still accounted for almost 4 percent of GDP and 10 percent of gross industrial output in 1977.[7] In Mexico the industry represented 6.8 percent of manufacturing value added in 1974.[8] Moreover, with important backward linkages to auto-related industries (including the steel, rubber, nonferrous metals, glass, and capital goods industries), the Latin American vehicle industries have been deemed "leading sectors in development strategies" in their national economies.[9]

At the same time the Latin American motor vehicle industries do share an important characteristic with other LDC industries that distinguishes them from the motor vehicle industries of the major industrial countries. In all the major industrial countries domestically owned firms play significant, if not dominant, roles. By contrast the role played by national firms in the Latin American industries is insignificant, if not nonexistent. The largest vehicle producers in Latin America by order of total production in 1975 were Volkswagen, Ford, and General Motors. Smaller producers included Chrysler, Renault, Fiat, Daimler-Benz, Peugeot-Citroen, Nissan, American Motors, and Toyota.[10] As this list suggests, the development of the motor vehicle industry in Latin America has been accompanied by its near total denationalization. By 1971 foreign-owned firms controlled almost 100 percent of Brazilian production, 97 percent of Argentine production, and 84 percent of Mexican production.[11] Furthermore the remaining national firms were state controlled, operating either under foreign license or with significant foreign participation. Not a single motor vehicle firm now remains under the control of private, national capital.

Coupling significant increases in industrial output with continued foreign domination, the development of the Latin American motor vehicle industry represents a seemingly successful illustration of what might be called "dependent industrialization." The development of the industry thus constitutes an important case study in the overall developmental experience of the LDCs. The primary task of this chapter is to analyze the dynamics of this pattern of development.

An analysis of the development of the Latin American vehicle industries must focus on the interplay between foreign motor capital and the Latin American host governments. A primary factor shaping this interplay has been the level of competition in the international vehicle industry. During the pre–World War II period, lack of competition in the international industry constrained the development of the local industry. During this time Ford and General Motors dominated the international industry. These firms were unprepared to develop manufacturing operations in Latin America, with the result that the operations there remained limited to the assembly phase.[12] Conversely the intensification of competition in the international industry in the 1950s had a favorable impact on the installation of manufacturing in Latin America. Indeed it was not Ford or General Motors that pioneered in manufacturing operations but rather smaller American and European firms intent on breaking into the Latin American market. Similarly the recent heightening of competition in the international industry has permitted the Latin American industry to assume an export orientation.

It is unlikely that international competition, acting alone, would have been sufficient to effect the installation of vehicle manufacturing in Latin America or the more recent adoption of an export orientation. In both instances carefully designed government policies complemented the impact of international competition. These policies had, and continue to have, a dual carrot-and-stick character. They have threatened foreign firms that refused to act in the prescribed manner with exclusion from the local market but have provided willing firms with highly attractive fiscal and tax subsidies that have reduced substantially the costs and risks of the prescribed actions. In the context of an increasingly competitive international industry, these policies have successfully induced—rather than compelled—changes in the operations of the transnational motor vehicle firms.

An analysis of the bargaining process between transnational corporations (TNCs) and host governments is central to an understanding of both the installation of vehicle manufacturing in Latin America in the late 1950s and the development of the export phase in the 1970s. In addition a focus on bargaining has a general significance in regard to the long-standing debate over the alleged willingness or unwillingness of the TNCs to develop manufacturing in the Third World. Nevertheless the utility of the bargaining focus is limited because it ignores the internal dynamics of the vehicle industries once installed. It is, however, precisely these internal dynamics that have been most problematic to vehicle manufacturers in Latin America.

Despite the growth of vehicle production since the early 1960s, the Latin American vehicle industries have demonstrated a marked tendency toward stagnation. Several common problems—especially the fragmentation of relatively small national markets along sector, company, product, and model lines—have defined industries with low-volume, high unit-cost production despite labor costs far below those prevailing in the developed capitalist countries. Under these circumstances the establishment and maintenance of conditions of profitability and growth have represented chronic problems confronting (to various degrees) all Latin America industries.

The internal dynamics of vehicle manufacturing in Latin America thus have impelled extensive state intervention and thereby made the relationship between the motor TNCs and host governments of continued, central significance to the development of these industries. This relationship, whether outside or within a formal bargaining framework, certainly has not been without conflict as the governments' interest in promoting national economic development and the firms' efforts to maximize profits on a global basis have clashed. Nevertheless these conflicts have not been primary and have not altered the mutual interest of the host governments and the TNCs in establishing and maintaining conditions conducive to profitability and growth. It is this underlying mutual interest that has led the host governments to intervene on behalf of foreign motor capital.

While state intervention has been required in all of the major Latin American industries, specific national patterns of intervention have varied considerably, reflecting to a significant degree the different local content requirements. In Brazil and Argentina very high local-content requirements (over 90 percent) exacerbated the high-unit-cost, low-volume character of the industry and made the success of the state efforts to create sufficient effective demand crucial to the expansion of the industry. By contrast in the Mexican industry, the far greater reliance on imported parts and subassemblies (as implied by the lower contents requirements) mitigated this problem somewhat while exacerbating balance-of-payments difficulties, thus prompting the state to emphasize export promotion.

Host government efforts to expand effective demand and/or promote vehicle exports have implied significant challenges to the working class in general and to the auto workers in particular. In practice these efforts have entailed the concentration of income and the tight control of labor costs at the point of production. The success of these efforts, and indeed their very formulation, has depended on the relative strength of both the auto workers and the working class as a whole (within which the auto workers often have played a vanguard role). In Argentina, for example, a militant working class effectively blocked the full implementation of these efforts and thereby limited the expansion of motor vehicle production. By contrast the defeat and/or containment of the Brazilian and Mexican working classes permitted the structuring of political-economic contexts highly favorable to the motor vehicle industry. Class relations are thus a second essential focus (in addition to the relations between host governments and TNCs) in understanding the development of the Latin America motor vehicle industry.

Assembly and the Transition to Manufacturing

Although assembly plants commenced operations as early as 1916, motor vehicle manufacturing—representing production with a high degree of local content—did not appear until the promulgation of a series of government decrees in Brazil (1956), Argentina (1959), and Mexico (1962). After decades of serving the market with a mixture of imported and locally assembled vehicles, TNCs responded immediately to the decrees by establishing major manufacturing facilities.

The assembly phase

Remarkably little is known about the assembly period. There is no detailed study of the economics of assembly operations; even factual data on the timing of investments, the size, value, and nature of production facilities are difficult to obtain. The evidence does suggest, however, that the assembly operations were profitable and that profitability was enhanced by state intervention.

The first firm to begin viable assembly operations in Latin America was Ford in Argentina in 1916. Ford had established a sales branch in 1914, and as its sales of imported vehicles increased, it initiated assembly operations in an effort to reduce its freight bill by transporting CKDs (completely knocked down units requiring only final assembly) rather than the bulkier and more costly finished vehicles.

Although the early Ford experience in Argentina suggested that assembly plants could be profitable without tariff protection, Latin American governments nevertheless began to construct tariff walls favoring the import of unassembled and semiassembled vehicles over finished vehicles. The main impact of these tariffs appears to have been to increase the TNCs' profit margins on Latin American sales. Imported finished vehicles continued to establish selling prices. By raising the price of imported vehicles, the tariffs in effect increased the margin between the sales price and the cost of locally assembled vehicles.

Consequently Ford, General Motors, Chrysler, and even International Harvester established or expanded low-volume assembly plants throughout Latin America in the 1920s and 1930s.[13] Hence the tariffs, which at least in Mexico were first imposed in 1925 at Ford's request, are best understood as a supportive government policy that increased profit margins on combined import and assembly operations rather than as a coercive policy designed to force reluctant TNCs to establish assembly operations.[14]

Although the evidence is sketchy, two additional factors seem to have reinforced the effects of the tariffs. First, the capital costs of the assembly operations were very modest, primarily because assembly was not particularly capital intensive during this period. Indeed "most overseas operations paid their own way, Detroit making virtually no investment in them. Cash was furnished for the first payrolls and for custom duties on the initial consignments; credit was also extended for these vehicles. Then the foreign branches and companies, as they sold cars, would pay their debts and from their profits invest in new equipment and plant facilities. Within a few months most overseas ventures did not need any added assistance from Detroit."[15] Second, the economies of scale were very low; plants assemblying no more than 3,000 to 4,000 cars per year were economically worthwhile.[16]

In short the assembly operations were generally small plants with very little machinery and equipment requiring little investment by the TNCs. Despite the modest scope of the operations, they generated significant profits. Ford declared profits in 1925–1926 of over $6 million in Argentina—a market that bloomed in the late 1920s into Ford's second largest foreign market—and $4 million in Brazil.[17]

During the 1920s the U.S. TNCs had no compelling reason to move to manufacturing. In fact they had very good reasons (including the restrictive size of the national markets and the absence of sufficient parts and materials infrastructures) to avoid making these investments. Furthermore they were not pressured in this regard by the host governments, and local sourcing of parts and components remained at a very low level.

The depression of the 1930s and World War II permanently transformed this situation. The collapse of commodity prices during the depression drastically reduced import capacity throughout the region. Motor vehicle imports, both assembled vehicles and CKDs, suffered a drastic decline. Data that illustrate this point are provided by Jenkins for Argentina and Mericle for Brazil; Mexican automotive imports also plummeted.[18] As motor vehicle imports declined, a local parts supply sector emerged, especially during World War II, in all three countries to service the aging stock of vehicles.[19] For the most part these firms were small workshops with artisan-type production methods and primitive technologies. Nevertheless they were important to the future development of the industry for they were owned by national capital and consequently provided the national bourgeoisie with a direct and immediate interest in the future development of the industry.

Despite the emergence of local parts production, there was no real opportunity for Latin American assembly operations to develop into manufacturing facilities during the depression and World War II. Local capital lacked the resources and expertise to establish a full-scale manufacturing industry, and the large U.S. firms were paralyzed by the depression. It was only in the postwar period that manufacturing became a realistic possibility in the larger Latin America countries.

Postwar developments

In the immediate postwar period the huge backlog of demand created by the low level of imports during the previous fifteen to twenty years generated a flood of automotive imports (finished vehicles and assembly material) into Latin America.[20] This surge in imports both contributed to a mounting import bill that threatened the balance of payments in Argentina, Brazil, and Mexico and imperiled the existence of the local parts producers. Under these circumstances the Argentine, Brazilian, and Mexican governments moved to adopt two sets of measures, although the timing of these measures varied considerably. On the one hand they limited finished vehicle imports by imposing high(er) tariffs and/or import quotas.[21] On the other hand they adopted measures designed to protect the interests of national capital in the domestic parts sector with, for example, both the Brazilian and Mexican governments identifying domestically produced parts that had to be incorporated in domestic assembly operations. These measures prompted an increase in the number of firms engaged in assembly operations and an increase in the local sourcing of parts and components that entailed, in the case of a few firms, operations beginning to approach true manufacturing.

The firms that took the lead in increasing local sourcing were not the big U.S. firms that had traditionally dominated the Latin American industry. Rather they were European firms that had recovered from the war, smaller U.S. firms, and state- and privately owned local firms operating under foreign license. The efforts of the three Latin American governments to promote local production thus coincided with and depended on the emergence of new sources of competition (to U.S. producers), which were both increasingly willing and financially able to invest in the terminal sector of the industry. At least in Mexico the investments made by these new rivals were relatively costless, "offset by generous tax and credit" policies that virtually exempted the firms from all taxes, while simultaneously providing them with some $46 million of credit in the 1953–1958 period alone, more than any other industrial sector. The firms may also have been drawn by the "enormous profits" that were available and freely repatriable in the "seller's market created by the government's restrictive import policies" and the absence of effective price controls.[22]

It was in this context of increased competition, strained import capacity, growing interest of the national bourgeoisie in the parts sector, and (at least in Mexico) government investment incentives that the three governments began systematic planning of the transition to manufacturing facilities. In fact the transition was well under way before the governments developed their plans for the future shape of the industry.

Transition to manufacturing in Brazil

The Brazilian plan for the transition to manufacturing was the first adopted (1956) and also the most restrictive, requiring 90 to 95 percent domestic content by weight within a period of three and a half years.[23] Taken at face value, this ambitious goal implied a very high level of risk for TNCs investing in manufacturing facilities, particularly given the underdeveloped state of the parts and materials sectors. In fact riskiness of the ventures was substantially less than appearances indicated.

Discussions concerning the establishment of manufacturing operations began early in the 1950s with the government consulting the existing vehicle assemblers "on production targets and methods of operation . . . and on the form that an incentive program should take."[24] The protective measures of the early 1950s represented a series of gradual steps that encouraged the TNC assemblers to increase their own local production of parts and their sourcing from domestic parts producers. The move toward manufacturing was thus neither unilateral nor abrupt

but rather a clear government policy long before the 1956 decree. The
pro-manufacturing policy thrust was given added impetus by the two
post–World War II entrants, Volkswagen and Fábrica Nacional de
Motores (FNM), both of which established operations that were substantially more than assembly facilities prior to the decree.[25] Thus on
the threshold of the decree, VW and FNM had already indicated a
willingness to move beyond assembly and stood as examples for the
other assemblers.

Despite the restrictiveness of the government's plans, all eight of the
existing assemblers plus three new firms decided to participate. As
Mericle illustrates in his chapter, the firms chose to begin manufacturing
for two main reasons. First, the plan effectively prohibited imports,
thereby providing the participating firms with a monopoly over the
domestic market. They thus faced a choice of either increasing investment or permanently losing the market. Second, the plan provided
the firms with a host of fiscal and foreign exchange incentives, which
drastically reduced actual investment costs. In essence the state under-
wrote the whole venture.

The government policies induced a surge in investment projects in
both the parts and terminal sectors of the industry totaling over $330
million for the period 1955 through 1960.[26] These investments in turn
propelled an enormous increase in output, with production jumping
from 600 vehicles with approximately 43 percent local sourcing in 1956
to 133,000 vehicles with over 95 percent local content in 1960.[27]

While differences and conflicts over the development of the industry
certainly existed in Brazil, with the firms generally preferring lower
domestic content requirements and a longer implementation period
than the government, these differences occurred within a broad consensus that accepted the passage to vehicle manufacturing in the context
of state guarantees of a protected market and extensive financial support.

Transition to manufacturing in Argentina

The second country to attempt a systematic and rapid transition to
motor vehicle manufacturing was Argentina. In 1959 the Argentine
government issued its Automotive Decree requiring 90 to 95 percent
local content on cars and 80 percent on commercial vehicles within a
five-year period.

As in Brazil the decree presented vehicle producers with the alternative
of manufacturing in Argentina or abandoning the market (and in the

case of the six existing producers, their previous investments).[28] First, the decree effectively prohibited the import of finished vehicles, foreclosing the possibility of serving the market from abroad. Second, it strongly discouraged continuation of simple assembly operations by imposing unequal tariff treatment on assemblers and manufacturers. Those firms that promised to meet the timetable and conditions spelled out in the decree were permitted to import parts and components at very favorable tariff rates during the five-year period, while nonparticipating assemblers faced prohibitively high tariffs.

As Jenkins points out, the response to the decree was overwhelming—twenty-three proposals to begin manufacturing in Argentina. For Jenkins, there are three key questions: First, why did the TNCs, especially the U.S. Big Three, fail to invest in manufacturing prior to the 1959 decree? Second, why were so many firms willing to invest after the decree? Third, why did the government permit so many firms to participate in the program?

Jenkins explains the failure of the Big Three to invest on the negative investment climate under Peron and a lack of effective competition from European producers. He attributes the overwhelming response to the decree to general improvements in the investment climate, including successful government efforts to curb the power of the labor movement, and to an oligopolistic reaction investment strategy on the part of the major TNCs in the world industry. He downplays the importance of the investment incentives as a factor encouraging firms to participate in the program. Jenkins suggests that the government's failure to limit entry was probably due to its eagerness to attract foreign investment in general and hence its unwillingness to take any actions that might appear hostile to the international investment community.

Our analysis shares much with Jenkins, although we tend to see less conflict, both actual and potential, between the state and the TNCs. We also attach greater importance to supportive state intervention—ranging from general investment incentives, to measures curbing union power, to direct incentives to the industry—as key factors encouraging participation in the program.

Like the equivalent Brazilian program, the Argentine decree did not mark an abrupt change in government policy or direction. Local production and sourcing had in fact expanded throughout the 1950s, prompted by government legislation. As in Brazil, the two firms that took the lead had initiated production in Argentina only in the postwar period. Daimler-Benz (Mercedes) began truck production in 1952, intending from the start to increase progressively the domestic content of its vehicles.[29] Even more important, Industrias Kaiser Argentina (IKA), a joint venture of the Argentine government and Kaiser (U.S.), initiated operations in the mid-1950s using manufacturing equipment shipped from the U.S. Kaiser plant. Initial plans called for a production of 40,000 vehicles per year with a local content of 60 percent of total vehicle value. These two projects established the future direction of the industry several years before the decree. They also served as an example for the larger U.S. firms that had dominated the market in the prewar period.

Other government measures (not part of the decree) provided further encouragement to participate in the move to manufacturing. Under a 1958 law foreign firms were able to minimize cash outflows by making their investments in the form of used machinery and equipment, patents, and other intangible property. This same law removed all restrictions on profit repatriation. General Motors made particularly good use of these provisions. The parent firm made no cash contribution at all to its Argentine investment, relying entirely on locally earned profits ($6 million) and used equipment from Detroit (capitalized at $14 million) to finance its $20 million investment.[30] The state thus reduced the riskiness of the venture by lowering real investment costs and facilitating the repatriation of any profit generated.

Profitability was virtually ensured under the system of preferential tariffs on imported parts. The decree permitted participating firms initially to import up to two-thirds of the c.i.f. (cost, insurance, and freight) value of vehicles at relatively low duties, thus minimizing the total cost of an Argentine-produced vehicle. In fact the reliance of the decree on value rather than weight as a measure (until 1965) meant that parts imports could be systematically underinvoiced, thereby increasing still further the percentage of cheap foreign parts actually incorporated. The low-cost vehicles thus produced could then be sold at very high prices in a protected market characterized by an enormous backlog of demand. These conditions permitted the participating firms to realize "a very handsome profit" that could be repatriated free of restrictions.[31]

Several of the twenty-three projects were really phantom proposals by firms that never intended to manufacture vehicles but "were simply taking advantage of the initial stages of the 1959 decree" to reap one-shot, windfall profits.[32] Other firms with long-run interest in the market used state support to establish manufacturing facilities at very low cost to themselves. In all, fifteen firms produced at least 5,000 vehicles each in the 1960–1964 period. The principal participants in the industry, and hence the principal benefactors of state support, were the six pre-decree vehicle producers and two other existing firms in related fields (Fiat with tractors and Siam di Tella with motorcycles) that had previously indicated a serious interest in motor vehicle manufacture. As postdecree output surged, rising from 28,000 vehicles in 1957 to 168,000 in 1964, these eight firms accounted for almost 90 percent of production.[33]

The timing of the key Argentine legislation suggests the effect of an additional set of factors—the dynamics of class struggle and domination—on the installation of manufacturing. Although the Peronist regime (1945–1955) represented a broad populist alliance, the industrial working class served as the government's main pillar of support. Working-class support reflected government policies that "legalized unions, implemented the first mandatory collective bargaining agreements and assured the participation of workers at all levels of government, including the Ministry of Labor."[34] Unionization spread to previously unorganized plants, and the number of union members jumped from approximately 500,000 in 1941 to over 3 million in 1951 (incorporating the majority of the economically active population).[35]

As working-class power grew during the 1946–1953 period, workers' real incomes increased in both absolute and relative terms, the distribution of national income shifted away from property income with wages and salaries increasing from 38.7 percent of gross national product in 1946 to 46.9 percent in 1952, and unit labor costs jumped substantially.[36] Relations on the shop floor were also transformed. As Juan Carlos Torre has observed, "Peronism conceded an implicit and broad leverage to the workers within the companies through the multiplication of internal grievance committees and the regulation of working conditions by way of 'convenios' or agreements."[37]

These developments created an investment climate that discouraged major, long-run commitments. With labor costs increasing and shop floor militancy spreading, foreign investors moved with caution. The working class also provided critical support for nationalistic legislation that further dampened the enthusiasm of the TNCs. Diaz Alejandro has suggested that the industry might have expanded immediately after the war if a political economy more favorable to foreign capital had existed.[38] While we cannot conclusively demonstrate that the relative power of the working class within the Peronist political economy was the decisive factor in delaying the investments, it is clear that the TNCs found Peronism more tolerable after Peron's swing to the right in 1952–1953. This shift in the orientation of the regime led to a decline in real wages and a new foreign investment law that liberalized restrictions on profit and capital repatriation.[39] Moreover it was only after a further attack on the working class by post-Peron governments that the 1959 automotive decree was issued and major investments occurred.

Transition to manufacturing in Mexico

In August 1962, three years after the Argentine decree, the Mexican government issued its automotive decree. The decree followed extensive discussions between the government and the existing assembly firms.[40] Bennett and Sharpe describe in detail the decree and the bargaining over its content. In essence the decree mandated that assembly firms prepare plans "for the local manufacture of engines and assembled mechanical components, [and provide] a timetable for the integration of the industry aimed at achieving, within approximately two years, a minimum national content equivalent to 60 percent of the direct cost of the vehicles."[41]

This relatively low sourcing requirement probably reflected the Mexican government's desire to avoid the high production costs associated with the 90 percent (or more) local sourcing required in Brazil and Argentina.[42] However, even the moderate 60 percent content figure implied a significant transformation of the existing assembly operations, which had grown in number from three in 1945 to nine in 1960.[43] Unlike predecree assembly in Brazil and Argentina where local parts incorporation approached intermediate levels of 40 to 60 percent, the approximate proportion of locally made parts and components in vehicles assembled in Mexico in 1960 was only 20 percent.[44]

The Mexican decree also differed from its predecessors by attempting to reserve a sector of the industry exclusively for national capital. The decree restricted the vertical integration of the terminal firms, permitting only locally owned companies to set up parts plants.[45] Had this restriction functioned effectively, an important sector of the industry would have remained Mexican. In addition the restriction promised to help the existing Mexican firms compete in the terminal sector. Mexican capital was incapable of financing the large investments that a vertical structure would have permitted. By contrast the subsidiaries of TNCs, relying on the parents' resources, could have taken full advantage of a vertical structure. The government-imposed horizontal structure promised to limit terminal sector investments to a level that Mexican capital could finance. Of the eleven assembly firms operating in Mexico, eight were small, wholly owned Mexican firms operating under foreign license, two were wholly owned Ford and GM subsidiaries, and the remaining firm was controlled by Mexican capital (in joint venture with Chrysler). Thus restrictions on vertical integration represented action by the state on behalf of the national bourgeoisie to protect its existing presence in the terminal sector and its potential domination of the emerging parts sector. In fact foreign capital increasingly penetrated the terminal sector and succeeded in evading the restrictions on vertical integration in the period following the decree and probably in evading revised restrictions imposed by the government in 1973.[46]

With the significant exception of lower content requirements, the Mexican government's attempt to promote vehicle manufacturing followed the Brazilian and Argentine pattern rather closely. It also closed off a profitable and growing market to imports and provided very attractive incentives that compensated TNCs for their investment. Indeed the government seems to have made available between $185 million and $225 million in subsidy payments alone representing 49 to 59 percent of the terminal sector's total investments and 175 to 210 percent of its investments in fixed assets in the 1963–1970 period![47]

Stagnationist Tendencies

The motor vehicle manufacturing industries installed in Brazil, Argentina, and Mexico following the promulgation of the national decrees in 1956, 1959, and 1962, respectively, soon confronted a set of problems peculiar to motor vehicle manufacturing in the Third World. Central to this set of problems was the high-unit-cost, low-volume nature of production. The solution to these problems was beyond the capacity of the individual producing firms, which were unwilling or unable to make the investments necessary to reap scale economies. State intervention to control costs and stimulate effective demand for vehicles thus became a necessary condition for profitability and growth. While the state did intervene on behalf of capital in all three industries, the mode of intervention and its success varied substantially.

High-cost, low-volume manufacturing

Unlike final assembly operations, many of the production processes and operations that together comprise true manufacturing (production with over 60 percent national content), let alone advanced manufacturing (over 90 percent national content), entail enormous economies of scale.[48] Failure to realize sufficient production implies sharply rising unit costs. The motor vehicle industries that emerged in Brazil, Argentina, and Mexico in the late 1950s and early 1960s failed to reach levels necessary for minimum efficiency.

The factors that explain this failure are well known and are reviewed in detail elsewhere in this book. Only the major conclusions are summarized here. In the first place, the demand for vehicles was severely restricted by the level and distribution of income in Latin America. With per capita incomes well below those of developed countries (in 1961, $267 in Brazil, $464 in Mexico, and $895 in Argentina) and with some 70 to 80 percent of the population failing to earn even these figures, effective demand for motor vehicles remained largely confined to the upper class and upper middle class throughout Latin America.[49] No Latin American country in the late 1950s or 1960s, including Argentina, contained a significant mass market for motor vehicles. Despite higher than average income levels and a distribution of income rather less inequitable than the rest of the area, only 3 percent of Argentine families accounted for one-third of all car expenditures in 1963.[50] This confinement of effective motor vehicle demand to a small segment of the population meant that the total market was very small. The entire Latin American market in 1957—the first year of the Brazilian program to install manufacturing—totaled some 310,000 vehicles (of which over 200,000 were imports).[51]

Second, national markets were highly fragmented among a plethora of producing firms, ranging from eight in Mexico to twenty-three in Argentina. The sheer number of firms in a relatively small market meant that most were very small. In fact the only firm in all of Latin America in 1962 to produce more than 50,000 vehicles in any particular market sector (cars, light vehicles, or buses and trucks) was Volkswagen.[52]

Third, competition between these firms typically took an oligopolistic form with many of the firms offering a large number of models with frequent model change (and limited parts standardization), which fragmented the national market still further.[53] By 1972 the Argentine industry numbered some 120 separate models, while the Brazilian industry counted 131 and the Mexican industry 76.[54] This proliferation of models, coupled with relatively short model lives, effectively limited (and continues to limit) most models to relatively small and costly production runs.[55]

Fourth, Argentina, Brazil, and Mexico experienced significant excess capacity in the postinstallation phase, which in turn raised unit costs and prices still higher.[56]

An indication of the relatively high production costs existing in Latin America can be obtained from Baranson's estimates of the costs of producing a light truck in 1967. Production costs in Argentina were 245 percent of U.S. costs; in Brazil, 180 percent; and in Mexico, even with its relatively low local contents requirements, 158 percent.[57]

High unit costs generated marked tendencies toward stagnation in both Brazil and Argentina immediately following the installation of manufacturing capacity. In Brazil production stagnated after 1962 and in fact declined between 1962 and 1965. In Argentina the completion of the installation phase of the industry generated a similar development. Production fluctuated substantially and actually fell in 1962, 1963, 1966, and 1967 while registering very slight growth in 1968 and 1970 (see table 9.1). By contrast production in Mexico exhibited consistent growth in the postinstallation period. In the decade following the 1962 decree, production recorded an average growth rate of approximately 15 percent. The contrast between this experience and the dismal record of the postinstallation Argentine and Brazilian industries requires some explanation.

Before turning to an examination of the Mexican experience, it is important to understand what the stagnation of the Argentine and Brazilian industries implied for the profitability and viability of those firms associated with national capital. As competition intensified in a stagnating market, secure access to credit (especially to finance advertising expenditures and installment purchases by consumers) became the quid pro quo for survival.[58] In this regard the foreign-owned firms were in a vastly superior position with greater access to both domestic and international sources of credit at lower interest rates than were available to nationally owned firms.[59] A wave of denationalization overcame the two motor vehicle industries. Mericle details these developments in Brazil in his chapter, and Jenkins does the same for Argentina. In both countries the terminal sector was virtually completely denationalized by 1971. The Mexican industry, in spite of its steady growth following the decree, also experienced some denationalization, although not on the Brazilian and Argentine scale. Foreign-owned producers increased their share of Mexican production from 62 percent in 1963 to 84 percent in 1971.[60]

State intervention in the Mexican industry

The relative stability of Mexican vehicle production in the decade following the 1962 decree cannot be understood outside of the framework in which it emerged and developed. State intervention structured this framework in several crucial respects. In the first place, the state instituted significantly different local content requirements in Mexico from those prevailing in Brazil and Argentina. Second, it acted to limit and control wage increases and other elements of total labor costs in the industry while also controlling prices.[61] Finally, for over thirty years it transferred income upward, concentrating consumer demand in the upper-class and upper-middle-class sectors of the population. Taken together these policies increased effective demand for motor vehicles sufficiently to offset any tendency toward stagnation resulting from the relatively high unit costs of Mexican production. It is worth examining these policies in detail.

The Mexican local content requirements are quite distinct from those of Argentina and Brazil. While the Brazilian and Argentine governments both required 90 percent or more local content (as measured by weight) within a relatively short period, the Mexican government set more modest goals in its 1962 decree and aimed to achieve "within approximately two years a minimum national [locally produced] content equivalent to 60 percent of the *direct cost* of the vehicles."[62] The 60 percent figure was itself misleading for it reflected the Mexican government's unique use of direct costs, rather than weight, to compute local production. By evaluating local production on the basis of local prices rather than relative to international standards, the use of direct costs inflated the true value and importance of local production. The 60 percent Mexican requirement thus represented a far smaller proportion of total value, measured in international prices. According to U.N. figures, national Mexican production in 1966 represented in fact a true participation (measured in weight) of some 40 percent of the total.[63] Similarly, a more recent study estimated that in 1971 Mexican national production measured in international prices comprised only about 36 percent of the total value of vehicles produced in Mexico. Indeed this same study suggested that this latter figure was itself inflated because of its failure to take into account the importation of parts and raw materials incorporated into nationally produced components.[64] Whatever the true figure representing national participation in Mexico, Mexican production—unlike both Argentine and Brazilian production—entailed the incorporation of imported parts and subassemblies to a very high degree. Consequently the Mexican industry enjoyed relatively low production costs compared to the other two major Latin American industries.

The Mexican state also sought to limit total labor costs in the motor vehicle industry. This effort corresponds with and must be located within the state's historical attempt to control the industrial working class through the subordination and integration of the trade unions. At the national level the most important labor federation, the CTM, comprises one of the sectors of the ruling party (the PRI). Its predominance largely reflects state support that has often entailed the repression of democratic elements that have tried to remain independent of the CTM and its corrupt, antidemocratic, and collaborationist leadership.

The general subordination and integration of the trade unions has had a significant effect on the development of the motor vehicle industry in Mexico. The predominance of collaborationist CTM-affiliated unions throughout the industry during the immediate postinstallation phase (until the late 1960s and early 1970s) permitted motor capital, often in conjunction with the state and the unions, to institute measures designed to constrain total labor costs by controlling militancy and ensuring managerial control in the plants. These measures included the development of wage controls imposed by or under the aegis of the state; the repression of strikes declared illegal by the state; the employment of a high proportion of temporary or day workers extremely vulnerable to company pressures; the widespread use of speedup; and the relocation of firms in areas with lower wage rates and more collaborationist unions. Roxborough's chapter describes the present operation of this system under the different styles of union leadership in the industry.

The absence of militant, independent unions and the predominance of the CTM affiliates thus limited the auto workers' ability to raise demands for higher wages and other forms of compensation. Even more significant, it permitted the firms to control the shop floor—determining work ratios, line speeds, etc.—without encountering major (and highly costly) resistance from either the union leadership or the rank and file.

The Mexican government also acted to control motor vehicle prices. Shortly before the promulgation of the 1962 decree, the government established a maximum pricing system for all automobiles under $4,000, excluding only the so-called luxury models. Prices were permitted to rise to a set percentage over and above prevailing prices in the home country of the producing firm; for example, the least expensive "popular" models were permitted to rise to 130 percent of their home country price. This system operated throughout the 1960s and early 1970s. It held prices to a relatively small increase during the installation of manufacturing while establishing a virtual price freeze after 1966.[65] The motor vehicle producers generally opposed this system. Nevertheless it complemented the attempt to limit production costs, increased the effective demand for motor vehicles, and thereby promoted the growth of the industry.

While this system limited price increases, motor vehicle prices in Mexico still significantly exceeded prevailing retail prices in the developed countries. With per capital income in Mexico in 1965 amounting to only 28 percent of comparable income in the United Kingdom (let alone the wealthier developed countries), the market for these vehicles thus would have been extremely limited had it not been for a highly inequitable pattern of income distribution.[66] For many years the Mexican state has sustained and promoted a pattern of income distribution through its monetary, fiscal, commercial, and, above all, labor policies that is highly concentrated. Indeed the income share of the wealthiest Mexican families seems to have risen from 1940 until the present time.[67] In the 1960s "Mexico continued to lead almost all other Latin American countries (including both Argentina and Brazil) in terms of income inequality."[68] By 1969 the income share of the poorer one-half of Mexican families had declined to only 15 percent, while the wealthiest 10 percent of all families received 51 percent and the wealthiest 5 percent received 35 percent of total national income.[69] The wealthiest 10 percent of families thus received an average monthly income in 1969 of more than twice the income of the second-ranking income decile and over fifteen times the income of the bottom half of Mexican families, while the relative standing of the wealthiest 5 percent was even more striking. It was precisely these upper-class and upper-middle-class families who, in attempting to duplicate the consumption patterns of their far wealthier North American neighbors, constituted the primary motor vehicle market in Mexico.

State intervention thus structured a political-economic environment within which vehicle production grew steadily in the decade following the 1962 decree. By limiting production costs, controlling prices, and concentrating income, the Mexican state generated sufficient effective demand to maintain a high rate of growth in the industry, although at enormous cost for the workers and peasants who failed to benefit from the production of cars (and other luxury commodities) designed for upper- and upper-middle-class consumption.[70]

State intervention in Argentina and Brazil

The relative stability and growth of Mexican motor vehicle production in the decade following the 1962 decree thus reflected the political-economic context within which the Mexican industry developed. Fashioned by state intervention, this context promoted vehicle production despite the relatively high-cost, low-volume character of the industry in Mexico. By contrast the political-economic contexts within which the Argentine and Brazilian industries emerged impeded vehicle production.

Two factors explain this crucial difference. First, the Argentine and Brazilian governments imposed substantially higher local content requirements than did Mexico. These requirements heightened the high-unit-cost nature of vehicle production and thereby exacerbated marketing difficulties. Second, the dynamics of class struggle and domination took a very different form in Argentina and Brazil than in Mexico. In Mexico the industrial working class (including the auto workers) did not seriously challenge either the overall growth model or the development of the motor vehicle industry. In Argentina and Brazil the industrial working class (especially the Argentine auto workers) displayed a militancy and radicalism in the immediate postinstallation phase that threatened profit rates, the existing distribution of income, and foreign investment itself—hardly the most propitious circumstances for the development of the industry.

The threat posed by the militancy and radicalism of the industrial working class drew the all-too-predictable response in both Argentina and Brazil. Military governments assumed power in both countries and instituted a series of policies—including outlawing strikes, replacing the existing trade union leadership with military intervenors, and arresting, torturing, and in cases murdering militants—aimed at crushing the workers' movements. While these policies were not designed exclusively or even primarily to promote the interests of motor capital as a special interest group but rather reflected the overall dynamics of class struggle, they nevertheless had enormous significance for the motor vehicle industries of both countries. By attempting to repress and then control the industrial working class (including the auto workers), these policies promised to concentrate income and limit total labor costs in motor vehicle manufacturing, and thereby restructure the contexts within which the two motor vehicle industries had been operating. In Brazil the success of these policies permitted motor vehicle production to soar in the 1968–1974 period. By contrast working-class resistance made it impossible for the military-dominated governments that ruled Argentina until 1973 to implement these policies successfully.

State intervention in Brazil

Brazilian vehicle production nearly quadrupled between 1967 and 1974, increasing at an average rate of over 20 percent per year (see table 9.1). This dramatic growth stands in sharp contrast to the industry's performance in the immediate postinstallation period when output stagnated due to political and economic instability and high unit cost that effectively limited market demand even among the wealthiest 5 percent of the population.[71]

The effective transformation of the Brazilian industry primarily reflected the success of state intervention following the 1964 military coup. It is worth emphasizing that the coup and the military's subsequent policies did not simply represent the interests of motor capital. Military intervention in fact represented an attempt to protect the interest of the upper classes in general during a period of increasingly intense class struggle. As demonstrated by the steadily rising number of strikes (including political strikes), the organization of rural workers, and finally the revolts of the sergeants and sailors in 1963–1964, actions by the Brazilian working class took an increasingly militant and radical form in the late 1950s and early 1960s. Trade union leaders began to demand radical reforms in a deteriorating economic situation in which "the left was growing . . . rapidly [and] the legitimacy of foreign investment and capital itself was being seriously eroded."[72]

As popular movements began to threaten the structure of wealth and power in Brazil, the army struck in March 1964, moving quickly to smash the organizations and weapons of the working class. Mericle details the means by which the labor movement was crushed and subsequently controlled. Humphrey's research clearly demonstrates that auto workers were unable to escape the constraints imposed by national labor policy in spite of the incredible dynamism experienced by the industry from 1968 through 1974. In effect the military's comprehensive labor policy made possible the extreme exploitation of Brazilian workers, including auto workers. Industrial workers failed to capture a significant share of the tremendous productivity gains registered by Brazilian industry (especially the foreign sector) during the boom period.

While these policies generally stimulated the Brazilian economy, they were particularly favorable to the expansion of motor vehicle production. As Mericle suggests, the military's policies effected a transfer of purchasing power to the upper and upper middle classes that was highly favorable to automobile production. Between 1960 and 1976 the top decile of income earners increased its share of total income from 39.7 to 54 percent.[73] This process revitalized and expanded the demand for motor vehicles. Government credit policy further stimulated demand by substantially expanding consumer credit, especially for automobile purchases.

The labor policies also favorably affected production costs in the industry. Humphrey notes that the auto firms seemed to have developed the practice of permanent job rotation after the state virtually eliminated legal job security measures in 1967. The firms have used dismissals and the threat of further dismissals to intimidate workers and minimize resistance to speedups. Moreover retraining costs have been minimal since the strategy has created a large pool of trained auto workers.

The various wage policies and control measures at work in the industry together have maintained the earnings of production workers at a very low level. According to one estimate, hourly wages of production workers averaged only sixty cents in the industry.[74] Wages have remained low despite impressive gains in productivity that increased output per worker in the terminal sector from 4.37 vehicles in 1966 to 8.41 vehicles in 1974.[75] The reduction in unit labor costs implied by these figures allowed the auto firms both to reduce prices (and further stimulate demand) and to reap large profits (used in part to finance new investments in the industry).

The labor policies of the military government thus generated, at least until the mid-1970s, a pattern of self-sustaining growth in the industry that increasingly allowed firms to transcend the high-cost, low-volume dilemma. On the demand side income concentration, credit availability, price reductions (estimated at 25 percent between 1966 and 1974), and the general increase in total economic activity, supplemented on the supply side by effective controls over total labor costs and the availability of profits to finance new expansion, together spurred production.[76] By 1974 Brazilian motor vehicle production had climbed to 867,730 units, compared to 225,000 in 1967.

State intervention in Argentina

During the first period of Peronist rule, the Argentine political economy (particularly before 1953) embodied elements that tended to discourage both the initial installation of motor vehicle manufacturing and the subsequent development of the industry. With the fall of Peron in 1955, the relationship between the national government and the working class was transformed. As the political economy of Argentina took on a very different character, both the (military) Aramburu (1955–1958) and Frondizi (1958–1962) governments attempted to institute two sets of measures favorable to the installation and expansion of motor vehicle manufacturing. First, the nationalist legislation of the Peronist period was overthrown with Law 14780 (1959), opening wide the door to foreign motor capital by fully abrogating the previous restrictions on the repatriation of profits and original investments.[77] Second, the post-Peronist regimes attempted to restructure the relationship between capital and labor.

With the overthrow of Peron in 1955, the Aramburu government, representing the interests of the old landed upper class, national monopoly capital, and foreign capital, launched an attack on the working class and the gains it made during the Peronist period. Government policies, including currency devaluations, trade union interventions, and martial law, attempted on the one hand to "reduce the share of labor in the national income" and on the other hand to overthrow the internal commissions and thereby permit capital to exercise complete control over the shop floor and the production process.[78] This dual attempt—initiated by the Aramburu government but sustained by Frondizi and much amplified after the 1966 coup—clearly presages and parallels the post-1964 Brazilian experience. Indeed had this historical project succeeded, it might well have duplicated the Brazilian experience in establishing a political-economic framework much more conducive to the expansion of vehicle production. Despite repeated attempts, the anti-Peronist governments of the 1955–1973 period were unable to realize this historical project. Although government policies did effect a limited concentration of income and an undermining of the internal commissions, working-class resistance prevented a fundamental restructuring of the relationship between capital and labor along the lines of the Brazilian experience.

The efforts of the Aramburu government to reduce the working-class share of total income and to weaken its organized power on the shop floor generated a period of intense struggle. While government policies were not totally unsuccessful—there was some decline in real wages and an erosion of shop floor control—nevertheless a wave of labor militancy "unparalleled in Argentine labor history" effectively blocked the Aramburu government.[79] The Argentine working class was in "an extremely combative and confident" mood as the new Frondizi government assumed power in 1959 (with Peronist support).

The following year witnessed a series of major struggles and defeats for the working class that marked the "beginning of a process of demobilization and demoralization."[80] In this new setting, as time lost due to strikes dramatically declined from 10 million days lost in 1959 to 268,000 in 1962, the Frondizi government moved to effect a "sharp reduction in real wage rates."[81] The demoralization, demobilization, and government repression accompanying the 1959 defeats further undermined the internal commissions. As James has observed, the 1960 metalworkers' contract contained for the first time a clause providing management with "a total carte blanche" to control the production process "with the union renouncing any right to interfere in manning, speed, quality control, or shift arrangements. . . . Within three years there was not a major industry without such contracts."[82]

The relative success of the Frondizi government in disciplining the working class in conjunction with the new legislation permitting unrestricted profit repatriation served to encourage the installation and early development of motor vehicle manufacturing in Argentina. Following the 1959 decree, investments in fixed assets in the industry rose substantially in the early 1960s, while output increased from some 33,000 vehicles in 1959 to 196,320 in 1965 (see table 9.1). To a significant degree, this increase in production was propelled by the backlog in demand caused by import restrictions over the previous twenty years. The elimination of this backlog by the first half of the 1960s slowed subsequent growth of vehicle production. In fact output fell in 1962, 1963, 1966, and 1967 as the Frondizi government and its successors failed to maintain sufficient effective demand. This failure in turn reflected the inability of these governments to restructure fundamentally the relationship between capital and labor along new stable lines.

Despite the importance of the events of 1959 through 1967, neither the Frondizi government nor the anti-Peronist governments that followed it were able to achieve sufficient control over the working class. In 1962, in the midst of a major economic downturn that resulted in the layoff of thousands of workers and provided employers with the opportunity to dismiss union activists, the CGT adopted the Program of Huerta Grande, demanding, most notably, the nationalization of the banks and other key sectors of the economy, the expropriation without compensation of the landed oligarchy, and the imposition of workers' control over production.[83] Moreover despite the increasing significance of collaborationist elements in the CGT, the Huerta Grande program became a *plan de lucha* that initiated a new era of labor militancy, with 3 million workers engaging in strikes and takeovers affecting 11,000 factories and work places in 1964.[84]

The military coup of June 1966 represented still another attempt to restructure class relations in Argentina. The new regime moved against the working class with a series of highly repressive measures while simultaneously implementing a drastic stabilization program that froze wages (while permitting prices to rise) and increased foreign penetration of the economy.[85] For a time these policies seemed successful. Both working-class real income and labor militancy declined (with the number of days lost through strikes falling from 1 million in 1966 to 15,000 in 1968).[86] However, a new surge of militancy and radicalism occurred in the late 1960s and early 1970s. Evans, Hoeffel, and James provide the details of this movement in the motor vehicle industry in their chapter. Automobile workers played an extremely prominent role, first in striking against the regime's economic policies in January 1967 and then in leading other workers and students in Cordoba in the massive insurrection of 1969 called the Cordobazo. The new surge of militancy and radicalism overwhelmed the regime's economic policies. As strikes, demonstrations, and guerrilla activity mounted and the economy fell into disarray, the military permitted presidential elections, which the Peronist candidate, Héctor Cámpora, won in 1973. Cámpora's victory generated an intensification of class struggle (within which the automobile workers continued to play a vanguard role) that produced an increase in workers' wages and a resurgence in the power of the internal commissions in 1973–1974. The anti-Peronist project of 1955–1973 had failed.

The failure of this project had a dual impact on the Argentine motor vehicle industry. On the supply side, by failing to discipline and control the working class, the anti-Peronist governments were unable to reduce total labor cost substantially through speedup, as occurred in post-1964 Brazil. While the evidence is not conclusive, working-class resistance seems to have blocked efforts to increase the intensity of labor. On the demand side, the anti-Peronist governments were also unable to concentrate income sufficiently in the hands of those upper-middle-class groups outside the wealthiest 5 percent of the Argentine population. The relatively small size of the Argentine population (21.5 million in 1965 compared with approximately 40 million in Mexico and over 80 million in Brazil) made this sector a particularly important element of the potential motor vehicle market in Argentina. The high level of class struggle adversely affected this sector with its relatively large number of salary earners.[87] While government policies in the 1953–1961 period successfully increased the income share of the wealthiest 5 percent of Argentine families to a percentage roughly commensurate with other Latin American countries, the income share of the next 10 percent of the population (from 5 to 15 percent) seems to have fallen during the early Peronist years and not to have recovered between 1953 and 1961. As a result this group received a significantly smaller proportion of total income than it did elsewhere in Latin America in the early and middle 1960s.[88] According to U.N. data, the average per capita income of this sector was $2,500 in 1961, considerably less than the price of many Argentine motor vehicles at the time.[89]

The anti-Peronist project thus failed to create a political-economic context sufficiently favorable to vehicle production to overcome the structural problems of the industry. In fact, the strikes, plant occupations, and slowdowns in response to the anti-Peronist governments exacerbated the high-unit-cost, low-volume characteristics of the Argentine industry by directly limiting motor vehicle production as well as by discouraging further investment throughout the economy that reduced overall economic activity and thereby—given the close relationship between per capita income and vehicle demand—diminished the overall demand for motor vehicles. Unit costs have remained well above international levels (with an estimated premium of over 100 percent in both 1967–1968 and 1978), while industry output has been unstable, with fewer vehicles produced in 1976 than in 1966 (see table 9.1).

Contemporary Problems and State Intervention

The nascent motor vehicle industries of Argentina, Brazil, and Mexico initially confronted a similar set of actual and potential difficulties that required extensive state support. The pattern and success of state intervention varied considerably, however, and by the mid-1970s the three industries had assumed very different shapes with very different problems. These problems, rooted in both past failures and successes, have prompted additional forms of state intervention in all three industries.

New contradictions in the Brazilian motor vehicle industry

During the mid-1970s the Brazilian motor vehicle industry entered a new phase of development. Between 1974 and 1980 output of the industry grew at an annual rate of only 4.3 percent compared to the 21 to 22 percent growth rate of the 1968–1974 period.[90] This sharp decline can be understood only in relation to the deterioration of Brazil's position in the international capitalist economy.

After the 1964 coup successive military governments closely integrated the Brazilian economy into the world capitalist order. Foreign direct investment poured into the country, with U.S. investment alone increasing by 500 percent between 1964 and 1977.[91] While the expansion of foreign investment helped fuel the Brazilian "miracle," it also implied mounting service payments (in the form of interest, profits, royalties, and technological fees), as well as an increasing reliance on foreign imports of basic materials and intermediate products. These outflows created balance-of-payments difficulties that began to manifest themselves in the early 1970s despite the very rapid growth of Brazilian exports. With the sharp increase in world oil prices in 1973, these difficulties assumed critical levels. The deficit in the Brazilian current accounts, which increased from $500 million in 1968 to $1.7 billion in 1973, jumped to $7.1 billion in 1974.[92] Net foreign debt increased from approximately $6 billion at year-end 1973 to $47 billion at year-end 1980.

Mericle illustrates how the growth of the motor vehicle industry in the 1968–1974 period contributed to the Brazilian balance-of-payments crisis. Prompted by a growing insufficiency of productive capacity and buoyed by growth in excess of 20 percent, the TNCs launched a whole new round of investment in the industry in the early 1970s. Once again

the government provided fiscal and tariff incentives that markedly reduced actual investment costs. All of the major firms launched projects
designed to expand production. In addition Fiat entered the industry
with a massive investment designed to make it the country's second
largest car producer (behind only Volkswagen). These projects promised
to increase the industry's installed capacity to approximately 1.5 million
units compared to 482,000 in 1968.[93] With the Brazilian capital goods
industry lacking the capacity and sophistication to provide the necessary
machinery and equipment, a huge demand for imported capital goods
resulted.

In addition the state-dominated materials sector could not keep up
with the vehicle industry's demands for steel, nonferrous metals, rubber,
and plastics, all of which had to be imported in substantial quantities.
The most dramatic impact on imports resulted from rising consumption
of increasingly expensive oil as the industry pumped hundreds of thousands of vehicles into circulation. In 1974 the cost of Brazilian oil
imports, representing 80 percent of total consumption, soared to $3
billion compared to $680 million in 1973.[94] The rapidly expanding stock
of motor vehicles consumed approximately 60 percent of these imports.[95]
Finally, as the firms' investment and debt base expanded, the potential
size of the industry's service payment outflow also increased
significantly.

The growth of foreign debt after 1973 left Brazil in a highly vulnerable
position in the international capitalist economy. In response to this
situation, the Brazilian government imposed an austerity program designed to maintain the confidence of foreign bankers and investors.
The general measures constituting this program have been drastic and
have included highly restrictive import controls, which held imports
in the 1975 to 1978 period at approximately their 1974 level; an intensification of export promotion activities, which yielded a 59 percent
increase in exports during the same period; and a skillful strategy of
debt management, which has permitted the country to refinance and
expand its debt.[96] Although these policies generally have been successful
in maintaining foreign confidence, they also have effected a deterioration
of the Brazilian internal economy—slowing the rate of growth while
increasing the rates of inflation and bankruptcy.

It is not surprising in light of the industry's role in creating the overall
balance-of-payments crisis that the austerity program has focused particularly on the motor vehicle industry. State intervention has entailed
three central aspects. First, the state has, in effect, frozen investments

in new large-scale production facilities by removing automobile production from the list of industries enjoying tax and tariff exemptions. It is worth noting that this policy is perfectly compatible with the interests of existing producers that have no interest in sharing what is likely to be a stagnating market with new entrants and little immediate interest in further expansion of their own facilities. Second, the state has attempted to promote motor vehicle exports. In the early 1970s, the state initiated a general program of lucrative export incentives and subsidies. After 1973, as the balance-of-payments crisis mounted, the state began to require export contracts, as well as link the granting of investment incentives to participation in the export promotion program. All of the major firms are now committed to long-term export contracts, and motor vehicle exports have soared accordingly, reaching $514 million in 1976, in comparison to only $3.9 million as recently as 1968.[97] In effect the state is pressuring firms to export but within a highly supportive and very profitable framework. The fact that the last round of investment brought several Brazilian firms up to production levels approaching technical levels of efficiency and that some of these facilities were constructed with export objectives in mind places Brazil in the forefront of Third World efforts to export motor vehicles and parts.

Finally, the state has adopted several measures to slow the growth of the domestic vehicle market and decrease gasoline consumption. It has, for example, tightened consumer credit terms and significantly increased gasoline prices (while encouraging the development of alcohol-fueled vehicle engines).[98] In effect the state has raised the income level necessary to own and operate an automobile at the same time as the slowdown in general economic activity has reduced the growth rate of per capita income. In addition the state has exempted the motor vehicle firms from the price control system and thereby further constrained demand, a measure that also has increased the firms' markups and per-unit profits.[99]

Austerity programs typically heighten both interclass and interelite tensions, which in turn may make implementation of a particular program highly problematic. The Brazilian austerity program seems to have produced this outcome. Class conflict has increased significantly. In a major challenge to the military's labor policy, the unions defied the government by engaging in illegal strikes in May 1978 and March 1979, the first important strike activity in over a decade. The unions are now openly demanding autonomy, as well as general political democracy. Humphrey documents the vanguard role that unions of auto workers have played in this movement.

Dissatisfaction with continued military rule, the country's development model, and the dominant economic position of foreign capital does not seem to be limited to the Brazilian working class. Indeed general dissatisfaction appears to be increasing among the middle class, segments of the national bourgeoisie—concerned that the austerity program will bring another round of bankruptcy and denationalization much as occurred between 1964 and 1967—and even within factions of the armed forces.[100] In this new political situation, it is not at all clear that the state can successfully manage its general austerity program and reestablish conditions for another round of accumulation.

The current political struggle will shape significantly the medium- and long-run fortunes of the motor vehicle industry. Throughout the boom period the motor firms counted on a labor program that, by controlling the activities of the working class as a whole, helped expand the auto market and that, by controlling auto workers, ensured the firms' control over production and contributed to their high profitability and rapid accumulation. The strike movements of May 1978 and March 1979 have challenged this labor policy directly. The movements raise economic demands for large wage increases that, if generalized, would signal a reversal of the income concentration process. They raise demands for trade union freedom that would dismantle the state's repressive labor control apparatus. Indeed they raise demands for democracy that would transform both politics and the state itself.

Both strike movements centered on the suburban São Paulo motor vehicle industry. In the first instance, state intervention was restrained, concessions were made, and selective repression of militants followed. In the second case, police and troops made hundreds of arrests, the union leadership was removed from office, and the union headquarters was seized. It is difficult to assess precisely the long-run consequences of renewed labor militancy. Nevertheless it is important to bear in mind that the economic situation is fragile and the dominant class is divided. Any significant democratization of the country will weaken the labor control system and strengthen the unions, particularly the metalworkers' unions, which represent the automobile workers and are potentially among the strongest and most militant unions in Brazil.

New contradictions in the Mexican motor vehicle industry

Despite its success in creating a context favorable to the expansion of the motor vehicle industry, the Mexican pattern of state intervention has also contained internal contradictions. After almost a decade of steady growth, these contradictions began to threaten the continued growth of the industry and have led the state to intervene once again.

Since the early 1970s state intervention has focused on the industry's mounting import bill. Although the 1962 decree was intended to reduce the value of motor vehicle imports and did in fact reduce the cost of imports per vehicle unit, in aggregate terms it failed. The absolute value of motor vehicle imports rose from $150 million in 1960 to $195 million in 1965 and $225 million in 1970.[101] These imports, comprising 10 to 12 percent of total Mexican merchandise imports from 1962 to 1972 and supplemented by substantial industry service payments, exacerbated Mexico's already serious balance-of-payments difficulties and threatened the continued expansion of both the industry and the economy.[102]

As a consequence the Mexican government acted to ameliorate the industry's impact on the balance of payments. The Automotive Decrees of 1969 and 1972 required the terminal firms to offset imports with increased export earnings, reaching a balance between the two by 1979. To induce the terminal firms to comply with this provision, the decrees further instituted both fiscal incentives and market sanctions (linking export performance and domestic sales).[103] These measures effected a substantial increase in motor vehicle exports, which rose from less than $1 million in 1965 to $208 million in 1975.[104] The ratio between industry exports and imports also rose significantly.[105] Nevertheless with Mexican production dependent on foreign parts, the industry continued to have a negative, net impact on the balance of payments. In fact the absolute difference between industry imports and exports increased, reaching $465 million in 1975.[106] As Mexico's balance-of-payments situation continued to deteriorate, with the current accounts deficits totaling $2.6 billion in 1974, the government issued yet another automotive decree in 1977.[107]

While the 1977 decree provided for a nominal increase in domestic content requirements—an increase seemingly contradicted by a new, more restricted definition of foreign production—its primary aim was to increase Mexican motor vehicle exports.[108] Like its two immediate predecessors, the 1977 decree required terminal producers to increase their exports (producing $1.10 in exports for every $1 in imports by

June 1981) if they wished to remain in the Mexican market. At the same time, the decree (in conjunction with associated legislation) increased the financial incentives available to exporters and, by abandoning the long-standing system of price controls, increased the attractiveness of the Mexican market.[109] The market's attraction has also been enormously enhanced by the discoveries of immense oil and gas reserves in Mexico. As a Renault executive explained the decision to expand the firm's investment in Mexico: "We believe that during the 10 years to come, the increase of oil resources will allow simultaneous development and diversification of the Mexican economy and its industries. We know that the automobile market grows substantially in these circumstances, because we have seen it in several other countries."[110]

The data are not yet available to assess the effectiveness of the 1977 decree. The Renault investment, the construction of export-oriented production facilities by GM and Chrysler, and preliminary export data for 1978 all represent encouraging signs.[111] They suggest that the decree may well succeed and make Mexico a net motor vehicle exporter. The development of Mexican motor vehicle exports and, in fact, the expansion of motor vehicle production as a whole will also depend on the resolution of a second internal contradiction. The state's long-standing reliance on a development model based on the production of luxury goods and the continued concentration of income has engendered widespread discontent among peasants, students, and industrial workers. All three sectors have launched mobilizations of "unprecedented militancy" during the past several years. Particularly prominent have been the struggles of workers in the electrical, railroad, mining, and motor vehicle industries to achieve union democracy—by mounting challenges to the collaborationist leadership of CTM-affiliated unions and by establishing new independent unions.[112] Within the motor vehicle industry, struggles for union democracy have broken out in almost all the unions since the late 1960s. These struggles have culminated in the creation of two independent unions at Nissan and Volkswagen and a rank-and-file victory in the CTM-affiliated Ford union.[113]

As the government's labor policies reduced real wages in the late 1970s, struggles for union democracy have intensified.[114] There has been a substantial increase in the number of strikes, many with "political trappings" and led by "independent worker groups."[115] As these groups have begun to present a serious threat to the CTM's continued dominance over the labor movement and to the government's labor policies, they have encountered heavy state repression.[116] It is important to recognize that these struggles, both in the motor vehicle industry itself and throughout the economy, could have major long-term implications for the development of the industry. They affect the distribution of income and the firms' continued control of total labor costs, a factor of particular significance to export production.

Continuing difficulties in the Argentine motor vehicle industry

In March 1976 the Argentine military staged a coup against the government of Isabel Peron, ending a revival of Peronist rule that had lasted less than three years. The new military regime encountered serious economic difficulties: stagnant industrial production, a soaring rate of inflation (335 percent), and a decline in foreign reserves that necessitated a six-month moratorium on the repayment of foreign debt.[117] These difficulties ultimately reflected structural problems. The industrial sector, which had emerged behind a wall of tariff protection erected by an import-substitution strategy, was inefficient and dependent on foreign capital. Frequent mobilization of the working class, as well as periodic balance-of-payments crises (generated by foreign linkages and a fluctuating commodities sector), constrained industrial expansion in the domestic market. Industrial expansion for the international market was limited by the inefficiency of domestic production.

In this context the new regime resurrected the essential elements of the political-economic project of the 1955–1973 period. The military again launched a comprehensive attack on the Argentine working class that included trade union interventions and suspensions, the jailing and disappearance of union leaders and militants, suspension of the right to strike, elimination of collective bargaining, and establishment of government-controlled wage policy.[118] These actions caused a sharp decline in real wages. According to one estimate, real wages fell approximately 40 percent during the military's first year of rule.[119] By September 1977 real wages were only 50 to 60 percent of their 1960 level.[120] As real wages have fallen, income has grown more concentrated. By early 1977 wages accounted for 31.0 percent of national income (compared to 44.8 in 1975), the lowest level since the end of World War II.[121] While real wages have fallen most dramatically in the state sector, the government's labor policies have also diminished wages and other elements of total labor costs in the motor vehicle industry. According to one account, "the cost-conscious terminal [sector firms] have been able to bring about substantial economies since the Argentine military government came to power in March 1976. . . . In some cases, such as at Ford, about 1,200 workers were dismissed, including many who were regarded as politically suspect. There has been a sharp drop in absenteeism and production-time losses through meetings called by shop stewards during work hours."[122]

At the same time labor militancy and resistance to the military continues. Small-scale strikes and job actions remain a frequent occurrence in the industry (particularly in 1978 and 1979), and a wide-scale flareup remains a threat to the regime and its economic policies.[123]

Like the military-dominated governments of the 1955–1973 period, the current regime has also attempted to encourage foreign investment. The government has eased restrictions of intrafirm royalty and technology payments; permitted firms to capitalize patented and unpatented technology (thereby inflating the book values of their investments and reducing their rates of profit for tax purposes); begun selling off its stake in approximately 700 companies; developed new legislation for hydrocarbon development; and eased restrictions on the entrance of foreign bank branches.[124] These measures have generated a substantial increase in total foreign investment, concentrated, however, in non-manufacturing sectors.[125] Indeed the substantial growth of foreign investments in the motor vehicle industry, which received more foreign investment than any other industry, is misleading. Seventy-five percent of the $168.4 million invested in the industry by foreign-owned firms between January 1, 1977, and August 31, 1979, simply represents the capitalization of credits granted to Argentine subsidiaries by their parent firms before 1977.[126]

The severity of the Argentine economic crisis has also led the current government to modify the economic strategies of the previous military regimes. In an effort to revitalize the Argentine economy, the government has begun to reduce protective tariffs and other trade barriers. By heightening competition, the government has hoped to force Argentine firms to produce more efficiently for both the domestic and international markets. While actual tariff reductions by year-end 1977 were modest, the government announced in 1979 a six-year schedule of more substantial reductions.[127]

Within the overall tariff-reduction policy, the motor vehicle industry has received special attention. As production plummeted to its lowest level in over a decade in 1978, a government investigating committee found the industry to be "inefficient, excessively dependent on subsidies and producing vehicles at double the unit cost of vehicles on the world market."[128] The committee made several recommendations designed to lower unit costs and revitalize the industry. These recommendations served as the basis of the 1979 decree reorganizing the industry. The provisions of the decree included: relaxation of the domestic content requirements of the current 96 percent for cars and 90 percent for trucks to 88 percent for cars and 75 to 82 percent for commercial vehicles by January 1, 1982; elimination of the "positive lists," which prohibited vehicle manufacturers from importing parts identical to those already produced in Argentina (regardless of any discrepancy in price); elimination of the virtual prohibition on automobile imports; and reduction of the tariffs on passenger cars from the current 95 percent to 75 percent in 1981 and 55 percent in 1982, with the 65 percent duty on commercial vehicles falling to 55 percent and then 45 percent.[129] The new decree thus embodies a two-prong strategy: it relaxes domestic content requirements and reduces restrictions on finished vehicle imports.

The decree's relaxation of domestic content requirements represents a victory for the TNCs in the terminal sector of the industry. The incorporation of cheaper, foreign-produced parts will increase profit margins in Argentina while also increasing the capacity utilization and efficiency of their parts plants outside Argentina. Conversely the additional import of parts will threaten the viability of the smaller, less efficient Argentine parts producers. It seems unlikely, however, that the proposed reduction in domestic content requirements will be sufficient to affect vehicle costs substantially, let alone make Argentine vehicles internationally competitive. Consequently the government may well consider a further reduction in content requirements, which VW (which now controls the former Chrysler subsidiary) and Mercedes-Benz—with their large operations in nearby Brazil—both seem to favor.[130] Additional reductions, representing a move toward the Mexican pattern, would entail an enormous risk for employment and production in the Argentine parts sector.

The decree's reduction of the barriers limiting finished vehicle imports is more complicated. At first it would seem reasonable to assume that an increase in finished vehicle imports would not be in the interest of the terminal firms (or, for that matter, the parts firms). There is good reason, however, to question this assumption. TNCs' increasing efforts to integrate their worldwide production operations suggest that an increase in vehicle imports may well correspond to the interests of the TNCs. Immediately after the ban on automobile imports was lifted,

Fiat announced that it intended to import several Italian-made models into Argentina while supplying its European market with the Fiat 130 Europa from its Argentine plant.[131] This reorganization, representing an intrafirm division of labor, will increase plant efficiency and lower unit costs for both the Italian- and Argentine-made models.

The new decree thus promises to heighten the integration of the Argentine motor vehicle industry with the world industry as a whole. While this strategy should reduce unit costs, it will also have another effect. With integration, the role and relative significance of Argentine production within a TNC's worldwide operations will depend on the attractiveness of Argentina compared to other competing areas. Consequently should the Argentine government fail to establish a highly favorable political-economic context for vehicle production, the TNCs will tend to limit the relative size of their Argentine subsidiaries and emphasize production in more favorable areas. The resurgence of trade union militancy in the vehicle plants (particularly in Cordoba) could threaten the future development of the industry once again.

Conclusion

We have attempted to demonstrate the centrality of state intervention in shaping the motor vehicle industries of Argentina, Brazil, and Mexico. During each phase of development, the three industries have relied extensively on state support. While the host governments and TNCs have not always shared common objectives, differences generally have been limited by their mutual interest in establishing and maintaining the conditions of profitability and growth. Host governments typically have attempted to resolve differences by inducing, rather than compelling, TNCs to comply with their goals.

Although state intervention has had a profound influence on the motor vehicle industry in Latin America, an exclusive focus on state-TNC relations is not sufficient to explain the patterns of development among the three industries. An understanding of the importance of the dynamics of class struggle and domination both at the national level and within the industry during each phase of development is also essential. At the national level the level of class struggle has had a critical impact on the creation of a market for motor vehicles, while at the plant level it has represented a key determinant of production costs, profitability, and growth in the industry.

During the installation phase in each country, the state provided significant incentives to induce TNCs to establish manufacturing facilities while simultaneously prohibiting vehicle imports. For their part the TNCs were not particularly reluctant to move in this direction, and some had already estalished intermediate levels of manufacturing. While the small number of auto workers present during this phase limited the significance of class struggle at the industry level, class relations at the national level did have an effect on the installation of manufacturing, most forcefully in Argentina. In Argentina the militancy and relative strength of the working class during the Peronist years—manifested in shop floor practices and relations, income redistribution, and nationalist legislation concerning foreign capital—discouraged investments in motor vehicle manufacturing until a military coup led to a partial transformation of class relations and the creation of a more attractive investment climate. In contrast both the Brazilian and Mexican working classes played relatively passive roles during the installation of vehicle manufacturing in their respective countries. Both lacked the power (and possibly the ideological inclination) to discourage or delay investments in vehicle manufacturing.

The newly installed motor vehicle industries confronted major difficulties. With relatively small and highly fragmented national markets, these industries were low-volume, high-unit-cost operations. Under these circumstances, state support was essential, and expansion and profitability depended on the success of government efforts to structure labor-capital relations in a manner conducive to the development of the industry. State intervention of this sort did not simply reflect the interests of motor capital but rather the broad class interests of capital as a whole. Nevertheless a transformation of class relations did promise a resolution of the low-volume, high-unit-cost dilemma by concentrating income and thereby expanding the effective market for motor vehicles, as well as by controlling total labor costs. In Mexico the implementation of this strategy did not encounter serious resistance from the working class, and the state successfully created a favorable environment for industry expansion. In Brazil the implementation of the strategy occurred after the military coup of 1964. The coup crushed working-class resistance and permitted the institution of a labor policy that concentrated income and controlled labor costs. In this new setting, Brazilian motor vehicle production jumped. Only in Argentina did the state fail to implement the general strategy successfully. Despite years of military rule, the level of class struggle remained (at key times) sufficiently intense to limit market expansion, inflate production costs and restrict profitability.

In the current period the three industries face somewhat distinct problems. In Brazil the industry's enormous expansion has generated new difficulties that center on the balance of payments and have required extensive state intervention. In Mexico state intervention continues to focus on the industry's traditionally negative trade balance, a direct product of the terms of the 1962 decree. In Argentina the industry remains a low-volume, high-cost operation. Plagued by stagnation, the Argentine industry has required still another round of government intervention.

While state support thus remains essential in all three industries during the contemporary period, the dynamics of class struggle also retains its fundamental significance. In Mexico and, especially, Brazil the level of class struggle has intensified, with the auto workers (again especially in Brazil) playing central roles much as they have in Argentina for the past fifteen years. This intensification of class struggle on the national level threatens the labor policies and possibly the general economic strategies of the Brazilian and Mexican governments and (by affecting demand) could have a profound impact on the two industries. In Argentina the working class is on the defensive. Nevertheless the situation remains unstable and potentially volatile. Any upsurge of working-class resistance might well mark the defeat of the government's latest attempt to revitalize the vehicle industry. Finally, the interest of all three Latin American governments in developing motor vehicle exports will increase the significance of class struggle at the industry level. As the governments attempt to induce the TNCs to develop export production, they must control total labor costs—in other words, the militancy and radicalism of the auto workers.

Notes

1. Rhys Jenkins, *Dependent Industrialization in Latin America* (New York: Praeger, 1977), p. 279.

2. For sources, see table 9.1.

3. Ibid.

4. Manuel Sobral, *High Growth Markets for Automobiles: Latin American Prospects to 1985* (Paris: Eurofinance, 1978), 2:18.

5. Kenneth S. Mericle, "The Brazilian Motor Vehicle Industry: Its Role in Brazilian Development and Its Impact on United States Employment" (unpublished manuscript, 1975), p. 168.

6. Sobral, *High Growth Markets*, p. 66.

7. *Latin American Economic Report*, July 28, 1978.

8. Rhys Jenkins, "The Motor Industry" (unpublished manuscript, n.d.), p. 1.

9. Ibid., p. 1; and Mericle, "Brazilian Motor Vehicle Industry," chap. 5.

10. *Latin American Economic Report*, December 16, 1977, p. 245.

11. Rhys Jenkins, "Multinational Corporations and the Denationalization of Latin American Industry: The Case of the Motor Industry" (paper presented to the Symposium on the Effects of Multinational Enterprises, Queretaro, Mexico, 1976), p. 6.

12. Alfred P. Sloan, Jr., *My Years with General Motors* (New York: MacFadden, 1965), p. 316.

13. During this period no European firm established assembly operations in Latin America, reflecting their small share of the Latin American market and their weakness compared to the U.S. producers.

14. William M. Gudger, "The Regulation of Multinational Corporations in the Mexican Automotive Industry" (Ph.D. diss., University of Wisconsin, 1975), p. 76.

15. Mira Wilkins and Frank Hill, *American Business Abroad: Ford on Six Continents* (Detroit: Wayne State University Press, 1964), p. 153.

16. Jenkins, *Dependent Industrialization*, p. 49.

17. Wilkins and Hill, *American Business Abroad*, p. 148. With the exception of the protective tariffs, the Latin American governments did not regulate the auto producers. Thus assembly plants could repatriate profits freely and engage in widespread transfer pricing.

18. Gudger, "Regulation of Multinational Corporations," p. 86.

19. For Brazil, see José Almeida, *A Implantação da Indústria Automobilística no Brasil* (Rio de Janeiro: Fundação Getúlio Vargas, 1972), pp. 8, 11. For Mexico, see Gudger, "Regulation of Multinational Corporations," p. 87. For Argentina, see *Motor Business*, no. 38 (April 1964): 47.

20. Mericle, "Brazilian Motor Vehicle Industry," p. 23; Gudger, "Regulation of Multinational Corporations," p. 89; Economic Commission for Latin America, *Economic Survey of Latin America, 1965* (New York: United Nations, 1965), p. 319 (hereafter cited as *ECLA 65*). See also Bennett and Sharpe in this book.

21. For Argentina, see Jack Baranson, *Automotive Industries in Developing Countries* (Washington, D.C.: International Bank for Reconstruction and Development, 1969), chap. 6; for Brazil, see Mericle, "Brazilian Motor Vehicle Industry," pp. 22–24; for Mexico, see Bennett and Sharpe in this book.

22. Gudger, "Regulation of Multinational Corporations," pp. 121, 136, 144–145, 148.

23. Almeida, *A Implantação da Indústria Automobilística no Brasil*, p. 38.

24. Lincoln Gordon and E. Grommers, *United States Manufacturing Investment in Brazil: The Impact of Brazilian Government Policies, 1946–1960* (Cambridge, Mass.: Harvard University Press, 1962), pp. 47–48.

25. Almeida, *A Implantação da Indústria Automobilística no Brasil*, pp. 12, 45.

26. Economic Commission for Latin America, *Economic Survey of Latin America—1964* (New York: United Nations, 1964), p. 300.

27. E. F. Gibian, "Establishment and Development of Automotive Industries in Developing Countries" (Proceedings of a seminar held in Karlovy Vary, Czechoslovakia, 1969), p. 57; and Mericle, "Brazilian Motor Vehicle Industry," pp. 26, 31.

28. The six firms were Ford, GM, Daimler-Benz, Chrysler, IKA, and DINFIA.

29. Baranson, "Automotive Industries in Developing Countries," chap. 6; *Motor Business*, no. 68 (October 1971): 36.

30. Jenkins, *Dependent Industrialization*, p. 153. Other foreign firms limited their outlays by forming joint ventures with locally owned firms.

31. *Motor Business*, no. 38 (April 1964): 45.

32. Ibid., p. 45.

33. *ECLA 65*, pp. 319, 321.

34. North American Commission on Latin America, *Argentina in the Hour of the Furnaces* (1975), p. 21 (hereafter cited as *NACLA, Argentina*).

35. Ibid., p. 57.

36. *NACLA, Argentina*, p. 28; and Whitaker, *The United States and Argentina* (Cambridge: Harvard University Press, 1954), pp. 204–206.

37. Juan Carlos Torre, "Workers' Struggle and Consciousness," *Latin American Perspectives* 1, no. 3 (Fall 1974): 80.

38. Carlos F. Diaz Alejandro, *Essays on the Economic History of the Argentine Republic* (New Haven: Yale University Press, 1970), p. 166.

39. Aldo Ferrer, *The Argentine Economy* (Berkeley: University of California Press, 1967), p. 202; and Whitaker, *United States and Argentina*, pp. 202–208.

40. Gudger, "Regulation of Multinational Corporations," p. 204.

41. *ECLA 65*, p. 325.

42. Gudger, "Regulation of Multinational Corporations," p. 208.

43. Ibid., pp. 123, 185.

44. Ibid., pp. 147, 197.

45. Ibid., pp. 275–276.

46. Ibid., pp. 274–279, 352.

47. Ibid., pp. 135–141, 224, 233, 253.

48. *ECLA 65*, p. 317.

49. Economic Commission for Latin America, *Income Distribution in Latin America* (New York: United Nations, 1971), pp. 12, 18.

50. Ibid., pp. 24, 42–48; Jenkins, *Dependent Industrialization*, p. 127.

51. Ibid., pp. 279, 281.

52. Baranson, *Automotive Industries in Developing Countries*, p. 29; and Mericle, "Brazilian Motor Vehicle Industry," p. 33.

53. Baranson, *Automotive Industries in Developing Countries*, pp. 46–47.

54. Rhys Jenkins, "International Oligopoly and Dependent Industrialization in the Latin American Motor Industry" (unpublished manuscript, October 1976), p. 12.

55. Jenkins, *Dependent Industrialization*, p. 210.

56. *Motor Business*, no. 68 (October 1971): 37; and Jenkins, *Dependent Industrialization*, pp. 210, 211.

57. Baranson, *Automotive Industries in Developing Countries*, p. 40.

58. Jenkins, "Multinational Corporations," pp. 7–13.

59. At least in Brazil government policy further strengthened the position of the multinational firms. Order 289 in early 1965 permitted some fifty of the largest foreign firms to obtain direct access to foreign sources of capital. "While Brazilian firms paid up to 48% in interest for the credit which they obtained inside their country, the foreign firms obtained loans abroad at 7 to 8%. . . . For many Brazilian firms, this was the decisive step on the road to bankruptcy." Eduardo Galeano, "Denationalization and Brazilian Industry," *Monthly Review* 21, no. 7 (December 1969): 14.

60. Jenkins, "Multinational Corporations," p. 6.

61. Total labor costs represent wages and salaries, fringe benefits, and training and recruitment costs, as well as any additional costs associated with labor turnover, absenteeism and strikes.

62. *ECLA 65*, p. 325.

63. Economic Commission for Latin America, *Economic Survey of Latin America— 1966* (New York: United Nations), p. 258.

64. Jenkins, "Motor Industry," p. 14.

65. Gudger, "Regulation of Multinational Corporations," pp. 177–179, 317–322.

66. Economic Commission for Latin America, *Income Distribution in Latin America*, p. 24.

67. Roger D. Hansen, *The Politics of Mexican Development* (Baltimore: Johns Hopkins Press, 1971), pp. 71–77.

68. Ibid., p. 74.

69. David Barkin, "Mexico's Albatross: The United States Economy," *Latin American Perspectives* 2, no. 2 (Summer 1975): 65.

70. Ibid., pp. 77–78; and Hensen, *Politics of Mexican Development*, p. 71.

71. According to ELCA's study, *Income Distribution in Latin America*, the average income of the wealthiest 5 percent of Brazilians was about 20 percent less than the average income of the same group in Mexico in the early 1960s. Simple manipulation of the data itself provides some rough estimates—$2,100 in Brazil, $2,660 in Mexico, and $5,595 in Argentina—of the absolute income received by this wealthiest group on a per capita basis. Economic Commission of Latin America, *Income Distribution in Latin America*, pp. 12, 18.

72. Timothy Harding, "A Political History of Organized Labor in Brazil" (Ph.D. dissertation, Stanford University, 1973), p. 567.

73. For 1960, see Carlos Langoni, *Distribuição de Rendas e Desenvolvimento Econômico do Brasil* (Rio de Janeiro: Expressão e Cultura, 1973). For 1976, see Marcos G. da Fonseca, "Radiografia da Distribuiçaão Persoal de Renda no Brasil: Uma Desagregação dos Indices de Gini," *Estudos Econômicos* 11, no. 1 (January–March 1981): 13.

74. *Economist*, June 10, 1978. In response to the *Economist* article, the association of terminal sector firms, ANFAVEA, claimed that wages of production workers averaged $1.56 per hour in their sector of the industry in July 1978. See *Notícias da ANFAVEA*, no. 294 (July 1978).

75. Mericle, "Brazilian Motor Vehicle Industry, p. 96.

76. Ibid., pp. 45–48.

77. See Jenkins in this book; NACLA, *Argentina*, p. 23.

78. Ferrer, "Argentine Economy," p. 202.

79. Daniel James, "Power and Politics in Peronist Trade Unions," *Journal of Interamerican Studies and World Affairs* 20, no. 1 (February 1978): 21, 27, 34.

80. Ibid., p. 22.

81. Ferrer, *Argentine Economy*, p. 202.

82. James, "Power, and Politics," p. 27.

83. Donald C. Hodges, *Argentina 1943–1976: The National Revolution and Resistance* (Albuquerque: University of New Mexico Press, 1976), p. 40; NACLA, *Argentina*, p. 13.

84. NACLA, *Argentina*, p. 13; Hodges, *Argentina 1943–1976*, p. 46.

85. Alberto Ceria, "Peronism Yesterday and Today," *Latin American Perspectives* 1, no. 3 (Fall 1974): 27; and Juan C. Portantiero, "Dominant Classes and Political Crisis," *Latin American Perspectives* 1, no. 3 (Fall 1974): 111.

86. NACLA, *Argentina*, p. 68.

87. Economic Commission for Latin America, *Income Distribution in Latin America*, pp. 94–97.

88. Ibid., pp. 16, 42. 46.

89. Ibid., pp. 16, 49; Baranson, *Automotive Industries*, p. 106.

90. Computed from data in table 9.1.

91. *Survey of Current Business* 58, no. 8 (August 1978): 28, and earlier issues.

92. The balance of payments consists of two main accounts: the current account and the capital account. The current account includes all international transactions relating to a country's current expenditures and current national income. The principal subcategories of the account are trade (imports and exports), investment income (interest, dividends, and profits), and other services (royalties fees and commissions, for example). Deficits in the current account can be offset by surpluses in the capital account. The principal subcategories in the capital account include foreign direct investment and foreign-held public and private debt. In Brazil the current account outflows have been offset by capital account inflows, resulting in expanded foreign direct investment and debt, both of which generate large future outflows in the current account.

93. José Almeida, "Perspectivas da Indústria de Veículos no Brasil," *Revista de Administração Pública* 8, no. 1 (January 1975): 299; José Almeida, "A Evolução da Capacidade de Produção da Indústria Automobilística no Periodo 1957–1969," *Pesquisa e Planejamento* 2, no. 1 (June 1972): 60.

94. Mericle, "Brazilian Motor Vehicle Industry," p. 61. *Conjuntura Econômica* 31, no. 1 (January 1977): 66–67.

95. Mericle, "Brazilian Motor Vehicle Industry," p. 62.

96. For trade data, see Mericle's chapter; for debt management, see "The Brazilian Gamble: Why Bankers Bet on Brazilian Technocrats," *Business Week*, December 5, 1977, pp. 72–81.

97. Ronald E. Muller and David H. Moore, "Case One: Brazilian Bargaining Power Success in Befiex Export Promotion Program with the Transnational Automotive Industry" (paper prepared for The United Nations Center on Transnational Corporations, New York, 1978).

98. "Petroleo aulera Proalcool," *Visão*, January 8, 1979, pp. 49–50; "Brazil: Gearing Up to Produce the All-Alcohol Car," *Business Week*, October 1, 1979, pp. 60–61.

99. *Latin American Economic Report*, October 7, 1977, p. 164. The price controls were later restored in the surge of inflation in 1979. See *Business Latin America*, April 25, 1979, pp. 129–130.

100. *Business Latin America*, February 22, 1978, pp. 58–60; *Boston Globe*, November 11, 1978; *Business Latin America*, May 31, 1978, pp. 175–176.

101. *La Industria Automotríz de Mexico en Cifras 1976* (AMIA, 1977), p. 164.

102. Gudger, "Regulation of Multinational Corporations," pp. 217–219; Jenkins, "Motor Industry," p. 16; and *Business Latin America*, May 12, 1976, pp. 145–147.

103. *Motor Business*, no. 83 (third quarter 1975): 36, 39; and Jenkins, "Motor Industry," pp. 17–19.

104. *La Industria Automotríz de Mexico en Cifras 1976*, pp. 160–161.

105. Ibid., pp. 160–161, 164.

106. Ibid.

107. *Motor Business*, no. 83 (third quarter 1975): 28.

108. *Business Latin America*, June 11, 1977, p. 194.

109. Ibid., April 27, 1977, p. 130, and March 7, 1979, p. 75.

110. Ibid., July 26, 1978, pp. 236–237.

111. *Automotive News*, February 2, 1979; *New York Times*, February 6, 22, March 3, 1980; *Business Latin America*, July 26, 1978, pp. 236–237; *Latin American Economic Report* July 14, 1978, p. 212.

112. North American Congress on Latin America, *Report on the Americas* 11, no. 6 (September–October 1977): 2.

113. Francisco Javier Aguilar Garcia, "El Sindicalismo del Sector Automotríz," *Cuadernos Políticos* (April–July 1978): 47–50.

114. *New York Times*, November 19, 1979, July 31, 1978; and *Business Latin America*, March 22, 1978, pp. 92–93.

115. *Business Latin America*, March 22, 1978, pp. 92–93.

116. *New York Times*, July 31, 1978.

117. *Business Latin America*, May 12, 1976, pp. 148–149.

118. Ibid., March 24, 1976, p. 89, May 5, 1976, pp. 139, 142, September 8, 1976, pp. 285, 287–288, January 5, 1977, p. 3.

119. Ibid., December 1, 1976, p. 381.

120. *Latin American Economic Report*, November 11, 1977, p. 202; *Business Latin America*, March 23, 1977, p. 91; and *Latin American Economic Report*, April 7, 1978, p. 104.

121. *Latin American Economic Report*, November 11, 1977, p. 202.

122. *New York Times*, May 13, 1978.

123. *Business Latin America*, February 1, 1978, p. 34.

124. Ibid., August 24, 1977, p. 268, October 31, 1979, p. 352; *Latin American Economic Report*, April 14, 1978, p. 105; *Business Week*, November 21, 1977, pp. 68–69.

125. *Business Latin America*, October 31, 1979, p. 352, January 9, 1980, pp. 12–13.

126. Ibid., October 31, 1979, p. 352; *Latin American Economic Report*, April 4, 1978, p. 105.

127. *Business Latin America*, December 7, 1977, pp. 390–391.

128. *Latin American Economic Report*, February 24, 1978, p. 57.

129. *Business Latin America*, June 14, 1978, pp. 190–192, February 14, 1979, pp. 52–53.

130. Ibid., October 17, 1979, pp. 330–331; *Latin American Economic Report*, April 6, 1979, p. 111.

131. *Business Latin America*, April 18, 1979, pp. 124–125.

Index